D1538712

# A Man Spoke, a World Listened

# A Man Spoke,
# A World Listened

## The Story of Walter A. Maier
## and the Lutheran Hour

*Paul L. Maier*

McGraw-Hill Book Company, Inc.

New York   Toronto   London

# Contents

# Preface

A son writing his father's life faces the pitfalls of bias and subjectivity, as well as the advantages of immediate access to primary sources and years of close observation. This book attempts to skirt the dangers and seize the advantages. I have not boiled all sympathy and involvement out of the story, for that would have left it sterile and vapid. On the other hand, nothing is more unfortunate in a biographer than hero-worship, be he son or not. Both credit and criticism are found in these pages, though if the one did not exceed the other there would have been less reason for this book.

Occasionally dialogue is incorporated in the text. It is not constructed, but reported as accurately as possible from original sources, diaries, and the consentient memory of those hearing, or involved in, such conversation. Documentation for important facts is provided in the Notes.

I am indebted to the following for their kind assistance in providing information about various periods in the career of Walter A. Maier: Emily Maier Eburne, Elmer A. Kettner, and Karl H. Maier—the early years; Adolph F. Krueger and Paul G. Prokopy—student days; Prof. Frank Moore Cross, Jr., and Kimball C. Elkins —Harvard data; Harriet E. Schwenk—professional detail; Herman and Emma Gihring, Dr. Herman H. Hohenstein, Prof. Arthur Carl Piepkorn, Eugene Bernald, W. A. Borkenhagen, Paul Friedrich, Dr. Oswald C. J. Hoffmann, Elmer Kraemer, Leo Shore, and Wilbur Wiese—broadcasting; Dr. E. T. Bernthal, Dr. Edward Buchheimer, and Dr. Gilbert T. Otte—Detroit Lutheran Hour; Herman F. Meier and Hugo Williams—Olcott days; Dr. Theodore H. Hanser—medical data; Ruth M. Elmquist, John Fish, and Prof. Chad Walsh—preliminary critique.

Special thanks for reading the manuscript and offering their helpful suggestions are due Dr. Eugene R. Bertermann, for years The

Lutheran Hour director and close associate of Dr. Maier; my brother, Walter A. Maier, Jr.; and Dr. Lloyd J. Averill, Dean of the Chapel at Kalamazoo College. Thanks are also given to my secretary, Virginia Slinker, who handled the typescript with efficient care.

Finally, my particular gratitude is extended to the woman who shared the life recorded in these pages, who was eyewitness and first source for so much in them, who had painstakingly organized some of the important materials, and who read the manuscript, providing valuable suggestions in its development: my mother, Hulda A. Maier.

P. L. M.

*Kalamazoo, Michigan*
*October 4, 1962*

And take the helmet of salvation, and the sword of the Spirit, which is the word of God.

Paul's Epistle to
the Ephesians 6:17

# Prologue

The voice had an extraordinary range, for each week it was heard around the world. In Shanghai it introduced a Chinese highway engineer to Christianity. In Illinois it caused a woman who was driving to an illicit tryst to make a U-turn on the highway. In Poland it preached anything but party line to a Communist functionary. And to millions of others across the earth, the voice had become a Sunday institution.

Coming through an elegant console in a New York apartment or the short-wave receiver of a bomber flying over Brazil, in English or via translation, the originating voice belonged to Dr. Walter A. Maier, founder and speaker of "Bringing Christ to the Nations"— *The International Lutheran Hour*. This program had become the largest regular broadcast—religious or secular—in the history of radio. More people could hear it over more stations than any other non-government radio program in the world. The Maier (rhymes with fire) messages were translated into 35 languages, aired from 55 countries, and heard in 120 nations and territories.

Walter Maier started broadcasting in pioneer style, over one low-power transmitter in a St. Louis attic at a time when radio was in its infancy. Eventually 1,236 stations beamed his sermons each week to an estimated 20,000,000 listeners in what was probably the largest "parish" in church history. Congregational response came, not in liturgical chant, but by mail, nearly a half-million letters arriving each year from an unseen audience.

His chancel was not always a radio station. At mass meetings across the nation, the voice became a person: the stocky-framed, tawny brown-haired, blue-eyed "Chrysostom of American Lutheranism."* Whether or not his was a "goldenmouth," he aimed to

* So *Time* styled him and footnoted: "St. John Chrysostom (the 'goldenmouthed') was a Fourth-Century Patriarch of Constantinople, famed for his eloquence," October 18, 1943, p. 46.

communicate Christianity in as persuasive and responsible a manner as possible, for he thought the church's proclamation of compelling importance for his age.

While striking his best-known stance at the microphone, Walter Maier led two or three other lives, as journalists often phrased it. He was also a professor of Old Testament, a magazine editor, and an author who penned thirty-one books plus a voluminous amount of devotional materials. In his meager spare time he tended a dozen different projects.

His story has its paradoxes. The man intended a private, academic career, but led a public life. He thought himself too busy for women, yet launched into so exuberant a romance that he wrote a book on marriage. He knew nothing of radio theory, but used it to record advantage. He could thunder as a prophet and charm as a father. He never had a regular pastoral charge, yet served a congregation of millions. His theology was unqualifiedly Lutheran, but his message was welcomed by clergy and laity in every faith.

Walter A. Maier was important to American Christianity for other reasons also. Much of church life in the United States was in spiritual doldrums when he began his ministry, and he became one of the chief spokesmen for a vigorous reassertion of classic Christianity as an antidote to the religious depression. That he helped occasion the contemporary "return to religion" seems clear, for by 1950 he had preached to more people than any other person in history. Such a grass-roots impact also helped to firm up orthodoxy at the theological level.

Because Walter Maier's message had penetrated in an unusual manner, Daniel Poling could call him "the pre-eminent voice of Protestant faith and practice,"[1] and Billy Graham speak of him as "one of Christendom's greatest leaders."[2] "Dr. Maier must be rated among the most influential clergymen of all time," editorialized the *Fort Wayne Journal-Gazette*,[3] while the *New York Times* acknowledged the "world-wide spiritual crusade" launched by "one of the world's best-known Lutheran preachers."[4]

Tributes and statistics hereafter remain peripheral to this account. Its core rather concerns a person who served a cause beyond reason without sacrificing intellect in the process; whose faith rested in God but was restless for humanity. Here is the life story of a man who read these final words of Jesus Christ and believed he could help fulfill them if God provided the means: *"Go into all the world and preach the gospel to the whole creation"* (Mk. 16:15).

# 1

# At the Hub

Walter Arthur Maier and radio were born almost simultaneously. On the day of his birth in Boston, October 4, 1893, any idea of transmitting messages through the air without wires was regarded by most people as wild fantasy. Yet the following year, a young Italian named Guglielmo Marconi invited his parents to the third floor of their villa near Bologna, where he pressed a button on a weird spark-generating apparatus and caused a receiving bell to ring on the ground floor *without* any connecting wires. Seven years later he would be in Newfoundland picking up the first transatlantic radio message: the letter S in Morse code (. . .).[1] Both the infant and the invention would mature together.

The parents of this Boston baby were Emil William Maier, professional organ builder, and his wife, Anna Katharine. They had been born in Germany. Emil was a native of the Black Forest, and as a young man he had erected and tuned organs in southern Germany and Switzerland.

A new church was going up in the Bavarian town of Rothenburg, and Emil had the contract to install the organ. He arrived in the community which, like the Brig o'Doon, had defied time and architectural change; though the year was 1878, Rothenburg belonged back in the Middle Ages. Even today its narrow, sloping cobblestone streets are still lined with ancient half-timbered houses, and the town is surrounded by a defensive wall. With Rothenburg prepared only for medieval warfare, Allied aircraft tried to avoid bombing it in World War II. Tourist attraction, calendar picture, a piece of living history, it remains a place where progress would spell disaster.

Young *Herr* Maier was only twenty-six, but the townspeople flocked to a local *Gasthaus* after the day's work to hear him tell of the wonders in the world beyond Rothenburg. Communications being what they were, any visitor from afar found himself transformed into a spellbinder. A *Herr* Loeffler was so impressed by the organ builder that he went home and regaled his stepdaughter, Anna Katharine, with tales told by this "man of the world." Naturally she was entranced, but so was Emil at reports of a certain pretty *Fräulein* Anna, for townspeople twittered that she would make a perfect wife.

Emil called at the Loefflers. There was Anna, and there was love. She, in turn, was charmed by the visitor, but lasses of that era often masked their affections. Anna used one dodge after another to avoid conversation with the organ builder, for what could she possibly have to say to him? At Emil's approach she was off to her aunt's, over at the neighbors', unavoidably detained baking cookies, and the like. But *Herren* Maier and Loeffler eventually cornered her, the suitor pronounced her cookies delicious, and the courtship finally got under way.

A simple, ungarnished romance it was, in the best traditions of nineteenth-century Germany. Every evening, against a tableau of Bavarian countryside coppered by the sunset, walked, not a couple, but a threesome! For there, two or three steps behind them on the meadows and lanes, was *Frau* Loeffler as chaperon, checking on whether the man of the world was also a man of God. Apparently she was convinced, for the evening walks soon saw only a twosome.

On one of their final excursions—as family tradition has it— Anna asked Emil a bit anxiously, "Haven't you completed your contract for installing the church organ?"

"*Jawohl!*"

"What will you do now?"

"Several organs are waiting for me in Ansbach."

"When will you leave?"

Emil breathed heavily and replied, "As soon as you will come with me . . . *as my wife!*"

Anna Katharine halted and blushed. Slowly she stooped to pick a wild flower, examined it with an expression of wonder, and consented to be *Frau* Emil Maier.

The wedding took place in the Rothenburg church where the new Maier organ could add to the festivity of the occasion. And what better guarantee that it was installed correctly than using it for the builder's own wedding?

After a tearful-joyful *auf Wiedersehen* to family and friends, the couple left for an extended honeymoon tour of Switzerland. The Alpine holiday was pleasantly prolonged by calls upon Emil's talents. Due to climatic extremes, some Swiss church organs proved cantankerous about maintaining pitch. Typically, Anna would sit at the console, playing the keys one by one, while her husband adjusted the pipes to proper tone up in the organ loft. For a couple deeply in love, working together was no work at all.

Two years passed, and ambitious Emil searched for fresh horizons beyond the fatherland. A cousin in Australia wrote of its advantages, but the couple preferred America, fabled land of opportunity for millions of young Europeans. With organs in the New World, there would be need for Emil's services.

After due preparation, *Herr* and *Frau* Maier arrived at Le Havre for embarkation. But the steamer for which they had booked passage was undergoing repairs and would not be seaworthy for some time. Rather than wait, the impatient couple boarded a small sailing ship with auxiliary engines which was about to embark for America, even though it was now November and they were warned that the voyage could be rough.

The elements waited until the ship was well out to sea, then joined in the howling violence of a winter storm in the North Atlantic. The face of the ocean became lathered in fury. Driving sleet soon shrouded the sails with ice, and the added weight proved too much for the rigging. Lest the entire superstructure collapse, the sails had to be hacked down with axes. The auxiliary engines were fired up, but steerageway could hardly be maintained. The ship was cast about like some overgrown lifeboat, groaning to the crest of a billow, then plunging sickeningly into the trough beyond.

Suddenly the sound of water gushing into the corridor outside the Maier cabin terrified Anna, who was now eight months pregnant. Certain that the ship was sinking, she clutched her husband as the beige carpet in their cabin turned a soggy brown from sea water trickling in under the door. Emil grasped her hand and flung open the door. They made their way down the passageway amid a chorus of officers' curses and commands, while panic took control of the ship. But it was not sinking. A large porthole near the water line had opened accidentally, admitting the violent Atlantic each time the ship listed to starboard. Several of the crew fastened it again.

Day and night for the better part of a week the storm raged on. Most of the lamps had been smashed from the pitch and roll. The few passengers who were not seasick made their way to the ship's kitchen for food, only to find that the cook had drowned his fears in alcohol and had to be chained. Cargo was jettisoned, and the water supply ran low when an epidemic commandeered the aft quarters. The waning morale of some passengers struck bottom. "*Herr* Maier," said one of them, "what if the ship lands on some hostile shore . . . *if* we ever reach land? Do you think they'll sell us as slaves?" Emil and his Anna could only pray.

The scheduled Le Havre-New York sailing time was about fifteen days. When the twentieth day had passed, the ship was given up for lost by New York port officials. By that time, however, the storm had subsided, and the boat was brought under control. On the morning of the twenty-third day, crew and passengers in wild jubilation sighted Sandy Hook. When the battered vessel had docked, a sympathetic harbor bartender passed out heaps of sandwiches to the passengers. "Help yourselves," he insisted, "you are the dead returned to life!" Emil and Anna quite agreed.

Since New York had more than its share of organ builders, *Herr* Maier had to work at several odd jobs before finding a position which matched his talents. And yet there was cause for joy: one month after the landing in America, baby Flora arrived, and Emil became "Papa" for the rest of his life. Soon, also, the new father broadened his skills to include piano building and now found favorable openings in New England. After a series of moves, the family settled permanently in musical Boston—by its own humble admission, "the hub of the solar system."

With the purchase of a two-family house in South Boston, Anna could supplement Papa's income by running a grocery and school-supply store on the first floor of their duplex. Emily and George were born, the latter distinguishing himself even as a toddler by trying to help his mother manage the store. A large-hearted lad, George had the expensive habit of handing customers not only items from the shelves, but also money from the cash register. Soon he was out of work.

This is the family into which another son, Walter Arthur, was born in the fall of 1893, and he howled his arrival quite emphatically. But within weeks of his birth, the new source of family pride was attacked by a virulent "milk sickness" which threw tremors into the baby and terror into his parents. "We thought he would die of convulsions," reported Anna years later. "The doctor gave him only a short time to live if the spasms didn't stop. Papa and I knelt at our bedside and prayed in agony. That night the fever broke and the convulsions stopped. We watched to see if they would return, but he slept on peacefully. Later we found that both of us were thinking the same thing at the time: perhaps God had some special purpose in sparing the child."

While this may seem pure maternal hindsight, George subsequently claimed that both parents always assumed little Walter would enter the work of the church. At any rate, from then on he was a marked man on more than one account: even later in life his forehead showed a tiny cluster of faint scars from that infant illness.

Anecdotes can be told about this, as any, childhood. If personality and character are charted in the earliest years of life, then these stories become previews of the future man as well as reviews of his heredity.

For example, with Black Forest–Bavarian ancestry and a Yankee environment, we should find traces of passionate individualism and self-reliance in the lad. It was the Fourth of July, and two-and-one-half-year-old Walter was playing with a set of blocks. His blond hair dangled down to his shoulders in the accepted coiffure for little boys at that time. It was very hot, and sister Em thought her perspiring cherub of a brother was looking less and less angelic. She seized his damp locks and wove them into two long braids, tying them with red, white, and blue ribbons, quite in keeping with the Fourth. The pocket-sized patriot examined himself in the mirror, scowled, and would have none of it.

Em pleaded, "But it's cooler this way, and besides, now you look like our good and wonderful President, George Washington."

Yanking the braids free, he announced, "But I don't want to be good and wonderful like George Washington—I want to be *me!*"

It was the following Fourth of July when to the virtue of independence he added that of diplomacy: if a hard, unsavory fact must be mentioned, at least couch it in tactful terms. It seems Walter had lit some punk in order to set off a string of small firecrackers, but then left it, still glowing, on top of his jacket in the bedroom. Soon jacket and bedspread were smoldering, and the room filled with smoke. He ran into the kitchen and reported, ashen-faced but diplomatic, "Mama, the house is a little bit on fire!" Mama beat out the flame, then followed through on her son.

But there was more than one way to demolish that South Boston duplex. One day he strutted into the house, looking very pleased with himself. "What have you been up to?" asked Papa. "I's a great big boy now!" Walter replied. "I can 'mash the cellar windows!" He had.

Walter received his elementary education at the Cotton Mather Public School in the Dorchester section of Boston, near the spot where Washington trained his guns on the city and forced the British to evacuate. His extant notebooks and lesson materials show a superior development, and he completed his eight years as class valedictorian. Finishing first in his class came to be a habit: he would repeat the performance in preparatory college and seminary.

Just when Walter became interested in church work is not certain. The only theological crisis in his early life occurred when the little girl next door announced that only Roman Catholics would go to heaven. He challenged her proposition on the grounds of logic: *he* was going to heaven; he was not Catholic; therefore heaven would have to include non-Catholics.

He participated with gusto in Sunday school and was surprisingly attentive during church services. "He actually seemed to understand the sermons even as a child," recalls Em. "He would prop up his chin with a stubby arm and gaze at the minister quite pensively." The Rev. Henry Birkner remembered well the ordeal with young Maier during confirmation instruction. While other students simply played back their memorized Catechism selections when quizzed by the pastor, Walter would pose some puzzlers of his own: Why did God allow Satan to exist? Did St. Paul ever get to Spain? Where is Nicea located? and the like.

Probably the greatest incentive to a profession in the church was the example set by his parents. Later in life, Walter said: "My earliest clear recollection is that of my father on his knees in the bedroom, praying." Even more a source of religious inspiration to the family was his mother. In church and community circles Anna Maier was now being called "the woman everyone loves." She saw to it that Christianity animated the life of her family and made no secret of her dream that at least one of her sons would enter the ministry. Years later, when asked to cite the most influential factor in his life, Walter replied, "The prayers, support, and outstanding example of my parents."

With this background, it comes as no surprise that he should seriously consider the possibility of entering the ministry. One day the Maiers attended a mission festival in Boston to hear an address by Dr. Henry Stein, professor at Concordia Collegiate Institute in suburban New York. It was his eloquent appeal for "more men to spread the saving gospel of Christ" which helped crystallize the determination of a twelve-year-old in the balcony to study for the ministry.

Preparation for the Lutheran ministry, however, demanded special language concentrations, even at the high-school level, in Latin, Greek, and German. To foster their son's plans, therefore, Emil and Anna encouraged his resolve to enter the Concordia Institute in New York, an academy combining both high school and junior college, as does a European *Gymnasium*. Walter made plans to attend the boarding school that fall.

The prospect of his further education at such a distance from home seemed lugubrious at best to the younger Maiers, especially little Karl, the brother who completed the family. Karl regarded Walter as his own patron saint; Walter delighted in providing him with a variety of trinkets, even though he had little or no capital at his disposal. But a resourceful wit more than compensated for lack of funds. Once Walter marched along with a torchlight political parade during the Kenney-Curley mayoralty campaign in Boston, and a parade marshall gave him two or three dozen red flares "for the younger set." Walter quit politics abruptly, and the flares served Karl as fireworks for many a Fourth of July after that.

Young Walter did his Christmas shopping not before, but after the twenty-fifth. "Why in the world should I pay a dollar for Karl's toy train signal when I can get it for twenty cents after Christmas?" inquired the boy economist. But the joy of celebrating on Christmas Eve was not to be sacrificed just because a German-American living in New England was acting like a Scot; so Walter cut a picture of the signal out of the train catalogue, wrapped it up, and presented it to Karl, who was even more thrilled by the anticipation for another day or two. It prolonged Christmas.

The Maier family spent its summers in northern New England. Flora and Emily, who were married by this time, had induced their respective husbands, Herman Hecker and Will Eburne, to purchase a vacant farmhouse near Canaan, New Hampshire, which was ideally situated on the shore of a lake framed by rolling hills and forests. Now this Canaan was far from the Biblical "promised land"; for Hampshire farmers it was more a wilderness of mean and rocky soil. The farmer who owned the property had gone West, with many others, to find better land.

The place was intended as a summer home for the family, but Anna took one look at the sprawling farmhouse, another at the panorama across the lake, and suggested that their real estate could double as a tourist haven for vacationers and so pay for itself. Soon the entire family was scrubbing, repairing, painting the structure, and finally an elegantly lettered sign was erected on the front lawn:

INN-BY-THE-LAKE
TOURISTS WELCOME

And they came. After several summers, Mama's managerial skills had more than paid for the place.

With a passion for improvements, Anna had the old kerosene lamps in the house replaced with the latest type of lighting system for areas without electricity: carbide gas lamps which were fed from a tank buried outside the house. One evening the lights started to go out because of low gas pressure. Mama was about to empty another bag of carbide powder into the water tank when her hired hand and a neighbor insisted that they could do the job. "All right," she said, "but *don't* light a match near that tank!" Anna heard them fumbling with the tank cap and went out to assist anyway. Just as she arrived, one of the men struck a match and the explosion knocked them all to the ground. Those in the house ran out to find the three terribly burned, Mama's face soon swelling hideously to twice its size with only slits left for eyes. Through prayer and sheer will power she retained consciousness—with all its agony—so that she could supervise first-aid operations from her prone position. Doctors later said that her directions probably saved all three lives. They recovered with only minor scars.

Later that summer a lightning bolt struck her kitchen, filling the room with a blue blaze and melting some of the metal objects in the place. Again she was swept off her feet, stunned yet safe. Anna Maier was down, but never out. The story of her later life was so remarkable in its own right that years afterward her pastor, Elmer A. Kettner, wrote her biography, *Grossie—The Woman Everyone Loved.*[*] And it was now that children born to Flo and Em were revising Anna's name from "Mama" to "Grossie," an abbreviation for the German *Grossmutter* (grandmother). "Grossie" she remained for the rest of her life.

The Maier boys romped through their vacations at Inn-by-the-Lake. As good New Englanders they loved the sea, but since that was beyond the mountains, one New Hampshire lake would do—their own Grafton Pond. Unfortunately, they had no boat for plying the middle waters, so six eyes began looking with ill-disguised envy at a small sailboat tied to the wharf of a neighboring estate. The tragedy of it all was that the *Mattie Weed* was rarely

[*] Elmer A. Kettner, *Grossie—The Woman Everyone Loved*, The Life Story of Anna K. Maier, the Mother of Dr. Walter A. Maier (Grand Rapids: Wm. B. Eerdmans Publishing Co., 1949).

sailed by its owner, the then-eminent author and divine, Dr. Louis Banks, of Boston. Later that year nature herself conspired to transfer ownership of the craft. Winter winds and high water snatched the boat out of drydock and deposited it again high on a small island near the center of Grafton Pond. From the moment the boys arrived in June, salvaging that ship was the all-consuming project. But simply taking it was risky. Given a body of water the size of Grafton, the owner might just recognize it.

Walter rose to the occasion. He composed a note and sent it to the august clergyman who had not yet arrived in Canaan for his summer vacation.

Dear Dr. Banks,

I am Walter Maier, who lives next to you in Canaan, New Hampshire, during the summers. Perhaps you did not know that your sailboat was blown up on the island this past winter. Would it be alright [sic] if my brothers and I try to repair and launch her?

The mast and sails are gone, but the hull seems seaworthy. You would make us very happy if you let us do this. If not, we will try to understand.

Thank you very much.                              Hopefully,
                                                 *Walter A. Maier*

The boy-diplomat all but anticipated such a reply as this:

My dear Mr. Maier:

Thank you so much for calling to my attention the sad fate of the *Mattie Weed*. My caretaker had informed me of this catastrophe earlier in the year, and I had thought the craft beyond repair. However, I am happy to note that you find the hull still seaworthy.

Since you will undertake salvage operations, I am pleased, as retiring admiral of the Grafton Sea, to make the following appointment: I name you, Walter A. Maier, Captain of the S.S. *Mattie Weed*, with all rights and privileges pertaining thereunto, and hereby convey full ownership of said vessel to yourself and your worthy brothers.

                                              Yours sincerely,
                                              *Admiral Banks*

An excited crew hovered over the *Mattie Weed* until she was seaworthy again. A new mast would have cost a year's allowance, but a thin and sturdy pine tree was shed of its branches and impressed into service. And why bother with expensive sailcloth when Grossie's enormous gray flannel comforter could catch the breezes just as well?

It was motley and makeshift, but a carnival for the imagination. Horatio Nelson, John Paul Jones, and Oliver Hazard Perry all managed several naval campaigns on Grafton Sea that summer. The creative flair, nourished by such adolescent fancy, would serve Walter well in the future even if he never got to sea.

The summer passed, and once again Inn-by-the-Lake had to be abandoned in favor of Boston. Each fall the family exodus was made more dismal by Walter's departure for the academy, since it left a stark gap in the close household circle. Yet Papa and Grossie considered it all part of a higher formula: take one son out of a Christian home, plunge him into study, mix in the varied milieu of life, wait a few years for creative interaction between individual and environment—and, behold, the man.

# 2
# Student Wam

Concordia Collegiate Institute in New York's Westchester County was a Lutheran academy which was trying to maintain stiff European educational standards in the New World. Such boarding schools probably offer a maturing experience, but many bewildered twelve- and thirteen-year-old freshmen often seem more like fledglings expected to fly before their feathers are dry. Nevertheless, the letters Walter sent his family show no discontent at having to study away from home. He rather looked upon the whole experience as a broadening adventure, his chance to make good.

At first, of course, he missed his family, George's pranks, and above all, "little Karl-boy," to whom he was constantly sending warm regards. But later letters show him completely caught up in the life of prep school, and some of them contain humble-yet-intentional references to high scores, top class ranking, and the like. A lusty *esprit de corps* charged his Class of 1912, and he described its outings, athletic prowess, and members who were now close friends. They called him "Beaner" in honor of his hometown specialty, Boston baked beans, or "Wam" (rhymes with Sam) from his initials.

Because Concordia's new Bronxville campus was under construction, the Class of 1912 was housed temporarily in nearby Hawthorne and New York City, where pairs of students roomed and boarded with Lutheran families. Wam and a classmate lodged at a home where the diet was not always adequate. His letters tell of hunting expeditions to neighboring hills in search of wild rabbits which they shot and roasted for a little extra protein. Sister Flo usually included a nickel or dime in her letters, which Walter delightedly acknowledged, once adding, "May I spend the nickel for U-Need-A Biscuits? Sometimes I'm so hungry!"

Any inconveniences, however, were forgotten when the class

15

moved into the proud new school in Bronxville, a complex of buildings in modified Georgian architecture. Since landscaping funds
had been depleted by extra construction costs, walks, shrubbery,
and trees still had to be added, not to mention a baseball diamond.
Now a shady college lane could be dispensed with, but certainly
not the field of glory for the Concordia nine. Class of '12, with
volunteers from the rest of the student body, decided to lay out a
baseball field for Alma Mater. The motto of '12 was *non solum
nobis* ("Not for ourselves alone"). "But predominantly!" upper-
classmen used to add in gibe. Here, then, was a project to prove
the motto.

With permission from the board of directors, one corner of
academy property was set aside for the diamond. Inevitably, it was
the corner where every square foot of ground was smothered with
rubbish and waste materials from the construction of the buildings.
Evidently the board was not only sports-minded, but aesthetically-
minded as well. Yet a series of student assaults with old wheelbar-
rows, shovels, and spare rakes paid off handsomely. No Polo
Grounds, certainly, but ". . . as fast and neat a diamond as is possessed by any prep school in Westchester County," boasts the yearbook.[1]

Center fielder for the Concordia team was "Beaner" Maier. His
batting averages and fielding proficiency are lost figures, the only
available statistics on the team being four wins, three losses, five
games rained out.

In order to earn most of his expenses at prep school, Walter
worked part-time in the campus kitchen washing and drying dishes.
His fondness for this chore is demonstrated by the fact that he was
never seen to touch a dishcloth in later years. Apparently, he also
had time for extracurricular activities. The yearbook lists him as
president of the Class of 1912, valedictorian, vice-president of the
student body, chairman of the press committee, Alma Mater correspondent, baseball player, and business manager of the yearbook.
He was also active in campus literary and debating groups.

The most representative view of Beaner, however, seems to have
been at study. His classmates remember him as a popular, per-
sonable, and outgoing chap who also had a "studious streak" about

him. The institute's library became a second home for Walter as he now indulged his concentrated reading habits.

Since Wam's was a pretheological curriculum, one of his subjects was Hebrew, the language in which the Old Testament was written. Almost immediately he nourished a growing interest in that tongue, which was terrorizing many of his classmates. They considered Hebrew the final indignity: after having been subjected to Latin, Greek, and German, this language with its twisted characters and odd alphabet, its multiple verb tenses and guttural sounds seemed only an academy-enforced detour from the ministry. Everything about it seemed backwards, including the way it was read: from the back of the book to the front, from the right of each line to the left.

Professor Heinrichsmeyer used to introduce his Hebrew course by devoting the first period to a spirited defense of the subject, and concluding, "At least you have the consolation that Hebrew is read from the top of the page to the bottom, even if everything else is different." This was usually greeted by a few hoots of discontent from the class, at which the professor drew himself erect, changed his benign smile to the frown of an Old Testament prophet and thundered, "This was God's language to His chosen people, and you will reverence it as such!" From then on the class learned Hebrew.

Another of his teachers, Prof. Henry Stein, Latin scholar and theologian, exercised the most profound influence on Walter both scholastically and spiritually. Ever since his mission sermon in Boston, Dr. Stein had shown special interest in Wam and now fostered his inclination toward the ministry. In later years, when patriarchal "Doc" Stein could appreciate his foresight in singling out *that* student, he always recalled the conference in which Walter announced his decision to go on to the seminary. That final resolve for the ministry came logically and normally; no brush with death shattered indecision, no mystical illumination intervened to change his life.

A few days before graduation, '12's yearbook, *The Echo*, appeared. In old English boarding-school tradition, the editorial staff delighted in cutting everyone down to size. By a minor marvel, Wam escaped with only the following:

The Hub of the Universe became too small to hold this young prodigy, so he left the bean-pots of Boston for Concordia's classic soup-bowls. Since his arrival "Beaner" has accumulated a vast store of knowledge by "grinding," though he is still behind in geography, having the idea that the world is bounded on all sides by Boston. He is as shrewd as the proverbial Yank; also a tireless worker, always occupied in doing something—or somebody. We say the latter from sad experience, and in order to get even we made him our business manager.[2]

The commencement exercises for the Class of 1912 took place in the proper old-world traditions, with musical selections followed by oratory in German, Latin, and English. Sitting in the audience on that warm June evening was Anna Maier, fresh from Boston; Papa could not attend because of an illness. Anna was proud—her son had the honor of delivering the valedictory address—and nervous—she had experienced this ordeal once before at grade-school graduation, when young Walter's pause between pages one and two of his speech seemed the longest five seconds in memory.

Walter now addressed the crowd in a manner which shocked Mama into the realization that six years had made a man out of her boy. He had learned voice control, modulation, and gestures, and spoke with confidence. After expressing the class's gratitude to the administration and faculty, he climaxed with a plea for the establishment of a Lutheran university in the New York area, perhaps with Concordia as nucleus. At the close of the address came his first ovation.[3]

After the ceremonies, the diploma-clutching graduates of '12 were congratulated by a phalanx of families and friends. Later in the evening, however, Walter was questioning the precise academic worth of the sheepskin in his hand. To be sure, the document stated in elegant Latin that he had graduated with highest honors. But with what degree? Although Concordia held to the demanding standards of European scholarship, it did not yet confer degrees which coordinated with the American system of secondary and collegiate education. Since it combined a high school with a two-year junior college, two more senior college years would be necessary for the regular Bachelor of Arts degree. Yet those who wished to study for the ministry now enrolled at Concordia Theological

Seminary in St. Louis, itself a graduate divinity school supplied by such junior colleges across the country as Concordia, Bronxville.

Walter, however, wanted to attain a regular college degree before starting at the seminary, because long-range plans involving postgraduate study were forming in his mind. But what university would accept him without an A.B.? Yet if he studied for the degree now he would fall two years behind his class at the seminary, not to mention the added expense.

The solution presented itself back in Boston after a conference with the dean of the faculty of arts and sciences at Boston University. Because of his performance in Bronxville, Walter was permitted to take almost a double load in order to complete his last two college years in one, *and* he was given a scholarship. So it was that the next June witnessed another graduation, as Wam received his Bachelor of Arts degree from Boston University.

In the fall of 1913, Walter left his native New England for Concordia Theological Seminary in St. Louis, soon to become one of Protestantism's largest divinity schools.

The pattern of seminary life was different from that of the academy, since students were now more matured in preparing for their professional future. A lengthy succession of courses was required, some of them so labeled that the very names struck dread in the hearts of neophytes: Propaedeutics, Exegesis, Hermeneutics, Isagogics, and Dogmatics. Within a month or two the first-year men had to master a whole new vocabulary.

Once again it was Hebrew Old Testament exegesis (interpretation) which especially engrossed Walter. Soon enough Professor Pardieck noticed that "the fellow from Boston" not only sliced through his quizzes and exams ruthlessly, but actually seemed to enjoy Hebrew. Old Testament studies fascinated Wam, and he determined to study Semitics on a graduate level.

As before, Walter invested much time in the library, although spare hours were claimed by various jobs since by this time he was entirely on his own resources. Back in Boston, Papa's health was failing, and he was confined to bed for long periods. The family remained solvent only through Grossie's skillful management of finances, but nothing was left for Walter's education. Through work and several business enterprises, however, Wam not only earned his way through the seminary, but even sent money home from time to time. Early Saturday mornings he would catch the first streetcar and arrive in downtown St. Louis at 6 A.M. to sell food and produce at the farmer's market. One morning the sleepy scholar arrived at 6:15 and lost his job.

Disappointment is the mother of alternative. Why not sell something more in keeping with the academic profession? Although the first typewriters appeared shortly after the Civil War, only now were they coming into such general use that even college students could afford them. Walter secured an Oliver franchise and formed the Concordia Typewriter Company. Sales boomed, and in a short time operations were broadened to include graduates out in the ministry. Ironically, the astute typewriter salesman himself used only the "hunt and peck" system for the rest of his life.

Another company he founded was The Seminary Press, which mimeographed lectures and materials for classroom use. That Wam had inherited Grossie's resourcefulness was shown also in his celebrated book transaction. Someone died and left a vast theological library which Walter and two classmates purchased with what capital they could muster. After combing the collection for titles they themselves wanted, the three put the rest of the books on sale and finally auction. Business was brisk, but when word got out that this Maier project had already realized its original investment several times over, all bidding ceased, and the entrepreneurs were treated to a touch of frost. Wam announced a final quotation of five cents per book for the remainder. Stony silence greeted his offer, and most of the useful works had, in fact, been purchased by now. Whereupon Maier and company stripped the books of their covers and sold the contents by weight for their raw paper value, since paper was a needed war material at the time. The salvage price alone more than repaid the original investment, and it was a happy son who could forward to Boston a check larger than usual. Evidently his popularity was not tarnished by financial success, for during his senior year he was elected president of the Concordia student association.

The problem of discipline did not loom very large at an institution such as the seminary, but parietal rules existed nevertheless. Since the administration frowned on late hours, the night watchman had students who returned after midnight sign their names on a special list which was totaled at the end of each semester and delivered to the dean's office. Old Franz, the watchman, had little schooling, but he was very conscientious and claimed that no student could sneak by him. And he had the list of latecomers to prove it; only the dean regretted to inform him that such signatures as "Julius Caesar," "Napoleon Bonaparte," "John Calvin," "Richard Wagner," and "Charles Darwin" were possibly not genuine.

Old Franz was like the watchdog retained by its owners for bark instead of bite. The students puzzled as to how he would react in any serious emergency, so they staged a holdup in which Wam was to be robbed by a disguised classmate brandishing a borrowed water pistol. The students howled for Franz. He came running up to the assailant, who suddenly shifted his aim toward Franz. The seminary night watchman was last seen running down the hall, shrieking, *"Ich bin geschossen!"* (I've been shot!)

Walter's favorite means of relaxation was to take long walks with head tilted downward. In such pensive pose he frequently found things. Once he spied a dollar bill under a policeman's foot, asked the officer to lift his right leg, and simply picked up the dollar. On another occasion he found a ten-dollar bill, a small fortune in pre-inflation days. He advertised in the local journal that a sum of money had been found and would be returned to the person giving the correct denomination and location of loss. Letters arrived claiming loss of various amounts, and one eccentric wrote how she had washed her ten-dollar bills and hung them on a clothes line to dry, but one had blown away! Since no description even approached the facts, Walter used the money to give a banquet for some of his classmates.

It was a memorable feast, especially because that was the last happy evening the host could spend with his friends for some time. The next morning Walter became ill with chills, nausea, throbbing headache, sore throat, and soaring fever. Later a typical rash appeared, and the disease was diagnosed as a virulent scarlet fever.

An ambulance was summoned, and Wam was carried out on a stretcher flanked by two lines of solemn seminarians.

The ambulance sped off to the Isolation Hospital, and "Walter A. Maier, Concordia student" had the distinction of being the last patient admitted to the antique structure. Walter's bed looked as if it had been used, but a nurse assured him that the sheets and pillow cases were just yellowed with age. Then, to climax his misery, a patient in the next bed struck up a conversation with the helpful comment, "Say, Mister, a man just died in that bed!"

Soon the worst was over: the fever broke to safer levels, and the rash gradually subsided. Two weeks later Wam was permitted to continue his recuperation at the dormitory, and in a short time he was back in class. Never again for the next thirty-five years would he be seriously ill.

The following June, Walter and his roommate-business associate, Paul Prokopy, had to remain an additional week after the seminary closed to finish some mimeographing. But they had not reckoned the extra days' expenses into their close budgets. After purchasing train tickets to New England, the two had only a few cents left between them, and it looked to be a hungry journey. Then came the idea. They invested their coppers in penny post cards and noted some crucial stops on the railroad timetable. Off went this message to four seminarians who lived in the cities they had checked:

Dear Classmate:
We are without funds and therefore without food. We shall pass through your city on June ___, and our train is due in the station at ___ A.M./P.M. Please tell your mother.

Your sincere classmates,<br>
*Walter Maier & Paul Prokopy*

The final day at the seminary they fasted, and early the next morning entrained for the long journey home, both now famished. Soon Decatur, Illinois, was announced—the first test. As the train lurched to a halt, there stood classmate Bob Heyne, big as life and with a box lunch to match! At Fort Wayne it was time for supper, and who should provide it but "Atch" Dorn with a suitcase-sized parcel. Atch's mother was so touched with the appeal-by-post card that she had prepared a chicken dinner for the occasion. At Adrian, Michigan, it was country sausage, and in New York State, beef. Not only did the post-card project function perfectly, the menu even showed variety. The two had so much food that they shared it with fellow passengers.

Aside from such capers and conviviality, the making of a minister is an earnest and extended process. In the course of his studies, the Concordia theolog faced a series of subjects from each of the five major departments at the seminary. He learned the Hebrew literature and history of God's dealings with humanity from creation to the time of Christ in courses taught by the department of Old Testament. Studies in the department of New Testament carried the record on through the Greek sources dealing with the life of Christ and the earliest history of Christianity. The chronicle of the church from its founding down to the present day was unfolded by the department of historical theology. Christian dogma, doctrines, and ethics were taught by the department of systematic theology, and the student learned the art of preaching as well as the sundry skills required of a pastor from courses in the department of practical theology.

Toward the end of his senior year, Walter was summoned for the interview which would determine his assignment, and he told the professor in charge of placement that he wanted to continue his theological study along with a military chaplaincy. Although he was informed that such a combination might be available, nothing came of it, and he applied for a graduate fellowship in Old Testament studies at Harvard University Divinity School. This was awarded him in recognition of his proficiency in the field.

Another day of commencement dawned in Walter's life, but this one carried with it more finality than the others. His Class of 1916 would now be separated, in a sense, for life, since no reunion could bring all the graduates together again. They were assigned their first congregations throughout the forty-eight states and Canada, while some received special calls as missionaries to Brazil, Argentina, China, or India. Ordination and installation would follow on their arrival at these scattered parishes, and they would be ministers at last.

# 3

# Back to Boston

Harvard—he always spoke the name reverently—was academic heaven to Walter. As a youth he loved to cross the Charles River and stroll about old Cambridge, dreaming of the day when he might study at America's first university. And now Harvard itself was making his postgraduate program possible, naming him an Edward Hopkins, James Savage, or Shattuck Scholar, depending on the particular fellowship awarded him annually.

As graduate fellow, Walter studied at Harvard Divinity School from 1916 to 1918, and at Harvard Graduate School of Arts and Sciences from 1918 to 1920. This shift was necessitated by his field of concentration—Semitic languages, literature, and history —for which the degree program was administered by the graduate school. His early interest in Biblical Hebrew had now blossomed into a study of the other Semitic languages, especially Babylonian and Assyrian, which were even more abstruse than Hebrew. Wam mastered the difficult wedge-shaped imprints of Babylonian cuneiform on clay tablets and soon learned to decipher also the linear wedge-writing of ancient Assyrian inscriptions. He enjoyed the challenge of translating those strange configurations.

To fulfill the conditions of one of his fellowships, Walter became a teaching assistant in the department of Semitics. He also studied Arabic, and Prof. James Richard Jewett was impressed enough with his performance that he engaged him to teach his classes in Arabic during the winter months while he was in California. For the first time Wam found himself facing a class rather than a professor. He relished the experience and resolved to include teaching in his eventual career plans.

During these semesters at Harvard there was necessarily much concentration on study. But one day in 1917 a friend dared him to enter the annual university-wide public speaking contest, and Walter accepted the challenge. In storybook fashion, he outstripped a large field of competitors and—by unanimous decision of the judges—won the coveted Billings Prize in oratory. But before the award of one hundred dollars was given him, someone remembered that the terms of Walter's fellowship precluded his receiving financial assistance from any other sources at Harvard. Since university authorities were unable to decide the problem, he was advised to bring a friendly suit against Harvard for award of the prize money. In this way, the issue would be presented to the Massachusetts courts for decision. Two years after the contest, the Bay State justices ruled that prize money could not constitute financial assistance in the sense intended by the terms of the fellowship, or such terms would involve unnecessary penalization. He won the suit, and the university treasurer released the prize money. The case of Maier *vs.* Harvard set a precedent for such instances.

Our Boston Demosthenes received his Master of Arts degree from Harvard University in 1920, having completed also most of his residence requirements for the degree of Doctor of Philosophy, as well as a first draft of his doctoral dissertation. He was now free to continue a career in the ministry while working up his thesis and preparing for the final examination.

Actually, Walter was little more than a half-time student during these years, for from 1917 to 1920 the theoretical scholar was also the very practical minister. On May 20, 1917, Walter Arthur Maier was ordained into the holy ministry at Zion Lutheran Church in Boston, and installed as assistant pastor of the church. Present for the solemn, liturgical ceremony was the Maier family, which now found a cluster of prayers and hopes formally fulfilled.

The Maiers celebrated the ordination with a gathering of the clan. Now a family man himself, George greatly admired his younger brother and predicted that one day he would exceed Phillips Brooks. Karl was so impressed by the ordination that his resolve to enter the ministry was strengthened. Grossie, of course, was glowing, and Papa sensed that he could now depart in peace, Simeon-like, since one of his sons was in the ministry.

For some years Papa's health had been failing, but at first he was not debilitated and so continued tuning pianos with high reputation as a specialist in that instrument. When the great Paderewski made one of his American tours, he invited Boston's Emil Maier to accompany him and make certain that his Steinway was always at tonal perfection. Papa also went on tours with the Boston Festival Orchestra, and one of his grand moments came the day he returned from a three-month concert circuit and handed Grossie his savings from the tour—enough that she could return to Europe for a summer and visit her mother, whom she had not seen for seventeen years.

Later, when a stroke paralyzed his left side, he designed a new set of tuning instruments which could be worked one-handed and so he carried on as best he could. Soon, however, he was confined to bed. As he grew weaker, his faith grew stronger, and he was never without his Bible or prayer book.

Shortly before dying, Papa was surrounded by his family. With halting breath, he paid his wife this tribute: "You have been my good angel. You prayed for me without ceasing. Under God I have you to thank that I am assured of the happiness of eternal life." After he had each son and daughter promise to lead a Christian life, he prayed with them and gave the Apostolic blessing to all present. Shaken with grief, Walter would not forget that benediction. Papa passed away peacefully, some twenty-six years before Grossie, and was buried at Brook Farm, the famed Transcendentalist haven which had been converted into a Lutheran cemetery.

Young life will replace the old. One of the newly-Reverend Maier's first duties as assistant pastor at Zion Church was to baptize an infant in the absence of his superior, the same Rev. Henry Birkner who had confirmed and ordained him. Since this would be his first baptism, he had rechecked the baptismal rite to avoid any slip-up. Before the sacrament is administered, questions are addressed to the sponsors who answer in the child's stead.

"Do you believe in God the Father?" he asked the godmother, who was cradling the infant, and the godfather.

"I do," they replied in the regular response.

"Do you believe in God the Son?"

Only the woman answered "I do." Walter looked anxiously at

the man, who finally opened his mouth with a resounding, "I do *not!*"

"Not during my *first* baptism!" Walter agonized inwardly, trying to imagine what in the world his seminary professors would do in a situation like this. The entire congregation was holding its sanctified breath.

Without changing his tone, and as if he were reading from the formulary itself, the officiant turned to the woman and said, "Please reply again, do *you* believe in God the Son?"

"I do."

"And *so do I!*" declared Walter as a hasty substitute sponsor. "Then you and I will answer these questions."

Blissfully unaware of the controversy it had stirred, the baby raised no protest and was finally baptized.

Fortunately, there were no such crises in the pulpit. Walter's first sermon to gain any notice in the press was, almost prophetically, a mission address preached in August, 1917, at Clinton, Massachusetts. In this he portrayed the increasingly widespread missionary activity of the church and stated that the goal of Christianity continued to be an announcing of the gospel message throughout the globe. One's highest privilege, he said, would be to aid that aim.[1]

The following October 31 marked the four-hundredth anniversary of Luther's sparking the Reformation by nailing his ninety-five theses to the church door at Wittenberg, and Walter was invited back to Clinton to give the quadricentennial address. This time the city newspaper supplied orchids in advance: "A special treat is anticipated in his address, for he is possessed of rare eloquence and is a forceful speaker."[2] At another celebration in North Plymouth it was reported that "Rev. W. A. Maier of Harvard University had the attention of his hearers riveted from beginning to end."[3] Other papers started referring to "the best Lutheran pulpit orator of Boston and vicinity." Now the "pulpit orator" was only twenty-four years old at the time—dangerously early for accolades—but apparently such notices did not turn his head. Of course, *someone* saved the clippings!

After trying to avoid it, America entered World War I in 1917. Although draft-exempt as a clergyman, Walter was anxious to serve both his country and his church at a time of crisis. A year earlier he had volunteered for the chaplaincy, and now the backwash of war splashed into his life.

Several German ships manned by three hundred officers and seamen had taken refuge in Boston Harbor to escape attack by the British shortly before America entered hostilities. When the United States declared war against the Kaiser, these ships were seized and their crews interned as enemy aliens on Gallup's Island in Boston Harbor. Since the Germans did not have a chaplain among them and were out of normal contact with the mainland, Dorchester's Pastor Maier petitioned the Commissioner of Immigration for permission to minister to the spiritual needs of these and other prisoners of war in the Boston area. His request was granted, and Walter soon found himself cruising out to the island on a government boat escorted by federal agents.

He had already determined the aims of his attempt at P.O.W. mission work: 1) as minister of the gospel, to serve the spiritual necessities of aliens and prisoners; 2) as patriotic citizen, to explain American democratic principles of government so that the captives might bury their grudges against the United States and its goals in the war; 3) as a humanitarian, to see that the internees were adequately supplied with food and clothing.

The harbor patrol boat docked and the government officers introduced the Germans to their new chaplain. The aliens scowled with suspicion. Perhaps the man was just "a plant" to spy on them for federal authorities. But Walter conversed with them in German and announced that regular church services would be held on Gallup's Island beginning the next Sunday. The congregation at "Island Church" for the first worship numbered only a few curious souls. But the Germans learned to their surprise that an American could deliver a good sermon in the mother tongue. After that the sailors attended en masse.

Because Grossie had insisted on learning English as quickly as possible, very little German had been spoken in the Maier family. However, any German-Americans of the time possessed a feeling for the language, and the grammar Walter had picked up at college. Suddenly his study of German had become far more than academic.

At her son's request, Grossie organized a group of Back Bay families to help supply the internees with articles of food and clothing. "While Grossie bought Liberty bonds, maintained a victory garden, and helped send packages to the soldiers, she also remembered the words of Christ, 'I was a prisoner and ye visited Me. . . ,' " her biographer comments.[4] She was grieved that the lands of her birth and of her choice should be at war.

Walter also initiated social programs for the internees on Gallup's Island as well as for unfortunates of all nationalities detained at the immigration station in Boston. In these he enlisted the help of brother Karl, who still recalls the weekly trips to the water front with a heavy 35 millimeter motion-picture projector which they set up for showing films "fearfully and wonderfully made as to plot," he writes. "That projector was operated by an 'armstrong' motor, the arm being mine, as I turned the hand crank endlessly."[5]

This religious-patriotic-welfare program, conceived entirely by Wam for people who otherwise would have been forgotten in their detention, brought results. The alien detainees learned that their physical and spiritual well-being were important to Bostonians after all, while the German officers and men on Gallup's Island soon buried their dislike of America and resolved to make the best of their circumstances. They busied themselves with building a chapel, laying out tennis courts, and even arranging trim—though beerless—beer gardens. A series of flower beds were planted with seeds which Walter brought them and fenced off with driftwood deposited by bay tides. Soon Gallup's was transformed into such a garden spot that harbor sight-seeing boats started swinging by the island. The YMCA now helped support Walter in his welfare work, appointing him a secretary of the organization.

In fact, when shortly afterward the government prepared to transfer the internees to Hot Springs, North Carolina, the seamen signed a petition requesting permission to stay in Boston Harbor, even though the bleak New England winter was approaching. But Gallup's Island was to be used for a military hospital facility, and the men went south.

Presently, Boston port officials and the secret service questioned the wisdom of ever having let a pastor of German ancestry minister to German enemy aliens during wartime. A censor had discovered that the young minister was apparently sending the internees cryptic messages in a code which no one could crack. Walter was called to the Immigration Authority headquarters, where he was greeted with cold formality and a telegram in German was thrust before him.

"Reverend Maier, did you send this?"

"Why yes . . . it's my Christmas wire to the seamen in North Car—"

"Would you please translate it for us—accurately?"

"Of course." He smiled as he saw that intelligence had already prepared a translation which the officer was studying. Rendered in English, the communication ended as follows:

Many thanks for all your help on the Island. May you fight the good fight of your Christian faith (I Tim.6,12), for you know that God will support you in your absence from loved ones in Germany. Always remember Rom.8,37-39. Christmas blessings in Is.9,6.

"Reverend Maier, I shall come to the point immediately. Perhaps we are not justified, but in wartime everything is questioned. Just what are those code references you sandwiched into what looks like a harmless religious message? This 'I Tim.6,12' or 'Rom. 8,37-39,' and so forth? What are you trying to communicate to those German seamen?"

Walter could hardly refrain from bursting into bewildered laughter. "Gentlemen, you know what *this* is!" he said, holding up his Bible. "Well, 'I Tim.' is simply the common abbreviation for the book of First Timothy in the Bible, while the numbers are chapter and verse." Then he thumbed to "I Tim. 6,12" and read aloud, "Fight the good fight of faith . . ." and so on.

Officialdom assumed its red face dutifully.

"Reverend Maier . . . this is very embarrassing for us. You see, it's just that . . . well in wartime . . ."

Walter chuckled, and then the whole office broke into relieved laughter. The officer concluded by thanking him for his part in helping the Germans become the orderly and cooperative group they were.

Early in the summer of 1918, the United States Army accepted young Pastor Maier as Protestant chaplain at Camp Gordon, near Atlanta, Georgia.[6] Although he was in the South for only a few months, Walter was delighted with Dixie until a smoldering summer descended; like any New England, he suffered in the heat. His services at Camp Gordon were well attended, but, more important, the stint in the Army gave him a first-hand acquaintance with military life which he would use to good advantage in the future.

After the armistice was signed, Walter returned to Harvard, Zion Church, and his welfare work. He was appointed chaplain to the Army's Camp Devens, near Boston, where he also saw opportunities for extending his P.O.W. ministry. Twelve miles from Devens was United States War Prison Camp No. 1 at Still River, Massachusetts, where one hundred German prisoners of war were incarcerated behind electrically charged wires. Before capture some had been sailors aboard the *Kronprinz Wilhelm*, a raider which had sunk thirty ships, and the rest were crew members of the German submarine U-58, which had been swamped by the American destroyer *Fanning*.

With permission from the Secretary of War, Walter determined to try his spiritual-patriotic-welfare approach here as well. At Still River, however, he met with frigid response; in fact, no one even appeared at the chapel room for the services he had announced. What to do with a congregation at zero was not covered by textbooks in practical theology, but clearly there could be only one solution: if the men would not leave their quarters for the chapel, the pastor would leave the chapel for their quarters. When Wam entered the barracks to talk with the prisoners, he was greeted by snarling suspicion.

"You are a preacher," rasped one of them in Prussian dialect, an officer, "and American preachers did as much to agitate for war as anyone else. We want nothing to do with you!"

"But I have not come to speak of war, but of peace—the peace of God."

Walter knew it would be difficult to convince the prisoners that his would be a different kind of message, but convince them he must. He told the men he would return a week later, a prospect they found less than enticing. On the way home he thought of a plan.

Approaching his mother a bit sheepishly, Walter suggested, "Wouldn't it be wonderful if we could bring a little Christmas cheer to the prisoners out at Still River?"

Grossie recognized the look in her son's eyes: another project was underway—and more work for herself. "Yes, Walter, but—out with it—what do you have in mind?"

"It's a big order, Ma, but I know it will work wonders. Could you knit a hundred pairs of woolen socks for the men? They need these more than anything else."

"*One hundred* pairs? By Christmas?" she gasped, then pondered. "Well, I'll try. Maybe some of the ladies will help."

Grossie's nimble fingers started flashing knitting needles, and soon others joined her task force. The goal was branded as "impossible," then "improbable," later "conceivable," and of course the women finished a few days before yuletide. Then they baked Christmas cookies and prepared a dinner which they would cater to the prison camp for a surprise celebration.

A car caravan set out from Dorchester on Christmas Day, 1918, led by the brothers Maier driving Wam's old Dodge, and it arrived at Still River despite a violent sleet storm en route. The group was admitted into the prisoners' stockade, and after singing a carol or two they distributed neatly wrapped packets of socks and small gift items. The dumbfounded Germans were then invited into a festively decorated mess hall and treated to their first Continental cuisine since capture, including hundreds of old-world Christmas cookies. Toward the close of the celebration, Walter announced that a Christmas service would be held in the chapel, and the hosts led the way by singing *Adeste Fidelis*. One by one the prisoners drifted into the candle-lit hall until all of them joined in the worship. All, that is, except Hans, the submarine gunner, who had vowed never to speak a word in front of hated Americans. He just sat in back sullenly, not quite believing what was happening. But when the service concluded with *Stille Nacht* ("Silent Night"), it was too much for Hans. Tears rolling down his cheeks, he too joined in. It was an unforgettable Christmas night for the Germans —and the Americans.

From then on the chaplain was assured of maximum attendance at his services. A few creature comforts, a little humanitarian outreach, and communication was again possible. In succeeding weeks, some of the men confessed that their neglected faith was reawakened by his preaching, and four or five found faith for the first time.

Having gained their confidence, Walter employed also at Still River the spiritual-social program which had proved itself in the harbor. The P.O.W.'s came to understand America's role in the war just concluded and now adjusted to their detention. The music-loving prisoners even formed their own German band. An old keg covered with oilskin was the drum, a couple of bones from ham roasts served as clappers, while a used-up banjo and some dented-but-donated brass pieces completed the ensemble. Somewhat more satisfying aesthetically was their glee club, which made the rounds of local army camps to entertain troops still stationed there.

One day word arrived that the prisoners would be repatriated shortly. To show their appreciation for Wam's work in their rehabilitation, they surprised him with many handmade gifts, which, though fashioned from crude materials and tools, were nevertheless handsomely made. Beautiful carved models of the *Kronprinz Wilhelm* and the submarine U-58—as well as two of the vessels they had sunk!—were presented to Walter. A great, yard-long replica of a clipper ship, accurate down to the thousands of knots in its weblike rigging, was designated for Grossie's fireplace mantel. Other intricate miniatures included a lighthouse, boats in bottles, and even a stately castle on the Rhine, complete with parapets and drawbridges. Walter was moved. He put the models on display at a series of church bazaars to aid European war orphans and then distributed many of them among relatives and friends who had aided his work with the prisoners.

The Germans did not forget young *"Pfarrer* Maier" after their repatriation, and some of them maintained a long correspondence with him. Several even arranged to send him a rare copy of an early Luther Bible, a second edition of the reformer's German translation published in 1541. That Bible remained one of Walter's proudest possessions.

The signing of the armistice in November, 1918, did not automatically reassemble the pieces of that puzzle called civilization which had been shattered by hostilities. Millions of altered lives and uprooted families now began the slow, sometimes agonizing, process of finding the path back to normalcy. Walter wanted to do his small part in helping accelerate this procedure at one spot on the globe. Because of his success at Gallup's Island and Still River, both German nationals in the Boston area and American governmental agencies came to regard the twenty-five-year-old as ambassador between the two groups. In many instances it was his good offices—like all these efforts, entirely on his own initiative and largely without remuneration—which eased the lot of people who otherwise could have been quite miserable during the war and its aftermath.

The Long Wharf Immigration Station in Boston Harbor had seen much of Walter. Many alien women and children, the families of men who were interned or captive at various points in the world, had been channeled to Long Wharf. Obviously, they would fare better if permitted the freedom to earn their own living rather than existing as wards of the state; but who could arrange for their parole? Probably no private individual, but perhaps a government. Walter knew that the neutral Swiss legation in Washington, D.C., was interested in easing the lot of such internees during the war. Upon applying there for assistance, he was commissioned as unofficial representative of the Swiss embassy in the Boston area.

Immigration authorities agreed to release the alien families if Pastor Maier, in the name of the Swiss Government, would act as "guardian, advisor, and cashier" for the entire group. He would. The families were paroled and comfortably housed among church people in the Boston area. When accommodations in the Hub finally dwindled, one missionary group from Borneo was sent to live at Inn-by-the-Lake up in New Hampshire.

With the end of the war, husbands were still separated from their paroled families. Particularly unfortunate was the case of Dr. Karl Muck, famed conductor of the Boston Symphony Orchestra. At the outbreak of hostilities, he had been arrested as an enemy alien, taken from his wife and family, and interned at Fort Oglethorpe in Georgia. Through the Swiss diplomats, Walter succeeded in arranging an early reunion and repatriation for the Mucks, as well as other German families in his charge. In May, 1919, he received a communiqué from the Legation of Switzerland, Washington, D.C., which began:

Dear Sir:

I have now the honor to inform you that the German Government has accepted the proposals of the Government of the United States for the repatriation of the personnel, officers, crews, of merchant ships, and interned civilians with their respective families. The Legation has already made arrangements with competent authorities for the repatriation of the above mentioned Germans and their respective families on the transport leaving Charleston, June 18. Transportation on this steamer will be at the expense of the German government. . . .[7]

Mrs. Karl Muck with the other paroled wives and families could now join their husbands and fathers at Charleston.

A farewell reception was held for the entire group, at which the internees expressed warm appreciation for the treatment accorded them in America. One of the company presented Em's little daughter Dotty with a huge doll house he had fashioned, all seven of its rooms furnished to the last detail, from tiny electric chandeliers to the wooden fish on the kitchen skillet.

A reporter from the *Boston Globe* came down to the harbor and did a story on the aliens who were embarking for Charleston. What impressed him was the fact that a youthful minister-student had occasioned all this on his own initiative; he included a sketch on "the one man who did more than anyone else in bringing about the happy arrangement."[8] In these months, other newspapers also published articles on Walter's prisoner work, applauding his small but meaningful effort in helping heal the fractures of war.

When Walter was awarded his Master's degree, several university teaching positions were offered him which would have facilitated his preparation for the doctorate. Naturally, his professors urged him to accept one of the offers. Here was one of the crucial decisions he would face in life. The alternatives seemed almost equally appealing: a career of scholarship, or service to the church in the active ministry. However, it was not a matter of choice; his ultimate goals involved *both* teaching and church work. But probably he felt that even a temporary secular academic career at this time would have lured him from the higher summons which had sent him through the academy and seminary. First, therefore, he would answer the call of the church, perhaps later the call of the university.

# 4

# League and Love

The call of the church came promptly—and surprisingly. The year of Walter's birth had also seen the founding of a Lutheran young people's organization called the Walther League, named after Dr. C. F. W. Walther, one of the fathers of Lutheranism in America. Formed for the purpose of furthering Christian knowledge as well as service to church and home through various projects, the organization soon grew to the point where it needed a national executive secretary at its helm. The League now appealed to Boston's Pastor Maier to accept this office.

Although he had not envisioned youth work as his primary calling in the church, Walter saw the critical juncture in the church's program for young people. The proffered post carried with it also the editorship of the organization's monthly journal, *The Walther League Messenger*. If youth were important to the future of the church, then so was this call to administration and to pen. He prayed over his decision, and said yes.

Again Wam forsook his cherished New England for the Midwest, since the national offices of the League were in Milwaukee. En route he stopped off at Fort Wayne, where, amid impressive ceremonies on the evening of October 7, 1920, he was installed as executive secretary of the Walther League.

His first responsibility in Milwaukee was to familiarize himself with every aspect of the organization's operations and multiphase program. The League's executive board had guaranteed him a free hand in formulating policy, but now made one important suggestion: rid the organization of a project which appeared too ambitious for it to maintain—a tuberculosis sanitarium at Wheat Ridge, Colorado, which was supported largely by the League. Presently it needed far more funds for capital expansion than the organization could provide, and so the new executive secretary had the sorry task of traveling out to Wheat Ridge and announcing the withdrawal of League support.

It was a miserable train ride, made worse by Walter's unhappy mission. Upon arrival, he was given a guided tour of the institution by an eager staff, which was totally unaware of the deeper reason behind his visit. Passing bed after bed, he saw patients in various stages of the steep climb back to health, and his distress mounted. What if some of them should relapse instead of recover because the League withdrew its support and the sanitarium had to close?

After the tour, Superintendent H. H. Feiertag told Walter of plans for future expansion. Wam's heart pounded. *He* had to call a halt to it all? That instant, without consulting his board or realizing how it was to be done, he pledged the League's full and continuing support of the sanitarium and more tangibly than ever before.

In the following months, the young people helped raise more than $200,000 for Wheat Ridge, saving what is today a flourishing institution of mercy.

Many other trips had to be made in behalf of League work, especially to various regional conventions of the organization. With an executive secretary who found his job exciting, an epidemic of enthusiasm soon spread throughout the League. Membership quickly shot upward, hundreds of new societies from coast to coast joined the national organization, and the circulation of the *Messenger* doubled in a matter of months. In less than a year Editor Maier substantially increased the size of the magazine, added features and pictures, wrote brisk editorials, and dressed it all in a fresh new format.

But this was only the beginning. Soon after arriving in Milwaukee, Walter stated, "The time is past when the Walther League must do big things in a little way." This keynoted his administration. He submitted an expansion program to the board which would have made it gasp were it not squarely behind the League's new look. He also suggested a spate of new projects for the organization: League support of foreign missionaries, sponsorship of an extensive Bible study program with a separate journal for this purpose, lengthening the chain of hospices in various cities—

Christian homes for working girls and travelers, establishing a separate student district of the League for colleges and universities, and participating in European relief work. Within a year or two each of these projects became an active reality for church youth.

The leaguers responded to all this in spirited fashion and made no secret of their admiration for a leader not much older than themselves. At regional and national conventions they now greeted him with prolonged applause; his speaking schedule was dotted with invitations. Clearly, rapport was no problem.

The executive secretary was twenty-seven, handsome, and quite single. By this time his boyish features were offset by a distinguished forehead and penetrating blue eyes, which contributed to an air of masculine determination. It was only natural that a number of feminine leaguers should find something more than spiritual inspiration in the man. The matchmakers were at work, of course, but Walter dodged their efforts. He regarded girls with a critical eye; a flaw in some attractive young eligible would thwart any possible romance. It was always "beautiful but dense," "character lacking," "no sparkle," or some such objection. Friends twitted him with being a perfectionist when it came to women. He said nothing in defense. At Bronxville, St. Louis, and Boston he had been too busy studying or working to be concerned with girls.

A charmer named Elsie from Boston's Jamaica Plain was the exception. Wam and Elsie began dating, and friends approved. However, this budding attraction was all but nipped by Walter's move to Milwaukee.

Any church young people's organization is liable to the charge of being a matrimonial agency. When critics said this of the Walther League, Secretary Maier fired back, "If, in the League's program of spiritual growth and service, boy meets girl and they fall in love, what in the name of common sense is wrong with that?" Of course he never thought this would happen to him. But it did.

One spring morning in 1921, a young suburban Indianapolis teacher boarded the interurban for her daily trip to school, carrying along the latest issue of the *Messenger* to read on the way. She had the unlikely name of Hulda Eickhoff. No crowd-follower when it came to naming children, her mother had found mention in the Old Testament of a Huldah who prophesied in Jerusalem (II Kings 22:14). A slender brunette with expressive brown eyes and a sparkling smile, Miss Eickhoff was probably the most attractive teacher Public School No. 54 had seen. This fact was not lost on her pupils, who regularly stampeded for the privilege of remaining after class to help her tidy up the room.

The magazine she was reading in the lurching coach had not always served as commuting companion, but lately something had happened which seemed to give the *Messenger* new life. The articles and editorials penned by the person who signed himself "W.A.M." not only contained a solid message, but were zestful reading as well. Evidently this "W.A.M." person was Walter A. Maier, the League's new director.

"What kind of man is he?" she mused. Most likely a mature individual in the middle prime of life; tall—he wrote tall-ly; happily married—how else could he write such articles on marital and family ideals? And probably he had at least four or five children; his knowing concern for young people showed that. From his writing alone she knew she would enjoy meeting such a person, but of course that would never happen.

Soon Hulda took up membership in the Walther League and was promptly elected secretary of the Indianapolis chapter. Before long the state board learned about the efficiency of a certain Miss Eickhoff, who also happened to teach the eighth grade. "Just the person for our new Junior department," suggested the League's Indiana district president. "If she can handle eighth graders she should more than qualify for our early teens."

Hulda was now given charge of all Junior societies in Indiana, which involved planning monthly programs for lower teen-agers along three areas of emphasis which she herself devised: spiritual, cultural, and recreational. Her program copy was sent to League headquarters in Milwaukee, where the man who wore the initials W.A.M. would approve her material.

One day Walter asked his secretary, "Lydia, do you know this Hulda Eickhoff from Indianapolis?"

"I've never met her, Pastor Maier, but the Indiana board seems quite pleased with her work."

"Too bad she's a girl—she would have made a good minister. Her writing is theologically sound, and she does a decent job of getting the message across to teen-agers."

Walter rose from his desk and paced the office pensively, then halted and said, "Wait a minute. You were at the national convention in Evansville, Lydia. Surely you must remember the Indiana Junior secretary." Already he was at the files and pulling out a large group photograph of the Evansville convention. Lydia was not certain, but did point to a girl in the front row with the officers. Walter squinted. Hulda's face was about one-eighth of an inch wide in the photograph, and he hauled out a magnifying glass. Typically smiling features showed through the grain of the picture. "So young. So lovely—I think. Of course, you could never tell from a photo this size."

A girl whom he had never even met began to haunt Walter. At a League function later in the spring he saw Alfred Huge, an officer of the Indiana district, and took him aside.

"Al, do you know a Miss Hulda Eickhoff?"

"Sure, she's our Junior secretary."

"Good one?"

"Doing a fine job."

"She's rather attractive, isn't she?"

"No. She's *very* attractive!" Al grinned.

"What does her father do?"

"He died about, ohhh, ten years ago. He was a nurseryman out in Five Points. Fine Christian family."

After a long pause, Walter managed, "Is she engaged?"

"I don't think so."

"Does she . . . have a friend?"

"I haven't been able to find out. Wish I knew myself!"

Walter ignited a glowing smile and said, "Well, we can both learn in May. I'm speaking at the district convention in Indianapolis."

"You wouldn't want me to make any introductions now, would you?"

"Easy does it, Al. But why not send her a post card by way of . . . oh, a greeting of some kind?"

While Al assumed an odd expression, Walter purchased a picture post card and thrust it in front of Huge with one hand, offering a pen in the other. Al managed some kind of casual message and signed it. Grinning and impulsive, Walter swooped down on the pen and added his own name in bold strokes.

The next day, the addressee found, to her delighted shock, that "Walter A. Maier" knew of her existence. She walked back from the mailbox staring at that signature, trying to see into the man behind it. Was it possible that he was younger than she had imagined, that he might *not* be married? Hardly. The League would never choose an unsettled bachelor as its head. Probably he was satisfied with her Junior program, and this was his way of passing her a little recognition.

Much of Hulda's time was soon occupied with arrangements for the district convention. At one of the committee meetings, she was glancing at press releases concerning the principal speaker.

"Why is there no mention of a Mrs. Maier and family?" she casually asked Al Huge, who was supervising arrangements.

"I don't know. That's a very odd omission. . . ." Hulda froze her features so they would register no trace of disappointment, while Al continued, "Then again, it's probably because there is no family. . . ." He paused for an eternal five seconds, then resumed, "and there is no Mrs. Maier."

"I wonder why not. It's too bad he never married."

"Well, give him a chance. After all, he's only twenty-seven!"

Trying to detract from a deepening blush, she blurted, "Do you think our housing arrangements are satisfactory, or should we anticipate a larger crowd?"

Al could no longer restrain a guffaw and said, "I think you would like to meet Pastor Maier—*and* vice versa—and not just on League business!"

"Nonsense! Well . . . I've enjoyed reading his material, but anything else is ridiculous. Why we've never even met!"

That remaining detail was effected in May, 1921, when the Indiana district convention was held in the Great Hall of the Athenaeum Club in Indianapolis. On stage during the opening matins was a mass choir singing "The Heavens Declare" from Haydn's *Creation*; Hulda was the soprano in the antiphonal quartet. From the corner of her eye she noticed a dark-haired man sitting near the center of the front row. Probably that was the executive secretary himself! Whenever the director was not looking, she stole a glance at the rather handsome fellow, whose eye she had also caught.

Mistake! Following the service she learned that Pastor Maier had not yet arrived and was not due until later in the day. The afternoon business session began with a report on Junior work in the district. Dressed in powder-blue French voile, Hulda was telling of progress with the early teens when a slight commotion developed as Walter and his delegation arrived. His train was late, and a sheepish executive secretary was escorted down the aisle to the first row and seated directly in front of the reporting Miss Eickhoff.

She paused momentarily and glanced at the tardy arrival, then continued her report. Now she read automatically, for her mind was occupied with other matters. Could *that* be Walter Maier? "He didn't at all correspond to what I'd had in mind," she later recalled. "I had imagined a tall man with dark hair and brown eyes. And here he was: medium height, tawny hair, and blue eyes! Not even his suit was dark, but a rather dull-looking oxford gray. And it needed pressing.

"But after my address came his, and soon I forgot all about the gray suit that needed pressing and the eyes that weren't brown. Occasionally they flashed in my direction as he appealed that the convention dedicate its talents to the Lord of the church."

The delegates were stirred by the message, and Hulda by the man. He spoke with compelling authority, quite unlike anything she had heard before. And he was not middle-aged, or married, or even bad-looking for a fair-complexioned man.

For Walter, that afternoon brought the opportunity of seeing Miss Eickhoff in some dimension larger than a tiny photograph. He found the life-size enlargement even lovelier than he had projected. Whatever variety of love it is which develops at first sight, Walter sensed that he was veering toward it. He must meet her.

According to his schedule, Walter was to leave for Nebraska that night. But the heart countermanded all such plans. The convention had arranged a social gathering for the evening, and here at last would come the chance to get acquainted with this woman.

There was a milling throng in the large Social Room of the Athenaeum, and nearly half the evening passed before incessant introductions finally yielded Wam the chance to meet the girl who had changed his plans. She greeted him with a cordial smile, exchanged a pleasantry or two, but then moved on to mingle with a group of friends. Left behind was a puzzled man, just warming up for further dialogue.

A short while later he sighted her through the crowd, sidestepped some feminine delegates who had closed in on him, and after some broken-field maneuvering managed to reach Hulda. However, she had caught a glimpse of his approach and now eased off into another direction with one of her friends. Walter began thinking that he would be well on his way to Nebraska by now had he not changed his plans so foolishly. A hand was on his shoulder.

"Why don't you write her a post card?" suggested Al. "That way you could at least communicate. I'll sign it with you!"

"Al, what is this curtain of ice? Am I *that* repulsive?"

"I don't think it's all that bad. We've kidded her mercilessly with the 'you'd make an ideal couple' approach, and she reacts violently. She's pretty—but proud. Why half the eyes in this room are focused in her direction, just waiting to see if she'll make a play for you."

Al had analyzed the situation correctly. This was indeed a kind of agony for Hulda. More than anything else she wanted to meet *that man,* but late-Victorian ideals of femininity prevented her from betraying the slightest interest. The game had to be played correctly, or she could never face the teasing of her friends. Somehow he would find a way.

He did. Very discreetly Walter arranged for a private luncheon "conference" with the elusive Miss Eickhoff the next day. And he was armed with the proper excuse: there was League business to discuss with her.

At the stroke of noon they entered the Palm Room of the Athenaeum and took a table at the far end. Fumbling with his napkin, Walter led off, "I've greatly admired your programs for the Indiana Junior Department, Miss Eickhoff."

"Thank you. But do you know what really lured me into League work?"

"What?"

"Your *Messenger* editorials."

"Well that should make us old friends. We read each other before we met each other!"

They toasted this friendship with tomato juice and plunged into the get-acquainted conversation each had experienced many times before, but never with such meaning and purpose. They learned as much about each other as they could during one luncheon, and both liked what they learned.

And yet there were massive reservations. Walter was a little starched and self-conscious about it all. Suppose she has only a professional interest in me? Perhaps I'm not her type? Hulda, catching herself lest she betray her feelings, tried to remain prim and formal. Her thoughts mirrored his. He keeps referring to my Junior work. His interest must be League, not love.

With the dessert, Walter grew serious and proved that League business was not simply a handy pretext for conversation with attractive women. He voiced concern about the expanding lower-teen program of the organization. "We can't lose the younger set," said he. "We must have a special, central secretariat for studying their needs and providing appropriate materials. At the July convention in Milwaukee I'm going to ask for the creation of a national Junior department with offices at our headquarters."

Hulda's eyes blazed with interest.

He squared off and confronted her directly. "If this goes through, would you consent to become the League's first national Junior secretary?"

"I? But I've had no professional training for such a position. . . ."

"The salary would probably be less than what you're getting now as a teacher, but there are other compensations."

"Salary is no object—I love church work. But I'm *very* concerned about my qualifications." And she proceeded to cite chapter and verse on her inadequacy for the post.

Wam would have none of this. "From what I've seen of your work—and with prayer—I know you will succeed."

No decision was expected that quickly. But as they left the dining room, he extracted her promise to consider the offer seriously. It was a dramatic concurrence of interests in the life of Walter Maier. He would have created that office had he never met this girl, yet now he could not imagine the office without her.

After the convention Hulda luxuriated in the new possibilities which had swept into her life. She was surprised at this man's confidence in her, excited by the thought of working at his side. However, there were considerations which sobered her surging mood. Why barter success for insecurity? She was happy in a teaching career and had been advised by the supervisor of schools to work toward a principalship, or more. As a step in this direction, she had already enrolled for the summer term in education at the University of Wisconsin. And now abandon these plans for a plunge into an unfamiliar field without professional preparation?

During her summer at Madison, a special delivery letter arrived from Walter eagerly requesting that she attend the League's national convention in Milwaukee. Below the typed message was a postscript in his wavy handwriting: "How about another dinner or two? We don't have any Athenaeum here, but we should be able to find something nice!"

Of course she would attend. Perhaps the results of the convention would guide her decision regarding a future career; and then there was that other incentive—Walter.

After arriving in Milwaukee she saw him again, but the welcome was brief and somewhat cooled by his whirling about like a dervish in tending to last-minute convention details. She had no thought of blaming him—this was his job. Besides, she had nearly decided to place Walter Maier on a pedestal chiseled with the legend: "Not For You." She did not want a broken heart.

The evening before the convention opened, various committees were concluding their work. As Hulda was about to leave with one group of leaguers, the overbusy executive secretary spotted her, broke in on the group, and announced, "I shall see Miss Eickhoff to her lodging place. There is work I wish to discuss with her."

That was both truth and pretext. There was much that Walter

wanted to discuss; some of it was business, most it was not. Their conversation resumed where the Athenaeum luncheon had left off.

All too soon they arrived at the home where she was staying. Walter was frustrated. He had had so few moments with this girl because of his responsibilities. Hesitantly he asked if she would enjoy walking a little longer, just as Hulda was hoping he would think of some way to prolong the evening. So they continued.

There was a dash of old-world flavor in their relationship. Walter recalled the Rothenburg romance of his mother, how continental courtship had been, above all, a walking experience. And here they were in old Milwaukee—that German city transplanted to the Great Lakes country—on the eve of a nineteenth-century romance in the "roaring twenties." Back and forth they strolled until the early hours of the morning, ignoring the doorstep as a malicious intruder.

The convention opened with a service in which nearly 2,000 young people participated jubilantly. When Walter entered the pulpit they stilled to a hush, for many had never heard him speak, and expectancy was the mood. Hulda described it later:

"Actually he looked rather small in that high pulpit, nothing more than another leaguer. His text was I Chronicles 29,5: *'Who then is willing to consecrate his service this day unto the Lord?'* After reading it he glanced knowingly at me for a moment, then began his sermon. At first his manner was gentle, almost timid; but not for long. Soon his voice picked up a vigorous crescendo, challenging us to appreciate the depth of the divine invitation and privilege to serve in the church. The congregation listened in total silence. I could not escape the feeling that this man spoke for God, in a way beyond explanation. For me the decision regarding League work was made then and there. If he still wanted me for the Junior office, I would now gladly accept the post."

Walter was radiant when he learned of her resolve. It lifted the major burden from an already weighted back, and he bounded through the rest of the convention in rare style. Now he was ready for anything.

This was fortunate, because on the preceding evening an otherwise-occupied Secretary Maier should have prepared a report concerning the League's Bible study project, and he had not had time to write a word of it the next day. When the convention chairman called for his report, Walter walked to the rostrum with a convincing number of pages clipped together. He gave a smooth, documented presentation, flipped the pages at regular intervals, and concluded with a tight summary. Then he handed his manuscript to the recording secretary, who leafed through it and turned white —each page was only blank typing paper. A note was smuggled into his hand: "Will submit a better copy tonight.—W.A.M."

The convention authorized the establishment of a Junior department, and Indiana's Hulda Eickhoff was appointed the new national secretary, which surprised no one. She was to begin work at Milwaukee headquarters that September. All anticipation, Hulda returned to finish her summer course at the University of Wisconsin.

One weekend Walter dropped by Madison "to discuss Junior work," and as background for such critical conversation the two chose a little pavilion near the student union overlooking Lake Mendota. No bronze plaque has since been erected—the pavilion has even been torn down!—but here the couple held hands for the first time.

Just after Wisconsin's summer session ended, the "Junior work" pretext, fractionally true as it was, also carried Walter to Indianapolis, where he met the Eickhoff family. Hulda's three brothers— Alvin, Arthur, Ted—and four sisters—Lydia, Emilie, Paula, and Edith—were much impressed by the rising young clergyman, though not overawed. There was instant rapport also with Mother Eickhoff, who shook with laughter at Wam's tales of escapades in student days. That weekend, almost as an afterthought, plans for the Junior secretariat were crystallized.

Walter formally presented his newest officer to the League at the New England district convention in late August. But a more important introduction took place when he exhibited his prize from the Midwest to a curious German-Yankee family named Maier. Em, George, and Karl were won over by Hulda at once, Karl demonstrating his approval at dinner by playing tricks on brother's new girlfriend. Flo thought Miss Eickhoff quite capable, but added, "You're both very self-sufficient, and she may be too independent for you," an opinion reversed by her romance-minded daughter Barbara.

Walter's Boston friends quickly became Hulda's as well, including her hostess—none other than Elsie, Wam's former interest! Etiquette experts or advice columnists would have stormed, and a legion of women cried "How cruel!" but this arrangement was Walter's way of breaking the news to Elsie in what he thought a politic manner! The fact that she has remained a lifelong friend is testimony to her qualities.

Grossie responded to the importee from Indiana with twinkling eyes and immediate approval, even though the two met each other under somewhat bizarre circumstances. When Walter brought Hulda "home to mother" it was actually to a waterfront warehouse, where Grossie was seated between barn-high stacks of used clothing, sorting socks. How Anna Maier got there is a tale in itself, the story of one of the large private war relief efforts long before the establishment of CARE.

Walter could not shake off the news about conditions in postwar Europe. Press accounts told of many thousands victimized by the war, freezing to death for lack of clothing and shelter. Letters from abroad begging castoff garments of any kind substantiated such reports. Once again Walter hatched a plan which involved his mother, only this time the order was far larger than a hundred pairs of socks. He inserted a large notice in the *Messenger,* asking church youth to collect clothing and shoes for European relief and send them to Boston in care of "Mrs. Anna K. Maier, 1 Waldorf Street, Dorchester, Mass." To Grossie he telegraphed:

LEAGUERS SENDING CLOTHING FOR EUROPE. HAVE SAME BALED FOR SHIPPING. DETAILS FOLLOW. LOVE. WALTER.

The response to his appeal was prompt and generous. The young people organized clothing drives, bundled used apparel in hundreds of church basements, and sent it off to Boston. Almost before the promised "details" were sent, Grossie received notice that whole freight-car loads of clothing were arriving in her name. The rail-road warned that if the cars were not unloaded within a few days she would have to pay stiff demurrage charges. And that was not the half of it. How was she to transport tons of material to a sorting and baling warehouse or arrange for shipping?

Grossie could only pray that resources would somehow be pro-vided on schedule. Her unique plight was picked up by the press, and two broad-hearted businessmen came to her rescue. A Mr. Loew, president of the New England Waste Company, put at Gros-sie's disposal his warehouse in Revere, which not only had ample storage space but a baling rig as well. And Mr. Burkhardt of Rox-bury's Burkhardt Brewery provided a fleet of his beer trucks to carry clothes to the warehouse and bales to the docks. Dauntless Grossie arrived at the Revere baling plant determined to start the job her-self, but visiting friends caught one glimpse of the mountains of clothing surrounding a tiny grandmother, and soon a multishift crew of volunteers was at work opening cartons, sorting, and baling. It was here that Walter proudly introduced Hulda to his wiry mother.

Inevitably, there were problems at the warehouse. Grossie's pastor came down to help, but at day's end he found that his new Brooks Brothers overcoat had been baled and sent off to the docks. A few of the laborers whom Mr. Loew had assigned to the project would occasionally pocket some choicer items under the assumption that charity begins at home. In fact, some of Hulda's time in Boston was spent with young Barbara in guarding against such theft. A daily closing ritual saw them briefing the foreman, who then stopped one of the workers at the door and announced, "Rosie, you've put on too much weight today. Now take off all those skirts!" Pouting, Rosie shed skirt after skirt.

After weeks of work, much of the operation was completed, and many tons of clothing and shoes had been sent to Europe. Grossie vacated the Revere warehouse, and 1 Waldorf Street again became relief headquarters for parcels which continued arriving in later months. Then she called on Mr. Loew to inquire about charges for using his facilities, equipment, and help. Biographer Kettner de-scribes the scene:

Once more Mr. Loew asked: "Who will get this clothing?" When told that it would be given to any needy person, regardless of race or religion, he expressed his gratitude. Then he asked one of his men to bring the cost sheets. A huge, bulky file with dozens of pages of detailed figures was laid before him. The last page presented a total running into many thousands of dollars. With a sweep of the pen, Mr. Loew marked the whole account "paid in full." What an indictment of Anti-Semitism! A Jewish gentleman had done without any charge what a half dozen agencies had refused to do even at full commercial rates. "When I see how faithfully you people worked for love and not for money, I couldn't charge you anything," Mr. Loew replied.[1]

In equally generous fashion, Mr. Burkhardt would take no reimbursement for his trucks.

A similar clothing effort was repeated annually for the next three years under the supervision of Grossie and son George Maier, while Messrs. Loew and Burkhardt continued charging the same benevolent rate. Many hundreds of tons of clothing, shoes, sheets, blankets, thread, soap, and foodstuffs reached needy families overseas, and grateful letters from abroad poured into League and Boston relief headquarters.[2] Six years later, Anna Maier revisited Germany and was formally received by the city councils in various towns and feted for her role in sending American aid to Europe at a crucial moment. Grossie modestly responded that she only baled what others had sent.

Upon leaving Boston, Hulda commented, "A book should be written about that remarkable mother of yours." Walter was pleased that the two women had hit it off from the start—a rare phenomenon in many romances—but even happier that their own mutual understanding was ripening.

The train trip back to the Midwest was punctuated by stopovers for speaking engagements and meetings with key youth leaders in New York City, Rochester, Buffalo, and Cleveland. Hulda could now observe her new boss at close range, inspiring enthusiasm for Christian youth work, and she noticed how he blunted all praise directed to himself. Whenever his message sparked commendation of any kind, he quickly changed the subject, almost ignoring what had been said. "Here is a man," she mused, "who has great talent without great pride. To such a person I could give my life."

The train was clattering into Chicago's Loop as Walter made final mental notes on the girl sitting beside him: "Here is a woman who combines beauty and intelligence with spirituality. Furthermore . . . I love her." The New York Central wove its way into La Salle Street Station and screeched to a halt. They stepped off the train. Walter put down the suitcases and stared at her. Against a setting of hissing steam, shrill whistles, and bumping coaches—and without quite knowing why—he caught her in his arms and kissed her.

# 5

# "For Better, Not for Worse"

It was in Chicago, not Milwaukee, that the couple-in-love administered League affairs. By this time the Milwaukee headquarters were too small for the expanding organization, and the Windy City seemed a better location as convention and rail center of the nation. Offices in Chicago were purchased, and new staff workers recruited, including Walter's seminary roommate, Paul Prokopy. With increased personnel, headquarters now hummed with activity. The League had come of age.

The new Junior secretary filled her responsibilities with predicted ease. To extend her department's program for the teen-agers, she made occasional speaking tours and contributed articles for the *Messenger*. Soon Wam had her editing a new *Junior Messenger* for the younger clan. She relished the work.

Walter also noted her interest in the sanitarium project, so one day he threw out a challenge: "Hulda, I'm sure the Wheat Ridge Christmas seals campaign could be far more effective if someone really organized it and put some steam into the effort." She detected the roguish glint in his eyes and discovered the "someone" without benefit of divination. Despite a lack of formal administrative experience, she soon set up a pyramidal sales structure throughout the League involving district and local seals managers. The arrangement worked—almost too well. For the managers remitted their proceeds to League headquarters just after Christmas, while the offices were closed for the holidays. On January 3 the staff returned to find heaps of mail with thousands of dollars in checks and cash lying in the open beneath a bulging mailbox. Chicago's gangland had missed an easy haul.

After seals proceeds were in, more than $13,000 could be forwarded to Wheat Ridge, and the next season over $20,000 was sent. Superintendent Feiertag rhapsodized in his *Sanitarium Review* about "a most wonderful young miss . . . Hulda Eickhoff" for whom the patients offered thanks to God and "three rousing cheers."[1] Her efforts in the Junior department were also receiving accolades from different corners of the church, which, of course, delighted the boss immensely.

During these months, the two relived their lives for each other, not on League time, but during many evening strolls through Chicago. Occasionally they invited "PGP" (Paul G. Prokopy) to join them, but he preferred playing cupid to chaperon and would vanish regularly. To the brunette beside him, Walter spelled out ideals, ideas, and plans, as well as his ultimate goals in life. She matched hers against his and there was no clash, just the complementary contrast of two personalities who now sensed that they were meant for one another.

Yet romance was not always idyllic. Rarely could the executive and Junior secretary coordinate their out-of-town speaking engagements, and some weekends split them apart. But now a new development threatened their courtship. Walter requested, and was granted, a leave of absence to continue his studies at Harvard. When he had accepted the League post, it was agreed that he would be given such a leave once the organization's new program was well under way. He had not lost sight of his doctoral project, and PGP could take over direction of the now-booming League pro tempore. Leaving Hulda was more difficult, but she did not wish to block his career in any way, and they could still see each other at intervals, especially during the summer. The "test of separation" they termed it at the time. Would it be "Out of sight, out of mind," or "Absence makes the heart grow fonder"?

They had the answer even before Walter left Chicago in February, 1922. Merely the prospect of separation seemed cruel as they kissed good-by at the station on the very spot which had witnessed such a scene before. Only this time Walter couldn't stand it. Just before the train started pulling out, he whisked a startled girl onto the coach, explaining that she could get off at Hammond, Indiana, and return by interurban. Wam always hated farewells, and this maneuver softened the blow.

Hammond saw the final parting, and as the train pulled out a strong voice could be heard above the sundry shrieks and groans of the engine: "Tell PGP to keep a high chin—and remember how much I love you!"

Courtship continued by correspondence. Walter's letters told of his reenrollment in the Semitics program, to the pleasure of departmental advisors; hers kept him in close touch with League affairs. Soon she had something momentous to report.

Hers was the responsibility of opening all mail which arrived at headquarters addressed to Wam. One day there was a large, registered letter from St. Louis for "The Rev. Walter Arthur Maier." Hulda knew she was opening an important communication, but what she could not realize was the fact that this letter would forever change Walter's life—and her own. For it was more than a letter. She pulled out a formal document entitled "Diploma of Vocation" and read it excitedly, speaking certain words aloud: " 'The Electoral Board . . . Concordia Theological Seminary . . . extends to you a Solemn Call to become Professor of Old Testament Interpretation and History . . . beginning in September. . . .' " Thrusting the document into the hands of PGP, she asked, "Is he really to be a *professor* . . . at so young an age?"

Paul read with pontifical precision: " '. . . Call to become Professor of Old Testament . . .' Yes, full professor. But that doesn't surprise me. Wam had it coming. Now he can serve the church in an even larger capacity."

With a thrill Hulda forwarded the letter air mail and spent the rest of the day absorbing its implications. On receiving the call, Walter was equally elated. He had a deep respect for the institution, which had now selected *him*, only twenty-nine, a mere stripling in the academic world. That would make him the youngest person ever to hold the rank of professor in the eighty-three-year history of Concordia, and without that scholastic *sine qua non*, the Ph.D. degree.

Here was precisely the rub which complicated what should otherwise have been an easy decision. He was now well on his way to a doctorate in Semitics. Was he to interrupt his advanced program a second time for immediate service to the church? His Harvard professors cautioned him against it, suggesting that he accept such a post after he received his degree. Another qualm was the League: had he finished his task there?

A supporting letter arrived from the seminary, urging him to accept the call, for the church needed a clergy adequately trained in Old Testament studies. The decision was especially critical this time, and Walter sought divine guidance.

Prayer and a brisk exchange of letters produced a good compromise of all alternatives. Walter would accept the call to the Concordia professorship; be granted a leave of absence for final doctoral study when necessary; and resign as executive secretary of the Walther League, but continue as editor of the *Messenger*. In this way no doors were shut, and he could even carry on part of his youth work in the new post.

Walter attended his last national convention as League executive at Omaha in July, 1922. When he formally resigned his office in a farewell address, everyone in the city's Auditorium seemed moved, most of all the speaker. After concluding on the happier note that he would continue with the *Messenger,* he was greeted by what newspapers termed "a tremendous ovation," with leaguers rising en masse to salute their departing chief.[2]

The young people esteemed him, and he them, and it had indeed been a profitable association, even if only for a two-year period. During his administration, membership doubled to nearly 50,000, as did the number of affiliated societies to 886. The hospice, foreign mission, Bible study, student, relief, and sanitarium projects were started or revitalized; headquarters had been expanded and transplanted; and one of Wam's final trips had initiated the League's new summer camp on Lake Michigan at Arcadia. In giving the benediction at the convention, Walter Maier was closing one phase in his life which he could never forget.

That September, he moved to St. Louis, while Hulda remained in Chicago. But the League work which had brought them together continued to play guardian angel for their romance.

The *Messenger* was printed by Northwestern Publishing House of Milwaukee, and the Junior secretary had had the task of traveling to Wisconsin each month as editorial assistant in order to "see the *Messenger* through," i.e., to deliver the magazine copy to the publishers and execute final make-up, read galley proofs, delete or supply fillers where appropriate, and the like. Now that the editorial office had moved to St. Louis, a personal liaison with Northwestern was more important than ever. The solution was rather adroit: once a month the Chicago editorial assistant simply *had* to see her St. Louis editor for magazine copy and instructions before taking them to Milwaukee. On such weekend visits, of course, time was divided about evenly between responsibility and romance. And even the days of separation had their compensation in the form of a flourishing correspondence.

When love takes possession of people they are known to act, at times, in a less than rational manner. Or if reason is present, it clearly plays second fiddle to emotion, as in this case history. During one of her St. Louis weekends, Hulda attended Vespers at Our Redeemer Church, where Walter was now part-time assistant pastor along with his professorship. While preaching for the service, he noticed that a seminarian sitting next to Hulda was paying far more attention to her than to his sermon. After Vespers and on the way to the station, Walter was sepulchral in silence. Hulda wondered what on earth had happened. He started complaining about the student who had "dared to make a play for" *his* girlfriend. He had seen them chatting at a dinner preceding the service, and perhaps she had even invited the student to sit next to her. Stunned, Hulda countered vigorously that she was unconscious of the student or his motives. But no assurance to the contrary was believed, and the evening ended disastrously as she burst into tears and boarded the train.

"Much as I had been hurt," she later recalled, "it was worth the ordeal. For two days later came his special delivery letter, so alive with regret and love that our relationship was immeasurably deepened." To share a few excerpts:

January 9, 1923

'My most precious Love,

I waited until the train was out of sight, and more than once I felt the wild impulse to run after it and go with you. It is always hard to part from you, but under those circumstances, terribly difficult. When are you coming to take complete possession of me and mine—and to stay with me without leaving?

Forgive me for my ugly mood, for doubting you for a moment! The mere suggestion that you might not be happy with me has caused me to suffer more than you realize, since by this time I know I want you at my side—always. I really wouldn't amount to much without you, because I need the inspiration which you supply. . . .

Do you think that I ever dream of the great things the Lord is going to permit me to accomplish for His Kingdom without invariably taking for granted that all this is inseparably and imperatively linked with my beautiful Hulda? You are the all-comprehensive object of every love-thought that asserts itself within me. . . .

The question which you and I must soon definitely decide is: when shall we be married? Please, Darling, write me when you receive this just when you want the happy day to come.

Your own,<br>Walter'

So it was that their first major quarrel virtually precipitated Wam's proposal!

Hulda read the letter over and over again. Was he actually proposing in these lines? Any remaining doubt on that score was dispelled by Walter's trip to Chicago that spring. After what had preceded, the proposal itself was a formality. Yet formalities need not be wooden reverences to convention. Walter made of his proposal a review of their happy relationship and an even happier preview of what would follow when they joined their lives. He concluded, "Even though the marriage vows read 'for better, for worse,' I'm going to modify them silently in our case, because—God helping us—no matter what may intervene in life it must be 'for better, *not* for worse.' Will you marry me?"

"For some reason . . . a mere 'yes' seems too simple a reply," she faltered, "so . . . let's say rather 'Amen.' "

He crushed her to himself in one of his boyish bear hugs. "You even answered me in Hebrew! *Ah-main!*" he shouted exuberantly, giving the authentic pronunciation and definition. "Certainly. So be it! It shall be so!"

That June, Walter asked Mother Eickhoff for the hand of her daughter and received a cheerful affirmative. He had captured mother's heart shortly after daughter's, and now it was merely a question of arrangements. He wanted the wedding in a few months, but the women thought it better to wait a year, in accord with the lingering proprieties of the previous generation. The suitor wished that he had asked earlier.

Because of their mercifully busy schedules, however, the months sped through the calendar, and soon it was only a matter of weeks before the wedding. Mother Eickhoff preferred modest, quiet nuptials, but Walter tried to argue her out of it: "The wedding is the happiest day of our lives, and surely we want to share it with our friends." Mother E. smiled and gave in.

A timely gift from a prosperous great-aunt put the expanded nuptial plans on a sound financial basis, and about five hundred friends were invited. They came from far and wide—League associates in various cities, delegations from Chicago, St. Louis, Detroit, and elsewhere. In their first trip West, Grossie, Karl, and Barbara represented the Boston relatives, and with enormous satisfaction Hulda introduced her mother and her mother-to-be. The *entente* was *cordiale* as it was instant, and the two were last observed strolling arm in arm along the wooded Eickhoff estate, chatting in spirited German.

The wedding was set for 7 P.M. on Saturday, June 14, 1924, at St. John's Lutheran Church in the Indianapolis suburb of Five Points. Barbara and sister Paula were bridesmaids, and another sister, Edith, the maid of honor. Ushers were PGP and Al Huge, with Karl as best man. Although it was a sultry evening, the flower girl and ring bearer caused no crises, and the bride looked fresh when she appeared. As reported, she wore ". . . a beautiful gown of white satin, trimmed with silk lace, and carried an exquisite shower bouquet of white roses and lilies of the valley. The train of the gown was adorned with a beautiful lover's knot, and the duchess veil was trimmed with orange blossoms."[3] Whether or not convention approved, Walter could not fight down a broad smile as his bride approached, radiant in the soft flicker of tapers which stood sentinel along the aisle of the crowded church. They joined

arms and faced paternal Pastor Wambsganss, who delivered the
wedding meditation. In the ceremony, bride and groom looked at
each other knowingly when the minister came to the words, "for
better, for worse." They said their vows without timidity and became man and wife.

Appropriately, a gala reception and banquet were held at the
very Athenaeum Club where the newlyweds had first met three
years before, and the joy of the couple was indeed a shared experience. Congratulatory telegrams were read, including two from
President Coolidge and England's King George V, though the
lettering on these was traced to Karl's typewriter. The wedding
party conspired to spring surprises, reveal secrets, and add to the
general gaiety. Finally, the two mothers wished their children Godspeed with maternal blessings, and it was done.

Because of broadening contacts, Walter had received invitations
to spend his honeymoon in various parts of the country, but one
alluring bid from California was irresistible. Neither he nor his
bride had ever been west of the Rockies, and these lines from a good
friend whet the imagination:

As our wedding gift, please accept the use of one of four new cottages
which we have just built in Santa Monica near the ocean. Make it your
home all summer if you possibly can. The rooms are fully furnished,
and they invite you along with the blue Pacific. You can make this your
base for exciting excursions up and down the West Coast. . . .

The writer was Dora Knief, a journalist by profession and a frank
person, always to be taken at face value. Gratefully they accepted
her generous offer, since the groom did not have to teach until fall.

After a torrid trip west on the Atchison, Topeka, and Santa Fe,
there was Dora, good as her word, waiting for the newlyweds at
the Los Angeles station. She whisked them off to Santa Monica
and drove into a flower-choked courtyard, stopping in front of
white and gleaming Cottage No. 1. "A hearty welcome to your
home for the summer!" she announced with a glad smile, thrusting
a key into Walter's hand.

*"Tante* [Aunt] Dora, this is undoubtedly . . . well, what I mean is. . . ." He was faltering badly.

"When words come hard for a preacher, editor, and professor, that *is* a compliment!"

"The place is far lovelier than you described. And the view!" Bride was filling in for groom.

"May you have much happiness here! But you must be tired after the long trip, so I'll introduce you to the rest of the family later. Now rest!" With that she was off.

As a salute to convention, Walter carried his bride across the threshold and into the living room. The cottage was perfection— handsomely furnished and generously stocked with food. They were consummately happy. And so began the summer of 1924.

Marriage books had warned of the crucial first weeks newlyweds spend in adjusting to one another, of how future marital success can hang in the balance during that interval. While this may be true, Professor and Mrs. Maier wondered what the fuss was all about, their marriage had launched itself without the predicted crises.

During these weeks, bride and groom instead charged the batteries of memory with prized experiences and so stored up reserve power to illumine whatever darkness life could bring in the future. A kaleidoscope of scenes, flashes of recollection would scintillate for years afterward: the daily beach sunning and ocean swim; the time Walter buried his bride in the sand, then sculptured gigantic legs on the mound with shoes propped up ten feet from her head, and how the people gaped; beach parties arranged by their hosts; "The grunions are running!"—the sport of catching the elusive silvery fish which rode the waves in at high tide, deposited their eggs in the sand, and swam back out to sea, unless caught and roasted at bonfires up and down the coast; meeting a host of new friends, like "Our Honeymoon Pastor" Troeger, who saw to it that a car was usually at their disposal; jaunts through palm-shaded Beverly Hills or the fragrant orange groves near Pasadena; moonlight drives through the Hollywood Hills, overlooking the electric panorama of crisscrossed diamond strands which was Los Angeles. Excursions to Capistrano and other Spanish missions were lessons in history, art, and architecture. Drives up and down the coast unveiled fresh vistas at every curve, with mountains plunging into the Pacific. Or the boat trip to Catalina, for which queasy Walter had dieted on Mothersill's Seasick Remedy; a few whiffs of sea air and he promptly forgot he was supposed to get sick.

If honeymoons bring out the husband in a man, this one also brought out the boy in Walter. Mastery of escapade was evidently a dominant Maier gene, for it afflicted brothers George and Karl as well. One day Wam contrived to have a visiting minister friend, whom his wife had not yet met, pose as a door-to-door salesman. The pastor-peddler played his part with such sincerity, that although this housewife would not buy his wares, she did invite the man to attend church. Holding his sides in paroxysms of laughter, Walter told her she had just won a Lutheran pastor for the Christian faith.

Another minister from Pasadena, a seminary classmate, and his wife drove them on a short jaunt into Mexico. On the return trip the foursome stopped overnight at a hotel on the American side of the border. At 1:30 A.M. Walter telephoned the adjoining room in a disguised voice, and led off:

"Is this the Reverend George Theiss of Pasadena?"

"Yes . . . ?"

"This is Director Arthur of the United States Department of Immigration. We've had our men tailing you today in Mexico. Would you mind answering a few questions?"

"Well . . . no," Theiss answered, perplexity in his voice.

"While you were in Tijuana, didn't you see a cockfight and look at gambling devices in operation?"

"Yes, but we didn't gamble, we just. . . ."

"Just wanted to see how bad it was, eh? When will you ministers learn?"

"Now see here. . . ."

"But what we really want to know is this: exactly who was that suspicious-looking character with the beautiful Mata Hari of a wife? You drove them out of Mexico."

"*Well!* I can certainly vouch for. . . ."

"First I should warn you that conviction for importing international spies in your case would also involve unfrocking and ex-communication, to say nothing of imprisonment and. . . ."

Theiss blurted in with a torrent of impassioned defense for his "great and good friend" until Walter could contain himself no longer and howled into the telephone. Finally Mrs. Maier got to sleep that night, wondering what kind of man it was she had married.

One day a telegram from Detroit arrived, and it was all over. The eight weeks of happiness on the West coast ended abruptly, and a large gathering of friends gave the couple a farewell dinner, then saw them off at the station. The wire read:

COME BACK, FUGITIVES STOP  YOUR SECOND HONEYMOON IS PRE-PARED STOP  WHEN MAY WE EXPECT YOU?    ED AND PGP

If California had its Aunt Dora, Michigan had its Uncle Ed. Edmund Kuhlman was a fair-haired, distinguished-looking personage who first met Wam at a League convention in Michigan, and from that moment on he remained one of his most loyal friends. It seems that Ed and wife Helen had conspired with Paul Prokopy and his Mathilda to do something which would be cordially condemned by any of the Post-Vanderbilt sorority—joining a couple on its honeymoon! If two newlyweds are company, three a crowd, what are *six*?

Yet the Maiers had been ready partners to the plot and would not let insipid convention prevent an automobile tour of New England with their closest friends. A beaming foursome met the second-honeymooners at the Detroit depot, and off they drove in Ed's temperamental, seven-passenger, Studebaker President touring car. The vehicle made at least the Detroit-Buffalo run without breaking down; but then, being ferried in the hold of a D & C liner on Lake Erie, it never really had the chance. Topside on the S.S. *City of Buffalo*, the three couples refreshed themselves in the gusts which swept briskly off the lake, reveling in a life which could never again be so carefree. These were the golden hours, the golden days, valued as much in retrospect as in experience.

After docking at Buffalo, the eight-cylinder pride of South Bend carried its passengers to Niagara Falls, then toured the panoramic

Finger Lakes country, the river glens of central New York, and the Catskills. Finally came the Hudson River and New England; to Walter it was more like crossing the Jordan into the Promised Land.

In Boston, the groom of two months proudly displayed his bride to the relatives and friends who could not attend the wedding. And here a final series of vignettes would crowd in on memory: the proud claim of swimming in two oceans on one honeymoon; more beach parties; Boston Pops Orchestra concerts; visits to the historic sites associated with America's birth; excursions into the White Mountains of New Hampshire.

But now the six had to call it an August, and they retreated to the Midwest. Eventually, the Maiers found themselves approaching St. Louis. The medieval castle which is Union Station loomed larger in the train windows, telling them it was all over. They were ex-honeymooners. Walter caught the mood, helped his wife off the train, and said, "Hulda, this has been such a towering experience that I wonder if the rest of life *could* be—a kind of anticlimax." She kissed him and objected vigorously.

Walter Maier was badly mistaken.

# 6

# Bridegroom—Professor

Two years earlier when both had speaking engagements in the city, Walter and Hulda took a stroll through south St. Louis, where Concordia Seminary was located. While looking about, they volunteered such comments as, "Fine people, but dull dwellings." "Where do all those soot balls come from?" "This surely is one city where we'd never want to live!"

Eating crow, the Walter A. Maiers gave out a new address: 3727 Ohio Street, St. Louis, Mo. It was one of a hundred thousand brick houses with green shutters lining the latticework of old streets and avenues near the Mississippi. Bordering its postage stamp-sized front yard was a buckling, split-level sidewalk which made one dim-sighted seminary professor think he was going lame in hobbling over what he imagined a level path. So little sunlight filtered down into the narrow canyons dividing the residences on Ohio Street that the new hostess had to turn on the lights whenever guests arrived, or risk the impression that she was conducting a séance. The first time he exposed his bride to the place, Walter almost apologized. But she ardently defended the house, since it was now haloed with special significance: "This is our first home!"

From then on, setting up housekeeping was as much a challenge to the newlyweds as if they were managing a mansion. Mother Eickhoff paid them a week's visit to help arrange the place and give her daughter a postgraduate course in cooking, and soon the cold, inanimate house became a warm and vital home.

Although a professor, Walter was teaching at a religious institution with a salary necessarily lower than he would have received at other schools where he might have taught. Consequently, the couple had to budget carefully in order to remain in the black, and the watchword of family thrift came to be: excellent quality without excellent price. Rarely did they embark on a purchasing expedition without the lure of a price-slashing sale. Groceries, especially canned goods, were purchased in bulk quantities for long-term saving, and there was as yet no car to eat its way into the domestic economy. In fact, at the end of the first year the enterprise of Maier and Maier could show a profit, since the honoraria Walter received from speaking engagements as well as his *Messenger* salary were channeled into a nest egg.

One luxury, however, could not be dispensed with—hospitality. Never during his seminary days had a professor or friend invited Wam home to dinner or a party. This was due largely to the European concept of the academic-social gulf which separated faculty and students. Walter resolved to do the very opposite should he ever teach, and one of the few requests he had made of his fiancée was that students should always be welcome in their home.

So it was that the Maier household was thrown open to seminarians on the first holiday occasion, Thanksgiving. Inviting five students home to sample a bride's premier roast turkey was clearly less than cricket, but the men seemed eager enough to give the bird a try. Proud of his wife's maiden culinary adventure, the host kept opening the oven door, and "Boys, look at that!" was the cry, ten times to the hour. The large brown fowl did surprisingly well, despite the temperature fluctuations in the oven.

Every state in the Union has clergymen who remember attending some of the student parties which Professor Maier scheduled for the rest of his life. Seminarians started admiring the man who was "a bear in the classroom, but a prince at home."

One of the memorable soirees on Ohio Street featured a four-course chicken dinner for the graduating class of 1926, 115 strong. Long tables were erected in the back yard, while the catering staff consisted of one heroic housewife assisted by a visiting Grossie. Entertainment was no problem. Whatever difficulty the professor might have in getting students to express themselves in the classroom, the host had no such trouble. As master of ceremonies, Walter invited each seminarian to summarize his life in a brief, humorous fashion, and soon the party was off the ground. After an evening of mirth, he closed with a prayer presenting the needs of his guests to a God who could supply them. This party format proved highly popular with each succeeding class.

But what of the other Professor Maier, the "bear in the class-room"? He won the distinction for two reasons: the subjects he taught and the way he taught them. Hebrew was the cross in the curriculum for many seminarians, the course with blue-ribbon honors in any "subject-we'd-prefer-to-avoid" contest. Unlike western languages, Hebrew has no cognates in English—there are no verbal similarities whatever between the two languages. However, after a year or two of study, the scholar who applies himself suddenly finds Hebrew coming alive, especially when used to ferret out the meaning of the Old Testament.

What does the Book of Genesis signify as an account of the origin of the world? When and how did God relate Himself to man by covenant? What about the Sinai experience? Is there a broader message in the epic struggle of Job with his conscience and his God? What is the poetic and the religious depth in the Psalms? Do the prophetic messages of Isaiah or Jeremiah or Nahum have contemporary application? To what extent did the Hebrews look for a Messiah? Questions such as these were discussed in courses which the young Semiticist taught in the department of Old Testament interpretation and history at Concordia.

If the subject matter was fascinating-but-formidable, so also the professor. He carried his academic standards directly from Harvard to Concordia with little modification. As lecturer, he knew his material cold and only occasionally glanced at notes in his deliberate stroll back and forth before the class. Sometimes his delivery was rapid-fire, and students had trouble getting it all down in their notebooks.

With lectures thorough, could the examinations be otherwise? It was common to see students bringing their lunches for one of his marathon final exams. The usual stint was 8:30 A.M. until noon for the brighter students, with the last leaving the classroom well into the afternoon. One hot day Professor Maier treated his examinees to a round of ice-cream cones out of sheer sympathy. Occasionally, a seminarian would spill a little of his gall onto the test paper, as the fellow who wrote in place of an answer: "This question is unreasonably difficult. Take off credit." The red pencil in the margin later replied: "We aim to please: —15." More than one student confessed that he spent as much time preparing for Wam's courses as all the rest put together.

Freshman Karl Maier arrived at the seminary a year after his brother had joined the faculty, and students watched to see if any favoritism would develop. "I was very hard put to keep up and get a decent passing mark in Old Testament," he reports, "I didn't receive any preferential treatment, I can assure you." It was a far cry from Boston days.

Mrs. Maier watched her husband preparing one of his quizzes and remarked, "Walter, have a heart! Don't you think that test is a little too long?"

"It is fairly complete. But I *must* help maintain high standards for the highest profession on earth. Doctors or lawyers have much to learn in mastering their professions; the same should certainly be true of the ministry."

"Yes, but remember, what appears easy to you is probably very difficult for the students."

"You win, O patron saint of students! I'll cut it down a bit."

Hulda looked over his shoulder and saw him drop just two parts of one question. "No wonder they call you a bear!"

"It's not all *that* bad, Honey. But I have a wonderful idea. My teaching schedule is heavy and I need assistance with grading exams. If you learned Hebrew you could help mark the tests."

"I? Hebrew? Are you serious?"

"Certainly. I'd be your private tutor!" Walter was waxing enthusiastic.

"*No!* Positively not! After all, there is a division of labor. Unless, of course, you help me dust, make dinner. . . ."

"I concede." Walter threw up his hands.

". . . and if you want less work grading, then shorten the exams."

He never did. Although some students objected at the time, they later thanked their former professor for having made them study hard because of their better facility in understanding the Old Testament as well as the mental discipline involved. One graduate wrote back eight years later that he regretted having made a satirical remark about Hebrew to amuse the class, because he found repeated recourse to his Old Testament lecture notes out in the ministry.

As student enrollment at Concordia mounted, so did the size of sections in Old Testament. Soon a gentile professor found himself in the paradoxical position of teaching probably the largest Hebrew classes in America. Professor Maier was becoming recognized as a Semitics specialist, and various academic centers and organizations invited him to address them. Fostering this involvement in Old Testament studies, he resolved to finish his doctorate in short order and undertake an archaeological tour of the Near and Middle East.

Walter A. Maier would probably have lived and died a significant scholar and author if radio—"the miracle of radio" he termed it —had not altered his life. The technique of sending electronic impulses through the air had been developing apace, and experiments by Reginald Fessenden resulted in the world's first "broadcast" at Brant Rock, Massachusetts. Significantly, it was a semireligious program in honor of the day, Christmas Eve, 1906.[1] Regular programming, however, did not occur until the improvements of Lee De Forest's triode vacuum tube and Edwin Armstrong's superheterodyne circuit. Then, one memorable November evening in 1920, Station KDKA in Pittsburg went on the air with the Harding-Cox presidential election returns, and radio soon took its place in the American scene.

Broadcasting intrigued Walter immediately, and just a year later he faced his first microphone when an address he delivered to a League convention in Louisville was aired. This was the era of the crystal set and earphones, or, if one had the money, the luxurious tube sets with "talking boxes" (speakers) which could pull in one or two pioneer stations amid much static.

Among the first St. Louisans to tickle his crystal with a cat whisker was an engineering student named Herman Gihring, who lived three doors from a newly arrived professor of Old Testament. Walter and Herman became friends and talked radio many an evening, although Grandma Gihring thought the two needed psychiatric help in view of their discussions about voices in the air. Herman clapped a pair of earphones on Grandma to prove his sanity, and they all listened with fascination to the early broadcasts of KSD, St. Louis' first radio station. There were dispatches with news fresher than the papers could print, music truer than scratchy gramophone disks could play it, but also programs with less than minimal entertainment value. Certainly radio would have other applications.

Presently the electrifying idea burned through Walter's earphoned head: broadcasting was ideally suited to communicate the Christian faith! For the first time in church history it would be possible for a minister to preach the gospel far beyond the confines of one auditorium or the audibility of the unaided human voice. With the future development of radio, there would be practically no upper limit to the size of the unseen congregation which could hear its pastor, or to the number of unchurched who would be reached with the Christian message simply because they chanced to tune in.

"Now we can get through to these people," Wam exclaimed to Herman. "Imagine the implications—masses could hear and even be brought to faith."

"Yes, but what about regular churchgoers? They might just get lazy Sunday mornings and prefer hearing a sermon in bed."

"Hardly! That's precisely where the concept of worship comes in. Services by radio could never be a substitute for worship; only a supplement." He paused a moment, then brightened with excitement. "And what about those who can't attend church because of illness, or age, or location? Now the church can come to them wherever they may be. . . . The fringe vocations, forest rangers. . . ."

"O.K., Walt, I'm sold! But you should check all aspects of this thing. What about the loss of visual contact with the speaker? Couldn't that hurt the effectiveness of his address?"

"True. We would lose one of the senses in radio." Walter furrowed his brow in thought, then continued, "But for a sermon, that could even be advantageous, Herm, because it's the message which counts, not the minister. And what better way to emphasize the message alone."

"Right. But just a final thought: what if radio stations refuse to take a religious program? The way a man feels about his God can be awfully controversial, you know."

Walter puzzled over this possibility. "Good point," he slowly reacted, "and yet to deny a religious program would somehow seem unconstitutional. In that case the church would have to build its own radio stations. Actually, that might be a good plan anyway."

After further conversation it grew late and the two called it a night. So ended one of the very crucial discussions in Walter's career. Many of the ideas which later would affect the lives of multitudes—including his own—were planted that evening and began germinating in the following weeks.

The thought of a Christian broadcasting station started to engross the professor in moments between classes, and one evening he confronted Gihring with the possibility. Walter felt that the church should move into radio "on the ground floor" and that as a first step it ought to establish its own station, at least on an experimental basis. Herman concurred, but cautioned against broadcasting only religious services: "Preach all the time and no one will listen." Walter chuckled and agreed. He thought the station could offer a variety of other worthwhile features besides a core of religious programming. Since the church should provide leadership in culture, hours of good music, drama, discussion forums, and book reviews might well be presented—and without advertising to hound the hearer. Probably the station could be supported by listener contributions as a charitable agency.

This marked the beginning of world Lutheranism's venture into radio on a regular basis. As it happened, Walter was not indulging in reverie, but charting something which became a quick reality. Later that fall, Herman attended an electronics exposition in St. Louis where he procured a brochure describing the new radio transmitters of the Western Electric Company. Walter examined the pamphlet and was amazed that the price of a complete broadcasting apparatus was not so prohibitive as he had imagined. Immediately he approached seminary officials with the possibility of establishing a station at Concordia. An improvised room in the sprawling attic of the seminary might serve as the first studio, and an adjoining chamber could house the transmitter.

Walter's enthusiasm, however, was not shared by all colleagues on the faculty. To some the project seemed too expensive, while one of the older men even questioned the future of radio. Herman suggested that perhaps Wam should abandon the scheme, "unless you don't mind fighting for it."

Walter did not mind. He prayed earnestly about broadcasting

and became only more convinced that radio was God's special gift to the church, and the church had better recognize it as such. Finally, he approached two key individuals: Concordia's dean, Dr. John H. C. Fritz, and the president of the (mid) Western District of the Lutheran Church—Missouri Synod, Dr. Richard Kretzschmar. They showed immediate interest, and when Professors Maier and Fritz then formed a "Radio Committee," the project was under way.

Meanwhile, Walter had publicized the necessity of a link between religion and radio in *Messenger* editorials, and by this time the interest and support of church youth had been enlisted. The Walther League now appropriated $7,000 for the project, and this sum was matched by Lutheran laymen, friends, and even seminary students. A 500-watt transmitter was purchased, and soon two tall masts connected by antennae projected above the roof of Concordia Seminary. The Federal Radio Commission assigned a 545.1-meter wave length and the call letters KFUO to the attic station. Walter interpreted these as "Keep Forward Upward Onward" and dubbed the station motto, "The Gospel Voice." On Sunday, December 14, 1924, KFUO began broadcasting at 9:15 P.M. with the words: "This is Station KFUO, Concordia Theological Seminary. . . ." It was an exciting moment for Wam.

A number of telegrams from listeners started arriving before the evening's programming had concluded, and within a week several hundred letters and cards from Missouri and twenty-five other states testified that KFUO was being heard. Clear reception was reported from as far away as Toronto and Havana. In those pioneer days of the uncluttered radio dial, such transmission, aided by the ionosphere bounce effect, was possible on just 500 watts.[2]

It was a humble but successful beginning. Walter had two weekly programs: a Sunday Vesper series, and a Thursday evening feature called *Views on the News* in which he commented on the major stories of the week from their political, social, and religious perspectives. It was his own idea and predated most regular news commentators by some years. Arrangements were at times makeshift in those early days. Once, despite the engineer's best efforts, the equipment started to falter during one of Walter's broadcasts, and he himself had to hold a wire to the grid-cap on one of the tubes for the rest of his show or be cut off the air.

He abhorred the possibility of making an error over the radio, and his record was nearly perfect until the day he addressed the faculty and student body in an Easter service broadcast from the seminary chapel. After working late the night before, Walter looked a bit sleepy as he entered the pulpit and began: "The text is from the Gospel of St. Mark, chapter 16, verse 3: *And [the women] said among themselves, Who shall roll us away from the door of the sepulchre?*"—which is not quite Biblical. Colleagues and seminarians tittered at the fumble.

KFUO was communicating. Mail from St. Louis and surprisingly far beyond commended the high cultural level of the station. Unchurched listeners started showing an interest in religion and writing to admit it. By the end of the first year on the air, thousands of letters had been received. Since broadcasting was still a novelty, city newspapers gave full coverage to KFUO programs, especially Professor Maier's lecture series on contemporary religious issues, which began in the fall of 1926. The radio pioneers could not know it at the time, but their attic studio would eventually mature into one of America's foremost religious and cultural broadcasting stations, with recorded extension services covering the nation and, in fact, the Western world.

The other half of Walter's vision also materialized in the next years. Secular radio stations and networks would indeed air religious programs, masses would be reached, and the Christian message transmitted as never before. There was more prophecy than optimism in Professor Maier's repeated promise: "This is only the beginning!"

The *Messenger* continued to grow in size, coverage, and circulation. Transferring the editorial office to St. Louis caused no complication, as feared, and somewhere Walter found the time necessary to edit a very creditable magazine. He regarded this task as more than a mere part-time responsibility, for the pen was too powerful an instrument to risk blunting it through halfhearted application.

During the quarter-century of his editorship, 1920 to 1945, the cross-sectional monthly issue contained an average of sixty-four pages with features on a variety of subjects, religious and secular, most of them illustrated. Included in each number would be at least three editorials and articles authored by "W.A.M.," which were not averse to dealing with the significant, if controversial, issues of the day. He also penned the "Turret of the Times" columns in the center of the journal, which surveyed the contemporary political and cultural panorama.

The articles which the editor published in his magazine dipped into everything from archaeology to Zwingli. There were excursions into the worlds of literature and education, music and the fine arts, science and medicine, society and entertainment, business and labor. Popular items such as serials, travel pieces, character sketches, and sports accounts were also included occasionally. More serious were the articles on national and international affairs from the religious, not merely political, coign of vantage.

The *raison d'être* of the *Messenger*, however, was to present thinking church people with the spiritual features not available in secular periodicals. Naturally, the religious department was broader than the others, and articles on theological, inspirational, and moral themes appeared in each issue, as well as accounts from church history, missionary exploits, and studies of other faiths, cults, and para-religious movements.

While the journal grew in popularity, there was also occasional criticism. If the editor brought Harvard standards to his classroom, he maintained them also for his magazine. The Indiana district board of the Walther League suggested that the *Messenger* was becoming "too heavy reading for the average League boy or girl." So far as the younger members were concerned, this objection was accurate, for the periodical had, in fact, extended its outreach. Editor Maier admitted as much in reply, but suggested that the *Junior Messenger* was intended for the younger set, and his journal for the thinking young adults of the church.

Evidently there were enough of these, for the circulation soared from 7,000 to 80,000 under his editorship. The *Messenger* soon became something of a family magazine in the church, since its official organ, *The Lutheran Witness,* remained predominantly doctrinal in tone. However, Wam's journal also attracted a sizeable non-Lutheran readership, as letters to the editor demonstrated.

Writing articles in addition to editorials is usually beyond an editor's call of duty, and where Walter found time to do so remains somewhat mysterious. He was, of course, relieved of administrative details by a series of efficient business managers at League headquarters. Probably it was also a case of Harriet flying back and forth to the files while he dictated like a dervish between trips.

Harriet E. Schwenk was Wam's personal secretary from 1929 on through the rest of his life. Slender, pleasant, and intelligent, Harriet readied the environment so that her boss could produce as he did. Walter had learned of an unusually competent graduate student who had just received her Master of Arts degree from Washington University, and friends assured him that she was precisely the person needed in his office. He checked her notebooks and literary work, hired her on the spot, and never regretted the happy decision. She quickly mastered the knack of helping on the *Messenger* and rendered valuable contributions as editorial assistant. Harriet was a versatile woman, and in that office she had to be.

These were also the years when Walter—even though not in the parish ministry—began preaching on a regular basis. Invitations to address large audiences had started appearing on his desk before he reached the age of thirty. Such requests were especially numerous for the days surrounding the Reformation festival in the fall and the Lent-Easter season each spring. In 1922 he was a featured speaker at St. Louis' American Theater Lenten Noonday Services—crisp worships tailored to involve downtown business and professional people in the Passion observance. Attending crowds found the events of the original Holy Week nearly contemporized by the eloquence of one who spoke "as if he had witnessed them himself," according to the committee in charge, which invited young Maier to return annually after that.

Word about Wam spread rapidly in church circles, and soon he was addressing capacity crowds at various special services in St.

Paul, Houston, Los Angeles, and other scattered cities. In following years, many of the mounting requests for speaking engagements had to be declined because of prior commitments. Omnipresence is not a human attribute.

Walter's message during the 1920s and how he projected it were highly significant for his future career. The kind of writing or preaching which provoked his irreverent yawn was that which remained solely in the Bible without applying Scripture to the present day. On the other hand, rarely could he open the Old or New Testament without finding stories, teachings, sermons eminently pertinent to the contemporary scene. Therefore he tried to relate all of Scripture to the whole political-social-intellectual milieu of his era. One result was that people found his articles and sermons, not dry as the dust of time, but vibrant with illustrations from, and relevance to, modern life.

Occasionally he was faulted for "bringing politics into religion," "using economic statistics," denouncing wrong and acclaiming right on any level of society, government, or religion instead of limiting his scope to local spiritual concerns. But he echoed his conscience in the matter: "You cannot divorce religion from the whole complex of life," or "You cannot compartmentalize Christ."

To make the faith relevant to his time, the "roaring twenties," was no easy task. Jeremiah would have felt at home during these years, since there was much room for a prophet's denunciation. And it seems strangely appropriate that one prophetic voice now raised in America belonged to an Old Testament scholar who knew the prophets well—St. Louis' Professor Maier. From now on and for the rest of his life, newspaper clippings report in detail his attack on the evils he found in contemporary society.

Sermon after sermon in the twenties lashed out against lax moral standards which were fathering rampant immorality, rising divorce statistics, and debasement of communications media; the dangerous dilution of personal values; agnosticism, atheism, materialism, communism, alcoholism, idleness, or the rising crime rate. He weighed the alternatives of militarism on the one hand, pacifism on the other, and found both badly wanting. As a conservative he opposed the only other major theological option current, the religious

Modernism of the twenties with its de-emphasis of the supernatural and its misplaced overemphasis on natural man. It galled him that Christian pulpits should feature something less than the classic Christian message, and he did not conceal his feelings.

Walter was especially concerned about the widespread breakdown of the American home, which, among other things, was yielding a bitter harvest of juvenile delinquency. In one address he stated, "The home of yesterday used to be a sanctuary of spiritual refuge, but today it is hardly more than a human filling station."

Because this voice was using modern language for modern hearers, the nation's wire services and press reacted with surprise that a Christian sermon could be something other than the then-usual extremes: a pleasant lulling of honeyed words, or a fire-eating sawdust harangue. Even the *New York Times* could not resist reporting the "human filling station" sermon.[3]

To his astonishment, Walter soon found some of his statements becoming aphorisms and finding their way into "Quotable Quotes" sections of magazines and newspapers across the country:

"Americans must learn to invest, not spend, their time."

"Education alone cannot instill morality: an uneducated thief will steal a ride on a train, while an educated thief will steal the whole railroad."

"A college degree is no charm against family troubles."

"Many youths regard fathers merely as their financial agents."

"Culinary clatter and dramatic razzle-dazzle called 'church work' is drowning out the testimony of the saving gospel."

"Modernism is not modern. It is rather as old as humanity itself."

However, a message which is uniformly denunciatory can wear very thin in a very short time, whether the denouncer be Old Testament prophet or new Semitics professor. This might have been a substantial danger in Walter's approach but for the fact that he was preaching Christian sermons, and these cannot be predominantly negative since their core purpose is to announce something quite positive indeed: the gospel ("good news") of God's salvation of humanity through Jesus Christ. If the first part in many of Wam's sermons uncovered the bad news lurking in the society of the twenties, the second always proclaimed the better news of remedy for the ills of the era in a renewed relationship with God in Christ. Walter would spend the rest of his life making this announcement clear to as many masses of people as he could reach.

His strictures, moreover, were not like those of some contemporaries who overcriticized America as "the new Sodom and Gomorrah," censures of a type he considered "exaggerated and misleading." For example, the flapperism of the era was not "a universal blight," as many claimed, but only "a dense smudge arising from a very little flame." And young people were not nearly so wicked as portrayed in then-current literature. Said he: "It is my personal opinion that short hair, short skirts, rouged cheeks, and all the rest of the 'flapper' paraphernalia is merely a pose, and that there is a sound kernel beneath."[4]

It was a time when sinners were very bad and the saints very good, sometimes in the "goody-good" sense, condemning in one fell swoop all movies, cosmetics, playing cards, and merriment. Professor Maier disliked such extremes and insisted, "Christianity is not a joy killer." With pen and voice he cautioned youth against immoral motion pictures, but would not issue a blanket condemnation of movies as such. Given a good subject, he enjoyed them. "Young folk must have their fun," he maintained. "Luther himself said that pleasure and happiness are more essential than food and drink."[5] And as for drink, he was no prohibitionist crusader, but later commented on the issue dryly, "The church has more important things to worry about than 3.2 beer."[6]

Unwittingly he caused a press sensation simply as a minister who approved of cosmetics! "If rouge and lipstick make a woman more attractive," said he, "their moderate use is all right." He was particularly nettled that young people were blamed for having invented painting and powdering ("thumb-worn 'sins' catalogued in the indictments of modern youth"), when such techniques were in fact as old as history. Above all he was not impressed by society critics' hackneyed resort to the "good old days," for, he declared, "these are considered 'good' only because they are too far distant to permit their inconsistencies and absurdities to be revealed."[7]

One year after marriage, the bridegroom-professor addressed his first mass meeting, a Luther Day Festival at Ocean Grove, New Jersey. On August 4, crowds of Lutherans from New York, New Jersey, and Pennsylvania descended on the Atlantic resort for a day of sunning and swimming, and in the evening they filled the great seaside Auditorium off the boardwalk, nearly 10,000 strong.

Up on the platform, Walter eyed the multitude a little nervously during the opening liturgy. He had preached a host of sermons by this time, but never before such a throng, nor such people—sophisticated urbanites from New York City and Philadelphia. What if he should do less than his best, or what if his best were not good enough? He mounted the rostrum and bowed his head in prayer. "America, Wake Up!" was the theme of his address, and he began at a deliberate pace.

We are living in America's most prosperous era. . . . There is in this country today the greatest accumulation of wealth ever known to man. The ancients used to stare with wide-stretched eyes at the mention of a Croesus, but a glance at the income-tax statistics reveals the fact that there is a small army of men in our country today who would consider the commercial holdings of Croesus a mere side line.

He was under way. The warm-up period was brief, but it always involved extra effort. Now the Auditorium reverberated with confident tones.

We have flourished and prospered; grown in power and authority and influence; grown in wealth and resources; grown in size and population. But, we pause to ask: "Have we grown inwardly? Have we prospered in morals, in honor, in individual and national virtue? Have we grown in the fear and love of God? Have we grown in grace?"

You know the answer. . . . we have not come closer to God; we have not grown in spirit and in truth. I say this not in a destructive or pessimistic or cynical manner, for there is nothing as cheap and as useless and as dangerous as pessimism. But the irresistible evidence of stubborn facts pictures before our eyes a tremendous away-from-God movement which is at once so startling and so damnable that the thunder of God's vibrating wrath shrieks to those who still have ears to hear: "America, wake up! Arouse yourself from the dream of delusion and from the sleep of self-satisfaction."

First and foremost, America must wake up to a consciousness of its great national sin, the worship of Mammon and the craze for gold. Take people wherever they may be throughout the country and ask them what they consider to be their purpose in life . . . and from all directions a mighty chorus of avaricious voices will croak: "Gold, Gold, Gold!" And thus it happens that the cancer which is eating into the very vitals of our national life is dishonesty and financial rottenness. . . .

After portraying other countrywide sins, as well as their solution, the address closed with a positive appeal for a return to the "faith of the fathers":

. . . The hope of our country lies along the path that leads backward past all the failures and fancies of deluded minds, through all the tinseled attractions and tarnished temptations of the present day, backward, to the glory-crowned heights of Calvary. . . . Let Christ reign in the homes of our land, in the hearts of our people, and in the sanctuaries that bear His name—and America will wake up and arise to a new sense of its God-given leadership and pre-eminence in the civic and religious affairs of the world.[8]

Only with the "Amen" did the audience seem a living thing once again. The fervent address had held the people in apparent suspended animation.

After the service came a sight which would become typical in the future career of the speaker: a large crowd waiting in line to shake hands and exchange a few words with him. Strangely, Walter never tired of clasping each hand cordially, however long the queue might be. It made little difference if the hand belonged to a man, woman, son, daughter, grandfather, or grandmother; the pleasantries were tailored to suit the individual. Critics may ascribe it to a little natural vanity, but the handshaking marathon has another explanation: Wam loved people.

Last in line was the dark-haired girl with the familiar smile whom Walter hugged excitedly, then chided for not joining him earlier. The Maiers were not allowed to forget Ocean Grove; the Luther Day committee invited Wam to address the midsummer festival on a nearly annual basis after that.

Actually there were three Maiers at the Jersey shore, not just two. How that happened is a story which began one day on Ohio

Street when Hulda informed her husband that he would be a father. Walter's elation was boundless; he fairly rhapsodized at the news. Children charmed him, and in the most unprofessional postures he would stack blocks with babies or run electric trains with young men. Yet how much greater the joy with his own boy —certainly it would be a boy; the matter was beyond discussion. Before long he could contain the information no longer and told colleagues proudly, "My wife is fulfilling Genesis 1:28" ("Be fruitful, and multiply . . ."), much as Luther had broken the news about his Kate.

When they had been married a year, the Maier couple prepared a celebration for June 14, their first wedding anniversary. The night before the open house, Grossie, who was visiting, helped Walter prepare the punch, while his Dutch housewife was finishing the last wisp of cleaning. Suddenly she straightened and felt a decided something which was not due for a week or two. In a minor panic, Walter hurried her three blocks down to Lutheran Hospital.

At 7:30 the next morning, Walter Arthur Maier, Jr. arrived, an 8¼-pound, dark-haired anniversary present—to the day.

It was quite an open house, even without the hostess. An ebullient father was in his glory, welcoming guests to the anniversary-birthday party with a shake at the shoulders and the question, "Can you guess where Mrs. Maier is?" Grossie, the nimble substitute hostess, was as thrilled as if it had been her own first-born.

Walter assumed his paternal role with a minimum of difficulty. Even the 2 A.M. feeding failed to bother him—so long as wife and baby were quiet about it. As for the diaper problem, far be it from him to interrupt maternal activities. The line was clearly drawn: she would not learn Hebrew, he would not warm bottles.

One day Walter came home with some exciting news. The cornerstone for the new Concordia Seminary was to be laid in October, 1925, and the whole campus would be ready about a year later. The old south St. Louis seminary was no longer adequate for the purposes of the church, and extensive building plans had long been in preparation. Faculty and students were told to have faith, for soon they would exchange the superannuated structures on South Jefferson Avenue for an entirely new complex of seminary buildings to be constructed on a high, rolling, 71-acre tract west of St. Louis in fashionable suburban Clayton. Three rows of faculty homes would also be erected at the new location, a prospect bright enough for the family on Ohio Street.

Came dedication day, and by any standards, new Concordia Theological Seminary was an architectural masterpiece, a classic example of rich Tudor-Gothic mode. It was one of Protestantism's largest seminary construction enterprises to date. The complex included seventeen new buildings—administration and classroom structures, auditorium, library, dormitories, and dining halls—as well as the series of faculty residences.

The new seminary was designed by the architectural firm of Day and Klauder, which had recently done part of Princeton University, and the Tudor-Gothic buildings very much resemble Princeton's except that the addition of pink Boulder stone and blue-gray Zell stone in the predominant limestone walls produces, many think, a more beautiful effect. Roofs are of thick, bluish slate, while the windows are latticed in lead, some with ecclesiastical heraldry at the centers. The buildings crown a rise which overlooks acres of woods separating the seminary from surrounding suburbs. Today the campus with its shaded quadrangles and sweeping Gothic arches and vaults is one of St. Louis' prime tourist attractions.

In the fall of 1926, faculty and students found themselves in an academic paradise. A fresh morale stirred everyone as seminarians determined to use responsibly this gift of the Lutheran Church–Missouri Synod.

Last to move onto the new campus were the professors' families, and when the moving van arrived on Ohio Street the Maiers paid solemn parting respects to the house at 3727. Now they regretted any unkind first thoughts they may have had about the structure, for it would always claim a special corner in their memories. Here love flourished, here was their first home.

# 7

## "With Flying Colors"

"Eleven Seminary Terrace" was a trim, two story house of vermilion and ochre brick with steeply slanted slate roof, standing at the far end of a lane that led into the woods west of the seminary complex. Professor and Mrs. Maier were delighted with it from the moment they saw it in construction, and the final product was Walter's home for the rest of his life.

The first months at the new address brought a few difficulties. Streets and walks, grading and landscaping could not be completed before winter set in, and the Maiers soon learned the meaning of mire—mud which coursed lava-like along the lanes after heavy rains, mud which slithered in great heaps over what would be the future front yard, and was tracked onto the new hardwood floors to the dismay of the housewife.

The following spring, streets and landscaping were being completed when the appropriation for this purpose ran short with the work 95 per cent finished. Inevitably, the remaining 5 per cent included the corner hillside lot at Eleven Seminary Terrace. This end-lane area had been used as a construction dump, and the western exposure of House Eleven looked out on a panorama of broken bricks and slate, tar, ruined lumber, cans, debris, and stumps.

It was late spring when Mrs. Maier took her husband to the windows after his day at the seminary, pointed to the mess, and asked, "When?"

"The Dean says we'll have to wait until more funds are available, and that's not for a while."

"The eyesore is bad enough, but that rubble is becoming a hotel for rats and mice. I'm afraid for Walter Junior."

"Honey!" There was a glint in his eye. "Why don't we clear away that horrendous heap at our own expense? It would be a grateful gesture to the church for letting us live here."

Her concurrence was impassioned. A pair of horse and wagon

teams were hired for two days, as well as a corps of students who were content with minimum compensation. Trash was trundled off by the wagon load, stumps were dynamited out, holes filled in. The teams then dragged graders along the precipitous terrain and finally molded a gracefully sloping hillside.

"Now there is a piece of real estate!" said a satisfied Walter, surveying the completed project arm in arm with his wife.

"Walter. . . ."

It was said in the kind of tone he knew would cost money. "What?"

"I know you'll think I'm extravagant, but just imagine what a little pond and rock garden would do for this hillside."

"Too expensive." Then he flashed a smile, "I had in mind *two* ponds, fed by a waterfall . . . and a small stream running from one to the other . . . underneath a little bridge in between."

After a great bear hug, Hulda was off to her horticultural library and a stack of *Better Homes and Gardens* magazines. She had inherited a green thumb from her nurseryman father, and the hillside now became Family Obsession No. 1. Stone steps were placed, a flagstone terrace laid, and ponds dug and cemented, while shrubs and plants were bedded into rich soil brought in from the seminary woods. "One of my big moments," recalled Mrs. Maier, "was to see that white-collared professor of mine with black, loamy hands, asking where a forsythia should go." It was a memorable Saturday afternoon when the small hillside cascade was turned on for the first time and the family stood on the garden bridge watching the ponds fill with water.

But there are no roses without thorns. After the former dump had been transformed into a campus showpiece, a delegate to one of the many conferences held on the seminary grounds was overheard to say, "If professors can afford to have thousand-dollar rock gardens, it's time to cut their salaries." Hulda was indignant. She and her husband had improved church property by hard work and only a shoestring of expenditure. Angry himself, Walter shrugged off the smallness, concluding, "At least the place looks like a thousand dollars."

West of House Eleven a rolling woods of tall oaks served as a sylvan insulation against bustling suburbs. Soon this landscape was pierced by two orange and white radio towers. Moving along with the rest of Concordia, Station KFUO had climbed down from its attic and was now a large, new building a quarter-mile west of the seminary complex, bordering the athletic field. The station boasted four studios, reception and control rooms, more powerful transmitters, and the latest electronic equipment. New KFUO was an outright gift of the Lutheran Laymen's League, an organization of men in the Missouri Synod whose purpose was "to aid Synod with word and deed in business and financial matters," later broadened to include fellowship, educational, and service projects. In a short while, Wam and the L.L.L. would begin a long, profitable association.

On the last Sunday in May, 1927, thousands of people gathered to dedicate new KFUO. In the principal address, Walter commended the church's Leagues for having impressed radio into service for God. Toward the close he glanced at the soaring towers which straddled the multitude and said, "In our church today only these towers transmit the Christian message on a regular basis. God grant that this is only the beginning, that someday many other such spires of steel may radiate Christ even as structurally they point to heaven."

In just a score of years, these words would be fulfilled beyond the hopes of an optimistic faith. By then not two, but approximately 3,000 such towers would be radiating the Christianity in his messages alone, not to mention other religious broadcasts.

There was a loose strand in the cable of Walter's career which was still not anchored, initialed "Ph.D." To his chagrin, occasionally he would be called "Doctor Maier," an understandable slip since a professorship is usually attained only after a doctorate. Lately, however, a decided danger was threatening his graduate program at Harvard University. Because life in St. Louis grew far more crowded than he had anticipated, the months of uninterrupted, concentrated study which he should have been devoting toward his doctorate never materialized. Teaching, editing, and preaching had commanded most of his time, and by now five years had elapsed since he left Cambridge. His professors had warned him that precisely this might happen.

During summer months he completed his dissertation and had already submitted it to the Harvard Semitics department. Entitled *Slavery in the First Babylonian Dynasty*, it analyzed the sources of ancient slave supply, as well as the economic, legal, social, and religious aspects of slavery in the days of King Hammurabi as a key to understanding the early Babylonians. The monograph had required research in a dozen languages and from primary documents which included hundreds of cuneiform tablets. To Walter's relief, the dissertation was accepted by the faculty of arts and sciences, and parts of it were later published by the university.

Only the comprehensive oral examination remained, the ordeal by academic fire when one professor-inquisitor might pass him a 3,800-year-old cuneiform cylinder and ask for a translation of the scramble of stylus marks on it. Another could demand, "Tell us everything you know about Ashur-etil-ilani," or "Shamash-shum-ukin," or tens of thousands of other possibilities. A third might care to know about the diggings in Mesopotamia, summer of 1843, and so on.

During the final months of preparation for this examination, Professor Maier returned to his seminary office every evening after supper to avoid interruptions, while his wife could honestly answer telephone calls at home by saying that he was not in and taking the message instead. But each night at eleven his grind would be broken by a secret staccato whistle (. . . —) from the quadrangle below. Hulda, nearly widowed by Semitics, was waiting for her moonlight walk. And such strolls furnished encouragement enough for the crisis ahead.

To attain a Ph.D. in the field of Semitics at a university of Harvard's caliber was frightfully difficult in that academic era. Since the founding of America's oldest college in 1636, a considerable number of students had attempted the Semitics doctorate, but by 1929 only nineteen had ever earned it—an intimidating average of one successful candidate every fifteen years! Certainly the field was less than popular because of the old-school mental discipline and enormous application required to master the departmental demands.

Even with a complete familiarity in Hebrew and a good Semitics background from his Master's program, Walter still had to build proficiency in other areas. His examination would hold him responsible for Sumerian, Babylonian, Hittite, Assyrian, Hebrew, and Arabic language, literature, history, geography, and archaeology, to say nothing of the already-tested reading ability in Greek, Latin, French, and German required by the department—a grand total of ten languages.

A measure of the man's scholarship in preparing for this examination is the set of twenty books of study notes which he wrote, all of them extant. These average more than one hundred closely typewritten pages each and bear the following titles:

| | |
|---|---|
| Arabic | Hebrew Syntax |
| Assyrian Babylonian History | Old Testament Bibliography |
| Assyrian-Babylonian Religion | Old Testament Geography |
| Pan Babylonianism—Clay, Art | Old Testament History |
| Cuneiform Literature | Old Testament Literature |
| Cuneiform Parallels | Old Testament Religion |
| Cuneiform Texts, Vocabulary | Old Testament Text and Canon |
| Decipherment-Signs—Sumeriana | Old Testament Theology |
| Excavations—Geography | Old Testament Topics |
| Hittite | Semitic Languages and Origins |

Professor Maier was passing himself through an academic wringer, and perhaps only toward the end of this ego-flattening experience did he sense the full pressures involved in his choice of school and field. He had selected one of the most rigorous doctoral programs in probably the most demanding institution of higher learning in America. For one of the few times in his life, Walter Maier was genuinely worried. Here it would not be a case of trying to persuade thousands by oratory, but an examining committee of seven savants solely by knowledge. He could fail, as many before him had.

The comprehensive examination was scheduled for May 29, 1929, but Walter kept this information to himself. That spring he dreamed of some deserted mountain top where he could study without interruption. Instead he was found preaching as far afield as Los Angeles, addressing mass meetings, personally organizing a new church in downtown St. Louis, and at dozens of other engagements in addition to his regular classroom and *Messenger* responsibilities.

On Wednesday evening, May 27, the Maiers drove down to Union Station in their first car, a new Model A Ford. Husband explained to wife that he had to "attend to some business in Boston" and would be back that weekend. To see him on or off a train was so standard a routine that she thought nothing of it, except for the way he said good-by. Walter was disturbed about something, but he brushed off any inquiries with a broad smile and told her to leave before the train did. Three times they went through the parting sequence, but whenever she started to leave Walter just stood there looking at her, until finally the train began pulling out and he scrambled aboard.

Wam was on his way to Cambridge, where he would "attend to some business" indeed. At the station he had been tempted to tell his wife the whole truth about the trip and ask her prayers, but finally he vetoed the idea. If he failed the exam he wanted no one to know, especially not Hulda. If he passed, it would come as an ecstatic surprise to her, and no one enjoyed springing surprises more than he.

When he arrived in Boston, Walter notified his advisor, Prof. David G. Lyon, and the examination was confirmed for the following afternoon. Although invited to spend the night at the Lyons', Walter preferred the impersonality of a hotel for his final bout with the books. At midnight he showered and went to bed. For the next hour he tossed about, trying desperately to sleep. Tomorrow his life would change for the better, or it would not, and his nagging consciousness did not let him forget it. Finally he prayed once again, asking not for superhuman intelligence and perfect recall, only for the grace to let God use him as He willed. Surrendering further concern, he slept like a child.

The next day he boarded the subway and clacked his way northward underground. The multicolored mosaic station signs flashed by: Park Street, Charles, Kendall, Central Square, until finally the crimson of Harvard Square appeared, followed by the conductor's call, "All out—Hahvud Squay-ah!" "Most educated subway in the world," mused Wam as he stepped off, ". . . goes to Harvard ten times a day each semester."

He walked through the green immortality of the Yard and arrived at the museum room of the department of Semitic languages and history about 1:30 P.M. Seated around a large oval table were seven university professors, an examination committee which included such men as Prof. James Richard Jewett, the nation's leading Arabic scholar; Prof. William R. Arnold, one of the foremost authorities in Hebrew and Old Testament literature; Prof. George Foot Moore, famed historian of religion; Prof. David Gordon Lyon, the father of Assyriology in America; and Dr. Robert H. Pfeiffer, the noted Semitist.

Professor Lyon presented the candidate and he was seated. There was a bit of small talk to take the edge off the situation. Professor Arnold was examining the bibliography which Walter had submitted. It contained hundreds of titles. "This certainly is a formidable array," said he. "Do you mean to say that you have read all these works?"

Almost apologetically Walter answered, "Yes sir," but then smiled confidently as if to say, "Try me."

And tried he was. The examination began with two or three questions which made him shudder inwardly, not because they were that difficult but because they were first. He managed appropriate replies. The questions continued, followed by even more appropriate replies. After the first crucial minutes had passed, Walter knew he was well prepared and moved back from the edge of his chair.

When half an hour had passed, Professor Moore took up the interrogation. The candidate now began not only to answer the questions completely, but to furnish related detail which had not been requested. In some replies he gave a review of the literature on a specific problem, citing which modern authors opposed which ancient authorities, what the latest archaeological excavations had shown, who, apparently, was correct, who in error, and why. Professor Moore's eyes seemed to widen with surprise. The candidate now sat back completely, scarcely believing that he was almost enjoying the exam!

No professor likes to have his questions answered easily. The demands now became progressively difficult. Walter countered by supplying even more detail. Unloading a treasury of knowledge which had been hoarded during years of study, his mind fairly raced to liberate information. He was enjoying nearly photographic recall.

His interrogators knew that sitting before them was a Christian professor whose interpretations of the Old Testament might be conservative. One or two of the younger men posed questions calculated to embarrass the conservative position, and, of course, they had full academic prerogative to do so. Walter answered these in a dual manner. First he provided a synopsis on which authorities said what, then offered his own interpretation, whether or not it differed from the majority view. When challenged on the latter, he furnished chapter and verse on new evidence produced by recent archaeological expeditions. Smiles passed between Lyon and Jewett.

Semitic history, law, literature, and religion were covered in detail, since this was a three-hour examination. During the Assyrian reading test, Professor Lyon had supplied his colleagues with translations "for the sake of accuracy," while Walter, of course, was given only the original text. He glared at the cuneiform characters, paused momentarily, then proceeded to read off a better translation, Lyon told him later, than the published versions he had distributed. When he finished, something unusual occurred. Walter scrutinized the Assyrian once again and offered a textual criticism of the printed cuneiform, even suggesting how several of the reconstructions might be improved. The committee was astonished, and Professor Lyon beamed. Two or three cuneiform tablets were then placed before him—pieces of ancient correspondence—which he translated with magnifying glass and a little effort. Walter volunteered that the reply to one of the letters was probably in the British Museum, and the other at the University of Chicago.

"No need of further questioning! I am satisfied," was the refrain of one professor after another as the examination continued. Finally there were only ten minutes left, but the committee decided that it was enough. The candidate was asked to step out of the room while the examiners conferred. A surge of relief swept over Walter as he paced the hall outside, for doubt and worry had now given place to near-certainty. Four minutes passed, four hours in emotional time.

Suddenly the door opened and the youngest examiner came out to summon him. Although he had been instructed to say nothing to the candidate, his smile broke the news, and he clasped his hands over his head in the victory signal. As Walter re-entered the room, seven internationally famed Semitics scholars stood up simultaneously and bowed to him, signifying that they now recognized him as Doctor of Philosophy and one of their own rank. For Walter, the joy of that moment was total.

Professor Lyon offered a few words of congratulation in Assyrian, Professor Arnold in Hebrew, Jewett in Arabic. They added that they did not expect him to understand what was said so rapidly, but Walter teased out a translation anyway, "Wasn't it 'Patience has its own reward'?" and the like. They nodded approvingly and before it was all over he had shaken hands with each about two or three times. They assured Walter that he was fully qualified to teach at Harvard and should let them know if and when he was so inclined. In case other universities came under consideration, he should feel free to use any of them as reference, and they would confirm just *how* he had passed his doctoral examination.

As the session ended, some of the professors invited him to their homes, partly perhaps to learn more about this man whose capabilities had amazed them. With thanks, he asked to postpone these visits until a future trip to Cambridge because he had to return to the Midwest that night.

The rush was due to his dictum, "Happiness must be shared." In exhilaration Walter found a Western Union office and dispatched a telegram to St. Louis, then celebrated with the surprised George Maiers and other relatives in Dorchester, who had no idea he was in town but now shared his elation. Later he caught the midnight train for St. Louis.

Earlier the same day, Hulda had welcomed Grossie, Em, and

daughter Dotty, who were in St. Louis to attend Karl's graduation with Master of Arts degree from Washington University. Just as she was showing them the house, a messenger boy delivered a telegram, which she laid on the hall table while continuing the tour of inspection. It was probably just another speaking invitation for Walter. Later, while the Bostonians were unpacking, she opened the wire to see if it involved anything requiring immediate attention. Only then did she notice that the telegram was addressed to herself and read:

JUST PASSED MY EXAMINATION WITH FLYING COLORS.
LOVE AND KISSES.

WALTER A. MAIER, PH.D.

Stunned, she could not believe the message until she had read it three times. So *that* was the "business in Boston." "People, look at this!" she shouted, "Walter just received his Ph.D.! Did you know he was going to Harvard for his examination?" They hurried downstairs to share the excitement. The doctoral project was finished at last, and this called for festivities.

The next day, Hulda and little Walter met their returning hero at the station. As the Boston train rolled to a halt, a beaming Walter hurtled down the steps and into the arms of his wife, a pose they held for some time. "I'm very proud of you, Papa Doctor!" said Walter Junior, tugging at his trousers and waiting to get into the act. Wam swooped him off his feet like the acrobatic team of yore and administered a bear hug.

On the way home, Hulda insisted, "I want to know everything about the exam, every last detail." She knew he would tell the story only once and only privately. He complied, and never again repeated the whole account. From the many notes Mrs. Maier entered in her diary that evening came the details of the examination, particulars which otherwise would escape a biographer.

Arriving at 11 Seminary Terrace, the family walked up to the front door. Over it hung an electrically-lighted sign:

WELCOME, DOCTOR MAIER!

The word DOCTOR was blinking on and off. "Karl's work," chuckled Walter as he opened the door and a houseful of cheering relatives, associates, and friends descended on him. Grossie hugged her son, Karl grabbed his hand, and colleagues reacted in similar fashion. Seminary President Franz Pieper embraced him cordially, as did his successor, Dr. L. Fuerbringer. Neighboring Professor Graebner congratulated him in Latin and Professor Arndt in Greek. Hulda had mentioned nothing of a reception—they had exchanged surprises.

Although final exams were lurking at the end of the week, the faculty and student body scheduled an academic celebration in Professor Maier's honor at the seminary auditorium. It was a jubilant affair, with speeches from the president of the Concordia student association, the faculty, and city clergy. For the next days a lingering holiday spirit hovered over House Eleven.

This was springtime in the life of Walter Maier. Just three weeks later the "newly baked Doctor" (as Europeans put it) addressed one of the largest mass meetings of his career, a throng of humanity many times greater than that which faced him at Ocean Grove. Probably it was the largest assemblage in the history of Protestantism to that time. On Sunday, June 23, approximately 70,000 people crowded into Chicago's mammoth lakefront stadium, Soldier Field, to attend the quadricentennial celebration of the publication of Luther's Catechism, for which Dr. Maier was the featured speaker.[1]

The service itself had to be conducted in heroic dimension, with music provided by a mixed chorus of 3,000 voices, a children's choir of 4,000, and a large band. In the course of worship, the entire assembly—surpassing the population of Springfield, the Illinois capital—joined in a mass recitation of the Ten Commandments and the Creed, then sang the sermon hymn.

On a large dais near the center of the great hippodrome sat Walter, glancing at his notes along with the hymn verses. At this point he was beyond apprehension since such a congregation was too enormous for concern, so his mind assured him. His pulse, on the other hand, accelerated on its own as he rose to the rostrum, bowed his head in prayer, and faced the ring-and-spring suspension microphones which made communication with such an assembly possible.

In solemn, at first slightly ponderous tones which re-echoed in the vast stadium, Walter quickly pierced to the core of his message. He styled the Catechism, familiar question-answer handbook to Protestant Christianity, as "the Laymen's Little Bible," a manual which had far outlasted all others in the history of literature. As a son of his church, he asserted:

The Catechism of Martin Luther is the most concise, most practical, most successful, most Scriptural presentation of the facts and fundamental truths of Christian belief that the world knows. After a lapse of four hundred years, the Small Catechism remains the basis of religious instruction for millions . . . all over the world. Few books, aside from the Bible itself, have had such a widespread and prolonged influence upon generation after generation of Christians.[2]

The sermon climaxed with a plea that Americans re-examine and repossess the truths anchored in the first words of the Catechism, "We should fear, love, and trust in God above all things." The appeal stirred thousands of hearers. The dynamic in it was less Maier, and more Maier's use of Scripture vigorously applied to the needs of the people. He never found Bible citation to be anything less than potent.

Following the sermon, 70,000 voices closed the service by singing the "Battle Hymn of the Reformation"—"A Mighty Fortress Is Our God." Startled sea gulls by the hundreds screamed at the thundering sound and flew in a frenzy toward Lake Michigan. Despite that unplanned touch, it was one of Chicago Lutheranism's finest hours.

This was among the first of the great anniversary celebrations which crowded church calendars during the next five years: 1929, because 400 years earlier the name "Protestant" was born at the Diet of Speyer, and the Small and Large Catechisms were published; 1930 was the quadricentennial of the Augsburg Confession, the foremost statement of belief in the Lutheran church after the ecumenical creeds; 1933 marked the 450th anniversary of Luther's birth; and 1934 signalized 1534, when the first edition of the complete German Bible was published. At many of these observances, Walter was the principal speaker.

Elsewhere in 1929, he addressed mass quadricentennial celebrations in Milwaukee, where a total 10,000 jammed Auditorium services to hear him, with thousands turned away; in St. Paul, where 8,000 filled the Auditorium; in Ocean Grove, with nearly 10,000 attending; and in Cleveland, before almost 8,000 at the Public Auditorium.

In his own St. Louis, well over 22,000 packed the galleries, poured onto the floor, and exhausted all standing room in the huge Arena to establish an attendance record. Set for Reformation Sunday, the service was similar to the Soldier Field observance: the choir of 5,000 children, an orchestra of Concordia students, mass recitation and singing.

"The Modern Protest of Protestantism" was the title of Walter's address, for which he turned church historian to underscore the significance of the term Protestant. It was on the nineteenth of April in 1529 that Lutheran princes, gathered with the Roman Catholic estates at the imperial Diet of Speyer, strenuously objected to demands by Emperor Charles V that Lutheranism be proscribed in Germany. They united in delivering this statement:

. . . "We protest by these presents before God, our only Creator, Preserver, Redeemer and Savior, and who will one day be our Judge, as well as before all men, that we, for us and for our people, neither consent nor adhere in any manner whatsoever to the proposed decrees in anything that is contrary to God, to his Holy Word, to our right conscience and to the salvation of our souls."

It is from the opening words of this declaration, the "We protest," that we have millions, even as you and I, who bear the title "Protestant" and bear it proudly. . . . Now four centuries have elapsed since that memorable day in 1529 and Protestantism has grown from a few thousand persevering followers to a mighty army of almost 200 million.

Yet the speaker was not there to foster self-satisfaction or complacence. He continued:

In many ways the Protestantism of 1929 is only a haggard specter of the Protestantism of 1529. The Protestantism which starts from that heroic figure of the Reformation, Martin Luther, is a positive, evangelical creed that bows submissively before the word of God; but much of Protestantism today is a negative, unevangelical system which, serenely but determinately, disregards the word of God. In many Protestant denominations there are today hundreds of ministers who really protest against the Bible, against the inspiration and inerrancy of Scripture, instead of protesting in behalf of Biblical truths and teachings as those brave men of 1529. . . . Let us remember the warning words of Daniel Webster: "If we abide by the principles of the Bible, our country will go on prospering, but if we and our posterity neglect its instruction and authority, no man can tell how sudden a catastrophe may overwhelm us and bury our glory in profound obscurity."

The rest of the address supplied a positive "restatement of real Protestant principles," according to newspapers the next day, which reported the sermon in detail and its effect on people attending "one of the largest indoor religious gatherings ever held anywhere."[3]

This citation illustrates one aspect of Walter's early addresses before mass audiences. It galled him that in the interest of updating and applying theology to a modern era, many clergymen had gone too far and were compromising the heart of the faith. "Christianity is spontaneously relevant in its classical message," he told his students. "While the technique, illustrations, idiom, style, application, and communication of its preaching must be modernized, the essential truths remain constant. Ours is a changeless Christ for a changing world."

In widening American church circles after 1929, Walter's preaching was being styled as "Luther-like,"* but he dismissed such remarks as kind but faulty flattery. Similar commendation he handled as an electric charge which was best grounded before it did any damage. For a dangerous potential existed now: pride. One thirty-five-year-old had personally addressed almost a seventh of a million people in only seven sermons, two of them before what were among the largest outdoor and indoor religious gatherings in history; Harvard had granted him his doctorate with highest honors in a difficult field; and his other efforts were meeting with a success usually reserved for later life. Achievement had arrived,

---

* So, also literally, thought Donald Grey Barnhouse, who wanted W.A.M. to be the "voice of Luther" and preach some of the reformer's most important sermons for his library of great preachers project. See *Time*, December 17, 1951, p. 73.

which meant that pride, achievement's first cousin, would be rapping at the door. Walter knew that if he let pride come inside it would nullify his ministry. Sensing that Christ was the Solution here as in any spiritual difficulty, he was mindful of John 3:30— *"He must increase, but I must decrease."* This battle was won, and remained won.

Walter's summers away from the seminary brought freedom and balance to an otherwise crowded career. A week after the Soldier Field celebration, the three Maiers spirited themselves off to the Blue Ridge Mountains of Virginia. The trip ended in a picturesque town called Waynesboro at the southern end of Shenandoah National Park, where they were greeted by brother Karl and his bride Esther. Karl had accepted the pastorate of two congregations in the area, and Walter had come to ordain and install him in his first charge. He preached on the text, *"Sanctify yourselves: for tomorrow the Lord will do wonders among you"* (Jos. 3:5), and the "wonders" did, in fact, take place. So productive was the relationship between Karl and his parishioners that he is pastor of Waynesboro's outstanding Bethany-Trinity Church and Christian Day School to this day. Probably it was his photogenic wife and children that led Karl into his avocation of motion-picture photography, which he subsequently used for Synod's visual education program.

From Virginia, the Maier family drove north along the Appalachian spine to eastern Pennsylvania and a large resort near the hamlet of Pocono Pines called Lutherland. The place had been founded by an association under the leadership of Henry A. Dahlen, a New York manufacturer and contractor who felt that the Ocean Grove excursions of one day were too short a time for Christians to relax together. A scenic, 500-acre resort in the wooded Pocono Mountains which was only 100 miles from New York and Philadelphia, Lutherland aimed to provide harried urbanites with an atmosphere of natural beauty in which to "make their faith a living, active force." Daily morning devotions and lectures were conducted by visiting clergy, while afternoons and evenings were filled with cultural programs, sports, and amusements.

Henry Dahlen first met Walter at Ocean Grove and had repeatedly invited him to serve as summer dean of Lutherland. He would have the responsibilities of supervising the resort's religious program and preaching for the Sunday services. At first Walter declined the offers, enticing as they were; he wanted the summer free for research on a contemplated book. But the association stressed the opportunities for the church which Lutherland provided, and such thinking was "the way to get to Wam." He finally consented.

Shortly after their arrival in the Poconos, Henry and Alma Dahlen took Dean Maier and his family on a tour of the resort. They were enchanted, for the place had something to offer every age group. The youngest toddlers were supervised at a garden playhouse; for boys there was Camp Chicagami; for girls, Camp Nawakwa, both on ice-blue Lake Tamaque, the water playground of Lutherland. Young people stayed at Walther League Camp Beaverbrook, ensconced in a pine forest; newlyweds were quartered in a row of rustic bungalows. Adult guests had a choice between the great, homey Inn, or luxury lodges farther in the woods. Flanking these was Lutherland Restaurant, where the best prime rib of beef *au jus* west of New York was served. Sports facilities included a golf course, tennis courts, and riding stable, while nature trails led to fishing streams through forests abounding in deer and wildlife.

The social center of Lutherland was the Casino—one, needless to say, without any gambling devices. Above its elaborate gift shop and tearoom was a large auditorium for purposes sacred and secular. Sunday and weekday mornings it was Lutherland Church; at other times, Pocono Playhouse, the concert hall, or theatre, depending on the evening's scheduled entertainment. The Casino never saw a dull summer day.

The Maiers were given the use of a spacious summer home near the Casino. As satellites around the resort complex, such houses were constructed by New Yorkers, Jerseyites, and Pennsylvanians who had made the mistake of driving to Pocono Pines out of curiosity. One visit was enough to riddle a family with Lutherlanditis, a disorder whose only treatment was moving to the place each summer.

Soon the dean was supervising a program of spiritual and cultural interest which remained the pattern for years to come. Guests were gratified that a vacation could relax the body, deepen the mind, and freshen the spirit—all at the same time.

Sundays at the resort were days of rest for nearly everyone but the kitchen staff and Walter. While visiting clergy conducted the weekday devotions, on Sundays it was Wam's pulpit, and Casino worship services soon became the high point of the Lutherland week. Then a pleasant problem developed. Word spread that the "Ocean Grove preacher" could be heard in the Poconos on a weekly, not just annual, basis. People began driving from East-coast cities for his morning service, staying through Sunday to discover Lutherland, and returning to tell their friends. Sunday crowds cramming the Casino auditorium were such that two serv-ices had to be held. Soon this was not enough, and the microphone came to the rescue while the congregation spilled onto the broad outdoor verandas of the Casino and participated in the services through loudspeakers. Eventually the large surrounding lawn was also requisitioned, as additional speakers were set up and the people were seated on long rows of folding chairs. When these gave out they sat on beach blankets. Even though visual contact with the preacher was lost by more than half the congregation, his addresses via electronics seemed to lose no force whatever—a prophetic phe-nomenon.

When Director Dahlen reported new attendance records of 2,500, soon 3,000 people, Walter was pleased, of course, but per-sonal credit for the crowds only irked him. Any nod toward a cult of personality could only obscure the higher cause. However, one participant in those services was falling into theologically dangerous hero worship. Once, following the sermon, a little man whose heart was brimming with pride informed an usher: "That was my *father* preaching!"

The preacher himself occasionally regressed to his youthful tricks in the Poconos, especially when the Karl Maiers visited along with the Indianapolis sisters-in-law. One day after lunch, the ladies were prevailed upon to show off their newly-purchased millinery. Opening prim bandboxes, they found instead hats which had sprouted old feathers, gaudy flowers, and clashing crepe-paper decor. But this was only a minor prelude. That night at 2 A.M., Paula was suddenly awakened by a horrific roaring from under her bed, while the bedroom itself broke into a ghastly chartreuse illumination which presently changed to a shimmering, fiery red. She sat up and gasped. Then trumpets blared, sirens screamed, and lights blinked. Charging out of the room in a frenzy, she stumbled over Karl and Walter, who were shaking with laughter. They had rigged vacuum sweeper, rotocolor floodlight, phonograph, and other gadgets to a separate fuse circuit.

North of the Casino, a woodland path led down to a beautiful outdoor chapel on Lake Naomi —Vesper Landing. A thicket of unusually tall pines had been thinned out, and the sloping bank graded into a natural amphitheatre with rows of benches facing a stone altar at the water's edge. Here there was a sense of worship possibly more sublime than in the grandest cathedrals, for they were only man's noblest structures, whereas the created elegance of an alfresco chapel was a function of the divine. Soaring pine trunks sprouting needled branches against a vault of darkening sky were the flying buttresses, the altar area framed by placid Lake Naomi constituted the chancel, and the whole tableau of nature's greens and blues, often haloed by a flaming sunset, substituted for stained glass.

Every Sunday evening, some 700 people gathered here for what soon became an amphibious Vespers, as one or two dozen canoes regularly paddled across the lake and put to at the landing during services. For his evening addresses, Walter prepared sermonettes on nature themes: "Seas in Scripture," "Mountain Messages," "God's Animals," and the like, demonstrations of how the Creator involves all of creation in His sovereign and saving will. After the benediction, Lutherlanders discussed the meditations over their arcing flashlights while walking back up to the Casino.

Labor Day came and the summer heard its own benediction. It was time for vacationland dean to become seminary professor once again. The Fred Nehrings, a New York family which struck up an immediate friendship with the Maiers, staged a gala farewell reception for them in their handsome lodge at the edge of Lutherland. Only the closest friends were invited, because in one summer

Walter and Hulda had managed to gain upwards of 250 "closest friends." Toward the end of festivities, Henry Dahlen made a speech of gratitude to the Maiers, insisting that they return to the Poconos every year. This prospect was not hard to face, since the resort seemed indeed "That Perfect Vacationland" of its motto. And they did return to Lutherland—each summer for the next eleven years.

# 8

# "The Impossible Church"

Another account begins in 1929, a year as important in the life of Walter Maier as it was catastrophic in the economy of the nation. This is no glory story—there is anything but grandeur in visiting poorhouses, or canvassing—but it discloses another facet of this career: a preacher to thousands could also be a missionary minister pushing doorbells.

Ever since his arrival at Concordia Seminary, Professor Maier had accented the cause of home and foreign missions among seminarians, with the result that a Students' Missionary Society was organized which soon rumbled with activity.[1] As faculty advisor, Walter suggested that mission work was not only a foreign enterprise conducted in such places as New Guinea or the Congo, but a venture which, like charity, begins at home, and he fired a fervor in the society to react accordingly.

Periodically, he led groups of students in canvasses, the familiar house-to-house religious polls. If enough unchurched people were found within a prospective area, the society suggested that a mission or new congregation be formed. With the blessing of church authorities, student pastors, teachers, and organists would then launch the mission. Today a number of thriving churches in Missouri and Illinois stand as results of these student efforts.

If no church building were available in a canvassed and promising locality, schools, stores, police stations, and even fire halls sometimes served the purpose. One Sunday morning, for example, Walter chartered a bus for Missionary Society members, and they drove to a community 15 miles from St. Louis in order to conduct Sunday school and church services above the local fire station. Just as the worship was concluding, an excited telephone call was followed by a horrendous roar of sirens from two trucks growling out of the garage below. A shaken congregation filed out. Inevitable comments were overheard at the picnic lunch which followed: "Wam's a fire-and-brimstone preacher!" "Holy smoke!"

As part of their practical training, seminarians visited hospitals, sanitariums, and mental institutions, as well as correction homes and jails. Ministerial technique had to be as broad as this, for it was the Master who said: "I was sick and you visited me, I was in prison and you came to me" (Matt. 25:36). The society sponsor was not too busy to demonstrate a bedside or even prison approach, since this was one of the roles of discipleship.

Then there were the social unfortunates who required a special outreach, people whom some would write off as useless dregs of humanity. In St. Louis a group of them resided at the Home for Homeless Men, a YMCA-sponsored haven for destitutes, transients, and vagrants of all kinds, a friendless and unfriendly lot. On Christmas days in the late twenties the Maiers visited here, along with small delegations of students singing carols and laden with presents.

"It was a picture of humanity which I had never seen before," reported Hulda, "uncouth, unkempt individuals apparently with no higher instincts than keeping fed. They were suspicious of everyone since they even stole clothing from one another. For protection they often slept in their clothes on those three-tiered beds, or stuffed them under the mattresses. Walter tried to put the story of the Savior's birth into language which they could understand, interspersing his approach with questions. Many had never heard of 'Jesus Christ' except as a curse, and few seemed to comprehend at first. But their comprehension increased by leaps and bounds when we gave them 'gifts from Christians who are sharing out of gratitude for God's own great Gift in Jesus Christ'—so Walter phrased it." At any rate, a beginning was made, and on successive visits there was less and less suspicion.

In later years, the story repeated itself at St. Louis' "Hooverville," a compressed collection of squalid and ramshackle huts sandwiched in between waterfront railroad tracks and the Mississippi River. A few of the hovels were no larger than huge shipping crates, simply because that is precisely what they were. Despite the dreary circumstances of economic depression, some families brightened at the caroling with memories of happier yuletides. In solid simplicity,

Walter explained that Christmas had a meaning for them larger than the present existence. He found that these messages always gravitated toward the Christian concept of hope.

Such efforts of the Students' Missionary Society and its sponsor set the stage for their most ambitious project: the founding of an "impossible" church.

It was a bleak day in February, 1929. Walter was riding downtown on the Olive streetcar, when a FOR SALE sign at Pendleton Avenue caught his attention because of the unusual object it offered to sell. The sign stood on the lawn of a large limestone church, handsome in modified Gothic with an Anglican look about it. The streetcar screeched to a halt, then droned on again. "We *should* have a Lutheran church in this area," mused Wam, "a densely populated district, but few people are reached. Olive *is* one of the main streets of the city."

After finishing his business downtown he returned on the same car line. This time he stepped off at Pendleton and walked over to the church. Of course; it was the Episcopal Church of St. George. He had read that this congregation was vacating its downtown sanctuary because members had moved out to the country, where they were now amalgamating with another parish. Walter walked around the church and peered through a window to see inside. Basically the structure was in excellent condition, "just broken in." He pondered the possibilities: "Should seat four or five hundred . . . probably good facilities in the parish hall . . . 'St. George Lutheran Church' . . . no, we'd have to change the name . . . no dragon-slaying in our tradition!"

He made an appointment with the Episcopal trustees, who showed him through St. George and even offered its use for preliminary services "if you Lutherans want to give it a try." Walter checked with the City Planning Commission for population statistics on the neighborhood and found that 40,000 lived within walking distance of the church. Next he marshaled the practiced talents of the Students' Missionary Society for a canvass of ten-blocks' radius from St. George. Before dispatching his seminarians, he rehearsed last-minute instructions: "Remember men, wear a friendly smile, and ask if the residents have any church connections. If they do, fine. If not, would they be interested in attending Lutheran services at St. George?"

Canvass results showed not only a number of unchurched Lutherans in the area, but a large percentage of the people with no religious affiliation whatever. Here, then, was true mission ground surrounding a church waiting to be filled. Walter approached his district mission board, the body which plans new congregations. The board replied that it could not sponsor such an enterprise because finances were not available at the time, but if the Missionary Society wished to proceed with the project—Godspeed. Then, in deference to an established church farther north, Walter suggested the mission as a daughter congregation of that parish, with the society carrying out the work of founding it. But the pastor replied that his church could not shoulder the added financial burden, and he saw "little material" in the canvass results.

Professor Maier discussed the mission with his students. To "go it alone" was a large order for the society, and he assured members that they could vote it down without losing him as friend or advisor. The seminarians courageously voted to go ahead.

Considerable criticism was raised about the venture. It was termed an "impossible church" for various reasons: there were too few Lutherans in the area; competition seemed considerable with prominent Second Presbyterian Church and the St. Louis Roman Catholic Cathedral near by; many transients lived in the neighborhood rooming houses, hardly church types. Some claimed that the territory was decadent—the Episcopalians had left, and we should now buy here? The project was too ambitious, starting on too grand a scale.

Walter and the society countered vigorously: this mission would grow through converts, not Lutheran transferees; the proximity of other churches demonstrated that the area was not decadent; in fact, property values were rising. As for membership prospects, Christianity is not tied to the social register, and the congregation would welcome transients or tycoons.

"Downtown churches sometimes sacrifice missionary opportunities by locating in the suburbs and leaving the large mass of population in the more congested districts untouched," stated Walter. "Since this church building is located in the center of the most densely populated section of the city, it is clearly a suitable place for a missionary experiment."[2] The experiment was to determine if seminarians could found, not just maintain, a congregation in the inner city. It would be a true "laboratory for theological students." The trustees of St. George would go along with the venture for a limited time, after which the church would have to be sold. The story which Walter later called "almost a missionary romance" had completed chapter one.

The Students' Missionary Society plunged into a resolute effort, and services were begun the last Sunday in April. Soon eighty communicant members—only eighteen of them transferees—constituted a founding nucleus, and the Sunday school was crowded with neighborhood children. Such results prompted the mission board to support the project anyway.

Raising the capital to purchase St. George, however, remained a considerable problem. The original asking price was $95,000, though the trustees implied they would be satisfied with substantially less. In case the price should fall lower, Walter applied for assistance to the church extension board, the agency which loaned funds for new missions, but at first the board seemed skeptical. The Episcopalians now needed ready money for their county church construction project, so the price started dropping. Almost daily a First National Bank vice-president telephoned Walter, quoting a new and lower figure, only to hear him say, "That's a *very* fair price, but I don't have that much money available." He was not trying to haggle with the Anglicans; he simply did not have the funds. Finally the price skidded to a fantastic $29,500. The replacement cost for St. George at 1929's prices would have been $150,000 at the minimum. A friend who was a St. Louis investment authority told Wam he *must* buy at such a price.

Walter appealed for assistance to the president of the Western District who, however, expressed his doubts:

. . . [Should] a new mission congregation that will not grow in leaps and bounds in such a territory really begin in such a pretentious church property? . . . I wonder whether the mission would not be served better if a house could be bought or leased and remodeled in that territory, perhaps more favorably located, with better prospects for the future? . . . Possibly it will be said for many years to come, "What a minor congregation in a major church!"[3]

Walter predicted that soon it would be a major congregation in a minor church. He replied the next day, answering the objections and pointing out that the entire church would cost little more than a house. He asked the president's recommendation for a loan of $10,000 from the church extension fund, then pooled enough money to secure the option.

Walter received his loan; he had requested only $10,000 because the balance was being raised in crazy-quilt fashion—little sanctified scraps and great pious pieces. One day, driving down Seminary Hill, he stopped to give a ride to an elderly stranger, who recognized him and remarked, "That's a fine project you have down on Olive Street, and I'd like to give you a thousand dollars toward it." Walter slammed on the brakes and asked, "What did you say?" He repeated the offer, adding "Is that too little?" Frank Mackensen was good as his word, and this godsend keynoted the venture. Walter mentioned the mission on his weekly KFUO broadcasts, and donations arrived from interested friends. The Louis Waltkes, father and son, of Waltke soap fame, lent and gave to the enterprise, and by now enough funds were accumulated. The Episcopal Church of St. George was purchased on January 17, 1930, and just in time. Two days later the bank called and offered to buy back the property at $8,000 profit! The answer came with the announcement that St. Stephen's Evangelical Lutheran Church was organized.

Before dedication, a full renovation of the sanctuary was necessary, and here also Walter's phrase, "missionary romance," justified itself. One of the first prospects he and a seminarian met in canvassing was Frank Snider. When they had stated their mission at Snider's door, he turned around and called upstairs, "Dorothy! Helen! Come down. You've been saying you'd like to join a church of some kind. Here's your chance." The consequences of that one canvass call should inspire any who weary of the often dreary routine: the Snider girls enrolled in St. Stephen's first confirmation class, the parents in the second, their boys joined Sunday school, and later Dorothy and Helen each married seminarians.

Moreover, Frank Snider was an interior decorator by trade, and the condition of St. George was just his meat. Refurbishing the sanctuary was his largest project to date, and his best. After he had physically transformed St. George into St. Stephen's, Snider presented the church council with a bill totalling $5,500 for materials and labor. Across it he had written "Paid in Full." His remuneration, he said, was a changed life in Christ, not cash. Snider's spirit was shared by other laymen and society students who gave hundreds of hours to St. Stephen's. And no one was paid anything, from the Reverend Walter A. Maier, pastor pro tem, to volunteer janitorial help.

Dedication day was Sunday, March 30. Three festive services were scheduled, but five had to be held to accommodate the crowd of 3,000 which attended. Walter preached on Stephen, the first martyr of the Christian church. The mission had chosen this name, he explained, not because St. Louis' eighty Lutheran parishes had nearly exhausted the prominent Biblical personalities in congregational nomenclature, but by reason of Stephen's role as the first layman actively engaged in church work. This was to be a laymen's church, like Stephen, "full of faith and of the Holy Spirit," a living example of how the "royal priesthood of all believers" could function at the heart of the inner city.[4]

Function it did, beyond the foresight of its founders. One of the most active members in the Students' Missionary Society, Arthur C. Nitz, was called as first pastor of the congregation, and his was a long and productive ministry. The various men's, women's, and young people's groups were organized, and the record of St. Stephen's since then is charted on a rising graph. In a short time it had repaid its debt to Synod many times over, and though deep in the inner city, its membership twenty-five years later was still 1,100, a shade less today. A Walter A. Maier Education Building and Christian day school have been added to the church structure, and now the capital plant is valued at $350,000. A downtown congregation flourished; it was not supposed to happen.

The larger influence of "the impossible church" is noteworthy.

At this writing, more than 1,000 people have been confirmed into the faith at St. Stephen's and 1,600 baptized. The parish also functioned as missionary gateway into the church for new arrivals in St. Louis, and well over 1,700 members were subsequently transferred to suburban congregations. "St. Steve's" also became the happy hunting ground for single seminarians, and an estimated 100 to 150 of them found their wives here.[5] The Maiers retained lifelong membership at St. Stephen's, and Walter preached the annual New Year's Eve services.

Occasionally, the "missionary romance" continues to inspire. Several years ago, for example, Mrs. Maier was relating city mission experiences to a women's rally in Cincinnati. One lady in the audience was a member of a young church which had disbanded for lack of interest, financial difficulty, and criticism. After hearing the St. Stephen's saga, she returned home to Dayton and stimulated a refounding of the mission. Today it is a large, thriving congregation with an impressive new structure.

In terms of long-range effect, it is difficult to guess how many lives were changed because Walter sat on the left instead of the right side of the streetcar and so chanced to see a FOR SALE sign one cold day in February.

One life in particular was altered rather tangibly by fledgling St. Stephen's. Two months after dedication day, a towheaded, blue-eyed son was born to parents who had waited five years for the event.

"We'll name him Paul for the Apostle," suggested Walter, "Luther for. . . ."

"For your hero," smiled Hulda, ". . . and Maier for mine."

Two weeks later, I was among the first babies baptized at St. Stephen's.

# 9

# The Lutheran Hour

During these early years of his career, Walter could not shake off his dream of communicating Christianity by radio. After frequent references to "radiotelephony" in earlier issues, the *Messenger* editorial of March, 1923—"Why Not a Lutheran Broadcasting Station?"—had marked the opening shot in his campaign of alerting the church to radio. By means of further editorials, articles, conferences, and addresses, this effort continued throughout the twenties.[1] KFUO was born, but two radio towers were still "only the beginning." Many more KFUO's were needed, or better, a short cut by which the church's message could be aired immediately over many existing stations by means of a special program on one of the national networks.

Now, four years after the pioneer broadcasts on KFUO, the second link was forged in the chain of events which would lead directly to such a Lutheran radio hour. It happened during Wam's first summer at Lutherland on the veranda of the Inn, where he was talking late into a July night with his old comrade of the crystal sets, Herman Gihring. A newly arrived resort guest, Gihring was now employed at the New York laboratories of R.C.A., and one of his functions was to assist radio stations in locating good transmitter sites.

"Wouldn't this be an ideal place for a Christian broadcasting station to cover much of the East?" Walter asked Herman. "We're high in the Poconos and less than a hundred miles from the coastal cities."

"Actually, this would be too far away for regular broadcasting, especially with the mountainous terrain. Short wave, perhaps, but but not the AM band."

"Well somehow we must cover America coast-to-coast with a religious program. I suppose the only solution is chain-broadcasting. . . ."

"That's right, the established networks: CBS, Blue, and of course our own subsidiary, NBC."

"Yes, it's NBC which carries Dr. S. Parkes Cadman on the *National Radio Pulpit*. NBC donates the time because his program is nondenominational and under the auspices of the Federal Council of Churches."

"And I suppose you're after a program with our church's message?"

"Exactly, a 'Lutheran Radio Hour,' preaching an authentic Christianity sometimes missing in a few of the 'modernized' versions I've heard, although it should have a very broad—not sectarian—appeal. But I'm afraid NBC would not donate the time to us because the broadcast would be sponsored by a specific denomination. They can give air time gratis in the three general areas, Protestant, Roman Catholic, Jewish, and keep religious peace, but. . . ."

"I suppose there would be dozens of separate requests for network time within Protestantism alone."

"Probably. So if our church did sponsor a program it would likely have to pay for it on a commercial basis. Have you any idea how much an hour of air time would cost on the chains?"

"An hour?" Herman calculated momentarily. "Oh, something like $10,000 on the major networks, depending on the time of day."

"For a series of weekly broadcasts?"

"For *one* broadcast!"

Walter paused and surveyed his shoes. "I think our Lutheran Radio Hour has now become the Lutheran *Half*-Hour, though we could call it 'Hour' in a broad definition."

"It would still be a very costly proposition—a far cry from that attic transmitter in south St. Louis!"

"I know. But somehow we *must* find funds to broadcast the faith across America." He stopped, then continued in lower tone, ". . . and perhaps across the world."

When Walter returned to St. Louis that fall, he discussed the necessity of network broadcasting with colleagues on the KFUO Radio Committee. His enthusiasm for a coast-to-coast Lutheran Hour was shared particularly by Dr. Herman H. Hohenstein, direc-

tor of KFUO, who had prepared an essay encouraging a nation-
wide radio outreach by the church. On November 15, 1929, the
committee resolved that a beginning be made, that ". . . Dean Fritz
and Dr. Maier confer in person with the officials of the various
radio networks at New York for the purpose of having Lutheran
religious radio programs broadcast over the chains."[2]

The project was under way. Soon after the New Year, Walter
was in New York City, discussing the possibilities of a Lutheran
network program with officials of the National Broadcasting Company. He got precisely nowhere. NBC explained that it donated
time for Protestant programming by arrangement with the Federal
Council of Churches alone, and that it could not supply time to one
denomination. Walter's objection that his church was not represented in the Council was not honored. Might Lutherans then purchase time for a network broadcast? No. As a matter of policy NBC
would not put religious time on a commercial basis.

Clearly the men were somewhat disturbed by the denominational aspect of the proposed program. "Do you really think a
Lutheran sermon is suited for the broad American public?" asked
one of the younger men. "Isn't Lutheranism primarily for the
Germans?"

Walter glared momentarily—as did the senior executives—then
regained composure and replied, "Is Presbyterianism only for the
Scots? Roman Catholicism only for Italians? Let me see . . . in the
past month I've talked with a Mr. Fitzpatrick, a Mrs. Rockefeller,
a Mr. Smith, Professor Polack, Mr. Calvin . . . and they're *all*
Lutheran. For that matter, if Lutheranism is primarily German
because of Martin Luther, then Christianity is primarily Jewish
because of Jesus Christ."

After a general chuckle, the conference concluded with a suggestion that Lutherans might be able to share the time allotted to
various Protestant bodies on a periodic basis, perhaps an eight- or
nine-week series. This meeting, however, further convinced Walter
that network time for a regular broadcasting season would have to
be purchased, instead of relying on a possible donated, but only
occasional, series, which would be far less effective.

Walter's Lutherland friend, Henry Dahlen, assisted him in the approach to CBS. Here the outlook appeared brighter. Columbia accepted paid religious programs, although it was now in the process of converting to a donation policy and planned to establish the interdenominational *Church of the Air* to implement the new approach. While a Lutheran Hour could hardly complement this policy change, CBS officials betrayed considerable interest in the project. However, only a few time slots were available in the network week, and CBS would have to charge full commercial rates, probably $4,500 per half-hour program over its thirty-four city network.

At last the enterprise had moved out of the hopeless category, even if network costs were prohibitively high. Back in St. Louis, Walter continued searching out other possibilities and making final appeals for noncommercial donation time. But there was no progress to report. The broacast would have to pay its own way, probably on CBS, and purchase radio time just like any manufacturer of soap, breakfast cereals, toothpaste, or automobile tires. And weekly costs of $4,500 would mount to well over $200,000 annually. This was not a matter of borrowing $10,000 for a St. Stephen's, but of spending ten times that amount for a minimum half-year's programming. Perhaps six months would be sufficient as a pump-priming period, after which listeners could progressively help defray expenses of the broadcast by sending contributions.

"To Aid Synod with Word and Deed in Business and Financial Matters"—the motto of the Lutheran Laymen's League rang in Walter's mind and now also guided the deliberations of the KFUO Radio Committee. Obviously that station did not have the funds necessary to sponsor a network program. Therefore late in April, the Committee resolved to turn the Lutheran Hour project over to the L.L.L.[3]

There was good reason to believe that the laymen would espouse the cause. The League had donated new KFUO and shown rising interest in religious broadcasting.[4] Moreover, the organization had high respect for Dr. Maier and his concern with radio—its board of governors included a number of his close personal friends.[5] In fact, nine months earlier the board had tendered Walter a call to become the first executive secretary of the L.L.L., hoping he could take a temporary leave of absence from his seminary professorship in order to mold the reorganization and expansion of the League. Although he found the call challenging, Wam felt that only Synod could grant him such a leave and so declined the offer respectfully. For the rest of his life, however, he remained very close to League affairs and now considered it especially appropriate that laymen should sponsor the network enterprise, particularly in view of the Reformation emphasis on the priesthood of all believers.

Responding favorably to the KFUO overture, the board of governors was encouraged by Synod in the radio endeavor and received permission to raise the necessary $100,000 within church circles. After further spadework in New York, board member A. A. Grossmann reported CBS' readiness to take the program, and this would probably be the last opportunity to purchase religious time on any national network. Therefore on May 31, 1930, the national convention of the Lutheran Laymen's League, meeting in Chicago's Palmer House, adopted the momentous resolution to sponsor a national Lutheran Radio Hour over the Columbia Broadcasting System beginning in the fall.[6]

Doctors Maier and Fritz served as advisory committee for the project, while Walter's friends and prominent laymen started raising funds by hosting pledge dinners in various cities. A tireless traveler in soliciting such financial support was Arthur Carl Piepkorn, one of Professor Maier's brilliant Semitics students, who now became corresponding radio secretary for the broadcast and later the noted theologian and author.

By late summer about $44,000 was received or promised from L.L.L. members and friends, as well as $50,000 pledged from the Walther League, which in effect gave that organization a partial sponsorship of the first season.[7] These totals were close enough to the $100,000 goal. On August 13, the executive committee of the L.L.L. formally authorized the advertising agency of Lyddon, Hanford, and Kimball, Inc. of Buffalo to contract with CBS for a weekly half-hour broadcasting series to be known as *The Lutheran Hour*, beginning in October. The minutes continue: "It was further resolved that Dr. Walter Maier be the first speaker."[8]

At the time, Dr. Maier was in the Poconos, and Dean Fritz wrote him a special delivery letter reporting his selection. Walter read the news with elation, not because he had been chosen speaker—this had been an open secret—but that now the final step was definitely taken. Linking Christianity and radio, the project which he had championed for eight years, had now come of age.

The contract was signed, and the program scheduled for Thursday nights at 10:00 (Eastern), 9:00 (Central), 8:00 (Mountain), and 7:00 (Pacific) standard time. A midweek evening was chosen because there was much concern that the broadcast might conflict with Sunday church services or be regarded as a substitute for them. The basic Columbia network would be used, plus five stations of the Don Lee Unit on the Pacific coast, comprising finally thirty-six stations in larger cities across the land. Simultaneously, short-wave outlets in New York and Philadelphia would carry the program beyond America.

The première broadcast was set for Thursday, October 2, 1930, and would emanate from Station WHK in Cleveland so that the noted Cleveland Bach Chorus could provide Lutheranism's finest music for the occasion. The evening before, the speaker entrained for Ohio in the ebullient mood which courses through anyone on the verge of something important. But as the Wabash clicked its way northeast into the night, he began to think and rethink the whole issue of broadcast Christianity. He knew there was also a dark side to the picture. Would people really tune in? They could hardly be compelled to turn on their radios and dial to the proper station. Would they continue to listen? They could scarcely stomp out of church in the middle of a sermon, but in the privacy of their homes they might easily give the tuning knob a flick of the wrist and banish any intruding preachers. Or what if hearers should use radio as a substitute for worship in church? That would be wrong theologically, and he could be the butt of much criticism. Would listeners contribute to the support of the broadcast? Probably some who listened faithfully, but so much money was needed. What if the Lutheran Hour should incur an enormous indebtedness in its first year? Likely it would not get a second chance. Already he could hear the slogans: "Maier's Folly" or "Where the L.L.L. Fell."

There was something even darker, as black as Black Thursday on the New York Stock Exchange the year before. What were the final implications of that terrible skidding of security values? Certainly a puncture was necessary, but this was an explosion. How low would the economy sink, and how could the program be supported in a deepening depression? What a time to begin broadcasting! Walter's head slumped in dejection. Finally, he consigned his cares to God, suffixed them with "Thy will be done," and went to sleep.

The autumn sunrise awakened him an hour before the train was due in Cleveland. Feeling more optimistic, he repeated his thoughts of the preceding night with a new inflection: *What a time* to begin broadcasting—just when people need it most!

Misery has come to millions who know no faith stronger than a trust in steel and stones and bank accounts. While bankers and politicians seek economic panaceas to quiet the growing unrest, social revolutionists and destructive theorists of many types are laying siege to our weakened social machine, like hungry wolves snapping at the hams of a wounded stag. . . . The Lutheran Hour proposes—

a faith built not upon the towering heights of skyscrapers, but upon the love of God;

a faith founded not on hoarded wealth and gilt-edged bonds, but upon the Scriptures and the sacred promise of our heavenly Father;

a faith that strengthens the mind and heart for every challenge life offers.[9]

The qualms evaporated like the frost on the meadows racing by. As never before, people needed Christ for the present crisis. And radio? It had to be a divine gift to the church, for what other means of communication could offer such enormous spread, penetration, and even economy considering its potential audience? Professor Maier applied to broadcasting the Old Testament Scripture, "Who knows whether you have not come to the kingdom for such a time as this?" (Es. 4:14)

That evening the final rehearsal took place at Station WHK, and even at this late hour the Lutheran Hour was almost abandoned. CBS was worried about the predominant sermon emphasis in a Thursday night program and had imposed a time limit on the address. Some of its stations were averse to broadcasting a longer sermon during the "amusement hours." Although preaching was the core purpose of the program, Walter had abridged his twenty-minute address to sixteen in compliance. But now, with just one hour till air time, CBS wired WHK that the sermon portion of the broadcast would have to be cut still further—to ten minutes. Walter was indignant and thought the additional reduction intolerable to the religious aims of the program. He informed the Columbia representative: "I cannot comply with this unwarranted restriction. I must refuse to broadcast!" The glare in his eyes was anything but bluff. It was a bad moment. With the minutes ticking away, CBS softened its stand, a hasty compromise was worked out, and Wam trimmed only about three paragraphs of his message.

He retired to his studio at 9:45 P.M. The last flush of insufficiency rippled through him, for this was no normal preaching assignment. The potential congregation numbered 55,000,000 people. Of course a majority of these would not be listening, but how many would? Suddenly he found himself in a posture he would repeat before every studio broadcast for the rest of his life—on his knees in prayer.

Meanwhile in New York, the network's hit mystery story, *The Shadow,* was just concluding. The red sweep-second hand of the master clock in the sprawling CBS studios rounded the nine, and simultaneously a warning impulse was sent to WHK's master control room. The STAND BY sign in the production studio flashed on. All eyes converged on the clock. At 10:00:01 P.M. the ON THE AIR sign glared, Director F. W. Strieter brought down his baton, and the Cleveland Bach Chorus responded with a rousing "Mighty Fortress." CBS announcer David Ross superimposed the words, "The Lutheran Hour—Bringing Christ to the Nation From Coast to Coast!" Following further identification of the program and its sponsorship, the chorus presented several sacred selections, including chorales from Bach's *Mass in B Minor* and *St. John Passion.*

Then came the address. It was titled "There *Is* a God!" and based on Psalm 14:1: *"The fool hath said in his heart, There is no God."* Walter opened directly:

This evening we are to dedicate the message of our first broadcast to the fundamental conviction that there is a God, that the great and infinite Father of the entire human race who has revealed Himself in many and remarkable ways is no fantastic formation of superstition, no creature of childish tradition, no will-o'-the-wisp of religious delusion; but that atheism, materialism, agnosticism, and all the many other similar theories which deny or question the existence of God are not only irrational and disappointing, but also anti-Scriptural and therefore destructive from every point of consideration.[10]

This opening paragraph contains but a single sentence! It seems that Walter hated to stop a surge of thought by resorting to something so paltry as a period. By generous use of the then-popular semicolon as well as comma pauses—plus a good set of lungs—the delivery came in rapid-fire flow, smooth and powerful.

The sermon proceeds to marshal demonstrations of God's existence from various sources: universal instinct, belief, and ethics; the testimony of nature from macrocosm to microcosm; the mathematical impossibility of chance creation; and history. Authorities are cited from Cicero to John Quincy Adams, infidels scored from Voltaire to the American Association for the Advancement of Atheism. Finally, the testimony of revelation is brought to bear on the question, revelation which climaxed when the world saw God in the person of Jesus Christ, believed that He was Savior through the convincing power of the Holy Spirit.

As the sermon was building to its summit, WHK's engineers nervously watched the needles in their VU meters jumping precariously into the red zones. They cut volume controls down a bit from pre-established levels to prevent overloading the transmitters, but Walter had asked them to hold such electronic tailoring to a minimum. Any moment they expected a call from CBS complaining about overmodulation on the network.

The speaker concluded his first chain broadcast:

Men can live without money, without fame, without erudition; they can eke out an existence without friends, without health, or without personal liberty and the possibility of the pursuit of happiness; but they cannot live in the fullness of a life that lives beyond the grave without God. Let them repeat their age-old challenge of blasphemy by standing up before large audiences to deny the existence of God and condescend to grant Him five minutes to strike them down dead! But in the crises of life and the pivotal hours of existence, only the Christian—having God and with Him the assurance that no one can successfully prevail against him—is able to carry the pressing burdens of sickness, death, financial reverses, family troubles, misfortunes of almost innumerable kinds and degrees, and yet to bear all this with the undaunted optimistic faith and Christian confidence that alone make life worth living and death worth dying.[11]

After concluding announcements and the signature theme, the first broadcast became history.

An encouraging number of telegrams arrived at the station soon after the program sign-off, but it was mail response which would now demonstrate whether or not the broadcast had reached the American public. In some rough proportion, few letters would indicate a comparatively small listening audience; many letters, a larger hearing. This was before the days of the Hooperatings, and fan-mail count was the only available gauge of the radio audience.

Two days later, Arthur Piepkorn excitedly reported to his former professor that a swelling stream of mail was arriving, and the rest of the week brought a torrent of letters and post cards to L.L.L. headquarters. After the first few broadcasts, well over 15,000 communications had been received, not including thousands sent directly to local stations or CBS in New York. Radio officials were surprised at the immediacy of the response, which they thought would build up only through months of broadcasting. Soon the listening audience was estimated at five million hearers, and after just two months on the air, network newcomer Maier was receiving more mail than such top secular shows as *Amos 'n' Andy*, or any other religious program in America.

Some letters objected that the sermons were too short, only a scant fifteen minutes in the early broadcasts, with the balance of time devoted to choral music. CBS had imposed this restriction, but when the popularity of the program was demonstrated, the limitation was lifted and the messages eventually took nineteen minutes of air time.

Succeeding broadcasts originated in other cities with excellent musical talent, but the majority emanated from KFUO in St. Louis. The addresses thrust into important contemporary issues for which Christianity had a message, and copies were requested by the thousands. Every fourth program was called *The Young People's Lutheran Hour* and slanted toward the problems of youth. This part of the series was supported by the Walther League.

More than eight hundred newspapers carried the story of the Lutheran Hour in its inaugural weeks. Both the *New York Herald Tribune* and *Post* regularly selected it as a recommended program for Thursdays, and editorials acclaiming its high quality appeared in various periodicals.

Postmarks on the arriving cards and letters comprised a geography course in miniature. From every state of the Union and beyond came the correspondence, written or typed on elegant stationery, letterheads, or common tablet paper; from Prince George, British Columbia, in one direction, to Mapiml, Mexico, in another; from the U.S.S. *Texas* in the Pacific, to the island of Bermuda in the Atlantic.

With radio still something of a novelty at the time, many listeners supplied anecdotes about how they first heard the broadcast. One woman was playing bridge in the forward salon of the S.S. *Bermuda Queen,* en route to Bermuda, and soft dance music from the ship radio was filtering through the lounge. Then, at 10 P.M., a middle-aged woman with more than her share of gall—or courage —stood up and announced: "Would you mind if I tuned in the Lutheran Hour on the Columbia chain? I never fail to listen, if possible." There were no objections, so the music faded and New York's WABC (-W2XE) came in clearly. The bridge player wrote that everyone in the salon stopped playing to hear what an urgent voice was telling them.[12]

It was a similar story in the lobby of Hotel La Salle in Beaumont, Texas, where forty-two guests listened as if chained to the radio, except for one hardy individualist who retired behind his newspaper. Some miles west in Giddings, listening to Dr. Maier had evidently become a municipal hobby. It was reported: "Practically every set in this little town tunes in on the Lutheran Hour, and we can go to a drug store, ice-cream parlor, filling-station, the office of a chiropractor—everywhere we hear the program. Usually a crowd is present. . . ."

In Lincoln, Nebraska, NBC's Station KFAB had studios in the Cornhusker Hotel and regularly fed its own programs into lobby speakers.[13] Yet by 9 P.M. one Thursday, the desk clerk had received seven requests to play the Lutheran Hour over the lobby radio. That evening NBC was not without honor except at its own station in Lincoln, where CBS was playing.

Evidently the Hour was getting an almost universal hearing despite its denominational name, for every race, religion, color, class, or national origin was represented in the mail. College presidents discussed the program, as did penitentiary inmates. It was endorsed by the man on the street whose job was being stolen by the depression, and by the scientist who only took a pay cut.

After Walter completed his thirty-sixth and final broadcast of the first series, more than 57,000 pieces of correspondence had been received. A majority of these were letters of appreciation from church-going Christians, but the rest fell into special categories. Many conversions were reported and often confirmed by local clergy. A woman in Rockland, Mass., joyfully told how she, her husband, and daughter were baptized on Easter Sunday as a result of hearing the broadcast. At the opposite end of the country, a sermon on immortality induced a man in Long Beach, Calif., to accept Christ, and there were many such instances in between. Similarly, an army of backsliders from Minneapolis to Miami were reconsecrated in the faith and recharged for the church, as they and their ministers eagerly reported.

Thousands of patients and handicapped blessed the broadcast, as a listener in the Los Angeles Home for Invalids who reported that the program was the highlight of the week for its 250 occupants, regardless of creed. The message penetrated senses which were largely dulled: a Chicago woman dictated, "I am totally blind, extremely deaf, badly impeded in my speech, and, in worldly possessions, very poor, but . . . a deeply appreciative listener to the noble and helpful Thursday evening broadcasts, which I can hear with the aid of head phones."

Those reeling under the blows of economic depression found hope and encouragement, as the man in Baltimore who wrote, "At the end of a long day of walking the streets in search for work I have often returned home tired and weary, to be much inspired by the . . . comfort coming through the ether during the Lutheran Hour."

Perhaps most surprising was the enthusiastic reception accorded a Lutheran broadcast by both clergy and laity of many different religious bodies. Its message reached the High Church—an Episcopal rector in Elizabeth, N.J., was moved to express himself in language which usually belongs to the revivalist: "What an hour! What religion! What preaching! It thrills, inspires, convinces, *convicts* and *blesses!* Such power! Such saving doctrine!" It also penetrated the humblest inner-city charity—in New York the McAuley Water Street Mission had to cut short its Thursday evening meetings because immediately after the benediction there was ". . . one big rush for the two club-rooms upstairs. 'Turn on St. Louis!' is the cry."

A Roman Catholic priest who was chaplain at the Michigan State Penitentiary in Jackson praised "the soundness of doctrine," and added, "It is to be regretted that the whole world could not have been blessed with the same privilege . . . of listening to your message." His words would be prophetic. A Jewish family in Chicago interrupted a party for out-of-town friends so that all could hear the Old Testament professor. There were thousands of parallel studies in interfaith outreach.

The excesses of religious Modernism were still rife during the thirties, and many of the laity who were disappointed in their clergy for "knocking out every prop of our religion," as a listener from Montreal put it, found once again a Christianity which believed in something besides man, which could inspire as well as instruct. Letter after letter from parishioners in Modernist churches reported "preaching about anything but religion," "a congregation that is diminishing rapidly," "Christ is not mentioned," and the like. Their gratitude at hearing a genuine Christian message once again was profound. Many clergymen voiced similar sentiments, as the Congregational minister from Somerville, Mass., who wrote, "I like your positiveness. It is a bit of encouragement to those of us who are fighting away in the midst of New England Unitarianism and destructive criticism."

Finally, there were also flashes of humor in those mail bags. Apparently, a few listeners did not hear or spell very well, judging from some of the letters which the post office miraculously delivered, although addressed:

| To the Minister of the Lutheran Church Missouri | Lutherun Raymond's Union Sant Lewis, Mo. | St. Louis Missouri Ratio Station that broadcasts the Dr. Walther Hour |
|---|---|---|

"Maier," of course, appeared in a wide variety of forms: Maya, Mars, Morris, Mere, etc., in addition to the normally manifold spellings of the *mī'er* sound.

Some letter conclusions were classic. A fan in Duquesne, Pa., added this postscript: "Please excuse my writing. I am a saloon keeper but no bootlegger." And at the close of her letter, a Bostonian explained: "I am a Roman Catholic and a real one, but I pray . . . that you may continue your wonderful sermons, and last and best of all, I do hope you may die a good Catholic."

Financial support for the broadcast averaged $2,000 a week during the winter months, and many contributors apologized that they could not send more because of the depression. However, Columbia network charges were $4,600 per program, not to mention office costs at Lutheran Hour headquarters. Radio time in that era was frightfully expensive. Today the same sum would purchase time on approximately 150 stations rather than just 36.

By February, most of the original cash on hand had been exhausted, and the L.L.L. owed CBS about three weeks' charges, or nearly $15,000. The situation now grew critical, for a Columbia vice-president came to St. Louis and informed the League that there would be no more Hour broadcasts unless financing were adjusted. A worried Wam sent off an S.O.S. to Henry Dahlen in New York:

PLEASE BE IN ST LOUIS MONDAY  STOP  LUTHERAN HOUR IN TROUBLE

Dahlen took the next train to St. Louis and attended a tense conference of the League radio committee, advisors, and prominent laymen. The meetings were slowly getting nowhere when Dahlen suggested that he and four wealthy laymen each deposit a note in the bank for $10,000 to fatten the broadcast treasury, which now lurked at a mere $365. But no one bought the plan since the depression had superimposed a question mark on all large financing.

By now it was 2 P.M. Wednesday, a scant thirty hours before air time. The Lutheran Hour was dying. "All right," said Dahlen, "I'll sign a note for $50,000 alone."

The Columbia vice-president, who was then brought into the meeting, replied, "Fine, but I don't know if we can honor the note with just your signature, Mr. Dahlen. We discount our paper with Chase National Bank in New York. I'll wire the bank to find out if they'll accept the note with your endorsement alone."

The meeting was adjourned until 8 P.M. As they left, Dahlen whispered to Walter, "Good Doctor, I think I should prepare you for bad news. I've never done a nickel's worth of business with Chase—mine's another bank—and with the depression and all they'll probably turn me down."

Because of the time difference, the telegram arrived in New York after the bank had closed, but it was forwarded to the Connecticut home of the president of Chase National Bank. Even though it interrupted his dinner, he wired back that Chase would accept the note with Dahlen's endorsement. Telegram in hand, the CBS executive walked into the committee session at 9 P.M. and announced that the broadcast could go on the next day as scheduled.[14]

This was as close as the financing ever came, for a special national Lutheran Hour meeting in Chicago the following weekend put an underwriting plan into operation by which a hundred guarantors in various cities each pledged $1,000 to continue the radio mission.[15] Dahlen never lost a cent for his faith in the broadcast.

In spring, however, listener contributions fell off alarmingly, and in proportion to the plunge of the national economy. By now the depression was worsening by the week. Many letters explained in distress that even the "widow's mite" was hard to come by. Added to the problem of financing was Columbia's decision to transfer the program to Sunday afternoons in the fall; church leaders still thought weekday evenings the better time. Therefore, the decision to conclude broadcasting was forced upon the League, and on June 11, 1931, Walter stepped before his microphone for what appeared to be the last time.[16]

Certainly this was a blow to him as founder and speaker of the Lutheran Hour, though the personal aspect concerned him least. The real damage was the massive setback in "Bringing Christ to the Nation" incurred by the suspension. What if the program should never be resumed?

The unseen congregation was stunned by the news, and months afterward letters arrived asking when another radio series would begin. In response to many requests, Walter's first book, *The Lutheran Hour*, rolled from the presses of Concordia Publishing House that fall. Dedicated "To My Mother," the collection of broadcast sermons proved to be at least a printed extension of his radio ministry.

Yet the network effort had been impressive enough. Though aired just nine months, the program had set new records in religious broadcasting. CBS received more letters at its New York headquarters concerning the Lutheran Hour than in response to any other network program. And after only one-half year on the air, Walter Maier received more mail than did *all* the programs sponsored by the Federal Council of Churches over the NBC network that entire year, even though these totaled nine times as much air time as the Lutheran Hour and featured such prominent preachers as S. Parkes Cadman, Harry Emerson Fosdick, Ralph W. Sockman, and others.[17] The paradox remained that these continued to enjoy free network programming, while apparently the most popular religious radio speaker in America was off the air because his broadcast had to be purchased at rates which were financially prohibitive.

Since the depression deepened, the Lutheran Hour would not be resumed until three and one-half years later. During this interval the speaker planned a relaunching of his broadcast. He negotiated with Station WOR, New York, which thought seriously of setting up its own special network to handle the Hour, and at rates far less expensive than Columbia's. He considered a parallel plan with WJR, Detroit. But there would be no resumption of the program until Walter was sure it would remain on the air. Until then he had faith that suspension of the Hour was temporary, not terminal.

# 10
# Other Irons

Radio was the largest iron in the Maier fire, but by no means the only one. Now that it was being tempered by a chilling plunge into silence, Walter could better tend other ingots in his career. Exciting events were edging into his life in the early thirties.

As a post-doctoral finishing touch to Semitics studies, he had planned a trip to Palestine during his first free summer. If facts about the ancient Near East were at his finger tips, he now wanted to "get dirt under his fingernails" on an archaeological expedition. The American Oriental Society had honored him with membership, and the facilities of the American School of Oriental Research in Jerusalem would be open to him. With the Holy City as base, he planned to make side tours as far east as the Tigris Euphrates valley and examine particularly *Tell Kouyunjik*, the mound site of ancient Nineveh, once proud capital of the Assyrian Empire which fell in 612 b.c. with one of the loudest crashes heard in antiquity. The fact that the Hebrew prophet Nahum had predicted this collapse so precisely intrigued him, and he began to lay plans for a book on Nahum.

But the trip could not materialize. Once again scholarship gave way to the practical needs of the church, in this case broadcasting. Perhaps another summer, he consoled himself, and it was back to Lutherland for the Maier family.

This second summer in the Poconos was interrupted by one of the very important addresses in Wam's career, which he delivered before the Institute of Public Affairs at the University of Virginia in Charlottesville on August 9. The institute was an annual forum at which national leaders in many fields met with renowned educators to discuss political, economic, and religious problems of the nation. Among those scheduled to participate were President Herbert Hoover, governors, senators, and representatives from various states, and special guests including Rear Admiral Richard E. Byrd of Antarctic fame.

Walter was invited to discourse in the ever-controversial area of church-state relationships. The fact that Thomas Jefferson had founded the University of Virginia gave him an idea, which he developed into one of his most significant essays: "The Jeffersonian Ideals of Religious Liberty."

Following a gala reception at Jefferson's Monticello, his evening presentation took place at the University's outdoor amphitheater, where a full moon illumined thousands of hearers. Professor Maier especially enjoyed this opportunity because here he could speak as a scholar without having to cast his ideas in a popular idiom. The address is a key to his political thought and to his criticism of Christianity in the early thirties.

He began by tracing the intellectual history of the First Amendment to the Constitution: "Congress shall make no law respecting an establishment of religion or prohibiting the free exercise thereof." That tocsin for the doctrine of separation between church and state had been sounded a hundred years earlier by England's Sir Henry Vane, and two and one-half centuries before Jefferson by the Lutheran theologians and princes gathered at Augsburg, who maintained: ". . . ecclesiastical power concerns things eternal and . . . political government is occupied with other matters. . . . Wherefore the ecclesiastical and civil powers are not to be confounded."[1]

However it was Jefferson's glory to have provided the first systematic application of these principles when he authored the Statute of Virginia for Religious Freedom, "the first detailed law in all human ordinances giving perfect freedom of conscience."[2] He regarded religion as "a matter between every man and his Maker, in which no other, and far less the public, has a right to intermeddle." Therefore he opposed any instance of such intermeddling by which the state would attempt to regulate the affairs of the church, or vice versa, so long as no lawlessness were involved.[3]

But Jefferson's principle of separation of church and state was being hazarded in the America of the early thirties. In some cities political patronage was being extended to one or another church group, and there was agitation that public tax revenue be used to support religious institutions.

Need I say that the world has not kept pace with the high standard which these Jeffersonian ideals have set? . . . We think almost instinctively of lobbies by religious groups in the national capital and in the political centers of our states . . . of the well-meant, yet nevertheless un-American tendency to make Bible-reading a compulsory part of our public-school curriculum; of the less commendable campaigns designed to make the American Sunday a replica of the Jewish Sabbath through the passage of dismal blue-laws. . . .

He [Jefferson] would disavow the outspoken pacifist tendencies of certain religious groups, the iron-fisted control which some churches wield in the petty circles of ward and city politics, the customary procedure of church bodies passing political resolutions or endorsing political candidates at their annual conventions, and the whole unholy relation by which the spiritual power of the church is prostituted, its appeal to the soul materialized, and its inner effectiveness hopelessly paralyzed.[4]

America's third President deplored sermons on politics, science, or the arts in place of religion. And yet:

A glance at the church advertisements in almost any one of our metropolitan dailies will quickly reveal that . . . American churches feature sermons on such topics as: "Is Mussolini the Man of Destiny?" "The Meaning of Dimension," "The London Naval Treaty—What It Means," "The Message of the Visiting Nurse," "Street-car Ventilation," or "Psychometric Reading". . . . It is the tragedy of modern American church-life that it has too frequently permitted its purely spiritual functions to be obliterated by patent bids for notoriety in political, quasi-scientific, and industrial subjects. Too many crusading pastors are political impostors; too many Scriptural texts are mere partisan pretexts; too many militant clergymen are really virulent policemen.[5]

The audience was listening in amazement and, it seemed, approval, though a few of the clergy were getting understandably warm under their clerical collars. Now, in intellectual honesty, a final, and logical, thrust had to be made. The Prohibition Amendment had been attached to the Constitution for the past decade and would not be repealed for three years yet. To fend off agitation for repeal, some churchmen had become politically vociferous on the issue, and the speaker did not hesitate to score this activity:

It is the duty of the churches to emphasize to their followers the virtue of temperance and the vice of drunkenness, yet such indoctrination under no circumstances is to assume a definite political coloring or to express itself in the maintenance of political intimidation campaigns or legislative lobbies. . . .[6]

In conclusion, Walter called for a thorough reapplication of Jeffersonian principles in questions of church and state, for this would minimize bigotry and national misunderstanding.

A thundering applause rose from the amphitheater, and the few who were frowning deepened their scowls as the ovation was prolonged. Reporters dodged out of the crowd and phoned in their stories. The next morning, many newspapers across the land gave the address headline billing with such variations as: "Church No Wet-Dry Forum," "Dr. Maier Attacks Church in Politics," "How Jefferson Would Stand on Prohibition," and the like. At any rate, the essay remained determinative for Wam's political thought, and it was later published.

One who shared Professor Maier's views on separation of church and state but agreed with him on little else in the area of religion was Clarence Darrow. The famed Chicago lawyer and self-styled agnostic who eloquently pleaded for impulse-killers Leopold and Loeb had added to his prestige in the colorful debate with William Jennings Bryan at the Dayton, Tenn., "Monkey" trial in 1925. In defending high-school instructor John T. Scopes for teaching the theory of organic evolution in the classroom, Darrow—in the eyes of many—had outmaneuvered "The Great Commoner" and so served to discredit a creationist view of human origin. Walter was disturbed by this development, the more so since Darrow was gaining wide repute as an agnostic orator. In reverie, Wam calculated how much of his Hebrew library he would surrender in order to debate with this man on the basic issue: the existence of God. Certainly he would use a different approach from that of Bryan, whom, however, he admired as an orator and a man of faith.

Five days before his appearance at the University of Virginia, Walter had told a mass meeting at Ocean Grove that the United States could duplicate Russia's destruction of the church if unbelief continued to flourish in America. He warned of such danger symptoms as "the formation of the American Association for the Advancement of Atheism, the organization of atheistic clubs and 'Societies of Damned Souls' in our colleges and universities. . . ."[7] The *New York Times* and the *New York Herald Tribune* had given the address broad coverage, which was relayed by newspapers throughout the country, including the Canadian press.

Several days later, Walter was opening his mail when he was startled by this letterhead in bold, black type: "THE ATHEIST SOCI-ETY OF CHICAGO—Branch of the American Association for the Advancement of Atheism." Beneath was the following message, dated August 11, 1930:

Dear Sir:

Having noticed your attack on the Atheists in the newspapers, I have the honour, in behalf of the Executive committee and members of "The Atheist Society of Chicago," to send you a challenge to debate any of our speakers on any subject you may choose to oppose us.

In addition to the speakers listed on the enclosed program, I can secure Olin J. Ross, noted Columbus O. Attorney-at-Law, widely mentioned as "logical" candidate for the presidential Republican nomination in 1932 or even the well known Clarence Darrow, to defend us.

If you are willing to have this debate in Chicago please let me know and I will make all arrangements.

Sincerely yours
*James E. Even*
[Secretary-Treasurer][8]

"Darrow!" exulted a beaming Walter. After weighing various aspects of the challenge, he sent off this reply, dated August 19:

Dear Sir:

Your letter addressed to St. Louis has been forwarded to me at this address, and I thank you for the honor of your invitation.

In reply let me say that I shall be happy to accept under these conditions: (1) that instead of a single debate a series of three debates be held; (2) that my opponent be Mr. Darrow; (3) that all details in regard to subjects, time, place, and manner of procedure be settled by mutual agreement after my return to St. Louis in the first week of

September; and (4) that the debates will be held in each of the following cities: Chicago, St. Louis, and New York.

I shall await further information from you.

Yours very truly,
*Walter A. Maier*

The mind of Clarence Darrow was razor sharp. It shredded any
ostentatious religiosity into mincemeat, and the man himself could
chew up several sincere-but-simple clerics before breakfast. What if
he should foil even a first-class intellect? This worried some who
read of a possible Darrow-Maier debate. The Chicago Lutheran
pastoral conference wrote Walter of its qualms. Less diplomatic,
perhaps, but more graphic was this written note:

Stanford University
Calif.

Say Man,
Don't make an Esel* of yourself. Clarence Darrow has more brains in
his little Finger than *all you Ministers.*

Yours truly,
*an Atheist*

Walter was not overawed by the prospect of facing Darrow. He
had brandished the debating lance since college days, and a decade
of public speaking had equipped him with as many forensic arrows
as Darrow had in his quiver. He knew the flaws in Darrow's brilliance: sometimes sarcasm, bluster, emotionalism, and plain wise-
cracks were used to disguise weak argumentation. But these could
boomerang against agnosticism as well. Above all, Walter resolved
that there would be no slogan-exchanging, no repetition of the
Monkey trial. The debate would be on the more essential level of
theism versus agnosticism, where Christianity could exchange its
posture of defense for a vigorous offensive with solid intellectual
respectability. He would even build on the positive humanitarian in
Darrow, a trait genuinely present in his colorful career. And when
the debates were over, it would have become apparent that religion
was far more than the "bunk" Darrow styled it,[9] not a sacrifice of
the intellect but its necessary complement.

* German for "ass."

Only later did the thought insinuate itself: what if Darrow would not debate? But the Atheist Society seemed sure enough of his availability. A letter arrived also from the American Rationalist Association, stating that group's readiness to sponsor debates of this kind.

Meanwhile, after newspapers learned of the possible debate, Darrow made a statement to the Associated Press: "I never issued any challenge of this nature and no one has been authorized to issue such a challenge in my behalf."[10] Shortly afterward, Walter received the following word from Even of the Atheist Society: "We had made no definite arrangement with Mr. Darrow and he . . . I am sorry to say, does not wish to accept this series of debates." However, the society would agree to a tri-city debate series, with Olin Ross, or Charles Smith, president of the American Association for the Advancement of Atheism, as opponents.[11]

Walter was deeply disappointed. In a spirited reply, he stated, in part:

Even now I am willing to concede that there may be some unavoidable misunderstanding of any arrangement between Mr. Darrow and your organization, but I do not think you should have asked me to meet "even Clarence Darrow" unless you were sure that he had consented to the use of his name. . . . And as I look over the situation, it seems to me that Mr. Darrow is the only speaker on your list who could help to bring out a throng of 20,000 with which we would pack the St. Louis Arena, for example. . . .

May I not suggest that inasmuch as the challenge to me to meet Mr. Darrow . . . is before the American public, that you see Mr. Darrow again?[12]

Even's answer was distressed: "We have pleaded with Mr. Darrow but, I am sorry to say, his last reply was, 'Anyhow, cut me out of the proposition.' . . . In using Mr. Darrow's name I have committed the 'crime' of believing that he should be willing to defend his position which he will not do, as I have since found out."[13] Another letter followed, suggesting that Darrow was getting older and "probably growing tired of so much noise and excitement," which possibly explained his disinclination.[14] At any rate, Darrow's refusal to debate—albeit defensible since he had not issued the challenge—remained one of the great disappointments in Walter's life.

One tangible result of this brush with organized atheism was his honorable billing as a "fanatic" in the "Opposition" column of the *Fifth Annual Report of 4A* (American Association for the Advancement of Atheism). But he was in good company—in the same column was a copy of the cablegram 4A had sent to Pope Pius XI in Vatican City, stating that a recent earthquake disaster in Italy only strengthened them in atheism! The Pope did not reply.[15]

If there was to be no drama with Darrow, drama of a literal kind was in store. A month later, Professor Maier was filling another, apparently incongruous role: that of a playwright who had penned what newspapers reported as one of the most ambitious dramatic spectacles in the history of the St. Louis stage. It was a historical pageant entitled *Truth Triumphant,* and its De Mille-like cast alone numbered more than the audiences of most theaters—well over 4,000 men, women, and children. This was Walter Maier's first and only foray into drama, but it was enough to demonstrate that professors can be versatile people outside the classroom.

Up in the Poconos, the idea had occurred to him of devising something special for the 1930 quadricentennial of the Augsburg Confession, the key Protestant declaration of belief. Trying a dramatic format, he developed a theme, and before summer was over he had completed the first draft of an enormous pageant.

When he submitted the project to the quadricentennial committee in St. Louis, it was greeted with unanimous shock. *Truth Triumphant* set the Augsburg episode against a background of religious history beginning with the Exodus from Egypt and extending to the present day. Needed for the four acts and fifteen scenes would be a cast of 3,500, a children's choir of 1,500 voices, the Concordia Male Chorus of 125, a women's glee club, an orchestra, and even assorted animals to add a touch of realism. Somehow the committee became infected with the idea and courageously buried its misgivings.

To produce this spiritual spectacular required a massive collective effort. The author, who fretted over the possibilities of chaos, was strategically assisted by A. A. Grossmann, producer, and Mrs. Frank Leach, director. They set up a general staff of forty-four subdirectors who supervised separate preparation of the various scenes prior to the grand rehearsal, which took place at the only building in St. Louis large enough to stage such a performance as this—the Arena.

An author's first play, an amateur cast and choruses of such awkward size, and only one full rehearsal form all the necessary ingredients for a dramatic disaster of heroic dimensions. One critic was worrying in advance about how to hang black crepe in his review of the pageant without offending St. Louis church life too seriously. Reporters would not believe figures on the size of the cast until the twelve-hour dress rehearsal.

On Sunday evening, October 26, *Truth Triumphant* was about to begin. Nearly 20,000 people filled every seat in the arena from the highest tiers to half the broad central floor, the other half constituting the stage. As house lights dimmed, a fanfare arose from the orchestra, ending with a flourish of ten trumpets. Then a lone arc light focused its blue-white beam on the Oracle, who would herald each episode and its significance from a small satellite perch above the stage. It was the author, dressed in his doctoral gown. He introduced a veiled figure, Truth, the allegorical theme of the pageant.

Act One, "The Quest of Truth," opens with yellow and red floodlights splashing on the luxurious palace of Amenhotep IV, the heretical Pharaoh of Egypt who dared to search for monotheism. Long processions of plumed Egyptian priests make their orisons before huge temple facades, as in the final chorus from *Aida*. The scene climaxes with the Israelite exodus, but fades out before the Red Sea crossing—and its production problems!

The second setting is Mesopotamia. Nebuchadnezzar's Babylonian court comes alive with queen's attendants bearing heaping trays of exotic fruit, and soldiers milling about Judean exiles. The king's successor, Belshazzar, gazes in terror once again at the ominous handwriting on the wall, and the Hebrews begin their second exodus from captivity.

Next, Greece, the third great civilization of the ancient world, parades her athletes, dramatists, and philosophers. Yet the tragic denouement in all three scenes is the appearance of Truth, veiled solidly as ever. Neither luxury, nor military might, nor intellectual search can uncover religious truth.

But then the One is born who said, "I am the Way, the Truth, and the Life," and the veil of Truth is finally lifted with the Nativity. The shepherds' scene found a star glittering from the ceiling of the arena, and for some moments the only sound heard was the bleating of twelve live sheep in the sawdust pasture below. After a lusty Christmas carol from the children's chorus, the act closed with the actor-shepherds trying to corral their straying sheep, whose baaing at the wrong places showed they were missing the point of the pageant.

"The Test of Truth," the motif of Act Two, traces Truth on trial in the crucifixion of Christ, the bloody persecutions, the missionary conquests of heathen Europe, and within the medieval church. Here realism might have become a bit lurid, but the press reported that ". . . there was no dwelling upon scenes of torture, and no seeming appeal to passion."[16] The Roman Catholicism of the time was portrayed without pope-baiting thrusts and with best foot forward, as, for example, Archbishop Boniface cutting down the pagan sacred oak and converting Germany. And yet the tragedies of Waldo and Huss: Truth is groping for light.

Act Three, "The Crest of Truth," centers in the events which had ignited the quadricentennial. The Reformation tableaus sweep from Luther* nailing his theses to the church door—and sending hammer blows ricochetting through the arena—to the spectacular climax at Augsburg in 1530. Here the enthroned Emperor Charles V† is surrounded by red-robed cardinals, papal legates, his imperial guard, the German nobility, and about a thousand townspeople. Before him approach the Protestant theologians and princes presenting the confession authored by Luther's associate, Philip Melanchthon. For half an hour a theological debate rages. Finally, despite the threats of emperor and church, the confessional constitution of Lutheranism is signed in a moment of supreme silence.

There was an additional, and unrehearsed, touch of drama in the

---

* Played by noted Concordia dogmatician, Prof. J. T. Mueller.
† L.L.L. Pastoral Advisor, Dr. Lawrence ("Lorry") Meyer.

Augsburg scene. As a prelude, Walter had managed to weave in the forces of evil, personified by the Four Horsemen of the Apocalypse: Conquest, War, Famine, and Death. This quartet was mounted on four of the famed Budweiser Clydesdale horses loaned for the occasion, but the spirited steeds obviously preferred pulling the familiar beer wagon through city parades rather than playacting. Finally, the horse on which Death rode had enough. It reared and threw the Grim Reaper, then bolted down the arena floor toward a horrified audience. At the first row it stopped short and started nuzzling the hat of a woman spectator, until her shriek sent the horse trotting off into a side exit where it was brought under control. The pageant lived on.

The final act, "The Blessings of Truth," brings the story up to the present by unfolding the broad heritage of the Reformation in missions, charity, art, music, and liberty. Here the cast included some who had played roles in Walter's life: Al Huge had moved to St. Louis, and here he was as Abraham Lincoln; the Rev. Arthur Nitz of St. Stephen's was Mendelssohn; secretary Harriet Schwenk, the Spirit of Liberty; Mrs. Walter Maier, the Spirit of Service, and the like.

One of the ways in which Lutheranism reached America was portrayed in a Mississippi riverboat scene with the familiar landing of the Saxon pilgrims in St. Louis under the leadership of Dr. C.F.W. Walther. The patriarch was accompanied by hundreds of immigrants, a covered wagon, dog, goat, and the same twelve sheep which had watched with the shepherds eighteen centuries before. When the company sang a hymn of thanksgiving, the collie barked and leaped in an obvious attempt to steal the show. That honor, however, belonged to a conceited goat attached to Walther's prairie schooner which refused to budge from center stage and had to be dragged off by the neck.

With the finale, the entire assembly arose and concluded with a hymn, while lights dimmed and an illuminated cross closed the pageant.

Then an ovation broke out which would not stop, for the crowd had found the three-and-one-half-hour production as stirring as it was spectacular. Reporters and critics shared the mood and shelved the epithets they had planned to use. Newspapers the next day styled this bird's-eye view of church history "a climax of color and movement," "elaborate and beautiful."[17] Perhaps L. M. Aldridge summarized it most soberly in the *St. Louis Times:* " 'Truth Triumphant' . . . was produced with an ease and reverence that brought tears of rejoicing and waves of applause from the crowd. . . . Humor, pathos and human interest marked the scenes of the pageant but did not detract from its reverence."[18]

Walter was pleased with the reviews, yet much relieved that it was all over. Drama was new to him; he had only experimented. Those who liked the experiment urged him to write more, but he was confident that the Lord had not called him to be a playwright, and this was his only Thespian venture.

As if to compensate for the fact that the Lutheran Hour was not broadcast from the fall of 1931 through 1934, Walter Maier went directly to the public. During the week his world was strictly Old Testament, but on weekends he filled some of the speaking invitations which crowded his desk. Files show, for example, that he had to decline ten separate address requests for September 27, 1931, because he was already scheduled for an engagement.

It is surprising to find how much space the nation's wire services and press devoted to the addresses, major and minor, of St. Louis' Dr. Maier during the early thirties. A polished phrase of his, an alarming statistic, a fresh spiritual approach to an important issue would soon rebound from newspapers to magazines, and vice versa. This was due partly to his reporter's sense of timing. If the nation were embroiled in an issue which had religious or moral overtones, he spoke out on the question and his remarks were published.

The appearances at Ocean Grove were exciting broader interest. *Time* magazine visited the celebration of July, 1931, and reported in part:

With the enthusiasm of a dozen Martin Luthers pelting a dozen devils with ink-pots, Rev. Dr. Walter A. Maier . . . flayed "this cynical, scoffing self-willed generation that bows down before the idol of profit and production, that knows not God and prides itself in this ignorance; . . . its penitentiaries, enlarged yet overcrowded; juvenile crime . . . divorce, with states like Nevada and Arkansas feverishly competing in the effort to make divorce easier, quicker and cheaper; apostles of free love and loose moral leaders . . . quicksand of companionate marriage, childless families . . . collapse of family felicity . . . professional impurity . . . commercialized vice. . . ."

Hotly he excoriated the "seven follies of church structure":

(1) The political church, which "either follows the dictates of an ecclesiastical head . . . or foists upon the free and sovereign people of our nation a program of selfish and sectarian ambitions."

(2) The sensational church, which uses "jazz bands, picked beauties as ushers and other bizarre attractions."

(3) The church "with the financial complex . . . raffles . . . roulette wheels . . . frenzied financing. . . ."

(4) The "epileptic church which institutes Bible reading marathons . . . churches that kick and scream."

(5) The "social church which fights against industrialism and capitalism . . . working for the body instead of the soul."

(6) The "inactive . . . smugly self-sufficient church."

(7) "Worst of all . . . the church with a craving for a modernistic creed, the passion for creating a new Christianity."[19]

The "Seven Fatal Follies" sermon was soon debated editorially far and wide. There was broad support; also some decided criticism, as, for example, that of Dr. Charles F. Potter of the First Humanist Society of New York, who found the address "medievalist."

Along with his critique, Walter offered positive suggestions for remedy. At an L.L.L. convention in Chicago he recommended that American churches adopt a code which would eliminate ecclesiastical abuses and re-aim them toward their primary duties. He also submitted a working brief for such a code, which was detailed by the Associated Press and again caused much reaction.[20]

The Reformation quadricentennials continued in various cities throughout the early thirties, and Walter was invited to address many of these "with the enthusiasm of a dozen Martin Luthers," as planning committees reminded him in jest. Detroit especially saw much of Dr. Maier during these years. In the fall of 1932 he and Michigan Governor Wilbur M. Brucker addressed some 11,000 in the Motor City's State Fair Coliseum to honor the bicentennial of George Washington's birth.[21] The following year marked the 450th anniversary of another important birth—that of Martin Luther—and for this celebration Walter spoke to a mass meeting of 16,000 at the Olympia Stadium in Detroit.

Probably the most colorful audience in his career awaited him at Olympia. Instead of harboring a fight crowd shouting itself hoarse over a pair of pugilists, the auditorium had been transformed into a vast cathedral for what newspapers called the largest indoor religious gathering in the city's history.[22] But what provided literal color was the chorus of 3,500 school children on the main floor, wearing different-colored caps. As they sat they formed a great red cross in a field of white, bordered by blue—an enormous living reproduction of Luther's coat of arms.

"A Mighty Fortress," sung by the chorus accompanied by a hundred-piece orchestra, opened the program. Then Walter delivered what became one of the famous sermons of his career, "Back to Luther!"—a serious plea for a twentieth-century Reformation through correction of destructive tendencies in the churches. *Time* published long paragraphs of the sermon without editorial comment. Two excerpts:

While [Lincoln] dealt with bodies in bondage and minds coerced by mental slavery, Luther threw off the shackles of . . . spiritual tyranny. . . . All Protestantism, yea, Roman Catholicism itself, as its eminent scholars have admitted, not only owes him an everlasting debt of gratitude but also needs the re-statement of many of his principles.

. . . Picture the cancerous growth of modern infidelity as ego-complexed pulpiteers, disguising the breed of the wolf beneath silk cassocks . . . read from the Scriptures with crossed thumbs, tongues in the cheek, and mental reservations, who place the Bible on the one level with heathen philosophies. . . . Think of the smooth, oily surrender of the deity of our Savior. . . . I still repeat the cry, *"Back to Luther."*[23]

Commenting on the address, the Roman Catholic weekly *Our Sunday Visitor* naturally viewed Luther in another light and proposed a counter slogan, "Back to Christ," suggesting a ". . . return to the beliefs and practices of pre-Reformation days."[24] This was skillful editorializing, yet Walter's Christocentric preaching was in little danger of Lutherolatry. And some years later *Our Sunday Visitor* would declare in an editorial, "We seldom miss listening to Dr. Walter Maier. . . . We believe that he has done an incalculable amount of good in his defense of the moral law, of right living, of the divine inspiration of the Scriptures. . . ."[25]

The same month of 1933 also saw a lengthy editorial in *The Western Catholic* entitled "Our Lutheran Friend," which led off, "There's a Lutheran gentleman whom we would like to meet, greet and congratulate . . . Professor Walter A. Maier."[26] The orchids were for excerpts of an address in which he had spoken out trenchantly on academic agnosticism. As syndicated by AP:

We nominate as America's Public Enemy No. 1 the notorious faith-wrecker who sits high in the council of academic distinction, scoffs at religion, denies the existence of God, and exterminates the spiritual life of the nation's youth and flower—the infidel teacher who receives popular plaudits and high salary, often paid by tax levies, for his cut-throat attacks on Christianity—the university professor who takes the pay of Christian endowments and of church-going taxpayers and then, a la Machiavelli, poisons the brain and the heart and soul of his students.[27]

Although too strongly worded for application today, the "faculty atheist"—now less missionizing in his presentation—was obnoxiously aggressive in those days and likely deserved such language.

Meanwhile Luther's birthday as a celebration was making the rounds of other major cities, and Walter enhanced the occasions on the rostrum. Finally the Reformation commemorations ended in 1934, the quadricentennial of the Luther Bible. To salute that publication, one hundred Detroit churches invited Wam to address a mammoth meeting on Belle Isle at the symphony orchestra band shell. Well over 25,000 people obliterated the hillside facing the shell that beautiful September Sunday, as Walter spoke on the significance of Scripture in general, this translation in particular. Making its own graphic contribution was the fat book from which he was preaching—the Luther Bible which the German war prisoners had sent him.

After the service thousands filed by to look at the volume. Published by Hans Lufft, the reformer's printer, the book was—and

is—in excellent condition despite its great age. The text contains
no verse divisions, but is well illustrated with elaborate woodcuts of
Biblical scenes. Or *are* they Biblical? The artist had portrayed
people in Palestine as sixteenth-century Germans in Europe. Moses
looks like Frederick the Wise of Saxony; David vs. Goliath is a
Bavarian farm youth opposing a gigantic knight in medieval armor.
While Luther was translating text, evidently his artist was translating pictures. At any rate, this is the book which largely determined the present form of the German language and served as the
font of much Protestant religiosity and culture.

A living link with the Reformation, the ponderous old Bible took
a trip on its own two months later, using means of transportation
which would have shocked its publisher. Walter had left St. Louis
for a similar quadricentennial at Saginaw, Michigan, when suddenly he called home en route: "Honey, listen carefully! I'm at
Decatur. I forgot to take the Luther Bible, and I *must* have it because Saginaw newspapers have featured it. Please take it to the
midnight Wabash for Chicago, give it to the conductor who knows
me, and tell him to give it to Pastor Kaub's son who will meet him
at Englewood station. He'll take it to Midway airport, where it'll
be flown to Detroit. Al Wilson will drive it from there to Saginaw.
Love you. 'By."

Though Mrs. Maier hardly had the chance to say "Wha-at?!" she
did as directed. Miraculously, the railway-airway-highway connections held together, and the Bible arrived in Saginaw just two hours
after its owner, some fifteen minutes before the program in the auditorium. After the service it was viewed with particular gratitude by
long lines of Michiganders.

From now on it becomes impractical to sketch even the very important addresses of Walter Maier. His schedule was crammed, but
variety was the saving feature. Weekends often found him anywhere in America, speaking at church celebrations from dedications
to golden or diamond anniversaries, as well as League, district, and
Synodical conventions; before business or professional organizations
and learned societies; at college, university, and seminary gradua-
tions; for convocations at universities from Harvard to Chicago,

Wisconsin to Louisiana; at civic centennials, national conventions of secular organizations; and, most typically, at religious mass meetings and rallies.

Yet none of this interfered with so much as a Hebrew quiz or *Messenger* editorial back in St. Louis. He never forgot that he had been called to teach and edit; nor, for that matter, would his academic load let him forget.

In 1932 the *St. Louis Globe-Democrat* planned a feature story on this brisk career for its Sunday magazine, but staff writer George Dent found Walter less than cooperative about it. Dent reported afterwards: "Dr. Maier is very retiring and modest. He does not seek publicity and was quite reluctant about being interviewed lest some of his statements might be presented to the readers in such a way that they would be construed as . . . self-applause for his own achievements." So the journalist had to mine the information out of scrapbooks and interviews with the lady of the house. When the story appeared in the *Globe*, it was bannered: "Dr. Walter A. Maier Has Crowded Much into His Life." But in view of what would come, this was "only the beginning." The article concluded:

Surely . . . Dr. Maier cannot possibly keep up the mad pace he has set for himself in the first thirty-eight years of his life, but after meeting and talking to this energetic personage one is inclined to throw logic to the four winds and boldly predict that if the story of his achievements and interests are written again a few years hence there will be a lengthy list of additions to be made.[28]

Dent was right.

# 11

# "The Happiest Home"

The seminary's House Eleven was the place where Walter recharged himself for "the mad pace." Here he found his maximum joy and a peace which braced him for multiple complexities outside. He was a family man—nearly the stereotype of the adoring husband, the devoted father.

Even though born into family life, couples often rediscover its felicity when they establish their own households. Walter had to share his "discovery" of the home with others in sermons, articles, a book, and a number of essays and booklets. In one of these, *The Happiest Home*, he says, is

. . . the one that lives closest to Christ. It need not be large, architecturally attractive, nor must those who dwell within its walls be blessed with money, social position, university training. Christ to guide the family, to lead the children, to avert the dangers of too much prosperity and sustain the household in days of need, sorrow, and sickness, will bring a joy that neither money, culture, nor position can ever bestow.[1]

Such references to joy reflected both the author's ideals and his personal experience.

The woman in charge of domestic affairs at House Eleven was finding less and less time to help her husband with *Messenger* work. Walter Junior was now in parochial school, but the new baby required the usual overattention. Editor Maier began to miss the criticism and proofreading his wife had provided in the past.

One day he walked into the kitchen wearing the look of a wronged child, and with almost the tone to match, he said, "Honey, if you can't read all of the *Messenger* any more, won't you please read at least my editorials?" She would, but an overactive doorbell and telephone were interrupting her uxorial, maternal, and editorial responsibilities. He was worried enough to suggest that they hire

144

household help, but she objected that a maid would disturb family privacy.

One evening they engaged a baby sitter and had to leave for a meeting at St. Stephen's before the dishes were washed. They returned to find that chore finished and the kitchen immaculate. "Now isn't this a welcome surprise?" said Walter, resuming his case. "Wouldn't it be grand if the dishes could always vanish in this fashion? Someone else can do housework, but only you can provide help on my literary work." With that he turned to the baby sitter and urged her to find someone for the position. The following Sunday afternoon she brought her cousin to House Eleven, a Miss Mabel Breckenkamp. Mabel was a shy but poised country girl in her late teens who had arrived in the city a few weeks before, and she made an immediately pleasing impression. And yet the thought of interrupting family privacy haunted Hulda. She groped for excuses.

"My husband probably can't pay you the salary you're getting from that wealthy family in University City."

"Salary isn't everything," Mabel replied. "The people and surroundings mean far more."

Mrs. Maier tried a final subterfuge. "Grossie is using our only spare bedroom and she won't be leaving until January."

"Then I'll come back in January."

Though his wife was reluctant, Walter hired Mabel on the spot.

One bright afternoon in January, 1931, Mabel arrived. With quiet efficiency she took over in the kitchen, and her first meal scored an instant hit. Walter Junior, excited to have more company in the house, shortly identified her as his "older sister," while the neighborhood children soon called her "the other mother at the Maiers'." And the original mother presently found Mabel, not the privacy-shattering intruder she had feared, but a godsend in the literal sense, "one of the great personal gifts with which God enriched our home, . . . the daughter we never had."

Now Mrs. Maier could function as wife, mother, and professional assistant at the same time. She was frankly delighted at her husband's rising recognition—but never showed it publicly—and saved newspaper and magazine clippings until 1935 when she had five scrapbooks full and quit. Because some out-of-town speaking engagements specifically requested Dr. Maier to bring his wife, they were not separated as much as might have been the case. However Hulda put a limit on these lest the children begin calling her the "other mother," and most of the time she could be reached at House Eleven. Visitors found her a genial hostess who had a knack of keeping them entertained while awaiting a break in the host's dictation when he would emerge from his study and greet them.

Hulda Augusta Maier was far more than a satellite in Walter's universe. Her criticism of his sermons and writings was a continuing help, and often it was she who chopped some of his marathon sentences into digestible segments. If he were in a playful mood while dictating and indulged in overalliterative phrases, she cut these down. Articles for the *Messenger* and other religious periodicals came from her own pen, and she hosted an inspirational-type breakfast show on KFUO, *For Heart and Hearth*. Ladies' groups often invited her to address them, and she discoursed on a series of appropriate themes at such affairs.

As often as possible, husband and wife worked jointly on a project, whether at home or out in the community. Some Friday afternoons they would don gloves and attack the garden, or unleash a home-improvement crusade. The basement was enlarged, and something was done about the corner porch which did nothing but harbor flies during the warm months when it could be used. A call was made to a carpenter friend, and soon porch became sunroom, with three great lattice windows filling the former open arches.

The family loved classical music, and one favorite relaxation called for a session in the darkened living room after supper to enjoy the highest fidelity available at the time, whirling 78 r.p.m. disks. Open evenings brought opportunities to attend concerts of the St. Louis Symphony, or the magnificent choral-orchestral presentations of the St. Louis Bach Society, conducted by a good friend, Dr. William B. Heyne.

In the spring of 1935, the Walter Maiers served as patrons of the arts for their city. The famed 700-year-old *Dresdner Kreuzchor*—the Boys' Choir of Holy Cross College in Dresden, Germany—was planning its first American tour, with a debut at the Metropolitan

Opera House in New York. Who would sponsor their appearance in St. Louis? No civic, cultural, or church organization seemed ready to make the effort. When Professor Maier learned of the impasse, he thought it unfortunate for his city to miss a musical organization which had been acclaimed by Melanchthon, Goethe, Bach, Mozart, Wagner, and others, and whose critical excellence in the modern era was rivaled only by the Vienna Boys' Choir. The Maiers discussed it and resolved to sponsor the concert. With the help of interested friends, the St. Louis appearance of the *Kreuzchor* was memorable—the Municipal Opera House was filled, the ovations were frequent, and the reviews enthusiastic.

The two chief sources of cheer—and anguish—in the Maier household were Walter Junior and Paul. Normal American boys, we lurched between the divine and the demonic. Walter Junior was so impressed by his father that more than once Mother had to reach across the pew and stop him from gesturing away in time with Father who was preaching. His school report card showed him bright enough—all A's, except for the glaring C minus in conduct.

Walt's favorite diversion was to "raise Cain" along with neighboring "profs' kids" on that 71 acre children's heaven called Concordia Seminary. It was Halloween all year for his group. The campus bell tower, for example, housed an enormous bell which was never rung —except by Walt and friends at some outrageous hour of the night. Skyrockets set off in the quadrangles while seminarians were cramming for finals was another standard caper, and when frazzle-nerved students gave chase, profs' kids went underground via Concordia's own version of the celebrated sewers of Paris: the seminary steam tunnels, heating maintenance links between the different buildings.

Usually, however, Walt preferred making money off the students to hounding them. His favorite scheme was to take me through the dormitories and announce that I, only three years old, would recite the first verse of the Bible in Hebrew for a penny. He himself would do Psalm 1 in the same language for a nickel. As a party joke to show off his "prodigies," Father had, in fact, taught us these verses in Hebrew, but little did he know we would commercialize on them. For seminarians, of course, it was a minor sensation to hear their professor's boys pouring out the same sounds they were agonizedly learning, and each new class of Concordians contributed handsomely to the piggy banks at House Eleven.

Few enterprises, however, were as profitable as the celebrated Grape-Nuts caper. Back in the middle thirties when the C.W. Post Company of Battle Creek, Mich., marketed the gritty-but-good cereal in the small yellow and blue boxes, a sales promotion offering prizes for box tops appeared on the packages. When Walt saw it his eyes bulged. There was Dizzy Dean with a smiling invitation: "Boys! Girls! Get my 49 valuable FREE PRIZES"—free, that is, if you had enough box tops. Zealously Walt read through the forty-nine options on the prizes: pocket flashlight for just three box tops and 25¢, or eight box tops alone; baseball catcher's mitt for 15 box tops and $1.25, or 35 box tops alone; bicycle for 100 box tops and $13.00, or 375 box tops alone, and the like.[2] Probably the Post Company calculated that no American boy could chew enough Grape-Nuts to buy the bike on box tops alone. It would take at least ten years of breakfasts. But Battle Creek businessmen had reckoned without the ingenuity of "Little Wam."

One afternoon he sidled into the office of Concordia's chief cook and dietitian, "Ma" Powers, and turned the conversation to breakfast cereals.

"Ma, how often do you serve the students Grape-Nuts for breakfast?" he inquired.

"Oh, once a week or so."

"Would you be kind enough to do a couple of things? Please save *all* the Grape-Nuts box tops for me—I want to get some prizes they're offering—and could you maybe serve Grape-Nuts a little more often? They're very nutritious."

Ma smiled and promised to do her best.

Now with 400 seminarians munching Grape-Nuts every morning for weeks on end, and Ma mixing in fruits to add variety, the outcome is obvious. Grinning at the tall forest of box tops stacked on the table in front of him, Walt gleefully thumbed through Post's prize catalogue. Mother shook her head in amazement, Father released his characteristic nasal snicker, and Mabel provided wrapping paper for mailing the tops. The scene repeated itself periodically;

naturally Walt always chose the alternative of all box tops—no cash. About once a month a great carton arrived from Battle Creek, filled with baseball suits, gloves, balls, tennis rackets, footballs, chemistry and microscope sets, games and flashlights for the other profs' kids —and all free.

After some months of this largess the Post Company wrote Walt not to send any more box tops, for the offer had expired. Little Wam took it stoically—he had received most of the prizes anyway—and later he claimed it was his shipments which closed down the promotion. At any rate, how many student lives were affected by the masses of niacin, vitamin B₁, iron, yeast, and malted barley in the daily doses of Grape-Nuts will never be known.

Father hated to punish us. When discipline was necessary he tried to shift the responsibility onto Mother, who naturally resented any monopoly on that chore. Finally they agreed on a division of labor: she specialized in light, incidental spankings, whereas he took over when angry enough to administer the rare full treatment.

Generally, he maintained a fairly even temper, though every man has his breaking point. During an automobile trip to Florida, Walt and I, then nine and four respectively, got car sick, always alternately, never synchronously. Furthermore, we serenaded our parents with countless choruses of "The Old Spinning Wheel in the Parlor" and threw in a little quarreling for good measure. At Coral Gables Father jammed on the brakes, evicted us from the car, and drove away, leaving us on the curb. We were speechless even after he rounded the block and picked us up again.

Christmas at House Eleven was an adventure in spiritual and material joy, a rite too rich to be celebrated more than once annually. December 25 is the climax of every year and approaching it is half the fun, and half the faith. For Advent, the season in the church year which heralds the coming Christ, translates a secular mood of "waiting for the holidays" to its original and higher purpose of "preparing for the holy days." Family evening devotions now centered in the coming Nativity, and the lighting of candles in the Advent wreath heightened household anticipation and made it sacred. Soon the first carols would be sung.

Advent also saw the mail swell and the packages arrive. One year a Christmas parcel arrived too early, about Thanksgiving. It was placed on the radio console, but after a week of frustrated glances Father could stand it no longer. He called us into the living room, ignored the "Do Not Open Until Christmas" labels, and tore into it with a guilty grin. We ate yuletide candy with leftover Thanksgiving turkey.

Opening Christmas cards became a ritual in itself. After dinner, one of the foothills in the mountain of cards was brought in. Walt would slit open the envelopes, I pull out the card and hand it to Father, who would announce the sender and pass it around for all to see. If it were exceptionally striking we rated it in the two-, three-, four-, or very rarely, five-star category. We boys felt that the women were far too generous in assigning the stars.

Mabel now commenced the time-honored ceremonial of the oven, filling the air with the fragrance of baking Christmas cookies, while Grossie, who often visited during the holidays, kneaded dough from wondrous European recipes. Some of the aroma drifted from the kitchen into the study, tantalizing the man who was supposed to be dictating. He would charge out periodically to assault the oven door for "cooky reconnaissance," insisting on first-bite privileges at testing time.

On Christmas Eve, after attending the St. Stephen's children's service, we wrapped and placed the last presents at House Eleven until Father rang the Christmas gong which inaugurated the family celebration. While he accompanied us at the piano, we joined in singing an old German Christmas folk song, "Kling, Glöckchen (Ring, Little Bell)," and formed a festive procession which wound throughout the decorated house during four or five choruses and ended with us seated in the living room. I recited the Nativity story according to St. Luke, Walt played a carol or two, and Father offered up his annual Christmas prayer. With the "Amen," the Maier brothers dashed for the sunroom, which the ladies had secretly transformed into the Christmasroom.

There, filling the corner with a multicolored blaze, was a spruce masterpiece in its season of glory, standing sentry over a mound of gifts. And outside the lattice windows, its snow-covered cousins, luminous in the moonlight, looked in on the festivities. The scene etched itself on the emulsion of memory too deeply to fade in one lifetime.

Father assumed his position on a hassock in front of the tree so that he could distribute the gifts one at a time. If anything disgusted him it was the mass assault some families made on Christmas presents. Why not share the excitement and prolong the happiness? In this way a reserve of gifts remained for a second celebration on Christmas night.

Nothing pleased Father more than to surprise us with some substantial and wholly unanticipated present, and never was he more successful than at yuletide, 1937. That November he had called us into the study and asked our "cooperation" in not going to the basement before Christmas Eve; then we would learn why, but meanwhile we were to trust him and not ask questions. For some time we obeyed, until the curiosity of seeing several students going in and out of the basement and making odd sounds downstairs was too much for us. One night Walt and I stealthily oiled the hinges of our squeaky cellar door and turned the knob. Such confidence Father had in us! The door was bolted.

After the longest Advent on record, the door was unlocked in the course of our Christmas celebration, and we were led downstairs blindfolded. Just as Mother untied the handkerchiefs, Father threw a master switch and a model railroad layout appeared which was so elaborately extensive it covered nearly half the basement. Four Lionel trains were running simultaneously over a track plan which boasted thirteen electric switches and four signals. Illuminated miniature houses, stores, stations, and street lamps filled areas between the tracks, while freight yards with an elevated railway were waiting for us to install them. In the background stood a mountain range, where a small train was circling the very castle which the German war prisoners had built back in 1918. And controlling all from a grand panel of switches and rheostats sat the beaming Reverend Professor Walter A. Maier, Ph.D.—boy engineer.

The thrill was almost too intense. I recall being able to do nothing more than jump up and down and scream. Walt grabbed

Father in a bear hug, while Mother and Mabel were smiling broadly. It was a grand moment.

How it had all happened was typical of Father. On Olive Street, just across from St. Stephen's, were some antique shops which he loved to haunt for bargains. During a visit to one of the stores, he asked what four large boxes in a corner contained, and the proprietor replied, "Oh, you wouldn't be interested in that. It's just kid stuff—some electric train equipment from the estate of a wealthy family." Father indicated that he just might be interested indeed, then pored through the boxes with growing animation.

"Well if you're *that* interested, I'll let you have the whole thing for $35.00." The value of the nearly new equipment bothered the dealer not a bit. It was out of his line—he wanted it out of his way.

"Sold!" Father carted the boxes home, sketched out a track diagram, and engaged two seminarians who were the campus Edisons to construct the layout.

From that Christmas on, the basement at House Eleven became headquarters for Concordia's profs' kids, and the trains a cornerstone in Maier family entertainment. Any guests under eighty-five were usually treated to a model railroad show before leaving the house. On evenings when Walt and I felt that Father had exhausted his quota of work for the day, a series of rumbles from the basement was usually enough to decoy him downstairs. Each of us controlled a separate train, and after one or two wrecks in miniature, Father would return to his desk, refreshed by this kind of tonic.

The student electronics wizards who had erected the layout, Walter Martin and Edward Stoll, casually mentioned one day that they owned amateur broadcasting equipment, but seminary authorities would not permit them to set it up in their dormitory room. Always fascinated by radio, Professor Maier readily offered the use of his basement, and soon Station W2AHO began ham transmitting-receiving from the cellar of House Eleven. It was another excuse for Father to interrupt his work periodically and talk to someone on a foreign continent, occasionally a missionary. The paradox remained, however, that what was soon to be the world's most broadcast voice could not tell the difference between a resistor and a relay. Father never learned radio theory.

Sharing happiness through parties continued at House Eleven. Every Advent season brought a series of receptions for the classes in Old Testament, typified by a wide, convivial circle of students, each interlacing his biographical sketch with references to how many lovely sisters were back home waiting to meet seminarians. Then mirth, games, chat, until the hostess announced refreshments and the men filed into the dining room to find a brimming smörgåsbord. "Everything must go!" their professor urged them, and nearly everything went. Finally the evening closed, as did all Maier soirees, with Father leading the group in prayer.

The month of May saw another cluster of receptions, this time outdoor garden parties for graduating seniors. Never were house and hillside set off to better advantage. Japanese lanterns illuminated the balmy St. Louis spring evenings, casting a warm glow over blossoming slopes, the waterfall, and ponds. On the flagstone terrace a small student orchestra serenaded guests, and the host also drew out other talents from seminarians by way of entertainment. In the growing Concordia student body were hobby magicians, telepathists, or actors just waiting to be discovered. Finally, although he always tried to avoid stealing the show, Father regaled guests with entertaining stories and emerged as the life of the party anyway, a contagiously happy man.

Periodically, the family spirited itself off on a brief vacation trip, and one handy weekend retreat was the Breckenkamp farm near Washington, Mo., home of Mabel's parents who extended us a lifetime welcome. When Father was not out "hunting" with his sons—usually old bottles blasted in the air with .22 caliber rifles— he enjoyed long chats with Uncle Julius and Aunt Elsie Breckenkamp, learning as much as he could about life and problems on the farm. It was a little frightening to realize that even on vacation his mind was running at a fast idle. Though relaxing, he was also storing up illustrations from country life and rural economy which he would use to good effect in future sermons.

Most vacation time was reserved for the Poconos. Despite the depression, Lutherland continued to attract greater crowds each year, and the winter hamlet of 200 inhabitants swelled with summer church attendance numbering up to 4,000 each Sunday. Some of the people who lingered after services to meet the speaker eventually became close friends of the family and have remained so ever since.

Following one hot service in July, for example, a stocky, light-haired gentleman and his wife waited to meet Father after he had changed his wilted shirt. Henry Dahlen came into the vestry with the news that the gentleman was none other than dime-store magnate S. S. Kresge, who regularly summered in Mountainhome, Pa., just across the Poconos. After hearty introductions, we had dinner together, and during dessert, Mr. Kresge leaned over to Father and proved his legendary affability. "Well, Dr. Maier," he said in the tone a kindly uncle would use for his favorite nephew, "it's true that we've only just met. But already I feel we know each other well enough that I want to call you 'Walter' "—Father's eyes flashed surprise—"and I want you to call me 'Sebastian.' "

"Sebastian it is!" exclaimed Father approvingly, and the two staged such a scene of hand-clasping that the ladies were startled. Walter and Sebastian they remained for life.

Years later, when the Maiers were vacationing in Ft. Lauderdale, they went on a cabin cruise with their physician-comrade, Dr. Theodore Hanser, and his wife. Father suggested to Dr. Ted, "We really should cruise down to Miami Beach and see a good friend of mine who has an estate on the waterway—he works in a dime store."

"And he has an *estate?*" asked Hanser with raised eyebrows.

"Yes," smiled Father, who liked to set up his humor. "He's S. S. Kresge."

"Go on! Do you really know him?"

"Know him? We're on a first-name basis."

"You're putting me on!"

Ashore, the Maiers telephoned the Kresges, who insisted that they all come down to Miami Beach the next day. Still somewhat incredulous, Dr. Ted piloted his ship down the Inland Waterway toward the Kresge estate. When the cruiser was still well out in the channel, Father grabbed a megaphone, raced up to the foredeck, and called across the water to a familiar figure on the Kresge pier, "Helllloooooooooooo, Sebastian!" Kresge cupped his hands around his mouth and cried, "Helllloooooooooooo, Walter!" Captain Hanser nearly shoaled his ship for surprise.

The Poconos, then, provided a catalyst which enriched the Maier world by admixing new friendships. Some of the most delightful hours in Father's life were spent after Sunday Vespers around the blazing hearth in our summer home with a living room full of friends. After drawing humor, witticisms, and stories out of his circle of guests, the host dipped into his own brimming reservoir. Meanwhile, people were so caught up in the cheer that they ignored seating accommodations, makeshift because of the overflow: orange crates covered with blankets, packing boxes, and the like. I can still see the distinguished Chicago cleric, Dr. O. A. Geisemann, perched on a small stepladder, part and parcel of the festivities.

Friends showed their appreciation in various ways, sometimes with personal monetary gifts which Father usually refused in favor of the church. It was a different story with the Maier boys. After an evening performance at the Casino, when half the resort population was milling about the gift shop below, friends often insisted on buying us some game or toy which we could select. Walt had a tried and tested formula for such instances: 1) drift away from Mother so she wouldn't make us refuse; 2) wistfully decline twice, to be polite about it all; 3) accept graciously, so we didn't lose out; 4) choose a very modest gift, and then, of course, be urged to select something more expensive instead; 5) thank profusely. His approach proved a great success.

It was high in the Poconos that Father seized on the idea. He honestly believed that no man in history was more happily married than he, though he never said this publicly because he felt that, ideally, every husband should be able to make the same statement. The love in his own union was finding a deeper, yet higher basis, but he knew this experience was far from universal. Some of the widely publicized opinions, agitation, and literature of the thirties showed that. Even supposed experts in the field were playing with the institution of marriage as if it were some experiment in animal breeding. As *Messenger* editor he was receiving more mail posing courtship and marital questions than in any other area. Obviously, there was need for a thorough study of the problem. The necessity of the day, therefore, as well as his own wedded happiness shaped his resolve to write a book on marriage. The interim in broadcasting also provided him sufficient time for research on the project.

During the next months, press clippings show Father speaking out on different aspects of marriage. When his investigation uncovered fresh evidence on the subject, he sometimes used the material immediately rather than waiting for it to appear in his book. Results were published also in the overseas press. In England, for example, the Manchester *Daily Express* began its article:

Professor Walter A. Maier, of Concordia Seminary, St. Louis, has brought statistics to bear on the bachelor controversy.

. . . "Recent German vital records show that married men and women live five years longer, on an average, than unmarried ones," he declares.

"Actuarial computation, sanity figures, and mortality rates in America also show that married men are less liable to disease, insanity, and the commission of crime than are single men. . . . The average mother, again, lives longer than the average spinster, and the death rate among bachelors in middle age is twice that of married men."[3]

It seems that women's page editors in some American newspapers were pleased with these statistics and quoted them frequently. Professor Maier started receiving fan mail from an entirely new quarter of the great public.

If matrimony was desirable, certain forms of it were not. Father was distressed to find that fourteen American states permitted legal marriage at the minimum age of twelve for girls and fourteen for boys, trailing India in this respect. Declaring this an "atavistic flareback to the Middle Ages," he was happy in this instance that the wire services did report his ire on the matter nationally,[4] and editorials on child marriage legislation soon followed. All such states have modified the minimum age upward since then.

Similarly, while addressing an international Walther League convention in the Poconos, he rapped philosopher Bertrand Russell for publicly teaching that physical infidelity was not serious, as well as former Judge Benjamin Lindsey, who advocated his "companionate marriage" program to ease divorce laws and repeal anti–birth-control legislation.[5] One of the most amusing reactions in the press came in "Cook-Coos," Ted Cook's King Features Syndicate column:

> Doctor Maier, what pretext flimsey
>> Prompts you to so assail Ben Lindsey?
> The judge enjoys his little theory,
>> So why not live and let live, dearie?
> Come, take a stroll by the ocean blue
>> And get a bigger, broader view.
>> *—Betty Fisher*[6]

Crowning the verse was a sketch of some lovely, lolling on a beach "by the ocean blue." Father chuckled and personally pasted that piece into a scrapbook.

He himself was not above using humor to convey a point and occasionally coined some quotable quotes which again gained wide currency. For example, to illustrate that good wives are good cooks: "What this country needs are calory-conscious wives who can prepare spinach so that the virtue of iron is not neutralized by the vice of sand."[7] Or, "Love flies out the window as the boy from the delicatessen delivers the cold meat and immature potato salad at the door."[8]

But humor also has its hazards, and publicity its perils. One day a reporter from the International News Service arrived at Concordia Seminary to interview Professor Maier on his marriage book project. *The American Weekly* wanted to do a feature on his findings and was also interested in what relationship existed between poor cooking and divorce. Father had serious misgivings about the Hearst Sunday supplement, but finally agreed *if* the article would not be sensationalized and the religious content of his views on marriage left intact. The reporter promised to comply.

Father remarked that a Lutheran Hour sermon on marriage had resulted in 2,000 letters from people who were wrestling with the divorce problem; the most frequent complaint from the men was "poor cooking" and related difficulties. He concluded that there was, in fact, "an inevitable connection between good cooking and marital contentment," and that divorces were often traceable to "atrophied domestic instincts of modern 'emancipated' young women." However, he then prepared a statement which emphasized that this was only one aspect of a complex problem with profound spiritual implications, asserting in climax:

I do not advocate materialistic philosophies of marriage which insist that the brute must be fed or that the avenue of easiest approach to the male cardiac region is by way of the alimentary canal. For the essential requirements of marital bliss are unselfish love, compatibility in Christian faith, and the happy spirit of camaraderie.

Concluding was a citation of Proverbs 31:10 ff., a Biblical description of the ideal wife, which he insisted be printed as part of his statement. The reporter promised to transmit the material exactly as it had been given him and that the religious content would be included in the article.

October 16, 1932, was probably the most embarrassing day in the life of Walter Maier. On that date *The American Weekly* carried the story with title, "How To Keep Your Husband," just over the sketch of an irate spouse glaring at his wife across a table laden with, among other things, "immature potato salad."[9] As a crowning touch, Professor Maier's own photograph was nestled in the midst of four portraits of glamorous divorcées, and accompanying this frenetic format was an article which had considerably drawn, quartered, supplemented, and misquoted material from the interview. The reporter had, indeed, transmitted his story faithfully, but the editorial offices of the *Weekly* apparently decided that religion would not sell, spice would. Most of the spiritual and ethical aspects of the divorce problem, including the above statement, had been cut out and the gaps filled with sensational substitution.

The result was a red and angry face at House Eleven and a small crisis at conservative Concordia. The mail started arriving from inflamed pastoral conferences, and perhaps the plainest language came from a district president who wrote:

When I read that article, illustrated with pictures of beautiful divorcées with that of our professor of Old Testament Exegesis in the midst of them, I was speechless. Polite language fails me even yet, and I can not characterize the article otherwise than as "slush, tripe, and baloney." In all charity I can not believe that you are responsible. . . ."

The professor in question spent an indignant October and November setting the record straight. His bristling letter to the editor of the *Weekly* pointed out all misquotes and pledges violated. The editor expressed his official regrets, and the Hearst papers carried Professor Maier's statement, as did the *Messenger* in an editorial, "Distortion!"[10] He had made a glaring error in not requesting proofs of the article before publication, but up to now the press had treated him admirably and his guard was down. Worn but wiser, he flexed all efforts to finish his book.

When the manuscript was completed late in 1934, the pages stacked nearly a foot high with well over a quarter million words typed on them. The author titled his book *For Better, Not for Worse* and dedicated it "To My Wife." As he lugged the sheaf of typescript into the office of Dr. Edmund Seuel, general manager of Concordia Publishing House, Seuel could only gasp, "Wam, you're not going to give us *this* long a manuscript, are you?"

Seuel knew his business—he had guided Concordia to its position as one of the largest religious book publishers in the United States. The house wanted a short, unscholarly volume for those who were contemplating marriage; publishing tradition for a book of this kind was brevity and simplicity. Obviously *For Better* violated both rules. Seuel suggested, cajoled, then pleaded that the manuscript be cut, all to no avail. "Well, if you want me to take it to another publisher . . ." began Wam, but Seuel's "No" cut him off. As a sheer venture of faith, Concordia would publish it.

Subtitled, "A Manual of Christian Matrimony," this would-be handbook, running to 504 pages in small type, assumed more the proportions of an epic. It begins with a theology of marriage and ends with heaven and immortality.

The book also deals with the serious contemporary offensive against Christian morality from such quarters as radical sociology, pan-Freudianism, campus scoffers, ultraliberal clergy, cultic zealots, and the smut in print and on celluloid. Essentially, two codes are in conflict: that of the church and of the world. The church honors marriage as a divine institution, whose prelude requires chastity; whose pursuit lies in faithful love, companionship, and the rearing of children; and to which there is no postlude of divorce except in extreme cases. At repeated times in history, however, the code of society has challenged the code of the church, but never so radically as in the thirties. The world regards marriage as an evolutionary development, whose prelude sanctions sexual experimentation to the final degree, whose pursuit might well avoid children or even faithfulness in given situations, and which may be terminated at any time by the most convenient arrangement available.

Having laid aside the prophetic role, the core of the book discusses various criteria for a happy marital choice and the central concerns of courtship, engagement, and marriage. A special section is devoted to various marital menaces, especially divorce and, surprisingly, birth control. The author's opposition to artificial birth control is unusual for a Protestant, but part of Father's personal persuasions. Among other things, he was worried that such regulated parenthood could induce a dwindling population—an anachronism today with its population explosion, though in the thirties the birth rate had reached new lows, probably due to the depression. But in ascribing to birth control an "anti-scriptural bias," Walter Maier clearly went further than the Bible, which is silent on the matter. Most of Protestantism today would certainly find his objections unwarranted, though some church leaders of the time seconded his position, including, of course, Roman Catholics. Cardinal William O'Connell of Boston wrote his "approval and appreciation" of Professor Maier's stand on marriage and home life.

Stylistically, *For Better, Not for Worse* shows the author using his favorite prose ploys. Just as in sermons, the same descriptive language and ample use of illustration are found here. Sometimes the illustrations are too good, and one is left with the vivid picture, having nearly forgotten the point being made in the process. For instance, to exemplify how wives can extricate their husbands from difficulties:

When the city of Weinsberg was besieged in December of 1140 and the brave women had finally secured permission from Conrad III to leave the city together with their most precious possession, they marched out in one of the strangest parades history has witnessed: each wife carried her husband to life and liberty. In a less dramatic manner many self-effacing wives have borne their husbands out of the siege of prolonged illness and chronic indisposition.[11]

After thirty-eight chapters, *For Better* closes its rather comprehensive study of marriage. Father hoped his book would demonstrate that wedded bliss was an attainable reality, not an outworn delusion.

Soon after publication in the fall of 1935, the book was reviewed by *Time*. Acknowledging that churchmen had a right to chagrin ". . . when they see the institution of marriage beset as it is in the U.S.," the article told what a "famed Lutheran" was doing about it, author-professor Maier, the "hard-driving, popular teacher . . . hard-working editor who dictates daily to three secretaries." The review cited twenty-three of the far longer cavalcade of sources used in the book, and concluded:

A tome of 504 pages, *For Better, Not for Worse* surveys the whole of marriage and many another subject. . . . out of one of the most remarkable memories and most capacious files in existence.[12]

In later, expanded editions, the topic index alone ran to thirty-four pages!

Other reviews followed suit. *The Lutheran Witness* (Missouri Synod) styled it the "American classic on marriage and sex,"[13] and *The Lutheran* (United) spoke of a ". . . treasurehouse of information on the subject of Christian Marriage."[14] While orchids might be expected from home, other periodicals were also kind, as *The Presbyterian*: "Few books present marriage on a higher plane. . . . Written in a strong style. . . . Not a dull page."[15] Or the interdenominational *Christianity Today*:

This volume is a needed protest against the pagan, despiritualized conceptions of courtship, marriage and family relations that find such wide-spread expression today. . . . It is much more than a protest, however. It sets forth the constructive contributions which Christianity makes to married happiness.[16]

But a few critics cited elements for worse, not for better:

Presumably the book is intended for young people who are contemplating marriage, but one wonders how many in this nerve-racked, hurry-up age will have perseverance enough to read so ponderous a tome. With characteristic German thoroughness the author has produced what might be called a college course in the subject.

—*The Augustana Quarterly*[17]

It certainly was a tome, and even with good reviews the publisher had cause enough for worry. However, Manager Seuel's fears soon faded into rosy embarrassment. He was so certain the book would not sell out its original printing that he had hedged against anticipated loss by destroying type immediately after publication. At least all that metal would not be tied up. Yet now he looked at early sales figures and gasped. There was a run on the book, the first printing had sold out completely, and orders were cascading in. Immediately he ordered a resetting and second printing of many thousands of copies more, but that should certainly exhaust demand, he reasoned. Shortly afterward he had to order a third printing.

Several months later the author answered a distressed-yet-contented phone call from his publisher. "Wam, I don't know why *For Better* is selling so well, but it is," said Dr. Seuel. "We're going to have to print it a fourth time, and I wonder if you wanted to make any changes for a new edition—you know, possibly cutting it down a bit?"

"Fine, good Doctor! Yes, I do want to bring out a second edition. I have more material and a new chapter on psychoanalysis I want to include. . . ."

"*Include?*"

"It shouldn't add more than . . . say . . . seventy-five pages to the book."

It almost seemed as if Edmund Seuel were moaning.

The new edition was ordered in mass quantities designed to obviate future printings, but a year or two later came the usual requests for still another printing, another edition. Once again the author expanded the book, this time without editorial protest. It finally was published at 598 pages—as if avoiding 600 from a psychological point of view—set in smaller type for more words per page.

This edition also sold out until a sixth printing was necessary. Wam had dared to credit the Christian public with the ability to read something not brief and not simple, especially when the subject was as important as marriage. His faith was not misplaced. *For Better, Not for Worse* conducted a separate ministry of its own, as a large reader correspondence demonstrated.

Of the human interest stories associated with the book only one can be cited here. Norwegian Arne Pettersen worked in the New York shipping industry, but his heart was back in Scandinavia with a Swedish girl named Ingrid. They became engaged, and to illustrate his philosophy of marriage Arne sent his fiancée a copy of *For Better, Not for Worse*. He also had a special interest in the author, whom he had met casually at Lutherland over the briefest handshake and was astounded to have Wam recognize him many months later in a line of thousands after a New York rally and ask, "Why Arne Pettersen, how have you been?" Meanwhile, Ingrid and her parents were impressed with a suitor who subscribed to the principles in such a book. When the transatlantic romance was fully ripe, the bride-to-be sailed across the mined and submarined ocean in May, 1941, during the week in which England's H.M.S. *Hood* and Germany's *Bismarck* went down. She had no friends, no relatives in America, but as a happy climax, Arne dared to ask the one other American she knew indirectly—the very author of the book on matrimony which she had studied—if he would possibly be in the East toward the end of June and could marry them. He would; he could. It was a delightful wedding, marking the start of a lasting friendship with the Pettersens. Their marriage fell strictly into the "For Better" category.

# 12

# To the Nations

When the Lutheran Hour went off the air in June, 1931, the question of the day was "Will it be resumed?" The answer was anything but certain, and the simple, sad story of depression economics was responsible.

One Thursday evening that fall, while the radio in Father's study was tuned to the CBS program which had replaced him, he wrote the following and signed it:

"Will the Lutheran Hour be continued?" It seems to us that an effort so signally directed to the fulfillment of the Savior's last commission to His Church, "Preach the Gospel to every creature," must continue. . . . And whenever and however the Lutheran Hour broadcasting may be resumed, it will be one of the most effective contributions . . . to the restatement and reemphasis of America's supreme need. . . .[1]

At the moment it might have seemed heady optimism, but the statement was as close to precise prophecy as Father ever came.

Not that he maintained total radio silence during the early thirties. In addition to local programs came invitations to speak on other religious broadcasts. The Detroit Lutheran Pastoral Conference had appointed a progressive radio committee under the chairmanship of the Rev. Adam Fahling, which had organized a seven-station network in Michigan and Indiana to beam out The Lutheran Hour of Faith and Fellowship each Sunday afternoon. Several times in 1932 and 1933 Dr. Maier was invited to speak on this program, which originated at imposing Trinity Church in downtown Detroit.[2]

Inevitably, he and the Detroit radio committee discussed the possibility of resuming the national Lutheran Hour, not, at first, over a prohibitively expensive coast-to-coast network, but on a smaller chain which could be extended in the future. Nucleus would be the Faith and Fellowship network emanating from WXYZ, Detroit, to which superpower WLW of Cincinnati could

164

be added, both stations affiliates of the newly formed Mutual Broadcasting System. At 500,000 watts, ten times today's maximum limit, WLW was the most powerful radio station in the world at that time and could be heard anywhere east of the Rocky Mountains. Spread could therefore be achieved even with a minuscule number of stations.

The committee resolved to inaugurate a second Lutheran Hour season with Dr. Maier as speaker. Some had qualms about scheduling the program on Sundays; others warned the committee of negative comparisons which would be made between the small, new chain and the original CBS network. Nevertheless, the Detroit Pastoral Conference proceeded with the effort, which was then supported also by the Lutheran Laymen's League.

However, substantial immediate sums were still required to underwrite the station contracts. Where to find these would have been a problem but for an appropriate suggestion from the Rev. E. T. Bernthal. One of the pillars in his church happened to be president of the Chevrolet division of the General Motors Corporation, William S. Knudsen,* who later became president of General Motors itself. Knudsen had expressed interest in religious radio, and a possible guarantee from him would prime the pump sufficiently to revive the Lutheran Hour.

One evening "Barney" Bernthal took Wam for a visit to the Knudsen estate. The self-styled "immigrant from Copenhagen now selling Chevrolets" warmed up immediately to "the Little Doctor," as the 6-foot, 3-inch Dane called him from that night on. The three had an animated conversation which ranged from automobiles' bodies to men's souls. Before it concluded, Knudsen cheerfully volunteered to underwrite the entire first series of broadcasts, though he wagered that listener contributions would "save him." At the door he put his arm around the Little Doctor and said in his Scandinavian accent, "Now you teach the people to look up to God—they've been looking down too much nowadays."

*Second Season* (1935)

On Sunday, February 10, 1935, the Second Lutheran Hour was

---

* Pronounced "Noodsen." He once told a woman who seemed annoyed at the silent "K": "You don't say Kuh-Nee Action, do you?"

born, the silence broken. In order to save wire charges and in deference to Mr. Knudsen's wish, the programs originated from his own Epiphany Church in Detroit. For each of the fourteen broadcasts of this series, therefore, the speaker had to commute by train from St. Louis, leaving on Saturday and returning Monday morning just in time for classes.

A précis of the program format that first Sunday is extant:

| | |
|---|---|
| 1:00 PM (EST) | Opening Chimes and Organ—Mr. Carl Munzel Announcement: Brace Beemer |
| 1:01 | "Beautiful Saviour"—Detroit Bach Chorus, Prof. Eduard Ossko, Director |
| 1:03½ | Prayer—Dr. Walter A. Maier |
| 1:04 | Chorale—Bach Chorus |
| 1:05 | Address, "Comfort for a Critical Day"—Dr. Maier |
| 1:18½ | Chorale—Bach Chorus |
| 1:24½ | The Fellowship Period—Pastor Edward H. Buchheimer |
| 1:27 | The Lord's Prayer |
| 1:28 | The Closing Theme and Station Announcement— Chorus and Brace Beemer |

Brace Beemer, the announcer, had another role: he was none other than "The Lone Ranger," radio's original masked man. Recognizing the voice, the younger set expressed delight that their hero was also so good a Christian that he announced on the Lutheran Hour. Detroit youth who came to Epiphany Church at broadcast time, however, were disappointed to find the Lone Ranger without cowboy suit, Tonto, or horse "Silver."

Beemer was also a dramatic actor with much professional training, and he soon set about trying to improve the oratorical technique of Walter Maier. Prebroadcast rehearsals usually heard the Lone Ranger telling the Old Testament professor how to modulate his voice: "No, no, Dr. Maier! You're too fast and loud here. Tone it down, but give it depth . . . dramatic pathos . . . engulf your hearers in the mood!"

The speaker would oblige by changing his delivery abruptly to pattern it after Beemer's demonstration. "That's more like it!" Beemer beamed. But when the signal-light flashed in the pulpit at

1:05, off went Wam in his own vigorous style, which may have been un-Beemeresque, but snapped an arrowlike message at the targets of intellect, will, and emotion in all listeners within range.

The mail showed that. Well over a thousand letters from sixteen states and Canada arrived after the initial broadcast. The WXYZ— six-station Michigan Radio Network—WLW hookup was penetrating far beyond Michigan and Ohio, and contributions enabled the chain to add new links. Soon KFUO; WTJS, Jackson, Tenn.; and KLCN, Blytheville, Ark., had joined this modest rebirth of the broadcast.

The weekend commuting to Detroit was very inconvenient for Father, of course. A 7:30 A.M. Old Testament class at Concordia faced him just minutes after his train arrived on Monday mornings. Later lectures could not be arranged, as the Detroit pastors had suggested, because of scheduling problems.

Yet the spiritual results of those weekends by Wabash immeasurably outweighed any personal inconvenience. From February through May over 16,000 letters arrived, bearing postmarks from thirty-five states and several provinces of Canada. Many listeners remembered the first season and now greeted the resumed broadcast like a lost friend. This letter excerpt from the Rev. A. S. Clark, a Methodist minister in Greenfield, Ind., is representative:

The Lutheran Hour was greatly enjoyed . . . some years ago, and when it was discontinued, I felt the public had lost one of the finest contributions to the national religious life. . . . We attend church in the morning, Methodist Episcopal Church, and then tune in your services through WLW as we await the serving of dinner. May God bless your work very greatly! With so many voices of the air appealing to the emotional fringes and the less important things in life, it is a hopeful sign on the horizon to find a great national voice calling us back to God and His plan of moral and economic recovery.

Clergy of other faiths expressed parallel sentiments, as did people in every profession. A professor at Ohio State University listened with his family while eating dinner; another at the State University of Iowa regularly called attention to the program in his classes.

The nonintellectuals and nonprofessionals also wrote, the response from all segments of society corresponding to the experiences of the First Lutheran Hour. And when finally totaled, the contributions did, in fact, "save Knudsen." Years later he jovially reminded Father, "That's one guarantee I never had to pay!"

As a token of appreciation for listener interest, the broadcast sent out its emblem, a little gold lapel cross, to those who wrote in. The crosses symbolized the Lutheran Hour from now on and made effective conversation pieces which later occasioned a whole category of "cross" human interest stories, including conversions.

The speaker also wrote a booklet of forty devotional meditations entitled *Beautiful Savior,* after the program theme, and a host of copies were distributed to the radio public that Lent. The project started what became a lifetime effort on the part of the author: to help erect "the family altar" in as many homes as he could reach.

The successful second season convinced the Lutheran Laymen's League to sponsor a resumed network broadcast, using part of the Mutual Broadcasting System. A new series would begin that fall. Since it was the Detroit pastors who had had vision enough to help revive the program, the speaker gratefully dedicated his next book, *Christ for Every Crisis,* "To My Brethren of the Detroit Pastoral Conference."[3]

For a time, the story of the man merges with the story of his enterprise. The one cannot fully be understood apart from the other. And the record of Lutheran Hour growth shows a venture of faith so remarkably successful—Walter Maier would say "divinely-blessed"—that even the highly ambitious motto "Bringing Christ to the Nation" was soon outgrown.

### Third Season (1935/36)

Scene One of this series takes place in St. Louis on the brisk Sunday morning of October 20. In his study at House Eleven, Father goes over his sermon for the final polishing, and about noontime he walks along the woodland path to KFUO. The fact that future broadcasts will originate one block from home rather than 450 miles away in Detroit is a substantial relief. After a prayerful glance at the radio towers, he walks into the station.

The new Lutheran Hour announcer, young and distinguished-looking Reinhold Janetzke, is pacing Studio B, repeating the opening words over and over again. Two blocks east in the Concordia chapel the Seminary Lutheran Hour Chorus sings for volume level adjustment into microphones amplified to KFUO's central control room. Here Chief Engineer Carl Meyer twirls a few of the dozens of knobs on the panels facing him, looking a little nervously at his VU meters and transmitter dials.

By 12:29½ P.M. (Central standard time), the speaker is ready in Studio C, and the local announcer concludes a recorded musical program with the words, "KFUO now joins the facilities of the Mutual Broadcasting System to originate The Lutheran Hour." Then absolute silence until A. T. & T. signals that the wires are cleared for the network program. At 12:30:00 a bell half-rings in the control room, as a station engineer at WLW, Cincinnati, flips a master switch simultaneously triggering other circuits in Stations WINS, New York; WCAE, Pittsburgh; WGAR, Cleveland; CKLW, Detroit-Windsor; WJJD, Chicago; KSTP, St. Paul; KFAB, Lincoln; and short-wave W8XAL, Cincinnati—and the Hour is on the air. A dark carbuncle of glass in the announcer's studio suddenly glows brilliant red and Janetzke's golden tones are heard: "The Lutheran Hour—Bringing Christ to the Nation!"

Another cue light flashes in the seminary chapel, where Director Norman Gienapp brings down his baton, and the chorus responds with a virile first verse of the program theme from now on, "A Mighty Fortress." Janetzke answers with an announcement describing the broadcast and its sponsorship, followed by several verses of a chorale from the seminarians.

Now comes the sermon prayer by the speaker:

Heavenly Father: In Thy name and for the far-reaching testimony to the love of Thy Son, Jesus Christ, the only, but all-sufficient Savior from sin and sorrow, we begin this series of broadcasts. Send us Thy Spirit, so that, as the hymns, prayers, and messages wing their way over the nation and beyond its confines, men may raise believing hearts to the cross and in Christ's ever-valid redemption find the divine answer to every question of body and soul. May Thy Word bring comfort to those who are afflicted by sickness and sorrow. May the promise of the Gospel raise the falling, cheer the cheerless, enlighten the doubting. O Father of truth and life, bless us, we beseech Thee; grant us through these months of broadcasting Thy saving grace. Consecrate all our powers of mind and body to this sacred task. Strengthen our weak efforts with a full measure of Thy power, so that all that we may do or say may be to the glory of Jesus' name and the salvation of many souls; and unto Thy name we will give all praise, glory, and honor, now and forever.

He says no "Amen." Rather, a choral Amen from the chapel closes the prayer for him. During that ten seconds he clears his throat for the last time.

Again the scarlet signal comes alive in the speaker's studio, and the voice of the Lutheran Hour poises to deliver the sermon.

As we inaugurate today the third season of this radio mission, you may ask in challenge: "What is the message of this broadcast?" With many and conflicting voices on the air, some that appeal to reason and intellect, some that would inflame passions and prejudices, we promise that these weekly broadcasts have no political aims. This microphone will not be employed to fan the fires of class hatred, bigotry, and intolerance. The facilities of our network have not been drafted to flood the American nation and our Canadian neighbors with economic theories, financial strategies, and social speculations. Rather do we acknowledge as our own the apostle's determination *"not to know anything . . . save Jesus Christ, and Him crucified"* [I Cor. 2:2].

Addressing you from the campus of a divinity school that for almost a century has dedicated its resources to the Christ of the Scriptures, I offer you in the name of the Triune God not the Christ of present-day compromise and concession, not the Christ of twentieth-century indifference and indecision, not the Christ of modern doubt and denial, who has been exalted in His humanity only to be robbed of His deity, but the Christ of the Cross. With my hand on the Bible, I dedicate this radio mission to the preaching of that Cross.[4]

And on to a nineteen-minute address covering that theme.

With the end of the sermon comes another choral rendition from the chapel, and then closing announcements by Janetzke. These include offers of professional advice from Dr. Maier for those troubled with spiritual problems, the little gold cross emblem, or copies of the sermon just preached. Finally, the signature theme is sung, two verses of "Beautiful Savior," with final humming of the hymn to accompany the sign-off code, "This is the Mutual Broadcasting System." All signals are cut, the master switch is thrown back at WLW, and the Lutheran Hour is off the air until next week at the same time.

With minor variations, this was the program format for the next fifteen seasons or more, a simple yet effective approach stressing the centrality of the Christian message and surrounding it with the best in church music.

The first broadcast had gone off without a hitch, the timing had not deviated too widely from the production script, and now only the waiting was left—waiting until the first mail arrived to indicate whether or not anyone had heard, the waiting while people reacted to this broadcast and its format. Was it too "pure"? The programming was reserved, not sensational; dignified, not firebrand. Would it therefore sacrifice popularity? And network spread was still nowhere near the first season with its coast-to-coast chain of thirty-six stations, so mail response would be moderate in any event.

"At least a playwright knows with the morning papers what will happen to his play, but we have to wait out a week," Father observed at dinner. Then the telephone rang and proved that he had not reckoned with communications faster than the United States Mail. It was Edmund Kuhlman in Detroit, reporting that the broadcast had come through "clear as a bell." Telegrams arrived later in the afternoon with similar messages, wishing the speaker well. Though pleased at the thoughtfulness of his friends, he had yet to hear from the public.

The following Tuesday, an excited call from Lutheran Hour headquarters reported that the first mail was arriving, and in quantities far larger than anticipated. Before the week was out nearly 3,000 letters and cards were delivered, with postmarks from most states east of the Rockies. And this set the pattern for the next twenty-nine weeks of the October-through-Easter series, as nearly 70,000 letters arrived, a substantial increase from even the first Lutheran Hour.

"If you have no church affiliation and are troubled by a spiritual problem, Dr. Maier will be glad to advise you." Evidently, many in the radio audience caught these words from the closing announcements, for thousands of letters now arrived asking specific help on every species of problem plaguing the human body or soul.

I admit that I don't believe, and I want to find out how to believe. Please give this letter your attention.                          —*Michigan*

Please send a message of comfort to a paralytic friend of mine. This girl is completely paralyzed, having no use of her arms or legs, and her throat is slowly closing up.                          —*Pennsylvania*

I am a young girl and would like to know your opinion about smoking and drinking in the case of young people.                          —*Indiana*

Many letters exposed the root concern immediately, or after just a few words:

Our home life is a shambles. . . .     I am an epileptic. . . .
God cannot exist. . . .     For years I have been blind. . . .
I don't care to live. . . .     A deafmute, I. . . .
My husband is an alcoholic. . . .     I am losing ground. . . .
I am all alone in life. . . .     I was crippled since. . . .

And many other varieties of distress.

Probably no category of effort commanded more of Father's time than answering problem mail. Even with staff counseling assistance, he now began dictating late into some evenings and had secretaries working on a shift basis. Mother cringed a little each Sunday when she heard the "Dr. Maier will be glad to advise you" announcement. It would mean mountains of work for her husband.

The nonproblem mail, of course, constituted by far the lion's share of response, and again it flashed a multicolored spectrum:

Being of the old Quaker faith, I was moved to give thee a word of encouragement. . . .                          —*E.J.P., Illinois*

It was one of the most eloquent and sensible discourses that have gone over this radio; it was filled with bristling thought and brilliancy. . . . I am a lawyer in this city.                          —*R.W.A., Illinois*

May I, as a Roman Catholic teacher, congratulate you? . . .
                          —*F.W., Ph.D., Indiana*

Sorry to say, I was a racketeer. . . . Pray for me.     —*T.G., Minnesota*

And many other contrasts, extremes, and polarities could be cited.[5]

Again the radio public requested the sermons in printed form, so *Christ for the Nation* was published, embodying the messages of the Third Lutheran Hour. Each successive broadcast series saw the publication of another such volume.

### Fourth Season (1936/37)

When the new series opened on October 4, a larger station chain was poised to carry the Maier messages. From now on Father had to broadcast twice each Sunday so that different sections of the country could hear at optimum times: at 1 P.M. (Eastern standard time) for stations in the East, and again at 3:30 P.M. (Central standard time) for the rest of the nation. Clearly, something had to be done about the Rocky Mountain area and the far West, which had not heard the Hour since 1930-'31. After a breakthrough in negotiations, KFEL, Denver, and nine stations of California's Don Lee Network were added to raise the total number of outlets to thirty-one, or nearly back to the broadcasting strength of the first season.

For the first time the mail showed a general spread across America, as more than 90,000 communications were received from every state of the Union and provinces in Canada and Mexico. The letters were sent from homes and schools, dictated from skyscraper offices or written during lunch-hour breaks in West Virginia coal mines, California gold fields, or Texas ranches. They were penned in ships at sea and in port, airplanes and airports, hospitals, eleemosynary institutions, A.A.A. hotels, and C.C.C. camps. Anybody listened, anybody wrote. "Your continued reference to better race relations does not remain unnoticed," commented a colored listener from Missouri, "and I am sure thousands of members of the Negro race listen to your broadcasts." "The Tonawanda Indians on the reservation near here listen . . . regularly," was the word from New York. In Indiana there were ". . . Greek Orthodox Catholics, very attentively listening," while a letter from Maryland began, "In spite of the fact that I am Jewish, I regard you and your endeavors with the highest praise. . . ."

Mail from a single city turned up one letter from the governor of the state, another from a convict in the state's prison. One writer added in postscript, "I have the honor of being the Mayor of Baltimore." The most satisfying of all correspondence, however, was that which showed the messages penetrating the unchurched: "My neighbor does not go to church, but he listens. . . ."—Illinois; or, far more welcome, "I know of at least three people whom your speaker's messages have brought to our church."—Ohio.[6]

In his *Fourth Lutheran Hour*, the author could now write, ". . . the broadcasting of the Gospel is no longer on trial as an experiment, since the unique value of radio as a supplement to the regular preaching of the Word has been proved conclusively."[7]

## Fifth Season (1937/38)

The number of stations doubled to sixty-two, in what was becoming a strong coast-to-coast network. Outlets in the deep South and the Pacific Northwest, areas hitherto blank on the radio map, came in for the first time.

This upward vault was done in historic Lutheran fashion—"by faith alone"—for speculation had been growing that a saturation point would soon be reached with response tapering off, since the program had now been established for several years. But it soon became evident that saturation was nowhere in sight. When the speaker signed off for the summer, more than 125,000 letters and cards had arrived, compared to 90,000 of the previous season. This was the largest annual mail count of any religious broadcast in the world up to that time, a first-place position which the Hour probably had occupied ever since 1935/36 and would maintain from then on.

The letters now heightened with dramatic interest. A sailor on an oil tanker 2,000 miles out in the Pacific wrote how the crew framed a Sunday church service around the short-wave broadcast. A lone prospector high in the Sierra Madres, Royal Canadian mounted policemen in Manitoba, the Governor of South Dakota, members of Parliament in Ottawa, and an Indianapolis beggar who listened in at the local fire station—all wrote Dr. Maier their warm appreciation, as did physicians, educators, state and national senators and representatives. An active mission congregation was organized in Pittsburgh as a direct result of a colored woman writing to the broadcast, and already it was receiving new members through confirmation.

Unitarians, Mohammedans, cultists, and almost all of the 250 American denominations and sects sent mail. For non-Lutheran ministers to suggest that their congregations tune in Dr. Maier after their own Sunday services became standard practice in some localities. Overheard at a club banquet in Omaha was the following bit of dialogue, started when one member heard another discussing the broadcast.

"I didn't know you were a Lutheran, Bill."

"I'm not. I'm Catholic."

"But you were talking about the Lutheran Hour. . . ."

"Wouldn't miss it . . . a lot of us down at K. of C. listen regularly. We even wrote in and they sent us their little gold crosses. My wife has hers on her rosary, and I've got mine here on my watch fob. Every night we pray for Father Maier."

Some correspondence came by devious routes indeed. Crew members on a banana boat in the Caribbean regularly tuned to the broadcast and now wanted to send a cash contribution by way of appreciation. Since there are no mailboxes on the open sea and they would not make port for some time, the men put their letter to the Hour in a lard pail, sealed on the lid, and dropped it down to coastal fishermen whom they knew to be honest folk. These fished out the can which had splashed into the Caribbean near their boat, removed the letter, and mailed it to St. Louis.

Not all missives, of course, radiated approval. A few took issue with the speaker on a rational basis, but there were also anonymous crank cards, signed messages of ridicule and sarcasm, and some notes with nothing short of blasphemy. Most of these argued from fanatic or sectarian motives. Yet all messages registering disapproval of any kind comprised only a small fraction of 1 per cent of the total.[8]

*Sixth Season (1938/39)*

About half the budget for the previous series had been contributed by the listening public. The other half was met by donations from congregations, societies, and individuals largely within the Lutheran church. In view of the economic recession of the late thirties, there was no financial mandate to redouble the number of stations, and the new radio season began with only four additional outlets.

Response, however, increased. Over 140,000 letters arrived, with contributions which now paid three-fifths the total network costs. The headquarters staff had to be enlarged substantially, and volunteer help was also provided by the Lutheran Business Women of St. Louis. Occasionally the ladies were rewarded by exciting moments when they opened correspondence from some notable on the American scene. Such a letterhead as this, for example, would cause a hubbub among the girls:

WARNER BROTHERS PICTURES, INC.
BURBANK, CALIFORNIA
OFFICE OF THE PRESIDENT

Signed by E. M. Warner, the letter began, "Enclosed herewith please find my contribution to your most worthy program, and I wish you an abundance of success in appreciation of your good work." Others in the entertainment world at the opposite end of the country—and salary scale—listened also, as the struggling young actor in New York City who wrote: "Being in show business, I, like so many others, never had time for church. Last Sunday I listened to your services over the radio and was deeply moved."

Other happy moments at headquarters came with the rare, oddly addressed envelopes which were inevitable among the thousands of normal letters arriving each week:

| | | | |
|---|---|---|---|
| Dr. Mayer | Lutern Priest | The Lucien Hour | Luter |
| Missouri | of the Air | Mutual System | St. Louis |
| | St. Louis | | |

Since the Lutheran Hour was the largest nongovernment mail receiver in St. Louis, the postal miracle is better understood. Addressed to some variation on the theme, "St. Louis, Mo." (sometimes only "Mo."), all of the following somehow arrived without delay at the right address:

Luther and Alvin

Dr. Myers Lourson Our

Luther and Co.

Dr. David Mayer

Missouri Senate [Synod?]

The Luke Hour

Mr. William Myra

Dr. Major Laughing Hour

Doc Morris

Happy Lutheran Houer

Lhuth Our Waler Meyer

Concordant Cemetery

Reverend Martin

Rufner Hour

The Lords Prayer

Then there was the fellow who did not want to miss—and did:

Rev. Dr. Walter A.

Caier
Coyer
Ceyer
Meier

With hearers in the millions, anything is possible.[9]

*Seventh Season (1939/40)*

In the fall of 1939, war in Europe lurched world history into a terrible turn for the worse. Yet the same months would also incline Lutheran Hour history into a wider turn for the better. Two steps of far-reaching significance forever altered the course of "Bringing Christ to the Nation."

First, the use of electrical transcriptions was introduced, which enabled strategically located stations not affiliated with the Mutual network to air an identical but recorded Lutheran Hour program at a convenient local time. Transcription technique was sufficiently perfected by this time that on home radios it was impossible to discern the difference between live and recorded broadcasts. Response was so favorable that within six months, 72 transcription outlets were signed in, raising to 171 the total station log.

The second and most noteworthy advance was the inauguration of foreign broadcasting. With the United States now comparatively well penetrated, the Hour looked beyond American boundaries. The speaker had envisioned an international outreach even before his broadcast was born and now waited only for the opportunity. Canada was obvious, and the first of many stations there were welcomed. But the initial "break" in foreign programming came when Clarence W. Jones, director of powerful long- and short-wave Station HCJB ("The Voice of the Andes") in Quito, Ecuador, chanced to hear the radio voice of Dr. Maier during a visit to the States and wrote him, offering the facilities of his station for English and Spanish broadcasts of the Lutheran Hour.

After dictating an enthusiastic reply in the affirmative, Professor Maier called several Spanish-American seminarians into his office, and before the conference was over Manuel Morales found himself Spanish Lutheran Hour announcer and eloquent Alfred Saez, translator and speaker. Thus the Hour's foreign program department was born, and Spanish became the first of fifty-nine languages in which the broadcast was eventually aired. Subsequently and until today, Dr. Andrew A. Melendez has been in charge of the Spanish department as regular preacher on *Cristo Para Todas Las Naciones* ("Christ For All The Nations").

Soon a number of short- and long-wave stations in Puerto Rico, Panama, Colombia, Venezuela, and Bolivia were also added for Spanish transmissions in Latin America. In a short time, most of the nations in Central and South America would be on the Hour's station log and responding with mail.

Four days before Christmas another overseas front opened when Father received a cablegram from the Philippine Islands, offering the facilities of KZRM, Manila, for Sunday afternoon Lutheran Hour broadcasts. He was elated. KZRM was one of the strongest radio stations in the Orient, and its short waves could be heard throughout a vast west Pacific quadrangle from New Zealand to Japan, to China, to Malaya and even India. The cause of this windfall was a former seminarian who had once learned his Hebrew from Professor Maier, now Rear Admiral J. Floyd Dreith. At that time he was a Navy chaplain in the Philippines, where his overtures secured the station for his onetime professor. Soon the program was beamed throughout the Orient in Spanish and English.

The following March, another former seminarian, Missionary R. J. Mueller, was enjoying a brisk afternoon in his compound at Wanhsien, China, a thousand miles up the Yangtze River from Shanghai. At 4 P.M. he decided to flip on his short-wave set, and after dialing through an audio-jungle of whistling, coding, and programming, he tuned in a chorus singing a very masculine "Mighty Fortress." "Just like we used to sing it at the Sem," he recalled. Then *that voice!* It sounded like Wam's—it had to be Wam's! His S.O.S. summoned other missionary families and Chinese seminary students in the compound, and a thrilled group of people on the other side of the world heard and later wrote the speaker, ten of the Chinese even penning their appreciation in halting English.

Mail now arrived also from such places as Hong Kong, French Indo-China, India, Australia, New Guinea, New Zealand, and the Philippines. When the season ended, exactly 176,508 communications had been received, an increase of nearly 40,000 over the previous series.[10]

## Eighth Season (1940/41)

International broadcasting was proving itself. What was projected as a possible future enterprise became a surprisingly present reality. In discussing overseas expansion plans with the Hour Operating Committee, the speaker sounded the keynote: "Fortunately God fathoms the future better than we can. If He has opened the door this wide we must go through it." Serious objections to extending foreign coverage would have been possible. What organization would ever enlarge overseas operations during wartime, except perhaps the Department of Defense? And because of the lower economies involved, broadcasting abroad would certainly bring in proportionately less contributions from listeners for the greater expenses of maintaining foreign stations. Yet sending many hundreds of missionaries to reach the same people—with a message needed in war or peace—would be almost infinitely more expensive. It was a case of praying and advancing.

During this season fifty-two foreign stations joined the twelve already in use. Clearly the program's motto had to be changed. Only one letter was added—an s—but it greatly expanded the purview of the project: "Bringing Christ to the Nations." While a majority of the new outlets were located in Latin America—Cuba, Dominican Republic, Nicaragua, Costa Rica, Paraguay, Uruguay, and

Chile, in addition to countries cited earlier—another westward thrust was made through short-wave KGEI, San Francisco, which could be heard as far as India; KGMB, Honolulu; KFQD, Anchorage; and XMHA, Shanghai. Negotiations were also begun with Generalissimo Chiang Kai-Shek for possible extension of a Mandarin broadcast throughout China.

International mail now increased on a soaring curve. There could be no doubt that the broadcast was beginning to penetrate two hemispheres, an enterprise which just five years before had started with only two strong stations. Lutheran Foreign Mission Secretary O. H. Schmidt toured the Far East and found that a surprising number of Filipinos listened regularly to the broadcast, many of whom previously had no idea of what a Lutheran or even Protestant might be. Missionaries now found easier entree among the populace, in some cases were even welcomed.

It was the same story in Latin America. In León, Nicaragua, for example, the owner of Station YNDG was so pleased with the *Cristo* program that he amplified it over loudspeakers set up in the plaza of the city park. On the following Sundays, announcements were made in the Roman Catholic churches of León forbidding the faithful from hearing such "heretical propaganda." After that the crowds were larger. And down in Montevideo, Uruguay, the same mail forwarded from Station CX16 supplied such extremes as an appreciative letter from the secretary to the President of the Republic of Uruguay, and a note from a sick girl of twelve.

Back in the States, meanwhile, the chain of network and transcription outlets had also lengthened, with a resulting total of 310 stations—a 500 per cent increase in two years. By the end of the season, about 200,000 letters had arrived, a record 13,000 communications were received in one week, 5,000 items in a single day. A sampling of these continued to be a sampling of the United States of America. Authors, artists, industrialists, and congressmen wrote enthusiastically, as did the labor leader who noted, "We are passing the word in our factories at Toledo that your broadcast is the one radio message that is genuinely interested in the working classes."

Thousands of vignettes materialized out of the mail bags. Commuting by train between mission stations in Wyoming, the Rev.

Paul Hansen heard his former professor over a portable radio in the coach, while a group of tough and swearing linemen in overalls toned down to interested silence during the program. On other railroads even more heard. A passenger agent on the Daylight Limited between Los Angeles and San Francisco wrote, "The radios were cut in on this crack streamliner all through the train and remained cut in all through your broadcast. I am sure most of the approximately five hundred on the train heard your straight-from-the-shoulder message." Whether or not a few passengers registered complaints at the end of the run is not mentioned!

A Los Angeles bootblack turns up his radio for passers-by as well as customers, while over in Pasadena the largest drug store in town plays the Lutheran Hour for lunching families. A station engineer at KTOK, Oklahoma City, writes that this is one program for which he does more than watch dials; he really listens, is happy to have a small part in its transmission. In the Pittsburgh Home for Incurables the patients cannot help hearing Dr. Maier because ". . . so many individual radios are tuned in and you have a such a strong voice, they can hear it across the hall if they don't have a radio in their own room." A Buffalo man writes that if he had not stayed home one afternoon to listen to the broadcast he could not have extinguished his blazing oil heater which blew up just at the "Amen," and his house would have burned down. In the same city a large newspaper ad begins, "WHOEVER YOU ARE: Listen to The Lutheran Hour . . . ," and at the bottom: "This advertisement donated by a non-Lutheran."

More than one suggestion reached the speaker's desk that ". . . you should be our next President of the United States," which always brought a chuckle. But he was "immortalized" in a different fashion—Atlanta's Oglethorpe University placed the transcription of his broadcast on February 4, 1940 into its "Crypt of Civilization," a time capsule containing a cross section of twentieth-century Americana, to be opened again in 8113 A.D. And so it went.[11]

*Ninth Season (1941/42)*

The European war was expanding. After the air Battle of Britain, hostilities had spread to Russia as well as North Africa. In St. Louis, the editor of the *Messenger* wrote: "No doubt can remain in the mind of any intelligent observer that the United States may be headed straight for active participation in the World War."[12]

Despite this background, there was no thought of retrenching Hour operations. New stations raised the total to 346, of which fully a third were located in twenty-five foreign lands. With the addition of Haiti, Mexico, Honduras, British and Dutch Guiana, Brazil, Peru, and Argentina, nearly every country in the Western Hemisphere now had a series of stations "Bringing Christ to the Nations" over long- and short-wave bands, in English, Spanish, and now also Portuguese.

But the International Lutheran Hour was not yet a global undertaking, since the continents of Europe and Africa had not been touched. One summer day, however, a cablegram arrived offering stations in Angola for Hour broadcasts in Portuguese, and the following spring the government of Iceland sent cabled word to a glowing Walter Maier, approving use of 100,000-watt Radio Reykjavik for his programs in English and Icelandic. This station beamed various frequencies also to the British Isles, and the Continent. For the first time the Hour would reach Europe.

Correspondence now arrived from thirty-six countries, emblazoned with such remote postmarks as Cape Town, South Africa; Coromandel, New Zealand; Bangkok, Siam; and Johore Bahru, Malaya. Listeners reported hearing Dr. Maier in spatial heights and depths. "I heard the Lutheran Hour 20,000 feet above the Brazilian jungle," wrote a bomber pilot, while a sailor told of receiving it on his portable radio aboard the surfaced submarine *Sail Fish*.

The more normal levels showed increasing penetration. Most American latitudes from Bering Strait to the Strait of Magellan now sent letters, many with verbal pictures: an Alaskan couple hurrying home on their skis so as not to miss the Hour; a tribe of Aztec Indians at Milpalta, D.F., Mexico, listening regularly to the broadcast, assisted by a bright young Aztec student who translates difficult Spanish terms into their Nahuatl language; a club of intellectuals at Ciudad Trujillo, Dominican Republic, tuning each week to *Cristo Para Todas Las Naciones* and discussing it afterward; plaza crowds hearing the program in Tegucigalpa, Honduras; a conference of Protestant pastors in Cuba playing Hour transcriptions in their churches after the eleven stations on that island have finished with them; Latin American newspapers giving the broadcast prominent, even front-page billing. The owner of Station CC133 in Chillan, Chile, skeptically agreed to give *Cristo* a trial hearing, yet after the audition he not only accepted the program, but secured additional outlets for it in Chile. And Latin American response was gratifying. From CX16 and CX24 in Montevideo came 582 letters in a single mail; from Radio Prieto in Buenos Aires, 543.

Both foreign and domestic correspondence revealed a phenomenon which had accompanied the program from the first, but was now assuming progressively larger proportions—conversions to Christianity. Hour headquarters had always been careful to handle prospects for church membership according to the following basic policies: 1) Prohibition of proselytizing—there was never any attempt to make Lutherans of those whose spiritual needs were satisfied by another Christian faith. A majority of financial support for the broadcast came from non-Lutherans as it was, and the speaker was careful never to "plug" his own church in sermons. Outside of the program's title, there was no repetition of the denominational name to give the broadcast a sectarian character, even if the theology in the Maier sermons was Lutheran Christianity. 2) Referral service—if a letter arrived from someone who had no church affiliation but desired it, he was advised that his name was being referred to the nearest minister in his locality, Lutheran if convenient, for follow-up work and instruction classes with a view toward church membership.

So many were the letters which arrived both from converts and pastors who confirmed them, that the speaker could write in the Foreword to his tenth book:

We cannot adequately thank our heavenly Father for the actual conversions and definite reconsecrations which the Holy Spirit has wrought through . . . broadcasting. It would take a volume much larger than this to recount the stories of those who attribute their conversion to God's grace as proclaimed in the Lutheran Hour. . . .[13]

Converts ranged from the Boston bootblack who regularly sent the broadcast part of his tips, to General of the Mexican Army Jose Gonzales Cantu, who joined the church together with his family of seven as a direct result of Hour-listening. Wives wrote joyfully of the conversion of their husbands, and vice versa, parents had their children baptized or enrolled in Sunday school, and pastors saw the results at the local level. One cleric in Oklahoma wrote:

. . . On March 1 we had the unusual and happy experience of accepting twenty-nine adults into membership through conversion and on April 12 another class of thirteen adults. Naturally, their decision is due entirely to the power of the Holy Spirit, through the Word . . . but humanly speaking, they were interested in listening to the Word after they heard the Lutheran Hour.

Amid the successes of the ninth series, however, came also a disastrous setback. This was the season of the attack on Pearl Harbor and America's plunge into war. Far East broadcasting was suddenly placed in mortal danger. Nowhere was the loss better symbolized than in the poignant cablegram from KZRM, Manila: "DISMANTLING EQUIPMENT JAPANESE INVADING." But the story of the Hour and the war will be told in a later chapter.

By season's end, the mail count stood at 260,000, as compared with 200,000 of the previous series. More than a quarter-million people had written, and since only a very small percentage of listeners to any radio program will take the trouble to send it a letter, the weekly broadcast audience was now projected roughly at 10,000,000 people, a figure corroborated by other means of audience measurement.[14]

Quite a congregation, this, and certainly a far cry from one lone transmitter in south St. Louis. On the eve of its tenth anniversary, the Lutheran Hour had shown a growth, penetration, and effectiveness for which radio authorities used the Madison Avenue term "phenomenal." The expansion of a small Midwestern project into an international enterprise reaching an area from the Arctic to the Antarctic and from England to China naturally caught the imagination of the public. Newspaper Sunday supplements in many cities did rotogravure features on "Bringing Christ to the Nations" and the speaker involved, whose voice had indeed "come a long way from St. Louis," after the then-popular ditty. But he always tried to deflect the spotlight away from his person and onto the enterprise. His favorite reason for doing so was once expressed thus:

Let any preacher who wants to feel how insignificant he is but how all-powerful and all-merciful God is try to broadcast to the nation every Sunday, and any thought of self-sufficiency will quickly vanish. More than any one else the radio speaker, deprived of some definite aids which the pulpit preacher has at his command, should realize that all honor and glory must be given to God.[15]

For Walter Maier, the experience in radio had corroborated the Scripture, "God . . . desires all men to be saved and to come to the knowledge of the truth" (I Tim. 2:4). From seminary days on he had interpreted the passage as a divine mandate for the universal outreach of the gospel. But only now could he appreciate how all-embracing was the faith, for the many differences or barriers which nature and society erect among men had faded in the common positive response to a Christian message. The response may have involved reconsecration or even conversion, counsel or even rescue, or—by far the largest category—the sanctification of normal Christians, but Christianity had communicated.

On the other hand, it would have been abnormal, in fact, impossible for every listener to have agreed with the speaker. Yet less than one-tenth of one per cent of the mail comprised letters of protest or criticism. This would seem too low for credibility but for the likelihood that most critics probably would not take the time to write in, or, for that matter, listen further. But the 0.1 per cent more than compensated for low quantity by good, bristling, acid quality. Since Walter Maier denounced evils and evil men wherever he found them in the society and culture of his day, he would have a significant number of opponents made to order for himself.

Occasionally atheists, "rationalists," or "humanists" wrote, making a spirited defense of their unbelief. They received personal replies from the speaker in which he discussed their arguments in detail and then supplied some of his own. Understandably, a few protests came from some in the Modernist ministry, and, very rarely, from non-Protestant clergy and laity. Then, too, periodic messages arrived accusing him of fascism for opposing atheistic communism, as he did from the very beginning.

Letters from fanatics and cranks came in grotesque sizes, script, and colors. There was also a small file of caustic correspondence criticizing everything from the speaker's faith to his oratorical technique. One classic card from California offered this bit of rhetorical advice:

"4 CHRIST'S SAKE, CHANGE YOUR VOICE. IT SOUNDS LIKE HELL!"

Father wanted to frame that one, but Mother would have none of it.

Sometimes a trap was set for the voice of the Lutheran Hour. One listener sent him a contribution of two dollars, explaining that the money had been won in a poker game. Father replied, in part:

Thank you very much for the interest in our broadcast which prompted your letter, as well as the contribution of two dollars you were kind enough to enclose. Since it is our policy not to accept funds derived from gambling of any kind, I return your two dollars herewith.

Moreover, since you seem to be in such financial distress that you had to resort to gambling, I am pleased to enclose also a gift of two dollars of my own.

A week later came a letter from the man's secretary, expressing the delighted amusement of their entire office staff. It seems our small-stakes "gambler" had told business associates that "any preacher will take any kind of money at any time," and wagered that this Dr. Maier would absorb the two dollars without a second pang of conscience.

Other challenges were far more serious and involved the existence of the broadcast itself. The question was frequently raised as to why the Lutheran Hour had to pay for every moment of its air time at full commercial rates, while religious programs on NBC and CBS were charged nothing. The answer was cited in an earlier chapter, but as "Bringing Christ to the Nations" assumed larger proportions, speaker and staff became less satisfied with that answer. Domestic network charges ate up the lion's share of the annual budget, and if this amount could be applied instead to foreign broadcasting, enormous strides would be possible—more languages used, more nations served.

Mutual could not donate the time, so once again NBC and CBS were approached. But, according to their established policy, neither network could carry the program on a sustaining (free) basis. More was involved than the denominational name of the Lutheran Hour. That, after all, could have been changed to its subtitle, "Bringing Christ to the Nations," as in most foreign broadcasts of the program.

The problem lay far deeper. One of the most unfortunate developments in the history of religious radio was the low quality and sensationalizing approach in a few of the programs. Just as there are good and bad representatives of any profession, so in addition to Walter A. Maier and other respectable network ministers there were also some radio preachers during this era who were inferior indeed. Religious confidence men, Elmer Gantries, faith healers, and "hot-gospelers" were using the air waves as well as the sawdust tent at the edge of town. Some were rabble rousers, thundering denunciation of anyone not belonging to their particular sect; others fed the fires of controversy. While most of these were, and are, contained on a local basis, some few got on the networks which, obviously, soon decided to donate broadcasting time to respectable religion rather than sell it to such.

The fingers of CBS in particular had been burned earlier in the decade by what *Time* called ". . . the rabble-rousing rise of blatant Rev. Charles Edward Coughlin as a paying speaker on its hookup."[16] Father Coughlin was, and is, a priest at the Shrine of the Little Flower in Royal Oak, Michigan, who by weekly radio programs and a party organization, the Union of Social Justice, had accumulated a national following in the thirties which thrived on political, economic, and social discontent. Professor Maier watched his rise with growing anxiety, but hesitated to denounce Coughlinism lest this be misinterpreted as an anti-Catholic attitude on the part of a Lutheran cleric. Finally, however, he could keep silent no longer. In the June, 1935 *Messenger* he stated his position in an editorial entitled, "The Clerical Conquistador." Avoiding the usual charges against the curate, he pierced the core of the issue: "We . . . protest against the interference of a Roman Catholic priest in the political affairs of the nation and his self-constituted leadership in a political movement which, by the regimentation of the masses, seeks to influence Congress and the legislation of our country."[17] Particularly in the relationship of church and state, the editor remained totally Jeffersonian. A year later his widely circulated "Reformation or Revolution" address at Ocean Grove made reference to Coughlin's political activities, asking that they be either officially approved or rejected by the Roman Catholic church. After rising criticism also within Catholicism, the radio priest was finally silenced.

But the damage had been done. Father Coughlin's demagogic intermingling of politics and religion had given commercial religious radio a bad name. And Judge Joseph Rutherford's militant use of paid broadcasting in behalf of the Jehovah's Witnesses had helped matters not at all. Accordingly, NBC, CBS, and Blue network policy avoided religious controversy by refusing to sell time and donating it instead to the three major divisions of organized religion in the United States: Protestant, Roman Catholic, and Jewish. Thus the *Catholic Hour* and the *Message of Israel* were broadcast gratis.

But who should speak for Protestants? Protestant programming was placed under the exclusive direction of the Federal Council of the Churches of Christ in America. This organization represented thirty denominations, but less than half of American Protestantism. Because the Federal Council was decidedly liberal in the theological controversies of the day, many conservative church bodies—including Dr. Maier's own—did not join it. And yet the Council's Department of National Religious Radio controlled all free air time allotted to Protestants in America. While it did some fine programming, it probably also erred in not scheduling at least one nonliberal on the various Sunday and weekday broadcasts donated to it. One of the Modernist preachers prominently sponsored by the Council frankly denied the deity of Jesus Christ. Thus, in order for millions of Christians to hear what for them could be the only spiritually satisfying message, one stressing the Biblical proclamation of salvation in Christ, they had to contribute dearly for it and have their broadcast come under the distasteful "commercial religious" category. For more than half of American Protestantism this seemed unfair discrimination and a less than tolerable situation.

What could the Lutheran Hour do about it? Appeal for free time to the Federal Council would be refused, because its program allotments were filled and it sponsored only interdenominational broadcasts on a regular basis. Now, since the networks would grant no further sustaining time either, Walter Maier grew increasingly perturbed. *Time* told the story in an article entitled, "Maier *v.* Council." Pointing up the paradox that, judged by mail response, none of the gratis programs on NBC or CBS was radio's most popular religious broadcast, the newsmagazine stated, "That distinction belongs to a . . . time-buying program—the Lutheran Hour. . . ." After portraying its speaker, the article continued, in part:

Last week, in a broadcast sermon at a Lutheran Rally in Manhattan . . . Maier declared that the Federal Council maintains a radio monopoly in the U.S., which he proposes to take up with the Federal Communications Commission. As documentation, Dr. Maier quoted a statement made by the Council's general secretary in 1929: "In the future, no denomination or individual church will be able to secure any time whatever on the air unless they are willing to pay prohibitively high prices. . . ."[18]

However, there is no evidence that the F.C.C. was actually approached on this issue.

Meanwhile, the problem of nonrespectable religious radio was being met by a new code of the National Association of Broadcasters, which barred programs involving religio-political controversy along with those attacking any race or religion. Moreover, the Mutual System became selective about which commercial religious programs it would carry, dropping any marginal or questionable ones.

This was still not enough for the Federal Council. It now addressed a petition to the annual convention of the National Association of Broadcasters and also to the Mutual Broadcasting System formally requesting that all paid religious programs be barred from the air, and virtually asking that all Protestant network broadcasting be placed under its direction. The Lutheran Hour speaker and staff were stunned and wondered to what extent the petition had been directed against their program.

The N.A.B. convention considered the request, then emphatically rejected it, ". . . partly to permit the Lutheran Hour to continue," so *Tide* magazine reported.[19] Mutual also dismissed the petition, refusing to discriminate against independent religious broadcasts.

Subsequently the Council addressed a similar petition to the Federal Communications Commission in Washington, and once again Hour officials held their breath in St. Louis. But this final appeal was rejected with the same emphasis.[20]

Asked to give a statement to the press, an elated Walter Maier emerged from House Eleven and said, "Christians of America have every reason to thank God that such totalitarian tendencies suffered this rebuke. Although the networks have not granted us the equal privilege of free radio time, we are grateful that the National Association of Broadcasters, the Mutual Broadcasting System, and the Federal Communications Commission have, by their action, served to uphold the constitutional principles of freedom of speech and religion."

Among the most persistent of other questions asked was, "Is the Lutheran Hour really the largest religious broadcast in radio today?"

Father smiled and turned to the program's director who was standing at his side. "Let's let Dr. Bertermann answer that one."

"Yes, it is," smiled Eugene R. ("Rudy") Bertermann.

"How do you know?" challenged a reporter.

"By any possible gauge: number and location of stations, area saturation, nations served, audience sampling estimates, and, of course, amount of letter response from listeners. This year alone we've received substantially more mail than Dr. Fosdick, Dr. Sockman, Monsignor Fulton J. Sheen, Dr. Peale. . . ."

"Hold it!" interrupted Father. "We'd better use President Roosevelt's rule—'Never give your "opponent" free advertising by mentioning his name,'" he winked. "More seriously, credit for the entire project goes to God alone."

Another newsman asked, "Dr. Maier, do you feel you've reached a saturation point by this time?"

"Just today the Lutheran Laymen's League approved a stated goal which we intend to reach with God's help: 'To use every available and suitable station on earth for the proclamation of Christ's eternal gospel.'"

"*On earth?*"

"Yes." He put an arm around Mother who had just come out of the house. "This is only the beginning."

# 13

# Why Success?

Communicating Christianity, the lifetime determination of Walter A. Maier, had materialized into radio's largest religious broadcast in a rather short time. His calling it "only the beginning" was both true and false. The sprawling network was far more than a beginning, and yet the next decade would send "Christ to the Nations" across the earth over four times the number of stations in many more foreign lands and languages. Soon the program would become the world's most extensive regular broadcast. Here, then, is an authentic success story, an episode in church, radio, and American history which stands by itself. How can it be accounted for?

Various explanations were offered. Some concluded that the Lutheran Hour had a ground-floor position in religious broadcasting and grew to preponderance accordingly. But NBC's *National Radio Pulpit* was the earliest network religious program and preceded the first Lutheran Hour season by seven years, the resumed second series by twelve. Again, it was suggested that there was little competition in religious broadcasting, few alternatives to the Hour, which therefore flourished in a vacuum. On the contrary, possibly no type of programming was so competitive as religious, since most of it was limited to a Sunday schedule which provided one, not seven, days to bear the broadcast freight. In Los Angeles, for example, seventy-six religious programs were aired on local stations from 7 A.M. to 11 P.M. each Sunday in 1944.[1] Besides the innumerable broadcasts of local church services which crowded the radio dial Sunday mornings in any city were the following national network programs: the *Catholic Hour*, the *National Radio Pulpit*, the *Message of Israel*, the *Church of the Air*, the *Old Fashioned Revival Hour*, the *National Vespers*, the *Voice of Prophecy*, the *Baptist Hour*, the *Pilgrim Hour*, *Wings Over Jordan*, the *Young People's Church of the Air*, the *Radio Chapel*, the *Back to God*

*Hour,* and others. Yet the Lutheran Hour exceeded any of these in broadcast spread, audience size, and response.

Another conceivable explanation was the backing of a mass sponsoring organization within a large church body. But L.L.L. membership was only 25,000 in the early forties, and the Lutheran Church–Missouri Synod then numbered some 1,500,000 members, only 1 per cent of the national population.

Perhaps the professional direction of the broadcast, mass advertising, or smooth scripts were responsible. But we find instead a group of radio amateurs happily violating many of the rules for running a religious program—and with splendid success. Had a professional consultant been brought in, his criticism would likely have been: too much sermon by a person who uses his voice too forcefully, stressing too much the same message of salvation in Christ. Even the name "Lutheran Hour" is wrong: too particularist, narrow, denominational. How can you expect a Methodist, or Catholic, or Quaker to listen to that?

But the surprising end more than justified the means. The speaker, director, and operating committee were amateurs only in the sense that they had never done this kind of thing before. Nor, for that matter, had anyone else in history conducted an international religious broadcast. They were pioneers in an uncharted medium who learned as they progressed and came off with professional results. Credit for these results must be distributed broadly, and no one was more conscious of this than the speaker, who, after God, invariably commended everyone associated with the broadcast, especially the staff and the participants.

## Behind the Scenes

Sponsors for the program throughout its history continued to be the Lutheran Laymen's League, whose support was loyal and dependable. The postmaster of Fort Wayne, genial E. J. Gallmeyer, was L.L.L. president during the crucial early years of the radio venture, which he warmly encouraged, as did his entire organization from board of governors to local members. The League executive secretary, T. G. Eggers, supervised Lutheran Hour headquarters at the Concordia Publishing House buildings in St. Louis. Affable "T.G." carried on a running feud with the editor of the *Messenger* because he allowed him only one or two of the magazine's sixty-eight pages to report each month on Hour progress. But Editor Maier wanted to avoid any "creeping nepotism" which might intrude from one of his careers into another.

In charge of the mail which poured into headquarters was the Rev. Herman W. Gockel, a man whose career was a living example in personal adjustment. Prior to joining the Hour staff, he was forced to resign his pastorate in Evansville, Ind., because concern over his responsibilities as shepherd of souls had affected his throat muscles and progressively interfered with his ability to preach. He now sublimated this concern into a remarkable ministry. For years his pastoral counseling by letter from broadcast headquarters served a congregation immeasurably larger than the one he had left. Today he is an author, as well as program director of television's *This Is The Life,* and his success story appeared in *The Saturday Evening Post* in 1953.[2]

Quiet and conscientious, Wilbur Wiese was, and is, business manager of the headquarters staff. A man who rendered faithful service through the years, Wiese could have capitalized on his administrative talent in the business world, chose instead to remain part of an enterprise he considered far more important. Martin Daib, as field secretary, drummed up financial support for the broadcast within church circles.

Chairman of the Lutheran Hour Operating Committee during formative years of the program was Homer J. Fitzpatrick, distinguished lawyer and close friend of the Maiers. Oscar Brauer and William Fenske also served in spirited manner.

Gotham Advertising Company of New York acted as liaison with the networks and helped publicize the broadcast. Dr. Arthur Kron, president of Gotham, far exceeded the call of duty in helping extend the Hour's domestic spread. His initial business contact with the enterprise ripened into spiritual pleasure as well, and he became a Lutheran convert.

The Hour lengthened its international station log with such apparent ease because Eugene Bernald, president of Pan American Broadcasting Company of New York, was especially active in securing overseas outlets. Himself a consecrated Christian, youthful "Gene" Bernald found Dr. Maier and "Bringing Christ to the Nations" true sources of inspiration in his life. And the man who supervised the pressing of hundreds of transcription disks each week was a self-styled "Lutheran Catholic," W.C. Hutchings, director of World Broadcasting Company's Chicago office.

Unsung heroines of the radio crusade were the host of secretaries and clerks at headquarters who processed the huge bundles of mail arriving from many parts of the world. Their number grew with the broadcast from twenty to approximately one hundred. A receiving staff passed the letters on to the reading department, which referred all correspondence to the appropriate offices. The bookkeeping division kept records on contributions. The personal correspondence staff handled letters which could not be answered with forms, while the mailing division sent out sermon copies and program mementos. The promotional department was responsible for posters, church signs, and similar advertising.

The volume of problem mail was channeled separately. Over the years, Professor Maier was able to classify human difficulties into 400 categories, and when letters fell squarely into these his replies were composed from forms he had prepared. However, all letters which could not be answered accurately in this fashion as well as those dealing with very serious personal or spiritual difficulties found their way to his desk, after transfer to a Lutheran Hour suboffice at Concordia Seminary.

Here Rudy Bertermann was in charge, formerly the Old Testament professor's brilliant class assistant. Before long Professor Maier had the tall, sandy-haired seminarian from Wisconsin working on broadcast matters. One spring afternoon near graduation time, Father saw him in the quadrangle below his office window and shouted, "Rudy, do you have a call yet?"

"Not yet. . . ."

"How would you like a permanent position with the Lutheran Hour?"

"I'd be delighted!"

It was that informal, that simple, but it marked the start of a lifetime association.

Rudy soon married one of Father's pretty secretaries named Ruth and acquired a Ph.D. Beginning as "Dr. Maier's Man Friday," he quickly proved an indispensable assistant in Hour operations, the necessary intellectual, the special counsel in the speaker's "cabinet." Seemingly Rudy was able to serve up a needed fact or statistic relevant to a decision on broadcasting simply by furrowing his brow and consulting the atmosphere. He seemed to thrive on collateral responsibilities. A typical Bertermann day, which began at 6 A.M., might find him dictating replies to a tall stack of letters, huddling with Father, sending off cablegrams to foreign stations, and flying to New York to trouble-shoot the latest network difficulty. Like as not, he would swing through Chicago on the return trip to check plans for a rally there.

Ever fiercely loyal to the man he always called "Dr. Maier" because of their initial teacher-disciple relationship, Dr. Rudy Bertermann was often at Father's side, whether in the privacy of his study or at the major public events of his later life. It was in their closeted discussions that the long-range policy and planning of the program were born. To no one's surprise, Rudy soon moved down to headquarters as chief of the entire broadcast operations with the title, "Director of Radio."

All serious problem mail and important correspondence soon found its way to Father's office, where Harriet Schwenk had the letter stacks readied for "The Boss." He, in turn, would read each communication, pause for a moment to structure his reply, then dictate the core paragraphs at a rapid pace, often leaving the introduction and conclusion to his secretary. She reported his office production as follows:

He read his correspondence eagerly and with amazing rapidity. . . . His mind magnetized the salient points from a letter, an article, a book, a report, a paper, and then vulcanized the facts into his memory. . . . Correspondence poured into his study not in piles of a hundred, but in stacks of linear feet. Yet he could remember isolated personal problems and tell us to look for "a letter from Ohio written in longhand on lined paper," or "a typewritten letter from Wisconsin with the initial 'J' in the upper left corner." Details were photographed in his mind.[3]

Harriet's job in the crowded seminary office became steadily more demanding, as she now found herself the personal secretary for three men: a professor of Old Testament, a magazine editor, and a radio speaker. A given morning might find her typing a Hebrew quiz, pasting up *Messenger* copy, or preparing sermon illustration files, not to mention handling the massive personal correspondence of the Boss. She also supervised the work of two or three additional secretaries, and in her rare spare time, Harriet contributed articles for the *Messenger* and other periodicals. Together with Mother, she also read Father's book manuscripts and proofs. Small wonder that he called Rudy and Harriet "my right and left hands."

Thousands of people away from St. Louis headquarters also worked for the progress of the broadcast. A special manual of instructions was prepared for "Lutheran Hour Keymen" across the country who helped publicize the radio mission. For that matter, anyone who telephoned a fellow citizen about the program was part of the effort, and the record is probably held by a woman in Memphis who made 2,262 calls one fall. Finally, the credits could be expanded to include the Protestant ministry in America, for the speaker commended the ". . . week-by-week help of our pastors and teachers. By their regular parish and newspaper announcements of the broadcast, their repeated endorsement of this endeavor, they have done much to strengthen our cause. To them, as also to the pastors outside our communion who have worked untiringly for the Lutheran Hour, we say, 'Thank you, and God bless you!' "[4]

## Before the Microphones

All program participants served without any remuneration. Tall, mellifluous announcer Reinhold W. Janetzke (now Janning) brought a cultured New England accent and cadence to the broadcast, which sounded as distinguished as the man looked and formed a soothing contrast to the voice which intervened between his opening and closing announcements. Transcribed announcer: L. Menking.

The assistant announcer was KFUO's Elmer J. Knoernschild, who later succeeded Janetzke and remains today the regular announcer and program director. Knoernschild's rich baritone phrasing of cold continuity leaves it vital and warm.

It was Martin Luther who called music the "handmaid of theology," and Lutherans have never forgotten it. Music had always played a prominent role in the program, and policy from the first was to offer only the highest variety. No sawdust melodies from frenzied arpeggios on piano or electronic organ, no gospel guitars, pious accordions, or theological trombones were permitted. Rather, the rich musical heritage of the Lutheran tradition was presented in its most representative form: the chorale, sung by a chorus *a cappella,* or occasionally with pipe-organ and orchestral accompaniment.

Most frequent of the many choral groups heard on the broadcast was the thirty-voice Lutheran Hour Chorus. Composed of Concordia students, the group had a spirited blend which projected chorales with such high technical quality that Fred Waring himself offered warm commendation. During summers, the chorus often went on concert tours throughout America.

Another group heard periodically was the St. Louis A Cappella Choir, a mixed chorus under the baton of noted Bach interpreter, Dr. William B. Heyne. When seminarians were on vacation, the St. Louis Lutheran Hour Chorus supplied the music, a group of laymen under the direction of E. W. Schroeter. And on Sundays when the Hour was aired from a rally in another city, the best local choruses were enlisted, sometimes 2,000 voices strong.[5] The musical ministry of the program evoked a special category of fan mail from listeners, some of whom were initially attracted to the Hour because of it.

Why success? Finally the question could be answered only by the millions who listened and wrote in. Members of the unseen congregation supported the broadcast with their gifts and prayers, and they were ultimately responsible for keeping it on the air. But why *that* program? The great majority of letters which offered any hint as to why the writers listened cited "Dr. Maier," "Dr. Maier's messages," or "the preaching" as the reason for their interest.

Father strenuously objected to personal acclaim for Hour success, insisting it was not his personality, qualities, or delivery which were responsible. His message? Perhaps, but only in so far as that mes-

*Walter A. Maier (1943)*

NELIDOFF

Protestant chaplain, U.S. Army, 1918.

(Top right)
W.A.M. at the microphone of Station KFUO, housed in "an improvised room in the sprawling attic of the seminary." The first broadcast took place on Sunday, December 14, 1924.

(Middle)
"This young prodigy," as the yearbook called him, at Concordia Collegiate Institute, Bronxville, N.Y., 1912.

(Left)
Walter Maier and Hulda Eickhoff on their wedding day, June 14, 1924.

W.A.M. at the throttles of an electric train "layout so extensive it covered nearly half the basement." Walt Junior on the left, the author on the right.

"One luxury could not be dispensed with—hospitality." Here the guests are the Lutheran Hour Chorus. Mother sits beside him; Rudy Bertermann standing behind.

*Father and Mother outside House Eleven, Concordia Theological Seminary.*

*Lutheran Hour Rally, 1949, W.A.M. preaching, Chicago Stadium, capacity 25,000. "Last minute crowds still tried to jam the world's largest indoor arena."*

sage was not his own, but God's word in application. In the forewords to each of his sermon books he reiterated a belief in the divine
factor, that God was using "Bringing Christ to the Nations" for His
own special purposes, and this alone could explain the nearly supernatural success of the venture. "If God were not blessing this broadcast, it would have plodded along or failed long ago," he stated
whenever interviewed. He culled Scripture for verses to neutralize
any personal plaudits. Most cited were: "Not unto us, O Lord, not
unto us, but unto Thy name give glory" (Ps. 115:1); and "He must
increase, but I must decrease" (Jn. 3:30), the passage with which
he usually deflected any praise intended for him. *Soli Deo Gloria*
("Glory to God alone") was the motto toward which he aimed.

Granted the divine factor as the core explanation for Lutheran
Hour success, we must still—unless God is Lutheran—answer the
question: why *this* broadcast, *this* speaker? What was it which
made Walter A. Maier by 1950 the "most heard preacher" in his
tory?

Several studies have been made on this question, including a
600-page treatise by Dr. Kenneth H. Sulston, "A Rhetorical Criticism of the Radio Preaching of Walter Arthur Maier."[6] However,
our problem is only to tease out—far more briefly than this favorable analysis—the three secrets of what evidently were highly
effective sermon preparation, content, and delivery. What was it
which gripped the unseen hearer, sometimes against his will, and
compelled his attention for nineteen minutes of, not suspense,
drama, adventure, but preaching? For many the very word sermon
conjures up a wearisome, one-way discourse, something to be en-
dured rather than enjoyed. But the radio listener does not have to
endure anything, and the sword of Damocles hanging over Father
in his studio was the realization that he was just a flick of the fingers
away from radio silence. Since his earliest efforts at the microphone,
therefore, he tried to develop a sermonic technique which would
make the listener forget about the On–Off switch on his radio—
forget, in fact, that there was a radio.

He took no course in broadcast preaching—divinity schools were
not to offer this until some years later. Moreover, formal instruction
would probably have changed his natural style as little as the Lone

Ranger's impassioned advice. What he developed for radio sermonizing was simply his own, normal, live-audience preaching. All
characteristics of his regular addresses were further honed and re-
fined for use on the air, since here the speaker was not assisted by
appearance, gestures, facial expressions, and the like. Here was only
the naked sermon, and it had to be good. He aimed to preach Christianity in a manner which would instruct, inspire, persuade, and
challenge his hearers without losing them in the process. All the
theology and rhetoric he knew were addressed to this goal, as will
be noted in tracing a sermon from idea to delivery.

*Preparation*

Early in the week, Father arrived at his sermon topic and Scripture text for the following Sunday. The subject chosen would
depend on a variety of factors. Many themes were rooted in the
Christian church year itself: Sundays celebrating Advent, Christmastide, Epiphany, Lent, Eastertide, and the Reformation suggested their own topics. Other subjects were doctrinal in nature,
such as those stressing the existence of God, the divinity of Christ,
the authority of Scripture, the essence of salvation, the hope of
immortality, the nature of faith, love, prayer, the church, and the
like. Another source of themes stemmed from the needs of his
listening audience. A quick review of the mail showed the speaker
what problems were uppermost among his hearers. Thus each
season included sermons on love and marriage, the home, family,
and youth. The problems of fear, pain, guilt, inner peace, immorality, meaninglessness, materialism, and death were other lis-
tener-inspired motifs. Occasionally the letter of but one listener
triggered a topic.

Sometimes the subject or a segment of the sermon derived from
national and international issues which had religious overtones,
and here the newspapers showed the speaker what to stress, how,
and when. Sermon titles from 1930 to 1950 such as "God's Program for National Recovery," "Light for the Lengthening Shadows," "For Christ and Country," "Full Freedom From Fear," "What
is God's Purpose in War?" "The Moral State of the Union," and
"Communism—Its Curse and Cure" were set against the moving

panorama of the depression, recovery, hostilities, postwar problems, and the cold war.[7] In the depression, hope and encouragement were stressed; throughout World War II, national repentance, rededication, and Christian comfort in bereavement; and during the postwar era, the necessity of divine guidance in the face of the Communist threat. Walter Maier recognized that the composite political, social, and intellectual scene was posing questions to Christianity, and he considered it his responsibility to supply answers, as well as to ask modern culture some questions of his own. But, in tailoring his preaching to the times, he did not—as some of his contemporaries—slight religion in the process.

On Fridays, after he had taught his last classes for the week, the professor turned preacher and had Harriet bring out files containing materials related to his subject. These included ideas, illustrations, facts and figures, special theological studies—whatever would help clothe the skeletal outline which was forming in his mind. Probably few preachers have had as extensive a filing system as his twenty-five four-drawer steel cabinets filled with thousands of entries. From student days on, his omnivorous reading "with one eye on tomorrow" had by this time deposited a vast, diversified store of applicable information. His editorship had also required enormous amounts of materials, and the harvest of catalogued data now did double duty. And the file was never static. On the corner of his desk was a continual stack of periodicals, newspapers, and books containing items marked for filing or copying. No sooner did Harriet clip and file one stack than another would appear.

After a brief prayer, the Boss studied the Scripture text he had selected, and its context, in the original Greek if the verse came from the New Testament, or in his beloved Hebrew if from the Old. Next, parallel and supplementary passages were compared, and finally he took a sheet of paper in hand, marked the letters "INJ" (*in nomine Jesu*—"in the name of Jesus") at the upper left corner, and sketched a rough outline of his address, including reference notes to supporting material from the files.

Now the sermon was ready for dictation, and that process, interrupted only by supper-break for a starving secretary, was completed Friday evening. The first draft was then revised Saturday morning, when additions and cuts were made, transitions smoothed, and style polished, resulting in the broadcast manuscript.

In later years Father dictated his sermons in the study at home, and well I remember the scene from watching through the keyhole—Mother had placed the study off limits during dictation time. In the corner chair, furiously attacking her spiral notebook with pointed pencil was Lucille Biehl, who came to House Eleven each week to take down the sermon and type the manuscript, refusing all remuneration as a gift to the Lord's work.[8] Father was pacing back and forth across the room, dictating sentence after sentence in a composed manner, as if glancing at some unseen Teleprompter through the windows. He dictated the punctuation as well, although in speaking the word "comma" we used to think he was just stalling for time in order to formulate his next thought. Occasionally he would stop at his desk, pick up a paper clip, hook it onto another, and move on. The chain of clips grew three or four feet long before he realized what he was doing. A colleague who once sat in on a portion of such dictation estimated that Father walked four or five miles in preparing one sermon. At any rate, the study carpet had to be replaced periodically.

Sometimes his concentration was so intense that he forgot he had dictated several hours on end and that his secretary might be near collapse. At this point, Mother would devise a means of stopping her husband without interrupting him. She would slip a small rug beneath the study door and shove it back and forth until Father's eye caught sight of it and he knew it was time to stop.

The completed sermon manuscript was taken across the street to the residence of New Testament Prof. William Arndt. Scholarly Dr. Arndt was Father's closest friend among the faculty, and he patiently read each of the hundreds of radio sermons his colleague delivered. Such a review assured the author of constructive suggestions, though Dr. Arndt usually gave his warm approval with very few changes.

Parts of Saturday evening and Sunday morning were spent in going through the manuscript orally, rehearsing any tongue twisters, and above all, in checking the timing and cutting. This was no mean task, since Father's final draft was almost invariably 100 per cent longer than he could possibly deliver in the nineteen plus minutes allotted him. The pica typescripts were twenty-two to twenty-four pages long, and even with his rapid delivery he could preach only the equivalent of eleven or twelve. The problem was that the dictating preacher never ceased being the painstaking scholar; if he dealt with a subject, he had to exhaust it. Therefore, in final preparation he had to decide which portions to use, which to sacrifice, and sometimes this decision came as late as the delivery itself. Since all sermons were later published uncut in book form, the extra text was not wasted effort. A comparison of transcribed radio messages and their printed counterparts shows that only supporting materials were surrendered, never main points.

An hour before air time, Father wrote out by hand the prayer which introduced each sermon. About noon Rudy Bertermann stopped by, and the two drove over to the seminary chapel where they prayed with the Lutheran Hour Chorus, then proceeded to KFUO. By now brother Walt and I had returned from St. Stephen's in time to join Father in his studio and assume our "weighty" responsibilities: Walt was official page-receiver—he would quietly take each page of manuscript after Father had finished preaching it—while I was time-signalman—four minutes before the end of the time allotted to the sermon I would hold up four fingers; three minutes, three fingers; and so on down to "CUT," when my arm would come down in a chopping arc.

Now witness possibly the most unorthodox preparation for sermon delivery since John the Baptist. Far from donning cassock, surplice, and stole, Father doffed coat, tie, and shirt, then began flexing his arms and trying out his voice level, dressed in trousers and T-shirt. No one could see into the studio, and he felt that this uniform gave him a desirable freedom of action before the microphone.

One minute before air time he checked his manuscript for pagination, cleared his throat, and chewed down the last Vick's cough drop, chasing it with a gulp of water. Then he led us in a very brief prayer, of which this is typical:

God our Father: Bless this broadcast mightily in the lives of all who hear it, that many may be brought to saving faith in

Thy Son, Jesus Christ, in whose Name we pray. Amen.

After opening announcements, chorale, and prayer, came the final flash of the signal light and time for the message.

*Content*

Since most of the 509 addresses he delivered over the Lutheran Hour have been published in twenty volumes, determining sermon structure is no problem. But because of the number and variety of the messages, only a representative sketch is possible.

Without using a salutation of any kind—he felt that "Dear Friends" or similar greeting would sound too stilted over the air— he launched directly into the introduction. This was usually brief and pertinent, serving to grasp audience attention and weld it onto the rest of the sermon. A startling story, a vivid excerpt from current events, a challenging statement or question served to rouse interest in what would follow. The speaker knew that if his introduction did not snag the ear of a random listener, he would have no second chance at him. After a lead-in paragraph which announced the theme and the Biblical text on which it was based, came the body of the sermon.

The message was structured in two, sometimes three, rarely four parts. One of the typical forms of organization was the problem-solution format, which well expressed both halves of the basic Christian kerygma or proclamation: the story of human sin and divine grace as revealed in God's Law and Gospel. The key communication which he spelled out in every sermon on record was this cardinal double core of Christianity: 1) that human violation of the divine Law is sin, sin which separates man from his Creator, incurring His dangerous displeasure as well as man's personal misery, and which would, in fact, condemn the creature but for the other half of the message; 2) that divine grace is revealed in the Gospel or good news that Jesus Christ, Son of God, atoned for human disobedience by becoming man, suffering, dying, and rising again for mankind, through faith in whom the sinner is justified— made righteous—in God's sight despite his own unworthiness.

Father felt that no Christian sermon was complete unless it expressed Law and Gospel in some form, and such expression constituted the heart of his preaching.

In his "Factors of Persuasion in the Sermons of Dr. Walter A. Maier," Concordia's Lester E. Zeitler charted as follows the distribution of paragraphs in one representative radio address which imply, state, or apply Law or Gospel, however major or minor the reference:[9]

Paragraphs 1  5  10  15  20  25

LAW

GOSPEL

(incidence shaded)

Generally, Law would be accented earlier in the sermon as the problems and needs of the listening audience were uncovered, and Gospel later, as the solution and answer to these needs. However, this was only one theological skeleton of the sermon, and the speaker did far more than elaborate doctrine. He rather brought all his resources to bear on the task of translating theology into a living message which pulsed with importance for people, which sought to persuade them that their relationship to God was the most crucial factor in their existence.

To do this he directed potent appeals to the reason, emotion, and will of any who chanced to tune in. To the intellect he addressed logical proofs of the truth of theism and Christianity in belief and practice, testimonies of renowned authorities in various fields, data, demonstrations, and special information on contemporary affairs which illustrated his train of thought. Regularly summoned was the evidence of past and present leaders in the worlds of politics, business, labor, science, and education to support secondary points in his argumentation. One paragraph, for example, might cite Sir Isaac Newton or Albert Einstein, Immanuel Kant or Robert Hutchins, George Washington or Franklin Roosevelt, and the like. But use of outside authorities never obscured reference to *the* authority in matters of religion: the word of God as revealed in Scripture, and

Father usually averaged one Bible verse per page of his sermons.

Newspaper material was sometimes introduced to add a touch of realism to the logical persuasion. Here his filing system proved of great value, particularly the dossiers of clippings he kept on current problems. If juvenile delinquency surged into the headlines he preached on the improvement needed in home and family life. If divorce captured the news he spoke on the sanctity of marriage. Corruption in business or government, racial bigotry, and the spread of evil isms would call for denunciation by the man who said frequently, "I must keep pulse on human affairs."

Involving the emotions of his hearers was legitimate, he felt, so long as this was done without overemphasis or sentimentality. For human action is too strongly motivated by universal drives and sensibilities to ignore the heart and the feelings of people. Did not Scripture itself refer repeatedly to peace, love, joy, and dozens of other emotions? Therefore in presenting the Christian proclamation he often also employed imagery and emotionally motive terminology.

At climactic sections of the address the will was challenged to respond to the message of the church. While every sermon did not necessarily crest with a literal call to a decision of faith, questions, even imperatives were frequently used to impel listeners toward action and resolve. Unbelievers were invited to accept Christ, believers to lead more consecrated lives, all through the power of God, the Holy Spirit.

The studies of Sulston, Zeitler, and others state that the Maier sermons utilized rhetorical tools with a natural, almost spontaneous effect: example, concreteness, iteration, contrast and comparison, alliteration and imagery, variety and illustration. It was an especially ample and timed used of illustration which intermittently recemented the hearer's attention to the message. However, a key quality of the addresses, they say, is authority: the man spoke with an apparently compelling authority; people could believe him. Introduced on the air each Sunday as "Professor of Old Testament Interpretation and History, Dr. Maier . . ." had credentials enough. But listeners really found these in what and how he preached, as one who earnestly believed his message and wished to share the faith purely out of concern for them. What other motive could he have had? He always insisted that his services to the Lutheran Hour be without remuneration.

The sermon ended with a conclusion which, like the introduction, was pointed and brief. Here the message was summarized, the listener invited to accept Christ, and a final appeal directed to God.

*Delivery*

Even the finest address will fall dismally flat if not projected through effective delivery, and it was Walter Maier's preaching technique which also captured the attention of the public and the fancy of writers who described it. Here are a few examples of journalistic flair:

Doctor Maier . . . locks himself in the studio of Station KFUO on the Concordia campus, strips off his coat and goes in swinging.—*Collier's*[10]

When the humble professor faces the microphone . . . he undergoes a metamorphosis. Gone are his normally soft voice and gentle approach. He shouts. . . . gesticulates emphatically. . . .—*Pageant*[11]

. . . He literally shouts into the microphone at a machine-gun pace. Radio engineers have tried all sorts of tricks to modulate the tone. Once or twice they persuaded him to slow down, but it took the punch out of what he said, people wrote in to ask if he was sick and fan mail dropped off 1,000 letters a day.—*Time*[12]

. . . The words pour out of his mouth—and soul—in a perfect torrent. A manuscript is before him, but often he forgets it as, with eyes closed, he climbs a mountain peak of inspiration and hurls wide and far his thunderbolts of warning to a lost world.—*Christian Herald*[13]

. . . The microphone becomes his audience, and to it he delivers his discourse, pointing his finger at it in stern warning, raising clenched fists toward it as he calls for penitence and spiritual rebirth, shaking his head at it intensely, as though it were the most miserable of sinners.—*The Saturday Evening Post*[14]

Perhaps most succinct was the comment of a Mutual network executive who called his speaking technique "the soapbox delivery of a Harvard script."

The above portraits are fairly accurate, although references to "shouting" and "swinging" are exaggerated. Journalists are prone to embellishment, and mention of Father in some magazines as "the Billy Sunday of the Air" who "bangs away at the microphone," and the like is pure balderdash. Fortunately, we can know exactly how the sermons were delivered, because many of them are recorded on transcription disks, and a sober analysis of these gives the true picture.

The key to his oratorical technique lay in his attitude toward the microphone which faced him. Here was not a wedge of perforated chrome, housing ribbon-foil between magnets converting sonic waves into electrical energy, but the symbol of thirty or forty million ears. And he had the responsibility of imparting the faith to all of them! Some would never before have heard the Christian message, others would hear it never again. Some needed just the proper words of guidance to alter a ruined life, others the solution to a problem which was nagging them away from religion, and still others a fortification of belief. The sense of his responsibility here was somewhat overpowering, hence the earnest prayer in the studio and the surge to address that metallic multiple ear with every shred of eloquence he could muster.

Convinced that the Spirit of God injected power into what he termed his "poor efforts," Walter Maier exerted the fibers of body and voice to send the message off as effectively as he could. Possibly "dynamic urgency" characterizes the sounds which filled the studio and the air. Sometimes pleasing, sometimes not, his voice often reached considerable intensity early in the sermon, violating the usual rule that radio speakers should use the volume level of a living-room conversation. The average rate of his fairly rapid delivery was 130 to 170 words per minute, and at times he introduced variety by raising pitch and volume as a thought cycle progressed, hitting the climax with emphasis, then tapering off for the denouement.

"Dr. Maier's delivery . . . is characterized by prophetic boldness," summarizes Zeitler. "The Gospel is proclaimed as though there were only twenty minutes left to bring millions to Christ. That kind of delivery is powerfully persuasive, for under it lies the ter-

rific earnestness of a dying man talking to dying men."[15] At all
events, the unmistakable thrust of the sermon was toward *you,* not
some other sinner, and once the voice caught hold it was difficult
to shake off. Above all, it never seemed to be reading a manuscript
and so preserved a spontaneous quality which makes any communication more effective.

After my "4-3-2-1" time signals and a rather frenetic "cut" sign,
Father usually got the point and managed his "Amen" some thirty
seconds after he was supposed to have stopped. Instantaneously and
mercifully, the scarlet cue light blackened, and the chorus was
heard on the studio speaker. Program Director Bertermann now
rechecked his stop watch, telephoned the chapel engineer to cut
one stanza from the hymn, and gave the announcer a circular
"hurry-up" signal. He obliged by quickening his pace for the closing announcements, and finally came "Beautiful Savior" with sign-
off at 12:59:59 P.M.

"Whew!" Rudy mopped his brow, "We just made it." Which was
always the way. With radio time eventually costing $1,000 per
minute, seconds counted.

The incidents, humorous and serious, which occurred over years
of programming could fill a separate chapter. One Sunday Walt
and I arrived too late to bring Father's water into Studio C, and he
suddenly found himself with a dry mouth and less than a minute
to go before his sermon. He signaled Elmer Knoernschild for water,
and the announcer was last seen running through the control
room, waving his arms. All he could find was a small vase, which
he hastily filled with water from a tap in the corner. Charging back
to the speaker's studio, he spilled half his burden and burst in with
what was left. To his horror he saw the signal light flash on, while
Father glanced at the dripping vase, then pointed a reproving finger at him and announced into the live microphone for all the nation to hear, "Too little and too late!" Knoernschild turned a horrific white and backed out of the studio. Only later did the shaken
announcer learn that "Too little and too late" were precisely the
first words of the sermon.

Then there was the rare broadcast when nothing seemed to go

right. The chorus came in late, the announcer bobbled a word or two, and between two paragraphs in Father's sermon I had the audacity to clear my throat loudly and intentionally. I was nine years old at the time and wanted to be heard coast-to-coast, in my own way, just like Father. He gave me a magnificent frown and continued preaching. But toward the end of the address he clicked his ring on the lectern, then clicked it again so that I, who had been looking elsewhere, would take notice. There he was, preaching but shaking a final page of manuscript where there should have been three more. I jumped up and searched through his brief case. By now he was at the end of his manuscript and continuing as best he could remember. After a paragraph of extempore, I finally located the missing pages, put them in front of Father, and he picked up again with a broad grin. I knew I had been forgiven for my coast-to-coast cough.

For several years in a row, the Second Sunday in Advent, which focuses on the cataclysms attending the Second Coming of Christ, saw minor upheavals in Father's own life. One Saturday afternoon while playing touch football with us, he slipped and fell on a stone which knocked him unconscious. We covered him with blankets and, to our vast relief, he regained consciousness while we were driving him home. The next day he preached despite doctor's diagnosis of a slight brain concussion.

Exactly a year later, I was out on the same athletic field when Father summoned me home for dinner by calling out in a great voice, "PAU-UL!" The strain caused a slight hemorrhage in a vocal cord, and a throat specialist told Father he would not be able to preach on Sunday. If he did, he might lose his voice for three months. Father pleaded. The doctor finally relented on condition that Mother join him in the studio and warn him to tone down where necessary by touching his arm. That sermon was delivered in a conversational tone, and a host of listeners wrote to find out what was wrong.

The following year Father was in the hospital with a brief, undiagnosed digestive upset, but on Sunday he insisted on being taken to KFUO for his broadcast. He preached, though wrapped in blankets, and was whisked back to the hospital just after his "Amen."

At the close of each radio season, speaker became author by re-polishing his sermon manuscripts and sending them to Concordia Publishing House, together with forewords which portrayed the response to, and growth of, the broadcast. In this manner *The Lutheran Hour* (1931) was followed by *Christ for Every Crisis* (1935), *Christ for the Nation* (1936), *Fourth Lutheran Hour* (1937), *The Cross from Coast to Coast* (1938), *The Radio for Christ* (1939), *Peace through Christ* (1940), *Courage in Christ* (1941), and *For Christ and Country* (1942). The books averaged some 350 pages each, and eleven more titles would follow in the next decade.

Both religious and secular publications gave the books very favorable reviews, as in these excerpts:

. . . sober, sensible, and fervent talks on religion . . . that have moved many people to serious thinking. . . .—*Boston Globe*[16]
. . . a clarity unusual in this day of foggy verbiage.—*Dallas Times-Herald*[17]
. earnest, evangelical, and absolutely sound. . . .—*The Christian Century*[18]
There is splendid muscular Christianity in the book [*Fourth Lutheran Hour*], no wishy-washy sentimentality; there is courageous trust and courage to go forward. . . .—*The Presbyterian*[19]

The books sold surprisingly well for sermon volumes and served as resource materials for many a Protestant minister. Nor were sales limited to the clergy. Aboard a train en route to Chicago, Father chanced to see a man reading one of his books very intently. Stopping to talk with him, he learned that the book was by a "powerful radio preacher." The reader, a dentist, apparently preferred getting back to his book. Though sorely tempted to inquire further about the radio preacher, Father identified himself instead. Blazing with surprise, the dentist placed an order for twenty-five of the books to use as Christmas gifts.

The theology of Walter A. Maier is implicit in these books and explicit in his other writings, ranging from articles on dogma to specialized monographs. Separate studies of his doctrinal position have indeed already been made. Here we need only sketch his theological contribution to American Christianity from the twenties through the fifties.

Maierian theology is perhaps best summarized as traditional Lutheranism expressed in an untraditional manner. "Student Wam" was educated in the conservative Lutheran Church–Missouri Synod, and this was reflected in his message whether voiced or penned. Now a man could react to such a theological heritage in one of several ways: he might become a renegade, claim the church was too traditional, and abandon it; contrarily, he could become a retrograde and join a few narrow-minded schismatics who out-orthodox each other in hunting heresy. But for the vast majority such training produced a ministry in the best traditions of Lutheranism: one which was informed by a Scriptural and doctrinal basis, as well as by the radical and realistic needs of a modern world.

At the forefront of this backward–forward-looking paradox stood Walter Maier. His theology was classical Protestant Christianity, yet he applied it, not in the time-honored terms and cadences of orthodox pulpitry, but in a fresh approach which sought to answer the contemporary concerns of moderns. There was little jargon and no pious pabulum in his message as it interpreted old truths for a new era. But he also maintained that a modern application of the gospel was not to compromise its authenticity.

How did this approach relate to the theological climate of his time? In future years, the first half of this century may well be noted as one of the very determinative periods in church history, not only by reason of the world-wide missionary extension of Christianity and the birth of the ecumenical movement, but also because of the theological struggle between liberalism and conservatism. The thesis of orthodoxy was challenged by the antithesis of liberalism, and whether any synthesis will emerge is yet to be determined.

At its sharpest, the struggle was called the Fundamentalist-Modernist controversy, and for a time there seemed to be no middle ground between what were becoming progressively extreme positions. Modernism sought to accommodate Christian theology to the unsupernatural demands of science and Biblical higher criticism. In the process, however, it often went to the extremes not only of reconstructing God in its own image—instead of vice versa—but much of the historic faith as well. Eventually its concept of salvation focused principally on the solution of social problems through education and a reliance on the "goodness" of man. Fundamentalism countered with a restatement of certain orthodox Christian doctrines as "fundamental" to the faith and rejected Darwinian organic evolution. But as it developed, the movement shifted to extreme literalizing interpretations of the Bible and a polemic attitude toward science and the less-than-orthodox. A Sunday school leaflet from a Fundamentalist church, for example, might date the Creation at 4004 B.C., while its Modernist counterpart could feature a large pussy cat to inspire the Christian virtue of gentleness.

Somewhere right of center between these two extremes, Lutheranism was less sympathetic with the Modernist pole, as could be expected. So also was Walter Maier. In radio sermons and *Messenger* articles he censured what he considered the Modernists' denial of the heart of the Christian faith. One of the considerations which had impelled him into a national broadcast was the opportunity to help satisfy the spiritual needs of masses who, he felt, were receiving only an emasculated Christianity from "pulpit traitors" who had modernized themselves out of the essentials of the faith. And a highly typical excerpt of listener mail during the thirties was this: "Thank you, Dr. Maier, for providing us true Christian sermons once again. The minister in our church has not yet mentioned the name of Jesus Christ this fall."

It is not surprising then, that Professor Maier should defend what Modernists were questioning or denying: the deity of Christ, His virgin birth, resurrection, and second Advent; the inspiration and authority of the Bible; and certainly also the cardinal Reformation emphasis on justification by faith. Only in the sense that he also considered these doctrines "fundamental" to the Christian faith did he occasionally permit himself to be called "fundamentalist" or "essentialist" in his theology, but—especially later on—not "a Fundamentalist." The lower case *f* was preferable for several reasons. The Modernist controversy had not split American Lutheranism as it had the Reformed bodies, and so "conservative Lutheranism" was a far better description of his position.[20] Moreover he could not agree with the excesses of Fundamentalism and its incorrect apocalyptic involvement, which, said he, ". . . sometimes shifted interest from the atoning Christ to speculations in millenarian conjectures."[21] Only twice did he even use the word "Fundamentalist" in any of his books, and then neutrally.

Subsequently the names Fundamentalist and Modernist were abandoned by nearly everyone but the extremists, and the polarity in Protestantism is now termed "orthodox," "conservative," or "evangelical"; and "liberal." Today the two camps tolerate a coexistence based upon mutual intellectual respect. Conservatives appreciate the necessity of confronting issues raised by critical scholarship and a scientific world view, while liberals have favorably reappraised their attitude toward the Biblical heritage of traditional Christianity. What changed the climate?

Theologian Karl Barth, of the University of Basel in Switzerland, sparked a world-wide theological shift from man-centeredness in religion back to God-centeredness. Some American liberals, among them Reinhold Niebuhr, reweighed orthodoxy, found it less wanting than they had imagined, and called themselves "Neo-orthodox." Traditional orthodoxy also shed its late-Fundamentalist excesses, and conservative theologians regained a general hearing.

Moreover in 1930 and from the late thirties on, orthodoxy gained further intellectual respectability on a nation-wide basis when the voice of Harvard-trained, Old Testament Professor Walter A. Maier informed millions in his radio audience that it was *not* passé to believe in the Scriptural concepts of God, Christ, salvation, or the afterlife. To gauge precisely his theological impact in helping conservatism rebuild its good repute after the Fundamentalist-Modernist controversy is, of course, impossible. But the many thousands of letters he received from clergymen, professors, even theologians who were involved in the struggle show that the Lutheran Hour speaker was regarded throughout the country as a champion of orthodoxy, whose influence was multiplied through the many leaders who listened to him. His even broader effect on the laity in those church bodies which were rent by the controversy was undoubtedly great, if the mass mail count dealing with doctrinal problems or expressing gratitude for a revived faith is any indication.

In summary, then, Walter Maier helped provide classic Christianity with an intellectual integrity which was often wanting after its encounter with Modernism. Similarly, Sulston concludes, with others, that Dr. Maier and his church lent to the conservative pole ". . . an intellectual and ecclesiastical respectability which it sorely needed."[22] Later in life he was commended also for his role in furnishing an antidote to the spiritual depression in American church life and helping to revitalize religion.

To this extent, his theology continues its influence today, for Protestant orthodoxy, far from being discredited, continues to grow in numbers, activity, and outreach in world Christendom, and at a rate faster than characterizes the liberal pole.

# 14

## "For Christ and Country"

Seaman L. M. Hinrichs came from Bend, Oregon, a town ninety miles north of Crater Lake near the majestic Cascades. Because he wanted to look beyond the mountains, young Hinrichs joined the Navy and was now seeing the world—or at least that part of the blue Pacific ploughed by his cruiser, the U.S.S. *Honolulu.* On Wednesday, December 3, 1941, the *Honolulu* was due in Pearl Harbor, but as it sighted Oahu the ship received sudden orders to heave to and drop anchor. An unidentified submarine had been detected in the area, and Navy patrols were making a search of the harbor approaches. When nothing was found, the *Honolulu* was permitted to dock two days later. Sailor Hinrichs spent the evening of Saturday, December 6, with friends on a taxi trip around Oahu and then returned to his ship at 11 P.M., since he did not have an overnight pass. Apparently there were too many seamen in port as it was.

Early the next morning the ship's crew went to the mess hall for breakfast, and Hinrichs took a seat near the radio so he could hear the Lutheran Hour, which was broadcast at 7:30 A.M. over KGMB, Honolulu. So it was that choral music from St. Louis accompanied chow, and then a familiar voice, which began, "In a critical moment like the present, when our country gropes on the jagged edge of long, protracted warfare, we ought to realize that neglect of divine instruction. . . ."[1]

"Look, these eggs are bad enough!" objected someone down the table. "Do we *have* to hear a prophet of doom at 7:30 in the morning?"

"Pipe down . . . this guy sounds interesting," countered another, so Dr. Maier was allowed to finish his sermon.

After the "Amen" at 7:55, Hinrichs left mess and went up to the ship's tailor shop. Just as he stepped inside he heard and felt a series of violent explosions which rocked the entire cruiser. He

216

lunged for a porthole and stared unbelievingly at a sky which was alive with Japanese dive and torpedo bombers. Eight battleships of the Pacific fleet docked across the bay were obviously the prime targets, and a ghastly inferno of orange flames was billowing up from where the *Arizona* was supposed to be. And it looked as if the *Oklahoma* were blazing and starting a sickening list to starboard. In the horror of the scene Walter Maier's prophetic words struck him: "present critical moment. . . . America groping on the edge of war. . . ." Now there was no more groping!

Only one seaman was hurt aboard the *Honolulu*, when a dud bomb scored a near miss and was deflected against the hull of the cruiser. But there were ninety-three other ships of the United States Navy in Pearl Harbor on December 7, and many of them were shattered or sunk, carrying away 2,000 American lives and wounding as many others. One injured seaman was insensible for exactly a week but regained consciousness at the strains of the "Mighty Fortress" theme and wrote, "I didn't know the Lutheran Hour was broadcast over a Hawaiian radio station until I woke in a hospital after the enemy attack."

Soldiers at Schofield barracks and sailors on other ships were also listening to Dr. Maier immediately before the Japanese bombardment. A seaman aboard the *Oklahoma* had tuned him in on his portable radio while dressing, and some of his cabinmates climbed out of the sack to listen too. When ship-shivering explosions punctuated that program, the group was awake and alert to meet the horror which followed. The *Oklahoma* had sustained direct torpedo blasts, soon listed badly, and then capsized with a loss of many officers and men. But the cabin congregation was able to abandon ship from the starboard rail, which was nearly awash, and swim over to the *Maryland* docked nearby. A chaplain later informed Father of the warm feelings the men had for the Hour and its spiritual fortification just when life was hanging by a thin thread.

In St. Louis, meanwhile, the person who spoke the last words over the bunk radio before sea water silenced it finished broadcasting and returned home for dinner. That Sunday, Mother and Mabel presented us with a main course of ham and Hawaiian pineapple, which prompted a comment from the head of the table: "You know,

KGMB, Honolulu, must really be getting through. We're receiving a surprising amount of mail from Hawaii, some of it from our military at Pearl Harbor."

After dessert, Walt and I played a cold game of catch on the front lawn, waiting for the dreaded call to wipe dishes, while Father turned on a classical music program from KFUO. Bach's *Toccata and Fugue in D Minor* was playing, and just at the final climax came a nerve-jangling fade-out and the announcer's agitated voice: "We interrupt this program to bring you the news that enemy aircraft have attacked the United States Naval base at Pearl Harbor in Hawaii. . . ." It was about 1:45 P.M.

Father summoned us into the living room and dialed furiously for further news. He called the Associated Press and received confirmation of the attack, plus whatever details were available. Then he went into his study and wrote an entirely new prayer and sermon introduction for the 3:30 broadcast. Less than an hour later he was before the microphone with this supplication:

Heavenly Father, Lord of the Nations: A crucial moment has come for our country with the reports of enemy bombardment; and we flee to Thee for refuge, strength, and the hope of victory. Humbly we bow before Thee to beseech Thy guidance during the heavy days before us. Direct the President, the Congress, and all responsible for the nation's future course along paths pleasing to Thee! Teach us individually to understand that we may be called to sacrifice life's most precious possessions for the defense of America and for the defeat of those who threaten to bring destruction within our borders! O God, who canst still break the bow and cut the enemies' spear asunder, we commit our cause to Thee, as we humble ourselves to confess our sins and for Jesus' sake beseech Thy pardon. Help us in this crisis hour to declare, "If God be for us, who can be against us?" Therefore, O Lord of hosts, be with us now as Thou wast with our fathers! We ask it contritely because we pray in Jesus' blessed name. Amen.[2]

The sermon began rather grimly with the new introduction: "We have just learned that our Pacific fleet at Pearl Harbor in the Hawaiian Islands has been attacked by unidentified enemy aircraft, probably Japanese!" For countless Americans, this was the first news that the United States was now embroiled in World War

11. Soldiers, sailors, and airmen in the radio audience who were on leave called or returned to their bases at once.

Listeners in Denver tuned to the Lutheran Hour but did not get it. The book *December 7—The First Thirty Hours,* by the correspondents of *Time, Life,* and *Fortune,* tells why:

Mutual Broadcasting Co. outlet station KFEL in Denver received a phone call from an irate listener who wanted to know why the Lutheran Hour was canceled. When told that some schedules had been upset by the war news, he snorted, "Do you think the war news is more important than the Gospel?"[3]

From that afternoon on, the life of every American would change, and so would the broadcast, a prospect seen only too painfully soon. The day after Pearl Harbor, the Japanese bombed Manila, taking the city three weeks later. Shortly before the invaders arrived, the management of Station KZRM dismantled its equipment, dynamiting what could not be carried off, and so the Hour's key Far-Eastern outlet was now silenced. XMHA, Shanghai, tried to continue the program for some weeks, but war pressures finally brought a halt to broadcasting in China. Similarly, the projected Dutch programs for Indonesia were precluded by the Japanese occupation, and the opportunities in Australia, India, and Africa halted by military restrictions and communications difficulties. While these doors were closing, others would open, as we shall see.

War itself did not surprise Father, even if the December 7 attack did. He loved history and studied its patterns and trends. When he superimposed these on the broad sweep of current events with which he remained in constant touch, the result was accurate foresight in repeated instances. His was one of the earliest voices in America raised against the dangers of communism, both Soviet and Chinese, as will be noted in a later chapter. Years before the event he also predicted the Arab-Jewish war in Palestine.[4] With even more precision he editorialized as early as 1934: ". . . there is nothing more certain on the horizon of international affairs than this, that there will be a second world war, which in some respects will definitely be more horrible than the first."[5]

His attitude toward the approach of such a conflict was anything but resigned. In *Messenger* editorials of the later thirties he argued for neutrality, urging that America keep out of war. He detested hostilities because of their ghastly effect on humanity as well as the work of the church, and suggested that only communism could benefit from another world war.[6] However, he was not a pacifist and took issue with many liberal clergymen at this time who were. While denouncing wars of aggression, he always maintained that defensive war was necessary and just.[7]

But there was at least one glaring flaw in his otherwise accurate political prediction. Back in the early thirties, Professor Maier, along with some prominent leaders of his day, was deceived by Adolph Hitler. He failed to recognize early Nazism for the menace it was. Certainly he was never pro-Nazi, yet as son of former German nationals, he was understandably against anti-Germans. Because much propaganda against the Kaiser in World War I was later proved factually false, from 1933 to 1935 he made the mistake of thinking that the rising anti-Hitler propaganda might also be exaggerated. Always ready for a good literary fray, and to balance the viewpoint on Germany, the editor carried an occasional article written by German churchmen which, among other things, revealed also a rare favorable facet of Hitler as *Autobahn* builder or one who purged indecent literature and stimulated his nation's economy through public works.[8] Yet he was not blind to the faults even of the early Nazism before Hitler was recognized as a menace. Already in 1934 he criticized the Nazis' marriage policy and, shortly afterward, their youth program.[9]

By late 1935, however, the mask started slipping from the face of Fascism, and Editor Maier reappraised his politics. Mussolini's rape of Ethiopia shocked him, and he registered editorial disgust and serious warning. Two years earlier he had termed his dictatorship a "nightmare of horror."[10] By 1937, the *Messenger* was on record against German, Italian, and Spanish Fascism in articles condemning such totalitarianism.[11] And when he learned details of Hitler's moves against Jewry, an angry professor of Semitics signed his "W.A.M." to an article entitled "The Anti-Semitic Shame," which scored the Nazis for their inhumanity.[12] He declared himself fundamentally opposed to the dictatorship, aggression, and restrictions of liberty, free speech, and worship that marked the Third Reich.[13]

So far as Japan was concerned, he voiced foreboding as early as 1934 over her growing navy and withdrawal from the League of Nations the following year.[14] He was also indignant that American scrap iron, machinery, petroleum, and military staples were aiding what was now obviously an aggressor nation. When the United States belatedly clamped an embargo on such materiel in the summer of 1939, he expressed editorial satisfaction: "Friends of peace, whose indignation has been aroused by the invasion of China, the bombing of undefended cities and the general terrorist practices by the Nipponese invaders, will rejoice in this action, which is unparalleled in American history since the days of the French Revolution."[15]

Just as this was being read, Hitler invaded Poland at the beginning of September. We were still in the Poconos at the time, and I recall Father hearing the news with straining eyes and furrowed brow. That night he paced up and down the portico of the Inn, praying that peace might still be preserved, but knowing that history and power politics excluded that possibility. England and France would not—should not—let Hitler go unchallenged. Mussolini would side in with his fellow Fascist. America's way into Europe had been paved in 1917. And then his latest editorial on Japan came to mind. What if. . . ? Two years later, United States entry into the war came as no shock, only its violent invitation.

In the weeks immediately following Pearl Harbor, Father told Americans via sermons and editorials that regardless of how they felt about war, they were now to defend their land and defeat the enemy with every resource at their disposal.[16] And while he looked upon war as divine chastisement for individual and national sins, the common patriotic goal could be nothing less than victory:

We have been attacked. Our task is to defend ourselves and to defeat our enemies. V indeed must stand for victory, but if it is to be a God-pleasing triumph, it will be a victory based on justice, righteousness, equity, with no room for personal profit, class advantage, or national aggrandizement. May God grant us that victory soon![17]

The war confronted the Lutheran Hour with problems more serious than the loss of key stations in the Orient. Church history showed that Christianity usually did not thrive during hostilities. Perhaps the listening public would dispense with the program as a peacetime luxury in its harried concern with the war. But speaker and staff remembered that the broadcast had been born in one crisis; it was now needed in another, more than ever "for such a time as this." Instead of retrenching, they resolved to expand wherever wartime restrictions would permit, especially in one very vital area: reaching men and women in the Armed Forces.

What follows is the account of a unique ministry, the first time in history that the church's message, aside from the chaplaincy, was delivered to troops fighting on many fronts by one of the most effective means possible under the circumstances. Radio could penetrate sea lanes and air lanes, reaching soldiers, sailors, marines, airmen in any vehicle from jeeps to bombers, in every shelter from foxholes to hospitals, in most encampments from barracks to shipboard, and in every condition from "just scared" to dying. Shortly after December 7, Father observed, "If the broadcast existed only to maintain the spiritual morale of our Armed Forces in this war, it would have been worth all our efforts so far several times over. *They shall not march alone!*"

New domestic stations were now chosen with one eye on their proximity to army camps, air fields, or naval bases. One week before Pearl Harbor, the Hour itself had "enlisted" when for the first time in radio a religious coast-to-coast program originated from a United States Army post, Fort Leonard Wood in the Ozarks of Missouri. In one of his most effective conclusions, the speaker climaxed:

Men of Fort Leonard Wood, soldiers, sailors, air men, marines throughout the country . . . for pardon and strength in your own lives, for the sake of your devoted parents, in behalf of your future husbands and wives, in the name of your unborn children, for our country's defense . . . I ask you, standing in spirit with me beneath the flag of our glorious nation and beneath the cross of our Savior, to repeat this declaration of loyalty:

"I pledge allegiance to the flag of the United States of America and to the Republic for which it stands, one nation indivisible, with liberty and justice for all.

"I also pledge allegiance to the Cross of Jesus Christ and to the faith for which it stands, one Savior-King eternal, with grace and mercy for all. So help me God!"[18]

The words were painfully appropriate. In seven days America would be at war; a few months later some of the very men in that congregation would be casualties.

This was the first of many wartime broadcasts which moved "on location" at military installations on the United States mainland. The Maier double pledge of allegiance evoked enthusiasm from both the military and the general public. Before long it was reproduced in newspapers and magazines, and recited on public occasions. Because of the demand, great quantities of small cards were imprinted with the double pledge and distributed on request.

Surprised at the popularity of his pledge to flag and cross, the author distilled it to motto size. In essence, loyalty was promised to country and Christ. He now reversed the two, for reasons theological and phonetic, and came up with "For Christ and Country." The expression soon became in religious circles what "Remember Pearl Harbor" was in secular.

When the motto reached general circulation, Father became an artist for the only time on record. He designed a small lapel pin which crossed miniature American and Christian flags with staffs constituting a V for victory, beneath which was a scroll embossed, "For Christ and Country." A specialty factory produced the pins in mass quantities for free distribution by the broadcast, and eventually they were worn from Corregidor to Casablanca.

The Lutheran Hour provided servicemen with items far more important than pins. Their letters expressed the need of portable devotional materials which would be light enough to carry anywhere, even into combat. The speaker responded by sending concisely printed copies of requested addresses and then writing his famed *Wartime Prayer Guide*. Measuring less than 3 x 5 inches, the sixty-six-page booklet with durable cover could slip into any pocket of any uniform. Included were special petitions, such as "For Air

Men," "For Chaplains," "Prayer when Seriously Wounded," and the like.

Few pieces of religious literature saw so much action as the *Wartime Prayer Guide*. Demands from home and abroad caused Concordia to publish several hundred thousand copies, and they turned up in duffel, sea bags, and even the jump gear of paratroopers. One copy was found clutched in the hand of a man killed in action. No denominational flavor was attached to the prayers: a Roman Catholic chaplain in Idaho announced at the close of his service on the base ". . . that the Lutherans had published a prayer book for servicemen, and he advised everyone to come to his office for a copy. He was soon out of prayer books . . . ," wrote one reader. The Hour also sent members of the Armed Forces pocket New Testaments, which were generously supplied by the Gideons, a Christian laymen's organization.

Naturally the Maier sermons from 1941 through 1945 often involved wartime motifs and illustrations in dealing with the needs of the day, and the program format was also tailored to the times. In the concluding announcements, listeners were invited to send names of military personnel to whom they wished the aforementioned devotional materials sent. Files were filled with letters of appreciation from servicemen who benefited from this gesture, especially those beyond reach of a chaplain. At the end of each broadcast, the speaker returned to the microphone for a minute and ten seconds to give a personal message to men and women in the Armed Forces, stressing comfort and courage in hardships. Wrote one soldier: "Your last remarks on the program do more for my morale than even a letter from home!"

Reaching the military was not always a simple matter, since some camps were located in sparsely populated sections of America or on foreign soil. Again electrical transcriptions were impressed into service. After negotiations with the War Department, large 16-inch Lutheran Hour disks were dispatched regularly to more than a hundred major United States military installations for local use, as well as to 50- and 100-watt overseas stations erected by the government to serve large troop concentrations abroad. Now the Hour could be heard at such widely scattered bases as those in the Aleutians, Guam, Iwo Jima, or North Africa. Also aired by these stations was another transcription series produced by headquarters entitled *Hymns From Home,* featuring choral favorites by the Lutheran Hour Chorus and a brief devotion by Dr. Maier. These and regular Hour transcriptions were also played weekly over amplification systems in military hospitals, such as Walter Reed in Washington, D.C.

The determination to reach service men and women in a time of crisis was thus high, but was it successful? Unquestionably, it was. The writer-listener ratio was greater in the Armed Forces than among civilians. Whether or not the aphorism is true, "There are no atheists in foxholes," there probably are far fewer than under normal circumstances. Evidently, personal religiosity is heightened in the emergencies of life, for many individuals who had been somewhat indifferent to the church's call now found themselves lending more than a sympathetic ear to the Maier messages. Many thousands of letters from the military bore this out.

They were another breed, these letters. Some arrived by regular post, others by microfilmed V-mail; many were uncensored, others well stamped and cut.

A few of the unreported skirmishes in the war took place when one group of men in a barracks wanted to listen to the Lutheran Hour while others preferred another program or peace and quiet. In a Florida camp, for example, the only radio in one army hut belonged to a corporal, who came in and found three privates lying on their bunks listening to the broadcast. The noncom didn't buy that at all and started shifting the dial. Yet all he could receive clearly on three or four other stations was a preaching Dr. Maier, so, angrily, he left him on. Wrote one of the privates, "That shows the Lutheran Hour is on almost every station, which is swell."

An airman in Iowa would let nothing interfere. He began with enthusiasm:

I haven't missed one of your programs since you started this season. I don't know of anything that I have experienced in my life that gives me the same satisfaction, peace, and assurance. . . . Quite a number of boys in my barracks do not believe in Christ. . . . One got so "brave" that he turned off the current this afternoon, but I have a portable radio, which is a plug-in or a battery set. I just turned it on with the battery with very little time lost, and your program went on just the same.

Elsewhere the Maier voice intruded with less resistance. These lines were written on the rolling deck of a light cruiser sailing off the California coast:

I am happy to inform you that as the program progressed, more and more shipmates huddled closer to listen. When I say your program will always be dialed on our radio every Sunday morning, I am not only speaking for myself, but in behalf of all my shipmates.

Allowing for due exaggeration, military mail nevertheless did report large numbers of listeners. After playing transcriptions on a Pacific troop transport, Chaplain Max Beck wrote that the Hour ". . . was carried over the ship's loudspeaker system and everyone on the boat was able to hear." Back on the mainland in Wisconsin, ". . . radios all over the barracks are tuned to your broadcast." However, the crowning proof of Hour outreach came from the private who wrote: "Even the first sergeant, who does not go to church, stopped to listen. . . ."

The place names in correspondence which somehow escaped the censor's scissors were a glossary of the war: ". . . aboard the U.S.S. *Shangri La,*" ". . . off Iceland in the North Atlantic," " . . . returning victoriously from Tarawa . . . ," "North Africa . . . ," ". . . Anzio," and a thousand others. One note had all the background and props for a future Broadway hit: "We are Seabees in Uncle Sam's Navy, just somewhere in the South Pacific. Some of my mates here expressed the desire to have a copy of your sermon. It was very touching to one of my mates in particular, whose wife had just lost a baby at birth." Richard Rodgers also wrote music for such a setting as this: "Where I am, under the Southern Cross, I, too, would like the small gold cross to wear to serve as a personal inspiration and to encourage the boys whom I, as a surgeon, am treating."

Tragically, there is more to war than humor and distant vistas. Horror, cruelty, suffering, and death are the more characteristic experiences, which macerated millions from 1939 to 1945. For some, religion was the first resort, for others the last. Especially in the extremities of agony, when life boiled down to one or two essentials, a radioed Christianity appeared to have etched itself on some souls. One father in Ohio wrote Dr. Maier: "My son, a sergeant in the 101st Airborne Division, was severely wounded in the Belgian Bulge. . . . As he lay helplessly wounded with shrapnel fire, he asked the Savior, mentioning your name, to spare his life, which He did. He is now home, his wounds healed. . . ."

For others, the only relief from anguish was release from life. One of the most tragic personal accounts in World War II is the story of the lingering death suffered by Lt. Hershel Horton, of Aurora, Ill., which was reported nationally over press and radio at the time. His patrol was cut down by Japanese snipers in the jungles of New Guinea, and while the rest of his men were killed outright, he lay in agony for eleven days with his right leg and hip shattered, just a few yards from the enemy, who thought him one of the corpses. A hole which he managed to scoop out of the ground filled with polluted water to slake his raging thirst, and he began a diary letter to his parents back in Illinois. After ten days of this, the Japanese noticed his movement, shot him again, this time in the shoulder and the neck. Still he did not die for another day, but wrote: "I have a pistol here, but I could not kill myself. I still have faith in the Lord. . . . God bless you, my loved ones! Keep the faith! Don't worry! I shall see you again some day. I am prepared to meet my Maker." When the War Department sent home his personal effects, the Hortons found among them a little gold cross from the Lutheran Hour, to which he listened faithfully. It remains in his family's scrapbook as testimony to a faith which sustained him to the end.

For those who lived, the broadcast served as a spiritual morale-builder. Mail from North Africa, for example, expressed thinking almost identical to that from the South Pacific, where one seaman phrased it clearly:

As I listen to your program, there is something that gives me a feeling of nearness to those I have left behind, for they, too, listen to your sermons, and in that respect we are worshiping in the same congregation; for, as your voice goes out over the air waves, it speaks to them and to me at the same time.

Most succinct was the comment of a front-line lieutenant in France who spoke in the name of his platoon, "If it wasn't for your program we could never stand up under it all."

Christian faith was proving to be a resource of courage and power in wartime crisis. This fact was borne out by chaplains of all denominations and, in the case of the Hour, by mail from every rank of officers and men. The buck private showed it in a letter home or a card to the broadcast. At the opposite end of the rank, General Mark Clark as well as Admirals William Halsey and Chester W. Nimitz also wrote the Hour their appreciation of the spiritual role in the war.

Armed Forces personnel can be very grateful people, and sometimes they expressed thanks also in a tangible manner. A flier with the Royal Canadian Air Force sent $5.00. A Wisconsin mother forwarded a contribution from her son in a Philippine foxhole. A group of servicemen in the Aleutians took a collection of $225.00 for the Hour, while another in Honolulu sent $328.38. Examples by the thousands could be listed. What moved the speaker most, however, was the genre of appreciation luminous in these lines from an infantryman in North Africa: "I do think personally that the interest of the Lutheran Hour in behalf of us boys in some of our darkest hours away from home and on strange soil, will be something long remembered after the present affair has passed."

Some of the most vivid stories, however, involve the enemy as well. Shortly after Pearl Harbor, the Japanese bombed Hong Kong and Singapore, and their invasion of Malaya followed. Finally, on Sunday, February 15, 1942, 85,000 troops surrendered at Singapore in what Winston Churchill has called ". . . the worst disaster and largest capitulation of British history."[19] Among these 85,-000 were Indian forces which had been summoned by the British for the defense of Malaya. On one of the following Sundays, a large group of Indian captives, many of whom understood English, heard an American broadcast in their Singapore prison. Bored

with their jobs, the Japanese guards had chanced to tune in a
Lutheran Hour short-wave broadcast over their radio. The Indians
listened until they determined that a Christian preacher was holding forth. Then they vented their displeasure, inasmuch as they
were Mohammedans from the region which is now Pakistan. A
sergeant major in their number asked that another program be
tuned in. Not only did the Japanese refuse, but spitefully turned
Dr. Maier on much louder! So it was another battle for the radio
dial, only this time *neither* side wanted to hear the broadcast. No
converts that morning![20]

"Bringing Christ to the Nations" reached even the enemy homeland, and far ahead of American forces. A Reformed missionary
who spent eighteen months at a prison camp in Japan had occasional access to a radio. One Sunday he was exhilarated to hear the
"Mighty Fortress" theme over a short-wave band. Following the
broadcast, he memorized the frequency and listened as regularly
as possible after that.

The Hour had a far easier time penetrating to P.O.W.'s in America. Transcriptions of German and Italian programs were cut for use
in the larger prison camps, but plans for Japanese disks were canceled by the end of the war. When letters started arriving even
from enemy prisoners during wartime, possibly the last straw had
been reached in the attempt to make the Hour—with St. Paul—
"all things to all men." The speaker could not help recalling earlier
days and his P.O.W. ministry in Massachusetts, when the approach
had been a good deal tougher.

Many Americans of Japanese ancestry who—in that blot on
United States justice—were removed to relocation camps for the
duration of the war tuned in nevertheless. Typical is this excerpt
from Idaho: "I have been an ardent listener . . . ever since the time
we have been sent to this War Relocation Center at Minidoka."
One Sunday, two residents of another relocation center were employed at a nearby poultry farm, but they warned the manager
ahead of time that they would have to take a half-hour break to hear
a preacher whom they had not missed for eighteen months. The
manager listened too.

World War II also had its "home front." One day Father appeared, wearing an aluminum Civilian Defense helmet and brandishing a fire extinguisher. He had been appointed air-raid warden for Concordia Seminary.

War altered the domestic scene in other ways, certainly, and Father's ministry saw new phases due to such changes. Many defense workers were pleased that the church had followed them to their transplanted locations—or Sunday working schedules—at least by radio. Gasoline rationing did not prevent urbanites from attending church, but in rural areas the situation was different. Typical was a family from North Dakota whose nearest church was 40 miles away. With only an A ration card, it could not make the trip regularly and so gathered around the radio with double appreciation.

One of the most painful, yet essential tasks Father had to perform during the war was to comfort families in his radio audience whose loved ones were beyond communication, severely wounded, taken prisoner by the enemy, missing in action, or killed in defense of their country. Here were the very difficult personal letters he had to write, answering listeners who were crushed, or helpless, or bitter in the face of loneliness and tragedy. Mail like this from a Virginia mother arrived with poignant regularity: "Six stars are in my window, and I have not had any word from any of my sons for so long. All are overseas. . . . pray for them."

But when blue stars turned to gold came the cruelest sorrow. Many listeners took it with noble character, others with less. If ever religion were put to a test, it was in such loss; but if ever the message of an immortal Christ who promised life everlasting applied, it was then. And this is a paradox of the faith: when it seems most difficult it is also most necessary. Expectedly, Father preached on resurrection and life eternal with greater frequency during hostilities.

The war years also saw him at the microphone for special broadcasts apart from the Lutheran Hour. The first time he spoke on a live round-the-world hook-up was in August, 1942, when the British Broadcasting Corporation linked its facilities with the Mutual System in America, the Canadian Broadcasting Corporation, the

Australian Chain, the New Zealand Network, and key short-wave stations in order to beam his message to all continents. The purpose of this special global network, arranged by Pan American's Gene Bernald, was to air his address, "Christianity and War," a discussion of the church's role in the crisis of the day. The Bishop of Chichester, the Rt. Rev. George Allen Bell, followed with the British view.

The transatlantic and transpacific broadcasting conditions were very favorable, as also the time, 7:30 P.M. in London. Response to the program exceeded hopes, as possibly one of the largest international audiences to hear a religious message sent letters from many parts of the world. BBC had given the special broadcast effective advance billing, and the English press devoted considerable space to it. One of the most persistent critics of the American accent or "twang," as he called it, commended Dr. Maier's for being less noticeable than most and applauded his sensible, spiritual approach to the problem of war.

For weeks afterward, masses of mail arrived from places with the most colorful names. The use of the special international broadcast had proved itself, and Father would employ it almost annually for future programs, especially at Christmastime.

The Lutheran Hour could also be heard regularly in wartime Britain via Radio Reykjavik as well as unbelievably ubiquitous Station HCJB down in Ecuador. For English radios HCJB was on the wrong side of the wrong continent near the wrong ocean in the wrong hemisphere, but its short waves came through with a clear, powerful signal. One suburban Londoner wrote:

Many is the time when we have had to leave our beds during a raid, and after the all-clear we have tuned in and picked you up. On one occasion in particular during a severe blitz on my home town, after the all-clear we tuned in and your chorus was singing. I cannot tell you in words what it meant to us at that time. It has been just like the voice of almighty God encouraging us.[21]

Nazi Germany also heard Dr. Maier later in the war. The Office of War Information requested him to prepare religious addresses, which government high-power short-wave transmitters then beamed to the cities and rural areas of the wartime Reich. He himself preached the messages in German. Direct reaction to these broadcasts was impossible of course, but during a postwar visit to Germany, some in the populace were pleased to meet the *Herr Professor Doktor Maier* whom they had heard secretly over American short wave during the war.

From all this the impression might be gained that Walter Maier would no longer speak before anything but a network microphone. This was hardly the case. The years which witnessed Hour growth were also filled with important mass public appearances too numerous to relate but for several illustrations.

One month before war erupted in Europe, he was invited to deliver an address in the Temple of Religion at the New York World's Fair. The mass meeting came off nicely, but it was a little old lady who provided the best story. According to the *New York Times,* she stopped by the Temple before the afternoon service and inquired at the information desk just when she could hear this Dr. Martin Luther preach. The receptionist replied with a twinkle, "I'm sorry, but Dr. Luther has been buried under the pulpit in the Castle Church at Wittenberg, Germany, since 1546." "My, my!" exclaimed the lady, thrown for a loss by her four-century *faux pas.* But, recovering quickly, she asked, "Well, who else is preaching here today?" The receptionist told her it was Dr. Walter A. Maier, so she trotted off to hear him.[22]

A year later, Luther's substitute addressed a throng of 10,000 gathered near the central symbols of the fair, the Trylon and Perisphere. He also spoke to overflow crowds at the Festival Hall of the Golden Gate Exposition on San Francisco's Treasure Island.

These years saw the development of a phenomenon which became an integral part of the "Christ to the Nations" effort—the Lutheran Hour Rally. Its formula was simple: take the usual religious mass meeting in a given city, add special emphasis on the radio mission, feature an actual broadcast, and garnish with sacred music and a little pageantry. What resulted was a religious attraction of the first magnitude. Often the rally began with a live, originating Hour broadcast, in which all participants—announcer, chorus, and speaker

–were on the platform. After air time, the program continued with music provided by mass youth and adult choruses and then crested with another address by Dr. Maier, this time his free-speaking self without manuscript or nineteen-minute restriction.

Although the first such rally dated back to 1930, radio mass meetings were not frequent until later in the decade. Once hostilities had prodded America out of complacency, however, a wartime public summoned Walter Maier to more rallies than he was able to address. Crowds at the major mass meetings were usually limited only by seating capacity, and thousands would often be turned away. From 1941 to 1945, attendance at Lutheran Hour Rallies—some of which are listed here—ranged up to 27,000, depending on auditorium capacity. Most of these were repeated:

| | |
|---|---|
| Boston Garden | New Orleans Municipal |
| Buffalo Stadium | Auditorium |
| Chicago Stadium, | New York Town Hall |
| Amphitheatre | Pittsburgh Memorial Hall |
| Cincinnati Music Hall | Rochester, Eastman Theatre |
| Cleveland Public Auditorium | St. Louis, Kiel Auditorium |
| Denver Municipal Auditorium | St. Paul Auditorium |
| Detroit Coliseum | San Francisco–Oakland |
| Indianapolis Coliseum | Memorial Auditorium |
| Milwaukee Auditorium | Washington, D.C., Uline |
| Minneapolis Armory | Arena, Constitution Hall |

However, mass meetings were not limited to metropolises. Small cities usually went all-out to invite rallies and furnished crowds from 3 to 10,000 strong. Often a substantial percentage of the citizenry attended—Sheboygan, Wis.: 20 per cent; Lockport, N.Y.: 25 per cent; while Bismarck, N. Dak., and Mankato, Minn., each sent 65 per cent of their populations. Occasionally Dr. Maier took to the country as well, and the first Rural Lutheran Hour Rally was held near Waconia, Minn., where 8,000 left their farms for the County Fair Grounds.

Mrs. Walter A. Maier accompanied her husband to many of the mass meetings and often addressed ladies' groups or other organizations on "The Human-Interest Side of the Lutheran Hour." In these talks she related the best stories and humorous anecdotes connected with the broadcast, and so entertained audiences that after forty-five minutes she would try to close, but there was consistent demand for more. Yet her major responsibility, she felt, was to shield her husband against anything from cold drafts to hangers-on. At testimonial dinners and formal banquets, his proudest moment came when he introduced "my beloved, beautiful bride!" Both "bride and groom" were, in fact, holding their youthful looks surprisingly well, give or take a few added pounds.

A classic example of the Lutheran Hour Rally was the series in the Chicago Stadium through most of the forties, especially that of October 3, 1943. The event was a tour de force of planning, to the credit of a committee headed by prominent Chicago businessman and churchman, W. F. Meyer. That fall, fifty strategic billboards advertised the rally, newspapers publicized it, and handbills were posted throughout the Windy City.

Came rally day and the exhausted committee could only indulge a bit of prayerful optimism. Although the program was to begin at 2:45 P.M., people started arriving at noon. By 2:30 every seat had been taken in the stadium galleries, boxes, and on the broad floor, which at other times supported anything from heavy-weight boxing championships to national political conventions. The attendance was now a capacity 25,000, but in the last minutes crowds still tried to jam into the world's largest indoor arena. Emergency seating and standing room were arranged for some 2,000 more, but the rest, estimated by police in the thousands, had to return home and hear the rally by radio. One usher said he had not seen such a throng since the nomination of Franklin D. Roosevelt in 1932.

Father had brought along the whole family for this occasion, including Grossie, who was now living with us at House Eleven. We were ushered through the crowds and along closed concession stands which otherwise would have done a brisk business in hot dogs, popcorn, and pop. Upon arriving at the stadium manager's suite, we were introduced to a friend of Father's who would have a part in the rally program, Governor Henry F. Schricker of Indiana. Gov. Schricker hit it off with Grossie immediately, and for twenty minutes the two chatted as if no one else were in the room.

"*Grossmutter*, aren't you proud of your son? Nearly thirty thousand people coming to hear him!" said the genial governor.

Grossie's eyes twinkled as she lowered her head and replied, "I am very grateful that the Lord is using him in His kingdom, and I pray that He will always keep him humble." Grossie was proud of "her boy," but she was never the doting mother. For her it was a long way from the days in south Boston when milk sickness almost extinguished the life of baby Walter.

Out in the stadium the scene was a little breathtaking. The vast reaches of the sprawling structure were filled with cascades of humanity and the sounds of sacred music played by Al Melgard on the huge stadium pipe organ. Behind the broad platform in front, a choir of 1,200 children and the Chicago Lutheran Hour Male Chorus ranged upward into the balcony, awaiting Director W. Sassmannshausen's downbeat. The stage was decorated with bunting, flowers, and a heroic cross of white chrysanthemums in the center rear. Since the rally motif was the spiritual-patriotic "For Christ and Country," many crossed American and Christian flags were in evidence.

The program began just before air time with announcements concerning radio decorum, for the premier broadcast of the new season was about to begin. Dr. Rudy Bertermann triple-checked the timing, waited for the signal from Station WGN, then cued Announcer Janetzke, who answered with, "Bringing Christ to the Nations—The Eleventh Anniversary Lutheran Hour!" This time the "Mighty Fortress" theme was mightier than ever, since everyone joined in singing it accompanied by the stadium seven-manual ("world's largest") organ. The effect was a bit overpowering.

When the time came for Father's address, he walked to the center rostrum, looking very small against that enormous expanse. Beginning with a tone of determination, he stressed the words leading into his theme:

After a year and ten months of the deadliest war this country has ever fought, we in the United States still have no day of national humiliation before the Almighty. We have observed special days of prayer, but America has not yet been on its knees before the Triune God, confessing its faults and faithlessness. If Lincoln's appeal for repentance and return to the Lord was necessary in 1863, it is a hundred times more imperative in 1943. . . . God alone knows what the future will bring; however, every American, and particularly every Christian, should know that the cry in this present crisis must be the call to repentance

AMERICA, RETURN TO GOD![23]

It was interesting to compare his platform delivery with what we had witnessed many times in the isolation of a broadcasting studio. It was nearly the same, except that here the gesturing arms, the facial involvement, the warning finger, the occasional slight raising of the right foot behind the rostrum were actions of a man clad in tailored navy blue serge, not casual T-shirt. We knew he would pay for this presentable attire in perspiration, and after such public appearances his shirts were damp and had to be changed.

The colossal congregation had learned its decorum well. Except for an occasional cough the stadium was deathly silent during the broadcast, as all eyes and ears were locked into the program in progress. With the broadcast sign-off, however, there was a murmur of relieved shuffling and stretching as the rally proper got underway.

Two hundred servicemen now participated in American and Christian flag-raising ceremonies, with the singing of the National Anthem and Pledge of Allegiance followed by the Lutheran Anthem and Father's Pledge of Allegiance to the Cross. Then the rally assumed more the features of a church service, with Scripture reading, confession of the Creed, and hymns. Again the man in dark blue rose to give the rally address, and this time his words flowed without limitations of manuscript.

After the offering, which raised $15,260 for the broadcast, Gov. Schricker briefly discussed the church in the postwar world, commending the international religious influence of "Bringing Christ to the Nations." Special commemoration was included for servicemen who had made the supreme sacrifice, and the rally closed with prayers and benediction. People seemed almost disappointed that it was over—after two and one-half hours.

For the speaker, the day was far from finished. At least two thousand filed down to the platform to shake his hand, and he cheerfully obliged, claiming that his arm never got tired. After more than an hour of this, with appeals from Mother and stadium lights flashing on and off, Father finally got the message and called it an afternoon.

That evening, a banquet was held in his honor, for the committee had discovered that the next day would mark Father's fiftieth birthday. With five hundred friends at the fete, it was a large conclusion to a large day.

Shortly, most of America learned about the rally. The *Chicago Tribune* featured the Maier address with front-page headlines, copious reporting, and large pictures.[24] *Time* foresaw that the mass meeting would be "the biggest religious event of the year" and had sent correspondents to do a story on Dr. Maier and his broadcast, which appeared two weeks later. Although the newsmagazine had carried articles on Father since 1929, this was its first larger story on his career.[25]

Each time they set foot in Chicago, Father and Mother were accorded an almost regal reception. On future visits for similar stadium rallies, they were lionized at parties and banquets by the city's churchmen. It seems safe to say that their grandest social moments were spent in Chicago, with Cleveland and Detroit tied for a close second.

The following June, the L.L.L. of northern Illinois tendered Father an enormous testimonial dinner in the Grand Ballroom of the Stevens Hotel just after he had concluded the season's broadcasting, and upwards of 1,500 attended. A year later when the Hour entourage was in Chicago for a postwar stadium victory rally, we were all spirited out to suburban Maywood and another gala birthday party for Father. Host was genial Otto H. Amling, Chicago floral prince, who had converted his colorful Flowerland into a glittering birthday palace. It was one of the grand events in any social calendar, and after an elegant buffet—"delicacies last seen in prewar days," chirped a columnist—humorous skits followed, through which Father laughed like a birthday child.

Otto Amling was a rare blend of wealth and wisdom, a man who knew how to enjoy life thoroughly and yet maintain a dimension of spirituality for himself and his family. He contributed substantial sums to the broadcast, but never with any fanfare. A warm friendship with Father had blossomed from the first, and "Uncle Otto" became his official host *extraordinaire* in Chicago, or wherever they might meet across the country. He represents a group of godsends in various cities who provided Father some of the happy hours in which he could regroup his energies. Regrettably, these cannot be listed here, but those to whom he dedicated his books are cited in a note.[26]

The war years augmented the power and population of one city on the eastern seaboard which had been significant enough even in peacetime—Washington, D.C. For years the *Messenger* had a special Washington correspondent, but during wartime some of the editor's activities personally focused on the nation's capital. Just one month before Pearl Harbor, he had led the House of Representatives in an opening invocation. As recorded in the *Congressional Record,* his prayer expressed gratitude to God for America's freedoms in contrast to despotisms abroad, and continued in part:

O Father, keep these legislators keenly mindful of the vital truth that our national preeminences are neither automatic nor irrevocable. More than ever before Thy divine benediction is sorely needed during these torn and twisted years. Thou, the God of our fathers, didst make America great, and only Thou canst keep us great in spirit, in service, in truth. Guard us against arrogant pride. Instead of parading our nation before the eyes of the world as a paragon of political purity, let us contritely confess our own sins. Bring us down on our knees in humble repentance.

As the lowering clouds of bloody conflict gather swiftly and ominously, help us understand that every war, be it ever so necessary and justified, is always a visitation from Thee. . . . Never, we beseech Thee, permit personal prejudices and passions to supplant unbiased judgment and unswerving devotion to the truth. Show us that righteousness alone exalts a nation, that sin is a reproach to any people. Keep the will of the Congress in harmony with Thy divine will.[27]

After he had concluded, several congressmen thanked him for offering an invocation appropriate to the gathering crisis.

Two mass meetings at the nation's capital in October, 1944, saluted the start of the twelfth radio season. The noon broadcast originated with the men of the Air Force at Bolling Field, where an ideal Indian summer day favored the assembly, and later in the afternoon seventy-five hundred Washingtonians crammed the Uline Arena for the rally. Senator Edwin C. Johnson of Colorado introduced the speaker as "the dynamic, eloquent pulpit, platform, and radio orator; consecrated seminary professor; widely known author and editor; profound scholar; understanding counselor; Christian gentleman, yet humble servant of God." What moved Walter Maier and his staff about this tribute was the fact that Senator Johnson had not been primed to say anything like this and had spoken with sincerity.

Busy, wartime Washington took time to value religion at a time of national crisis, and this as well as succeeding rallies there received good coverage in press and radio. The Maier tocsins for the necessity of national repentance were being heard. One day he received a letter from Congressman Brooks Hays of Arkansas, which began:

Members of the United States Congress associated in the weekly gatherings of "The Breakfast Groups" at the Capitol, recognize with deep concern our need of national repentance, prayer and dedication. Our President, his Cabinet and all of us in positions of leadership need the guidance and strength that only God can give. We are joining with other laymen throughout the country for a period of spiritual inventory, prayer and dedication on January 21 through January 23 [1945].[28]

The idea was sponsored by the prestigious National Committee for Christian Leadership, whose executive director, Abraham Vereide, further informed him in an accompanying letter: "The Congressional Committee in charge of this program greatly desire you to be the 'Voice of the American People,' giving the special address at the public meeting in the Departmental Auditorium, Washington, D.C. . . . calling our nation to repentance, prayer and dedication."[29] The cited Congressional committee included Senators Alexander

Wiley and Raymond Willis, as well as Representatives Everett Dirksen, Walter Judd, and John Sparkman. If such national leaders "greatly desired" his address, Walter Maier did not search for alternatives. His acceptance was announced in the House of Representatives.

The speech before the National Dedicatory Assembly was another of the very significant addresses in his career. Present in the auditorium were United States Representatives, Senators, and government officials. The Roosevelt administration and cabinet were represented, as well as leaders of the Washington community.

Evidently the address had arrived in more than one important mind, for Director Vereide wrote, in part:

. . . Your message was re-echoed at the Breakfast Group Meetings both at the House of Representatives and the U.S. Senate. We thank God for you.

A new impetus for the work locally and an inspiration for the cause of Christ at large have been the results of your coming. A new broadness . . . a re-kindling of faith in the Lord Jesus Christ, and new commitments to Him have been registered among the men. We want to assure you of our whole-hearted cooperation in your nation-wide ministry. . . .[30]

These, then, had been years to serve God and government, Christ and country.

# 15

# Meanwhile,
# Back at House Eleven...

"Dr. Maier is perpetual motion personified," commented one of the journalists who interviewed him at home. "I'm amazed that he has time for regular family life." Actually, the situation was not yet that extreme. Because of classroom commitments, the head of the house was absent at rallies only on scattered weekends, and, except for long hours spent in the study, he indulged his roles as husband and father with gusto.

Both our parents were concerned that Walt and I live a normal youth despite the danger that Father's growing recognition threatened to make a goldfish bowl of House Eleven. Occasionally, photographers caught the family in candid shots at home or on vacation, and when these appeared in Sunday newspaper rotogravure, the parents kept a wary eye for any symptoms of swelledheadedness in us, clamping down swiftly when necessary. Sometimes others took care of that. Once when a family photograph was published in the *Hongkong Telegraph,* I was so excited at appearing in print halfway around the world when only ten years old that I called in my neighborhood pals and displayed the prize clipping. Entirely unimpressed, they merely pointed thumbs in my direction and observed dryly, "Ge-et *him.*" I plummeted out of the clouds.

The multifarious activities of Father made for a very exciting youth, and dull days at House Eleven did not exist. What life at home sometimes lacked in privacy because of frequent visitors, it gained in zest and fullness because of them.

By this time Walt had undergone a metamorphosis from teenage Cain-raiser to serious student. High school had done the trick, after which he followed family tradition in graduating as valedictorian of his class and going to Harvard on a scholarship.

Here he now prepared for an eventual career either in medicine or the ministry.

Following him up the educational ladder five years behind was brother Paul, professional adolescent. My most creative efforts at the time were to build an eyesore of a tree house in a precarious oak near KFUO, and fill Walt's large shoes as mischief-maker—with help from profs' kids. The Four Horsemen of the Seminary Apocalypse in my generation were Dick "Destroyer" Hoyer, Gene "Rip" Rehwinkel, Paul "Rocket" Schick, and Paul "Streak" Maier, though our activities were far less delinquent than our names.

Grossie had come to live with us on a permanent basis since the beginning of the war. Silver hair now crowned a face aging with dowager dignity, but her mind remained razor-sharp. At eighty-three, she kept tab on world events and was never a cipher in family mealtime conversations. The day after her tete-à-tete with Governor Schricker in Chicago, Grossie presented Father with the following birthday letter. It would be her last.

My Son Walter,

I thank God that again I am permitted to celebrate your birthday with you, and I would like to give you a very worthwhile gift, one which will never decrease in value. I am always reminded of the Bible passage which was given you at the time of your confirmation as a motto for your life, Ephesians 6, 16-17: "Above all, taking the shield of faith, wherewith ye shall be able to quench all the fiery darts of the wicked. And take the helmet of salvation, and the sword of the Spirit, which is the word of God." In fervent prayer I asked God to grant you faithfulness, courage, and perseverance to use these weapons in His service and to His glory.

In all the following years my prayers accompanied you, and our faithful Lord granted them beyond all hope and expectation. He held His hands in benediction over you; He gave you power and opportunity to preach His word in many lands and languages, and to bring many souls to Him. . . . The Lord gave you many loyal friends, a faithful helpmeet and dear children. . . . I know that your heart is filled with humility and gratitude to Him.

My prayer now is that the Lord would continue to be your Help and Support, and that, even if dangers should threaten our beloved church,

God may protect you from all harm and danger, and that through you many more unbelievers may be made a heritage of the Lord.

Your loving, praying,
*Mother*

One day shortly after this, Grossie was shaken by a violent chill while climbing upstairs to her room. Mother bedded her down immediately and called the doctor, who diagnosed her condition as a heavy cold. The cold worsened, pneumonia set in. We whisked her off to Lutheran Hospital, where she was put under an oxygen tent. Grossie tried bravely to respond and smiled at us warmly through the celluloid of the tent, but no one was more prepared for death than she. One day while sewing, prior to her illness, she noticed how large her stitches had become. Cataracts were forming on both eyes, and she prayed God to take her before she became a burden on anyone, as if that were possible.

Now, over a little bedside radio, her tent opened temporarily, she heard her son's broadcast on the final Sunday of her life. She even commented on his sermon briefly when he returned from KFUO. Two days later, November 30, 1943, with a grieving son and daughter at her side, Grossie passed away peacefully at 3:15 A.M. Just like the Old Grandfather's Clock, her little wristwatch stopped ticking at the same time.

The following Sunday, in the only reference to a family member he ever made in a radio address, a bereaved son portrayed, as a brief sermon illustration, the prayerful passing of the Christian woman who was his mother. After a funeral service at St. Stephen's, in which the Lutheran Hour Chorus sang Grossie's favorite hymns, Father and Mother accompanied her to Boston for final services and interment next to Papa at Brook Farm. In order to be present there on the Sunday following, Father missed his first broadcast in the history of the program, and Rudy read his sermon instead.

"Rothenburg, 1860" was the first signpost on the road of Anna Katharine Maier, and from there it wound a long, hard, colorful way from the Old World of the nineteenth century into the New of the twentieth. Especially in her golden years she knew that common-but-greatest benediction of motherhood: having successful children "rise up and call her blessed" (Prov. 31:28). Six years later, *Grossie* was written with spiritual warmth and wit by Elmer A. Kettner, and published by Eerdmans.

Mother and Grossie had been unusually close, and the last three years had seemed like one extended visit in which their chatting shifted from English to German and back again, but never really stopped. Now the sense of loss might have been a little difficult for Mother, but for the busy atmosphere at House Eleven. As a matter of fact, by this time it was getting *too* busy at home, and she grew increasingly concerned about Father—clearly he was over-exerting himself. As magazine editor, full-time professor, and radio speaker he was literally doing the work of three men. Certainly he had the ability to hold down three positions at once, so long as these were normal posts. But one of them, the broadcast, had multi-plied into something as unsparing in its demands as it was para-mount in importance. Something had to go or at least be lightened. What until now was a youthful face started showing the strain of long night hours of work.

To complicate the problem, his teaching responsibilities had in-creased with the surge in student enrollment, so that by this time he was lecturing to jammed Old Testament sections on a schedule heavier than that of most other professors at the seminary, in addi-tion to serving as Old Testament department head. Since his field was so specialized, younger associate professors and instructors had been hard to find. Yet even though the situation was becoming in-tolerable, he would not complain. Mother, however, and the L.L.L. respectfully suggested to the seminary board of control that some-thing be done to lighten Dr. Maier's professorial load in view of his other responsibilities.

The issue reached the board of directors of Synod, and President John W. Behnken wrote Father that the board approved a solution which was favored by all concerned, especially Father. He would be granted a full and extended leave of absence from teaching so that he might devote his major energies to the Lutheran Hour. How-ever, he could continue to live in House Eleven, use his seminary office, and otherwise maintain regular connection with Concordia. His professor's salary would be reimbursed by the L.L.L., since he received nothing from the broadcast itself. It was a sound solution from every point of view, and Prof. Walter Roehrs arrived in 1944 to take over his sections in Old Testament.

Though relieved, Professor Maier did face his final classes somewhat wistfully. For twenty-two years he had taught his beloved Old Testament in Concordia's classrooms and now wondered whether radio responsibilities would ever let him return to the lecture hall. As it happened, broadcasting involvement only increased, his leave was necessarily extended, and he never resumed teaching.

Further relief came in 1945. After twenty-five years as editor of the *Messenger,* he resigned that position with his silver anniversary issue. Two reasons guided this decision. He had devoted a long term of service to the magazine, it was at peak circulation, and now he had to apply himself full time to the pressures of the Lutheran Hour. There were also several differences with the Walther League executive board. The president at the time objected to what he thought an overcritical attitude toward communism in certain Maier editorials—this was the World War II era of pro Russian sentiment —while the editor disapproved of some of the advertising accepted in the journal. So far as the Communist issue was concerned, in just two short years history would prove Walter Maier dead right.

So ended his quarter-century with the *Messenger,* which had seen circulation climb more than 1,000 per cent and attain a readership of nearly half a million. Through his editorials, "W.A.M." had been enabled to express his thoughts on politics and culture, which necessarily were less accented in his sermons, and so he found a forum for his wider-ranging and secular concerns. Perhaps Editor Maier had tried to do too much with the *Messenger* in making it both a young people's journal as well as a magazine of general interest. However, after he laid down his pen the circulation dropped substantially, and the magazine eventually gave spiritual birth to two successors: a revised *Messenger* which concentrated solely on League affairs, and *This Day* magazine, a church feature and pictorial monthly of family and general interest.

For the first time in his adult life, Father had one job instead of two or three—or did he? That the man was not content unless involved in manifold projects was evidenced anew. He could not abandon his first love, Semitics and Old Testament studies, and now resumed an endeavor which he had started but neglected for lack of time: writing a book on the prophet Nahum.

Another project which he had been tending stemmed directly from his concern with "the family altar"—daily devotions around the dinner table which might include a hymn, Scripture reading, meditation, and prayer. This brief household worship had followed supper in our home ever since its founding, and no pressure of time or presence of guests could suspend it.

Occasionally this made for less-than-solemn situations. On some evenings my neighborhood friends waited patiently outside the back door until we had concluded at the table "so as not to get roped into devotion." Periodically, Father would open the door and heartily invite them inside as if everything were finished. Once they were safely in the kitchen he gave Walt the high sign to lock the door, while I passed out hymnals to an augmented devotional circle.

Usually, however, visitors participated on a more voluntary basis and often arranged such devotions in their own homes. One dinner guest we can never forget, a St. Louis churchman who could do everything for his Lord but carry a tune. While he had a fine speaking voice, singing was quite beyond him. During the devotional hymn, the good man more than compensated for his endowment as a monotone by emitting a booming bass blast which vaguely answered the rhythm, but he himself remained oblivious to any cacophony in our breakfast nook. Although Walt and I tried to think of death and monstrous tragedies to keep from bursting with laughter, we lasted only one verse before we had to cut away from the table and muffle our roars in another room. Somehow able to control himself, Father looked at the rest of his family with a faint half-smile, and this was enough to drive Mabel and Mother away as well, leaving host and guest to finish up in a raucous duet. The man took it all good-naturedly, even if hospitality at House Eleven that evening left something to be desired.

Since few things inject faith into daily life so effectively as family devotions, Father stressed the practice publicly. One day the opportunity arose to further the cause in a special way. Ernst Kaufmann Publishers of New York had been pioneering a new format for home devotional literature: calendar leaflets for each day of the year with a Scripture text and 200-word meditation printed on one side, a prayer and hymn verse on the other. The 365 (or 366) leaflets were housed in a cardboard stand and entitled *Day by Day with Jesus*. The publishers now approached Father in person, asking him to author the series, and he readily consented. He suggested adding a special "Thought for the Day" to the leaflet, a key illustration to make the day's theme more graphic. Again his filing system supplied enough resources for years of writing this annual devotional calendar, which was fortunate since the project required great quantities of material. Each of the twelve *Day by Days* he produced was the equivalent of a 300-page book in the amount of text involved.

Only a few thousand copies were published in 1940, the first year of his authorship, but widening demand over the next decade raised sales to 50,000 copies annually. Father enjoyed writing these devotions as an almost effortless hobby. Although he turned them out in short order, quality control in his production must have been adequate, since each annual *Day by Day* received favorable reviews. The leaflets conducted a separate ministry, especially when recirculated, and some have been republished in tract format and enjoy continuing usage. Record albums entitled *Your Thought for the Day* were also produced, with Maier meditations and hymns by the Lutheran Hour Chorus.

The family gathered around the table remains the most vivid memory of our twenty-three years at House Eleven. The breakfast nook or dining room became a theater of comic relief for a busy head of the house and a workshop for welding family solidarity. Our parents saw to it that mealtime was not merely an ingestive act, but an adventure in conversation to which everyone contributed. Usually it was an animated scene, with each skirmishing to edge his comments into the dialogue. Discussions ranged from exciting new developments in the broadcast to the latest predicaments in which we boys were ensnarled.

As we grew older, Father would prod us into debate on deeper issues, sometimes theological. Walt and I thought this was just a crafty attempt to interest us in the ministry as a career, though

Father claimed innocence. He never made any formal suggestions regarding our future professions, yet when Walt finally announced his decision for the ministry, Father's neutral facade was cut by a vast smile. We found keen delight in challenging something he said in a sermon, but that only pleased him, for it was proof positive that his formidable critics were at least listening to his preaching.

Father made his share of "fluffs" in public and private life, and no one identified them sooner than Walt or I. Occasionally he bungled a phrase in a radio sermon and I cringed for him until he corrected it. Rarely, a wandering negative accidentally added to, or substracted from, an orthodox sentence in his address would transform it into pure heresy.

But social blunders are more striking, and a favorite dinnertime story was this. Once after Father had dedicated a classmate's church in Iowa, a farmer held up the reception line by telling him in detail about the blue ribbons his prize hog had won. To start the queue moving again, Father eased the man over to his host and said, "Pastor Mueller, I want you to meet . . . What's the name, please?" His one-track mind focused only on the prize porker, the good man replied, "Poland-China." The famous breed of pigs was unknown to city-bred Dr. Maier, so he made the introduction, "Pastor Mueller, this is my new friend, Mr. Poland China." The story still lives among Iowans to this day.

Hospitality remained a feature of family life, and nothing proved quite so rewarding as this, since guests at our table often helped stimulate the atmosphere. Important scholars, scientists, churchmen, educators, musicians, businessmen, and foreign dignitaries; yet also good common folk, servicemen far from home, students, and friends were all equally welcome.

Conversations with interesting visitors often resulted in interesting projects. A St. Louis layman and hobby stamp collector, George Snarr, and his wife were having dinner with us when he and Father hit upon the idea simultaneously: why not establish a philatelic project to aid the church's foreign mission program? Used stamps have commercial value even after the United States Mail has washed its hands of them, and in sufficient quantities they brought substantial prices at specialty houses. The effort was publicized, and people were invited to send any used stamps to the St. Louis headquarters of "Stamps for Missions." Soon cartons arrived from different parts of the nation with stamps of every category, though most were canceled domestic. Snarr served as director of the project, and Lutheran Business Women trimmed paper from around the stamps each Friday evening at Concordia Seminary, while a group of students sorted them. The endeavor brought results: Stamps for Missions has $50,000 in its mission fund from sales of otherwise useless bits of colored paper, possesses a horde of unusual issues saved for their mounting value, and undertakes special efforts from its proceeds. Last year, for example, Stamps sent 3,000 Bibles to India and provided funds for Lutheran Hour tracts in Korea.[1]

On another occasion it was a blind lady from Minneapolis, Mrs. Bertha Schroeder, who had dinner with us. A veteran Hour listener, she soon found a unique means of serving it. Some of the blind wrote to the broadcast in Braille, and Mrs. Schroeder, as new director of the department for the blind, assisted in answering such letters. She also transcribed Father's sermons into Braille and prepared other specialized materials, making a blessing of her handicap.

One Sunday our guests were Otto and Katherine Kuntze from California. An indefatigable worker for the broadcast, Otto had some unusual ideas for promoting it. His most successful project was The Lutheran Hour Pencil Club, an organization which advertised the program on pencils along with the slogan, "Tune in —Write in—Tell others." The idea caught on, various branches of the Pencil Club were organized across the nation, and by now 5,154,000 pencils have been distributed with legends in English, Spanish, German, Arabic, Japanese, and Tamil. These practical wood-and-lead Hour announcements have traveled to many parts of the world and resulted in people tuning to the program who might otherwise not have listened, some of whom even joined the church. The distance record probably belongs to a pencil which somehow found its way to Ceylon, where it was left at a bank teller's window. One of the bank officials found it, tuned in the broadcast, and later joined both Pencil Club and church, as did two of his associates.[2]

Father was always ready to help launch any new endeavor which would extend the work of the church. So it was that the founding nucleus of the following organizations met in our home: a Women's League which later developed into the international Lutheran Women's Missionary League, the Lutheran Business Women, Holy Sacrament Church of St. Louis, and St. Luke's Church of Newfane, N.Y.

Other collateral projects stemmed from Father's continuing interest in young people. When time permitted he still addressed Walther League conventions, and also demonstrated a special concern for the Christian ministry to students at institutions of higher learning. Back in 1934, he had been one of the founding fathers of Gamma Delta, the International Association of Lutheran College and University Students, and now saw the organization grow to more than a hundred chapters. For students of Hebrew and the Old Testament he founded '*Aleph Beth Gimel*, Semitics honor society. Other endeavors were also affected by what a colleague called "Wam's spiritual Midas touch."

Requests for public appearances before various academic, civic, business, and religious gatherings across the country continued to grow. He now had to decline an average of thirty to fifty such invitations per week, although he tried to accept one or two because he valued contacts with leaders outside his church.

Sometimes the request was of a more permanent nature, nothing less than a call into other fields of endeavor. Perhaps the most remarkable one had come in 1937. Fashionable and thriving Central Presbyterian Church in St. Louis County was without a minister, and its session warmly invited Lutheran Dr. Maier to fill the post. It was more than an ecumenical gesture, for the Pulpit Supply Committee had listened to him regularly and shared his theological stand. Committeemen assured him that he could, and should, continue as Lutheran Hour speaker in the new position. He much appreciated the good will and confidence of the Central Presbyterians, but replied that theological problems would arise were he to accept such a post. Moreover, he was not ready to part with teaching and so declined the offer respectfully. But he always felt a special warmth for that congregation.

Two years later he was offered the presidency of Valparaiso University in Indiana. This was America's first Lutheran university, and Professor Maier had always shown much interest in it, carrying an annual article or editorial on the school in his magazine and serving on the university board of trustees. The call to the presidency was tempting, for he expected great things of the institution. However, while the post would keep him within the academic community, it would necessarily restrict his broadcasting activities. For such an opportunity he might possibly have traded his Semitics, but he could not abandon the radio enterprise just when it was in fact "Bringing Christ to the Nations." He declined with regret.

Other schools also recognized Dr. Maier, one from the distance of another hemisphere. In 1943 Concordia College and Seminary of Adelaide, South Australia, awarded him the honorary degree of Doctor of Divinity in recognition of his multiple ministries. Two years later he was invested with a Doctor of Laws degree by New York's Houghton College.

A portrait of the man at his prime would show two profiles which do not often coexist in one personality: he was both a vigorous extrovert and a disciplined intellectual. There was no doubt that the man with the jovial face, steel blue eyes, and ruddy complexion loved people. When introduced to them he offered a handshake which Hartzell Spence describes as ". . . monumental. He takes your hand in an iron grip with the sweeping motion employed in Indian wrestling, and follows through with a yank and twist. . . ."[3] He diffused the kind of heartiness which disarms the most timid, and he regularly captured the hearts of children, on whom he lavished pet names. Characteristic of the outgoing personality, he continued to enjoy his little jokes. When preparing to leave somewhere with friends, for example, he would switch hats, planting his own large size eight on the smallest head in the group and not look as it sank down to the man's eyes and ears.

There was also no doubt that he loved the world of the mind, and much of his life was claimed by reading and dictating. "There was rhythm, speed, and drive in Dr. Maier's work," reports Harriet. "He found joy in working and continued in long, sustained periods of production without surcease." Before leaving on a long trip, he usually dictated late into the night, brushing aside suggestions that he get a few hours' rest with, "I can sleep on the train." If he did get tired he would rub his face rapidly and vertically with the palms of his hands, a maneuver which shocked him back to alertness.

Clearly he was an energetic personality in either direction—outgoing or ingoing. What caused the fire, the drive which pulsated through his careers and projects? For one thing, his body was well matched with his character—a sturdy, stocky, 5-foot, 8-inch, 170-pound, muscular frame which answered, perhaps even enjoyed, the demands made on it. This may help to explain his brisk personal pace, his kinesthetic preaching, or his performance in otherwise-fatiguing reception lines. Another clue is the armor-plated will power he could unleash when pursuing a goal, a determination which would brook no wasted time, take no circuitous routes in reaching its objective. The dominant aim in his life was his spiritual mission; for it he harnessed his energy. It was a matter of personal dedication.

The externals and incidentals of life, then, were trivia to him. He had five watches, but rarely wore one. In wardrobe he was anything but a dandy. For years, half his suits were blue serge because a friend in a quality woolen mill sent him the fabric and he could give his tailor a multiple order. Mother had to tell him when to haul out a new suit, when his shoes needed shining, when to get a haircut. He did, however, favor broad-brimmed hats, which were gifts from Texas friends, dark crimson ties, and—his sole item of jewelry—a gold wedding ring.

Similarly, he was not a theological purist. He tolerated such paganisms as Santa Claus, the Easter bunny, Wagner's "Bridal Chorus" or Mendelssohn's "Wedding March," and his unliturgical preference was a black, V-neck preaching gown rather than cassock, surplice, and stole. Only rarely and under duress did he wear a clerical collar. If unusually busy, he was not above stepping outside the back door when the telephone rang so that Mother could answer literally, "He's not in."

But one of the better ways to plumb a personality is to see it under attack. Honor or success tell only part of this life story. Their antonyms also play a role and expose other facets of the man.

# 16

# Cranks, Criticism, and Communism

It was an overcrowded day in March before Professor Maier had been given his leave of absence from teaching. Harriet was readying some correspondence for the Boss, who would soon return from class. Suddenly a man stormed through the office door and thundered, "Where's Dr. Maier?" While catching her breath, Harriet stared at a figure dressed in chinos and a coarse blue shirt, no tie, and then answered, "Why, he's in class lecturing. . . ."

"He's a false messiah preaching a false message!" bellowed the intruder. His black hair complemented two beady eyes, which were focusing on her with wild concentration. "*I* am the *true* Messiah! Look at the nail prints on my hands. And I can show you the slash in my side!"

The frightened secretary glanced at hands which had no print at all. One of them now fumbled in his pocket for a jackknife, which flashed out a 4-inch blade. Carefully the man sat down and laid the knife on the desk before him. Then he threw his hands into the air and exclaimed, "God help me go through with my mission!"

Harriet blanched and said, "But Dr. Maier is out now. He won't be back until. . . ."

"I'll wait for Dr. Maier until doomsday if necessary!"

"Excuse me a moment please," she said, sweeping past him into the hall. She found Rudy Bertermann and told him to call the police, then returned to the dreaded task of humoring the fellow until help arrived.

Suddenly, systematics Professor Laetsch walked in, smiled at the man, and whispered to Harriet in German, "You are in great danger . . . I followed him up here. Keep cool and *don't* cross him, while I warn Dr. Maier." With that he went to classroom E and whispered to his lecturing colleague, "Under *no* circumstances leave this room . . . there's trouble down the hall. Meanwhile, let me have one of your strongest and most levelheaded students." An able-bodied specimen followed Dr. Laetsch from the classroom, and they joined Harriet in a tense wait for the police. The man sat quietly enough, but mumbled menacingly from time to time.

Back at House Eleven, Mother and Mabel were startled when both front and back doorbells rang simultaneously. At each entrance stood police, who asked excitedly, "Where's Dr. Maier?" They had come to the wrong address! Mother directed them to the seminary, but before she could ask what had happened they raced off in their squad cars. Trembling with fear, she telephoned Harriet. With the man glaring at her, Harriet could only comment that it certainly was a cold day for March. Mother detected the duress, asked whether she needed the police.

"Yes . . . immediately!" she said, without arousing suspicion.

"Well, they're on their way. I'm coming too!"

Just then the police burst into the office. After frisking the man for concealed weapons, they found nothing more than the knife. They invited him to come with them, but he refused and kept repeating, "Help me go through with my mission!" Carefully the officers removed their revolvers so the man could not lunge for them in a scuffle and then forced him out of the office. It was no mean struggle, and passing students finally assisted police in working a strait jacket onto the deranged man. He was taken away for psychiatric examination.

As the squad cars were driving off, class recessed and Professor Maier now learned the nature of the trouble "down the hall." Harriet and Mother were a little shaken by it all. Father thanked everyone for maintaining equilibrium, but was concerned about the unfortunate fellow and called the hospital to inquire about his condition.

Sighed Harriet, "Today a possible assassination attempt, and only yesterday we received a picture of a baby named 'Walter Maier Cranford'! These things don't happen unless you're really in the public eye!" At this point it seems the Boss would have preferred obscurity.

Few public figures in American life have not encountered the "crank phenomenon," but famed church leaders are often especially hounded by this problem, since the unbalanced intellect occasionally seizes on religion as a release for pent-up fanaticism. Now with a congregation in millions, the crank problem is somewhat multiplied. Accordingly, Harriet had to learn how to humor the annual crackpot who wandered into the office.

Once she was confronted by a man who wore five sweaters and claimed, "All the troubles in this world are due to those four Volswartzes hanging from the roof of the *Post-Dispatch* building downtown!"

"What in the world are '*Volswartzes*'?" inquired Harriet. Evidently the man thought that was a nasty question, for he started chasing her around the desk. Finally she mastered the situation by announcing, "You know, you're right . . . the world's troubles *are* caused by those Volswartzes!"

The fellow beamed and sat down. Just then the Boss entered his office and a quick-witted secretary made the appropriate introduction: "Mr. Jones, this is Mr. _____, and it seems those Volswartzes are acting up again." Father got the message, and it was the springboard to a harmless bit of counseling which did not require police assistance.

Mother also had to indulge the occasional eccentric at home. One Sunday the bell rang and the door opened on a middle-aged man from Michigan who was a barber by vocation and an eye-fancier by avocation—that is, he had made a lifelong study of eyes because he felt they could see into the future. His research had carried him from fish eyes to birds' eyes, and now he was on the verge of a great scientific thrust into human eyes as well. Surely with all his vast connections, Dr. Maier could supply him with corpses for extracting the human eyes? Mother expressed her doubts, but invited the fanatic *friseur* to hear the afternoon Lutheran Hour broadcast. She was considerably relieved when Father returned from KFUO and just as diplomatically showed him the door.

Another year it was a woman in slacks who wore a long veil, draped madonna-like over her head and shoulders. She had come all the way from Minnesota "to learn from Dr. Maier's own lips how to become a saint." Or the time Mother answered the door and found a strange fist being shaken in her face with the words, "Your husband's sermons contain false doctrine! *I* should know . . . *I* am the Son of God!"

There was also the crank-by-correspondence, rather than in person. Periodically, a few letters would arrive, spelling out in grotesque lettering the news that the writer had personally received a message for Dr. Maier from the Angel Gabriel. Postcards announced apocalyptic conclusions from current events. Some letters, which obviously stemmed from neurotic or psychotic troubles, claimed visions and preached occult philosophies. Others were less than coherent, if not hopelessly meaningless. In such cases Father replied in as sympathetic a manner as possible, then wrote to the minister nearest the troubled individual, suggesting a personal visit for counseling and possible psychiatric assistance. One of the special joys in his ministry was to learn of some instances where such people dramatically improved or were cured following pastoral counseling and psychiatric therapy. After years of broadcasting, however, the file entitled "Religious Fanatics" remained astonishingly small, for such correspondence arrived at the rate of only one per many thousands of normal letters.

A success story is always in danger of becoming a hybrid between Pollyanna and Horatio Alger, a bed-of-roses tale of how the protagonist either sees no opposition, no evil, or banishes it in some painless manner. Such careers—if they exist—are possibly as boring as they are successful. The life of Walter Maier is not one of them, for it has also what Chad Walsh calls "the necessary dash of bitters," the admixture which makes final success virile and worthy.

The man knew bad moments in life, occasional distress, and a few ordeals which tested the fibers of faith, mind, and body. He frequently experienced the bitterness of opposition and criticism. Of course, "To avoid criticism: say nothing, do nothing, be nothing," as some sage has phrased it. Human nature being what it is, the greater the achievement, the more occasion for jealous faultfinding, as well as justified criticism—prices which anyone who would succeed must be prepared to pay. What made them a little high in this case, however, was the fact that a man acting as editor, professor, and radio speaker necessarily invited stricture from three different avenues.

*Messenger* criticism, of course, had been inevitable. When Editor Maier assumed a Jeremiah-like role in pouring inked wrath on what he considered the evils of his day, a few letters would storm in reaction. But this was hardly serious, nothing more than the common fare of all editors worth their salt. The replies to such correspondence were courteous, although occasionally little more could be said in substance than: "While I cannot agree with what you say, I was very much interested in learning your point of view."

In his role as seminary professor, opposition came not from faculty colleagues, most of whom were close friends, but from one or two members of the Concordia Board of Control, the administrative committee which governed the school. In fairness to them it must be stated that they did have a case against Dr. Maier if a professor's total energies were to be directed to his teaching duties and nothing else. Yet Father's conscience and that of the church had by this time summoned him to wider responsibilities, and he was granted a leave of absence, as noted. But now came a letter from a member of the board, which, indiscreetly, he had written on official stationery to express only a personal opinion. It was based on his mistaken conclusion that we were planning to move to permanent living quarters elsewhere, and the core paragraph stated:

This undoubtedly means that you intend to vacate the home on the seminary grounds sometime in the near future. Could you let the Board know as soon as possible *when* this will be? We must make definite arrangements at the present time to relocate and house a number of professors. Therefore we would appreciate an early answer from you.[1]

Father replied that he was "vacating" House Eleven only during the summer and had no plans for moving away from the seminary. He cherished his chair at Concordia and intended to return to it eventually after retiring from radio. Transferring all his personal papers, files, and books elsewhere would entail unnecessary difficulty, and was not justified in view of Synod's decision to let him use the residence.

The board member was not satisfied and joined with one or two others in bringing the case to the 1947 Synodical convention in Chicago. Before Committee Number 1, the large body which dealt with the educational institutions of Synod, the opposition claimed that an increased teaching staff made the seminary housing situation critical, and ". . . at present, Dr. Maier is keeping nine other faculty families out of House Eleven." Immediately the man under discussion arose to protest: "Mr. Chairman, I object. By sheer mathematics it would be impossible for me to exclude more than *one* faculty family!" The committee chuckled en masse and later upheld the position that "Dr. Maier stays in House Eleven," as did the convention.[2]

The opposition he encountered in his own Lutheran Church–Missouri Synod was rare and exceptional, but it smarted, because the criticism came from home. If Maierian theology was "traditional Lutheranism expressed in an untraditional manner," it was only natural that he, as one of his church's leading progressives, should come under attack by the ultra-orthodox. Synod's ultra-orthodox were a dwindling splinter group, but a very vocal one. While they approved the Lutheran Hour speaker's battle with Modernism, they also censured him for addressing non-Lutheran groups and praying with them! Interpreting this as "religious unionism," their heresy-hunting organ, *The Confessional Lutheran,* did Walter Maier the honor of attacking him. Naturally he made no reply, for he would not do battle with brethren of constricted mind.

But just as the one-tenth of one per cent negative radio correspondence cannot typify the listening audience, so this opposition is not in the least representative of the Lutheran church. From president down to least parishioner, probably 99 per cent of Synod was proud of its massive radio mission and its speaker. Lutheran pastors throughout America, many of them Professor Maier's former students, gave the broadcast grateful and enthusiastic support, as did the laity, and on most Synodical church lawns stood a small yellow-and-black sign, "The Church of the Lutheran Hour."

In his capacity as radio speaker, Dr. Maier soon discovered the same thing any parson learns in any parish: there is no such thing as a perfect sermon, pleasing to all parishioners. And with a congregation of millions he had a chance to learn this on a larger scale. A few listeners found too much doctrine in his addresses, others not enough; some, too much Law, others, too much Gospel; a few objected to his involving Christianity in contemporary issues, other critics said he did not do enough of this; some claimed he was preaching above the heads of the people, about an equal number said he was speaking below the intellectuals. And so on, proving the platitude "You can't please everybody," but for the fact that sermons are not, as such, preached to please. While some of the mailéd criticism cut to the quick, the speaker always regarded it as a miracle of grace that so small a fraction of listener response was negative, and he felt there should have been far more.

Occasionally, also, there were differences of judgment with the L.L.L. Lutheran Hour Operating Committee. More than anything else, this was a conflict between idealism and realism. Some of the laymen were hardheaded businessmen who at times wanted to reduce the number of foreign stations in the broadcast network, because some of these brought in comparatively little listener contribution for the expense involved in maintaining them. Countering this view were Doctors Maier and Bertermann, who wanted faith to surmount business considerations and consistently favored increasing the international station log. More than once the speaker had to tell the Committee, "All right, tell me which station you want to drop and I'll raise the money elsewhere." Usually this kept the outlet in question on the log, though he did not win every round. This encounter, however, proved creative: both idealistic faith and realistic business sense were necessary in an enterprise of this magnitude. And just as the speaker and director were sometimes sobered by financial considerations, so the Committee and the L.L.L. were fired by Dr. Maier's contagious faith in the Hour and adopted bold resolutions for expanding it in Europe, Africa, and the Far East.

A separate book could be written on the account of Maier versus communism. One published preliminary study has been made by his secretary and editorial assistant, Harriet E. Schwenk, "Dr. Walter A. Maier's Undeviating Stand Against Atheistic Communism."[3] "Undeviating" does, perhaps, best characterize his attitude, which remained utterly consistent from his first criticism of the movement shortly after the revolution of 1917, to one of his final radio sermons some thirty years later, "Communism—Its Curse and Cure."[4] During the same period, the attitudes of some contemporary politicians and even churchmen can, most charitably, be described as vacillating.

To have opposed communism seems far less impressive today, for ever since 1947, when the Truman Doctrine and the Marshall Plan finally recognized international communism for the menace it is, an alerted United States has registered its own massive opposition. In the twenties and thirties, on the other hand, a few groups of American intellectuals, including certain clergy, as well as some depression laborers flirted with Marxism, and the attitude of the general public seemed a benign indifference. Then, during the early forties, it became patriotic to praise Soviet Russia since she was fighting on our side, and even after the war a heady idealism for a time proposed a docile attitude toward "our Red comrades." Consistent opposition to communism before 1947, then, was less than obvious, and the opposer could even be branded as anything from a fanatic to a Fascist, as will be noted.

Ultimately, it all depended on why a person was anti-Communist. Professor Maier distinctly expressed his reasons, the most important of which was on a level above socio-economic-political ideology. In commenting on the collectivism of the early church, he stated in one sermon:

. . . Saint Luke summarizes, *"They had all things common* [Acts 4:32]." That was real communism. Don't let anyone tell you that the Church opposes communism in itself! The Church has no business to condemn any social, economic, or political arrangements which do not disregard the rights of God and man. If people of their own free will want to abolish private property and share their money, that is their privilege.

With such communism the Church, which is certainly not exclusively the capitalist's friend, or in any way the workman's foe, would have no quarrel today; but it is irreconcilably opposed to the atheism, the ridicule of religion, the blasphemy, the mockery, the persecution, which mark modern Communism.[5]

The difference, then, is between communism and Communism, the free socialistic experiments which arise from time to time and the malignant, military, politico-economic expansionist movement since 1917, which is not free and which aggressively opposes theistic religion. Professor Maier frequently cited Karl Marx' dictum, "Religion is the opiate of the masses," and Lenin's echo, "Religion is a kind of spiritual intoxicant," to demonstrate that the church's attitude is categorical: communism is anti-Christian, Christianity is anti-Communist.

He scored communism also for other reasons. Its anti-religious crusade removed the basis for personal ethics and the independent integrity of character, while its political principles submerged individual rights. Therefore it was to be resisted on a moral and political as well as religious basis. As a citizen he also considered it "fundamentally opposed to the foundations of our American commonwealth and . . . antagonistic to every form of representative government."[6]

He was at Harvard when the Bolshevik Revolution succeeded in 1917-19. Blame for the revolt he deposited squarely at the door of the Czarist regime, whose tyranny, decadence, and corruption had infiltrated the Russian Orthodox church itself. But communism was a very sorry substitute, and henceforth in sermons and *Messenger* articles he sounded a perennial warning against the godless Marxian program of Lenin and his successor Stalin.[7] Immediately after our government officially recognized the U.S.S.R. in November, 1933, the editor penned his classic denunciation of communism, "The Church Will Never Recognize Atheism."[8] Three months later he suggested prophetically that exports of hard goods to Russia could some day be used against America,[9] and as early as 1925 he recognized the Bolshevik danger in China.[10]

Throughout the thirties he continued voicing concern over communism, particularly because he felt that Marxian infiltration

of the United States was a possibility if more educators, churchmen, labor and youth leaders served as dupes of the Communist
party. Significantly, in the very first Hour address at Cleveland he
had noted that ". . . organized atheism, sitting in the high places
of . . . Russia, has supported with official fanaticism the greatest
away-from-God and away-from-the-Bible movement that history has
ever recorded, only to produce the supertragedy of modern times."[11]
And paragraphs on the Marxian menace are found in all his sermon books as well as in each annual *Messenger* volume of this
period.

World War II found the United States and the U.S.S.R. fighting a common enemy, and since it seemed not cricket to criticize
an ally, wartime public opinion in America was moulded to view
only the favorable side of the Soviets. Certainly this was understandable and perhaps necessary in the arena of world politics. But
principle remains principle, and Walter Maier never sacrificed an
inch of conviction before any pressures of the moment. He considered international communism dangerous either as an ally or an
enemy, but ". . . never more dangerous for us than when the masses
of our country regard [it] as harmless and inconsequential."[12] Yet
this opinion could not always be broadcast.

Wartime censorship affected the mass communications media as
well, and one day the Mutual network requested that a copy of
Dr. Maier's weekly sermon manuscripts be forwarded to its New
York headquarters for censorship before each Wednesday. This advanced sermon preparation one week and involved the frequent
ritual of opening a telegram from Mutual on Friday or Saturday,
which read: "KINDLY DELETE THE FOLLOWING WORDS FROM PAGE
—— . . . AND PAGE ——. . . ." Occasionally the wire was one or two
pages long, and in most cases it was references to Russia, the
Soviets, or communism which were censored so as not to offend the
allies.

The pen conveyed the message even if the voice (except at
rallies) could not, and deleted portions were reinstated for the
sermon books. The *Messenger* was not censored, of course, and
each year in the forties saw an article or two on the Marxian
threat.[13] In one of these near the close of the war, the man who had

predicted six years earlier that war would advance the Communist cause now charted the alarmingly expanded boundaries of what Winston Churchill would soon call "the iron curtain." But he also proposed a positive seven-point program to counteract communism.[14] Then, after the war ended, the eastern European satellites orbited perforce into the Soviet universe, and America finally realized the depth of the danger which Walter Maier had foreseen and warned against for a quarter century.

Communist sympathizers usually did not oppose him openly, reacting instead with occasional anonymous cards, unsigned threats, and poison-pen letters. We learned of these only indirectly, since Father never carried his troubles home with him. However, a periodic toxic telephone call at House Eleven, warning him to soften his stand on the Communist issue, alerted us to the problem. Once an anonymous voice breathed off a few threats and snarled, "*Every word* you say over the radio is being recorded to use against you!" To which Father replied with a grin, "Fine! But I'd be glad to save you the trouble by sending you transcriptions of the broadcast!" The voice muttered something and hung up.

To oppose communism is far easier today and requires no talent beyond the ability to read a newspaper. Before Russia made its move in eastern Europe, however, it sometimes demanded an amalgam of clairvoyance and courage. For besides Father and other respectable leaders in church and state, various unsavory groups were also opposing communism in that era, including Fascists, pro-Nazis, and pro-Czarists. Isolationists and the followers of Gerald L. K. Smith or Father Coughlin were also anti-Communist, as were various intellectual reactionaries, fringe groups, race-haters, and radical rightists. Often the slipshod, or malicious, mistake was made of identifying in one heap those whose only shred of agreement was opposition to Marxism, and that for entirely different reasons. Voices were raised, for example, which made the flagrant error of implying that Walter Maier was a Fascist simply because he was against communism, and this on a religious basis.

In July, 1945, Leon M. Birkhead and his organization, the Friends of Democracy, Inc. of New York, sent identical letters to the Federal Communications Commission, the Mutual Broadcasting System, and the National Association of Broadcasters demanding a thorough investigation of Dr. Maier's weekly Lutheran Hour programs, charging that he had disseminated ". . . political and controversial propaganda, much of it in opposition to our government's foreign and domestic policies." The organization further asked Mutual for radio time to reply to what it alleged were Dr. Maier's "anti-Semitic," "pro-German," "anti-Catholic," "anti-rationing," and "Red-baiting" pronouncements.[15] *Billboard* magazine promptly ventured a forecast: "Trade . . . feels that the expiration date of his [Maier's] contract, September 9, 1945, will find him off the air."[16]

Leon M. Birkhead was a Unitarian minister from Kansas City who resigned his charge in order to fight American Fascist tendencies and became director of the Friends of Democracy. The organization did some good in helping unmask pressure groups on the extreme right wing, as well as a few Communist-front efforts on the left. Birkhead himself was a flamboyant figure, whose positive efforts eventually suffered from the very tactics he sought to oppose. Sometimes he resorted to the propaganda misstatements, half-truths, innuendoes, and quotations out of context which were specialties of the right fringe, and, on the other wing, more than once found that he had unwittingly espoused a Communist-front effort, from which he subsequently resigned. This totally unjustified attack on Walter Maier and the Lutheran Hour was a case of watch hounds barking up a very wrong tree.[17]

As the wire services picked up word of the Friends' allegations, a mild furor was generated in several quarters. The Russian Embassy in Washington, D.C., interested itself in the charges brought against Dr. Maier and telephoned Concordia Seminary to make inquiries as to his connection with the school. Meanwhile, the seminary faculty resolved to back their colleague under attack, and letters to newspaper editors from a stunned listening public launched the first wave of protest.

So far as the F.C.C. was concerned, there had been thought at Hour headquarters of mobilizing a defense through Senator Forrest Donnell (Mo.) or even President Harry Truman, who as Senator had befriended KFUO before the F.C.C. But this proved unnecessary. It was only a matter of documenting the Birkhead charges as manifestly false, and Rudy Bertermann flew off to New York with a pile of evidence demonstrating the numerous anti-Nazi, pro-tolerance references in the Maier sermons and articles. There were nearly a hundred such passages in the Hour addresses. These and other materials gave the lie to the irresponsibly false anti-Semitic, anti-Catholic, etc. charges. His opposition to communism, however, Dr. Maier left unrefuted, even if "Red-baiting" was Birkhead's swear-word for it. Obviously, it was another case of erroneously identifying all anti-Communists in America as men of the same stripe.

Mutual's General Manager, Robert L. Sweazy, made a thorough study of the Friends of Democracy's charges, as well as the evidence submitted by Dr. Bertermann and Hour headquarters. His conclusions by letter to the Birkhead organization denied network time to the group since this was neither in the public interest nor dictated by fair play. Numerous inaccuracies were cited in the allegations, quotations out of context, false insinuations, and the like. As to such "evidence" that Gerald L. K. Smith had quoted from a Lutheran Hour sermon, ". . . if any use has been made of Dr. Maier's broadcast material by those you term the 'vermin press,' it has been without his knowledge and consent."[18]

Following suit, the N.A.B. and the F.C.C. also emphatically rejected the Friends' charges. The victory cleared the air for an embattled Walter Maier and demonstrated that a patriotic American could legitimately oppose communism on theological grounds, without being a bigot or Fascist at the same time. Lenin himself foresaw the logic of such a stand when he said, "A dedicated clergyman, being a man of God, is a mortal enemy of communism."[19]

The problem remained, however, that extreme right-wing groups in America, which were anti-Red along with being anti-everything else, occasionally quoted this "mortal enemy" or involved his name —without his approval and to his disgust—perhaps in an effort to enlist support from his national following. The same thing was being done with the names of J. Edgar Hoover and other leaders whose opposition to Marxism stemmed from anything but bigotry.

When such groups quoted "Dr. Walter A. Maier" to prove a point against communism, newspaper readers could draw the implication that he was in reciprocal sympathy with their entire platforms. Even Eleanor Roosevelt, as late as 1949, unintentionally made the same mistake in her widely-syndicated *My Day* column of September 9.

The article dealt with the activities of Lawrence P. Reilly of Detroit, founder and director of an organization called the Lutheran Research Society. Reilly, whom I remember as a likeable student at Concordia Seminary, gave up the ministry for a religio-political career of alerting Christians to the "enemies of religion," Communist and otherwise. His publications occasionally quoted Father, his former professor for whom he had provided office assistance, but soon showed the prejudice-peddling influence of Gerald L. K. Smith. No Lutheran church body had any connection whatever with the Lutheran Research Society, despite its name, and Father wrote Reilly his deep regret that he had been misled by the ultra-rightist approach to anti-communism instead of following a career in the ministry. He also forbade the use of his name or that of the Lutheran Hour in any connection with his activities.

Nevertheless, the Friends of Democracy's attack had misrepresented Father as one of Smith's and Reilly's confreres, and it was Friends' materials which had come into the hands of Mrs. Roosevelt when she was preparing her *My Day* column. Accordingly, she wrote, in part:

. . . Some of the other people whom he [Reilly] supports are Gerald D. Winrod of Wichita, Kan., a minister who is both anti-Catholic and anti-semitic, and Walter Maier, a somewhat fanatic fundamentalist who shortly before V-E day was still insisting that the Germans were a bulwark against Communism![20]

The unfortunate misassociation and nearly-libelous identification were a delayed bolt-from-the-blue, especially since the Friends' attack was discredited and now four years old.

Mrs. Roosevelt's column came as a shock to unnumbered Americans, not least to the immediate family. Walt and I first learned of it while driving along Lake Erie, listening to the radio. The 5 P.M.

NBC news announced: "Mrs. Roosevelt again in dispute with religious leaders. In replying to a reference made to Dr. Walter A. Maier in her *My Day* column, Lutheran Hour officials . . .," and so on. The "again" referred to Mrs. Roosevelt's controversy with Cardinal Spellman that summer over her opposition to federal aid for parochial schools.

Meanwhile a statement in Father's defense had been issued simultaneously by the Lutheran Department of Public Relations in New York City and St. Louis headquarters. He then sent a letter to Mrs. Roosevelt at Hyde Park, expressing regret at the misinformed reference and asking that she publicly retract the statement in her column. The press reported further details of the communication as follows:

I must emphatically disavow your implications when you call me "somewhat fanatic." I thank God that I am fundamental in that I stand unswervingly loyal to the cross of our Lord Jesus Christ. . . . But I deny emphatically being "fanatic." This is a dangerous term, and, I am reliably informed, borders on the libelous.

I expressly disavow any connection whatever, past or present, with the Lutheran Research Society. I am informed that its publication reprinted one of my radio addresses without my knowledge, just as scores of papers in various countries have. The fact that this periodical has quoted sections of one of my messages does not in any sense infer that I am identified with the Lutheran Research Society, or sympathize with the men whom you have listed in your column. . . .

It is also utterly false to declare that "shortly before V-E day" I "was still insisting that the Germans were a bulwark against Communism." This is absolutely untrue, and an examination of my radio messages (all of which have been reviewed by the Mutual Broadcasting System and are now in print) will bear out this statement. Please be fair enough to examine the record. I have denounced Hitlerism widely and unsparingly.

Your late husband thought enough of me to have his secretary telephone me personally, and ask me to come to Washington in connection with the Supreme Court issue.*

---

* The FDR telephone call occasioned one of the very humorous incidents at House Eleven. Mother answered, and the conversation went as follows:

"Is this the residence of Dr. Walter A. Maier?" inquired a distinguished voice.

"Yes. . . ."

The letter concluded with an acknowledgment that Mrs. Roosevelt had, no doubt, been misinformed and only unwittingly had included him in such a reference.[21]

Indeed she had. The Friends of Democracy material on Reilly had been forwarded to her in a letter from the president of another church body, who had neglected to read his enclosure and now wrote Mrs. Roosevelt his embarrassment and regret. A substantial amount of protest mail and telegrams also arrived at Hyde Park.

Eleanor Roosevelt displayed her integrity by publicly retracting her reference to Walter Maier through a later *My Day* column. While reiterating her stand against Reilly's activities, she explained that she had been furnished with entirely erroneous information so far as Dr. Maier was concerned and concluded: "Any misunderstanding of his position might hurt his spiritual leadership."[22]

Back in St. Louis, Father made a concluding statement: "I am deeply grateful for Mrs. Roosevelt's retraction. . . . Now that the matter has been brought to this happy conclusion, I thank Mrs. Roosevelt for her courageous, straight-forward statement and wish her a joyful holiday season in Christ."[23]

In postscript to this episode it should be stated that Lawrence Reilly broke with Gerald L. K. Smith and his approach to anti-communism and has returned to church work.

Walter Maier was not blind to criticism or hardened against it. Whenever there appeared to be a grain of validity to some particular charge, he called in the opinions of colleagues or neutral authorities and weighed all aspects of the issue. If certain objections

---

"This is the White House in Washington, D.C. I should like to speak to Dr. Maier."

Mother paused for a moment, then smiled and said, "Oh, Alvin, you can't fool me! I know it's you." It seems that brother Al from Indianapolis delighted in testing her gullibility each time he came into town by calling under such aliases as Charles Lindbergh, John L. Lewis, or the Duke of Windsor.

"But madam," the voice continued, "this *is* the White House calling Dr. Maier."

"Alvin, now really. . . ."

"I am the Secretary to the President! I wish to speak to Dr. Maier!"

"All right, Alvin, have it your way. Here's Walter."

Father picked up the telephone, and when his smile changed to an embarrassed frown, Mother—well, even the word mortification is not strong enough.

seemed justified he tempered his viewpoint and was grateful that they had been raised.

He wanted to be fair, to see both sides of a problem as clearly as possible. Therefore he could be objective enough to point out rare favorable aspects even of Soviet communism. For instance, his *Messenger* editorial, "Reds Draft Strict Family Laws," impartially credited the Russians with strengthening the home by passing statutes on divorce, illegitimacy, abortion, and pornographic literature which were more stringent than in America. In this respect, he said, the United States could learn a lesson from the U.S.S.R.[24]

But unjustified criticism and carping always hurt. They hurt Walter Maier. Whether from the back by someone presumed to be a friend, or from the front by ideological foes, some of this cut deeper than he would admit. But he never bore a grudge and learned to view such hazards in perspective: they made of life a spiritual battleground rather than a playground, and both church and churchmen are in better condition in combat than at rest.

A hidden resource remained his first and last line of defense: existential reliance on the words, *"If God be for us, who can be against us?"* (Rom. 8:31). He had staked his life to a career for Christ. And the very fact that he was "for God" in this manner signified theologically that God was already "for him." The conclusion had to follow: who, in the final sense, could be against him? He dared to take God at His word.

And so should others, he was convinced, for every Christian had his own good fight of faith. When asked for his autograph, he usually added, below his signature, "Rom. 8,37." Then he would say, "That verse is far more important than my name." People would check their Bibles and read: *"In all these things we are more than conquerors through Him who loved us."*

# 17

# World's Largest Broadcast

All the while, "Bringing Christ to the Nations"—The Lutheran Hour had been radiating over more stations in more nations. The decade of the forties saw the listening audience, mail count, contributions, number of foreign countries served, and headquarters staff double in size; the log of radio stations quadruple; and the number of languages employed increase twelvefold. The war, postwar, and cold-war years provided anything but a settled background in which to extend such an enterprise. Yet, after the master ledger at headquarters balanced out each series with a slight figure either in black or red, the speaker, director, and operating committee united on the annual decision: expansion. "To use every available and suitable station on earth . . ." was an impressive-sounding goal. Only they intended it literally.

*Tenth Season (1942/43)*

Honoring "The Tenth Anniversary Lutheran Hour," from now on the program was aired on a year-round, fifty-two Sunday basis, instead of the October-through-April schedule of previous seasons. Although network expenses were nearly doubled by this extension, twelve-month programming has been in effect ever since. Even if most star-studded shows deserted the radio dial during summer months, the church's message took no vacation, especially in wartime. Dr. Maier now extended his preaching season from October through May or June, while various Lutheran leaders delivered the addresses during the summer segment of the broadcast.

The special wartime role of the Hour during this and succeeding seasons has already been portrayed. Despite restrictions at home and the military loss of key outlets abroad, the tenth series saw the number of stations rise from 346 to 450, and the mail tally mount from 260,000 to 330,000 letters.

World hostilities did not interfere with the penetration of Latin

America, and some of the unusual missionary stories started arriving in greater number. One of them concerned the Rev. J. Reifsnyder, who carried on a remarkable and solitary ministry among the Indians near Tarma, Peru, along one of the Amazon headwaters. Less than civilized, the Indians were at first frightened by the portable radio which the missionary carried with him, wondered what manner of evil spirits resided in the "talking-box." But Reifsnyder translated the odd sounds into a message about the great Christ-spirit who was their Friend, and the choral music also scored a hit with the natives. From then on, gathering around the "Christ-talking-box" became almost a tribal ritual. The missionary was so moved by the phenomenon that he had a photograph taken which he sent Dr. Maier along with the message:

Far in the interior, where few civilized men penetrate, the Red Men gather around the portable radio to hear about the living God. Unconscious of the fact, through the interpreter, you occasionally speak to Indians in the remote regions of the Amazon jungle. The radio messages, true to the Gospel, bring much personal encouragement to me when I am alone in the hinterland among the semi-civilized and savage tribes, sometimes a week's journey or more beyond the bounds of civilization. . . .

Bundles of letters arrived daily from Central and South America, many of them teeming with interest. A member of the Catholic Action in Uruguay helps promote the broadcast, a Colombia medical student inquires, a Jamaican writes the circumstances of his conversion. Sometimes the listener is a bit difficult to classify—a resident of the Dominican Republic begins, "I write you in Spanish, but by nationality I am a Chinese and, of course, born a Buddhist," then states his resolve to study for the Christian ministry! A hamlet elsewhere in that country boasts only one radio, but its owner hangs a supplementary loudspeaker in a grove behind his villa, and each Sunday villagers bring their lunches and assemble beneath the speaker for spiritual dessert courtesy *Cristo Para Todas Las Naciones.*

As mail volume increases, North American listener response now shows total variety. The outreach to the Roman Catholic church continues to expand. A nun contributes her small token from Immaculate Conception Convent; visitors to a Trappist monastery hear a radio tuned to the Lutheran Hour; a Franciscan friar from Ohio finds more genuine Christianity here than in "all the pious piffle" of some other religious broadcasts. A Catholic family in Ontario does not listen to religious programs, "but for some reason we cannot dial you off." A priest in North Carolina tunes in regularly "when not engaged in my own official duties," and writes for copies of sermons he missed hearing. Another priest in South Dakota encourages his congregation to listen to the broadcast in announcements after High Mass. Then there is the story of a twelve-year-old girl who attended a Roman Catholic parochial school on Prince Edward Island off Nova Scotia. She wrote that her teacher, Sister Elizabeth, reminded classes to listen to the Lutheran Hour so that they could discuss it in school each Monday. She wondered if she could have the little gold cross memento. She could, along with a complimentary cross for the good sister.

Many non-Lutheran Protestant clergy regularly ". . . announce your broadcast from my pulpit," or ". . . use some of your material in my sermons." "We have offered prayer for Dr. Maier in our Sunday worship services" is a repeated phrase. Ministers send personal contributions, so do congregations. One Church of the Nazarene pastor even sets up "an offering box in our chapel . . . for the Lutheran Hour," while Presbyterian Dr. John Hawkes in Wisconsin preaches a sermon entitled, "Why We Welcome Dr. Maier to Merrill Today."

Other reports are a simple slice of Americana. A New York City furniture store on Tenth Street, which is owned and operated by Jews, has a loudspeaker over the doorway playing the Hour every Sunday for passers-by who often "stop, look, and listen." An Indian sachem from Missouri shows himself tender yet magisterial: "I love your sermons more than those of any other preacher. God bless you. And let me hear from you, please!"—Chief F. B. Standing Horse. In California it is Maier versus the funnies: "You seem to preach about me every Sunday. You hit me so hard I can't read the Sunday newspaper while you're on the air!"[1]

*Eleventh Season (1943/44)*

Nearly a hundred more outlets were added, bringing the total to 540. As in each series since the second, all graphs pointed upwards, and 335,000 communications were received.

Since these summaries aim to show different facets of response for each season, though all categories would apply to every series, we focus now on conversions. Those who were won for Christianity through the broadcast continued to mount in a total which "only eternity can reveal." Either through their own initiative or referral from headquarters, interested, unchurched listeners were contacted by clergymen and invited to instruction classes, baptism, confirmation, and church membership—by no means always Lutheran. For example, a man ". . . won through your radio mission . . . has now joined Tremont Temple in Boston," while a woman in Maryland ". . . has become a member of Christ's Protestant Episcopal Church" after hearing the program. They represent a host of others.

Some of the circumstances under which faith was born had an extraordinary quality. A number of case histories showed a late decision, as this report from a minister in Maine:

In this town live a brother and sister, the brother eighty-six years old, the sister somewhat younger. As a child the sister . . . began to pray for her brother's conversion. . . . For seventy years she continued her petition to God for the salvation of her brother. About three or four weeks ago, at the close of your broadcast, he switched off the radio and said he wanted to be a Christian. You can imagine the holy joy in that home. . . . a very clear and definite conversion at eighty-six.

Near the end of another life, and under less happy circumstances, this note was sent from the death house of the Massachusetts State Penitentiary. The writer was a murderer who had accepted Christianity after one of the broadcasts and corresponded with Dr. Maier ever since.

I just wanted you and the students to know that I walk and talk with Him day by day, praise God! Remember, I told you I lived a life of crime and, instead of walking the last mile for the State (I was in the death house fifteen months [pending appeal to the Supreme Court]), I am walking the last mile hand in hand with my Savior. . . .

Others gained faith during imprisonment of another kind, as the Arizona woman who wrote from her sanitarium bed: "Dr. Maier, if I never get well, I will say I am glad I had T.B., because it brought me to Christ with your help."

Unusual conversion reports arrived also from the entertainment world. A noted cabaret singer at one of the elite night spots in Quito had become a favorite of the fast, risqué set in the Ecuadorian capital and was leading the life of a hedonist. He recounted:

. . . However, it just so happened—why I did not know then, but now I realize that it was the will of God—that I tuned in HCJB of Quito, which was transmitting the esteemed spiritual program called *La Hora Luterana*. The divine word, the special message which seemed to be directed to me especially, moved my heart immensely. It kept me preoccupied and restless. . . . Then I decided to turn my life into other pathways and, trying to find the best way, I kept on tuning in *La Hora*. After three sermons, . . . falling down on my knees, I accepted the Lord Jesus Christ.

Parallel converts included a well-known singer holding forth at the time in a Florida night club, and a West Coast band leader who sent a $100 check to demonstrate his gratitude.

Probably no happier letters arrived for Dr. Maier than those which told of a husband or wife converted after hearing him. An unchurched husband in North Dakota habitually stormed out of the room when his wife tuned to the broadcast. One Sunday he stayed, but hid behind a newspaper he appeared to be reading intently. Only the pages were never turned. Finally he dropped the pretense, became a regular listener, and joined the church. Conversely, a husband in Pennsylvania tried to win over his unbelieving wife and reported, ". . . after ten years she has finally decided to become one of us. Your sermons helped her make this decision." Many such homes across the nation were gladdened by couples finally united also in one faith.

Unnumbered thousands who had strayed from church but were recalled and reconsecrated formed another category, typified in this message from Michigan: "Some years ago I heard you say that it wasn't enough to belong to a 'church of the air.' I felt guilty, so I went back to my own church, and now I feel that my soul needs are being filled." A Texas rancher ". . . partook of Holy Communion for the first time in eighteen years," while an Ohio businessman returned to church ". . . after an absence of twenty-four years."

Then there was the correspondence which defied classification. A woman in Washington, D.C., wrote that Dr. Maier was the only preacher to which her drinking husband would listen, although the conversion was not quite complete: "He still gets a bottle and hides it in the cellar, but it is a half-pint a week, while formerly it was a half-pint or more a day." A Bostonian, however, used the "beverage of moderation" and reported, "I was sitting in a beer garden when your program came on the air. . . . Please send me a copy of today's sermon." Another less-than-ecclesiastical environment was a pool hall in Kansas where ". . . the owner does not belong to church or attend services, but when it is time for Professor Maier all players must stop and listen quietly to the Lutheran Hour!"

Some of the mail flashed enthusiasm along with humor. A Presbyterian minister from West Virginia noted: "Your messages are so soul-gripping that I am sure God permits Martin Luther to hear, and I am confident that Luther has shouted a joyful 'Amen!' to so many precious truths. . . ." More miraculous would be the request from Ciudad Obregón, Mexico: "May God grant us the privilege of hearing you forever!"

Special honors awaited the speaker in upstate New York: "Did you know . . . about the new society formed at the Potsdam State Normal School, known as 'The Dr. Maier Club'? You are their favorite on the campus." In St. Paul, Concordia College students joined one of two oratorical societies: The Demosthenians or The Maierians. And from Ciudad Trujillo, Dominican Republic, came word, "You have been given honorary membership in our Touring Club, a distinction you merit, and I hope you will accept."[2]

## Twelfth Season (1944/45)

During the history-making months which witnessed the victorious conclusion to World War II, the station total increased to 609. The additions included new FM outlets, a broader concentration in Canada, and reopened opportunities in Africa through six-wavelength station CR7AA in Mozambique, Radio Leopoldville in the

Belgian Congo, and, a year later, superstation CR6AA in Angola. Yet the biggest news of the season was the addition of a forty-six-station Australian network which covered much of the continent, including the island of Tasmania. It was Father's old friend, now-Lt. General William S. Knudsen, who helped expedite the transcription disks to Australia across a wartime Pacific.

The twelfth series, however, began amid shock and concern, for the Mutual network had imposed serious restrictions on all its religious broadcasts, including the Lutheran Hour. Because of certain substandard programs, the Federal Council of Churches had continued agitating against all Protestant radio beyond its purview, and Mutual also wished to eliminate less responsible paid religious broadcasts from its chain. Accordingly, MBS adopted three measures, two of which necessarily affected the very responsible Lutheran Hour as well: 1) all religious programs were restricted to the Sunday morning period concluding with 1 P.M. (Eastern war time); 2) no broadcast was to exceed one-half hour's duration; 3) "No commercial announcements which involve any solicitation of funds will be accepted. Any phrase which suggests, however indirectly, that contributions are desired from the listening audience . . . will not be permitted."

These developments plunged headquarters into a mood of grave concern. With broadcasting expenses met by a generous radio audience, how was the Hour to continue paying its way if listeners should now perhaps conclude that it was being granted free network time? More serious was the apparently less favorable Sunday morning hour necessitated. A large segment of the radio audience had always been composed of good churchgoers who certainly would not—*should not*—forego worship services in order to hear the broadcast instead. While the proposed new time of 12:30 P.M. would not interfere with Eastern church services, Central, Mountain, and Pacific times would each carry the program an hour earlier into a crowded Sunday morning. Until now a second afternoon broadcast for the Midwest and Far West had remedied the difficulty, but now this had to be canceled.

Prominent Hour supporters were alarmed, including several governors who wired their concern to Mutual along with others. MBS was courteous to such appeals—it regarded the Lutheran Hour as a top quality program and gave it the latest possible time slot under the new schedule—but the restrictions had to stand.

The season's opening broadcast, the first under the revised arrangements, was the rally at Bolling Field, Washington, D.C., in October, 1944. That morning Walter Maier awoke prematurely in his hotel suite and paced back and forth with corrugated forehead. His eyes probed nervously out over the awakening capital, and the same tight worry gripped him as it had the evening before his first broadcast in Cleveland, fourteen years earlier. He prayed that the God who had caused the enterprise to succeed in the first place determine whether it had accomplished its purpose and should cease for lack of support, or expand into an even wider ministry. Although the latter now seemed impossible, somehow God could still provide the means. Never did petitions two and three of the Lord's Prayer carry so much meaning: *"Thy Kingdom come; Thy will be done. . . ."*

What happened in the course of the critical twelfth series was astonishing. Mutual's apparently hard policy turned out to be a blessing in disguise. Instead of losing a majority of its audience, the late morning-to-noon program reached an entirely new group of unchurched listeners, many of whom had never before heard the Hour, and a multitude of letters now arrived from religious neutrals. Moreover, much of the churchgoing audience could still tune in the afternoon transcription broadcasts. About 340,000 pieces of correspondence were received, only a slight increase over the preceding season, but far exceeding the number anticipated in view of the restrictions.

Similarly, dropping the contribution announcement caused no insuperable hardship. As it was, the Hour had never harangued its hearers for money, and the statement that the radio mission was supported by freewill offerings had been brief and dignified. Despite the fact that even this was now eliminated, listeners contributed substantially more than in any previous series. Not only did the veteran audience continue its support, but new listeners seemed to sense that their contributions were necessary, and the season even ended with a modest surplus. By all normal rules of radio, this phenomenon should not have occurred, and the speaker could only conclude, "The Holy Spirit assumed full responsibility and touched the hearts of our listeners as never before."[3]

How "Bringing Christ to the Nations" was supported is a separate account in its own right, and we only sketch it here. Network, production, and office expenses of the Hour soared from a $7,000 budget for the second season, to an annual $1,500,000 operation by 1950, or $29,000 per program. Direct listener contributions, unsolicited and solicited, provided about three-quarters of the expenses. The balance was raised through Lutheran congregations, church districts, organizations, rallies, and miscellaneous efforts. Although the budget was expanded each year, the expenditure-receipt balance was very close. Naturally all books were audited regularly by public accountants.

Where did the millions of dollars come from? From one penny sent by a Sunday school child; from the largest personal gift given to the broadcast, a check for $10,000 from the Charles G. Langs of Baltimore, and from every variety of source in between.

Typical of the large contributors, Mr. and Mrs. Lang were dedicated people who regarded the Hour as "one of the greatest missionary endeavors of the church" and wanted to help it as God had blessed them. A familiar name in the pickle industry, the Langs annually sent a check in the multiple thousands along with the request that they not be mentioned as donors. Upon learning of Mutual's restrictions on fund solicitation, Lang wrote Father from his Maryland farm that he would be willing to sell one of his prize bulls, worth $37,500, and forward the proceeds should the broadcast become financially embarrassed.

The vast majority of contributors, however, were of the one- to ten-dollar category, who sent the sum out of appreciation and a desire to help the cause. Some are charged with pathos. After her fiancé died, a Wisconsin nurse sold the linens in her trousseau and mailed the proceeds to the Lutheran Hour. A widow sent the $1.25 found in her husband's pocket when he died; an Iowa mother, the 21 cents in her deceased son's piggy bank. Another mother explained, "The enclosed contribution was sent to me by my son as a Christmas present in his last letter. He was an aerial gunner on a

B-17, but was reported missing over Germany." In the State of Washington, the girlfriend of a Marine killed on Okinawa asked that the money he had sent his parents as a birthday present for her be donated to the broadcast.

Some contributions were raised in unusual ways. One man sent the $20 he received for giving blood. An Illinois housewife hacked five cents a day off her grocery budget, sent the savings, and wrote, "We never feel it." A New York City bus custodian contributed all the coins and tokens he found while cleaning the vehicles and sent a $40 money order, another for $60 several months later, courtesy of money-dropping Gothamites.

Timing was important. Once when the freewill offering sentence was still permitted, a Tennessee listener heard a jingling sound at his radio just after that announcement. "The lower door to my dime bank had mysteriously opened—and piled on the radio were $2.50; so this goes to the continuance of your helpful program."

Usually, however, the gift was more premeditated. One spring afternoon in Kansas, the Herkimer Softball League All-Stars played the Wheaton All-Stars. But before the game, both teams arranged that a freewill offering first be taken for the Lutheran Hour. On a fall morning in South Dakota, a church men's club staged a rabbit hunt and sent the proceeds of $23.77. A choir in Sioux City contributed the collection taken at its annual cantata concert.

Gifts from listeners in foreign countries were lower by comparison, but so were the economies in such lands. Yet the contributed pesos, cruzeiros, bolivars, pounds, gulden, francs, and later rupees, kroner, marks, lire, and other monetary units eventually found their way into significant amounts of American dollars. Sometimes overseas stations paid for themselves, as in Hawaii where the steady contributions of one island listener maintained the outlets in Honolulu and Hilo.

Other income derived from rally collections, memorial wreath cards, an annual Easter seals campaign, annuity agreements—for those who needed the interest from sums donated during their lifetime—as well as bequests for the Hour in wills. Another idea which Father suggested was "Acres for Christ," a plan by which farmers pledged some fraction of their crops to the support of the radio mission. In raising these funds there was no resort to commercialization or pressure.

A less expensive foreign station could be sponsored for as little as $300 a year, and it was not uncommon to receive this amount, together with such covering lines as: "This is from the Adult Bible Class and friends of the Evangelical and Reformed Church, Salem, Oregon. Please let me know the station purchased, so that I can tell the donors where it is located, and we can make special prayer for it." Today, some two hundred stations are supported in similar fashion.[4]

## Thirteenth Season (1945/46)

During the first, turbid postwar year, the International Lutheran Hour took the largest stride forward in its history. Two hundred more outlets were added, raising the total to 809, with new stations in Morocco and the Fiji Islands, as well as the resumption of programming on KZRM and six other Philippine outlets.

With 809 stations, Walter Maier could safely issue this statement: "Our mission of the air is now the largest radio broadcast regularly in use for any secular or religious program, commercial or sustaining."[5] A world record had been set for the broadcasting industry, not by a news commentator, singer, comedian, or actor, but by a minister. To be sure, when the American President or the British Prime Minister addressed the world, the networks for such special programs were larger, but these were not regular broadcasts.

Mail was arriving in massive quantities, as high as 10,000 letters a day, with a season total of precisely 403,367. The St. Louis headquarters staff had a task ponderous enough just with domestic correspondence, but the mounting foreign mail—by this time from seventy countries—involved translation and special attention. The solution came with the establishment of Lutheran Hour branch offices in various parts of the world. Trial offices had already been set up in eastern and western Canada, and their success now sparked the institution of further branches in Rio de Janeiro, Buenos Aires, and Adelaide. Later, other offices were founded on different continents, until there were ten by 1950 (see Appendix II). International correspondence was now handled more efficiently, although important mail was still forwarded to St. Louis.

With letters in the hundreds of thousands, the number of those with vivid stories necessarily multiplied. Father and Rudy Bertermann published brief excerpts of the best of these (without signature) in the *Messenger* and the *Lutheran Layman,* as well as in the forewords of sermon books. Because even these could not provide enough space to feature the least cross-section of mail response, from 1944 on Rudy edited a new periodical, *The Lutheran Hour News,* which also contained pictures and news stories on the broadcast. And still the sermon book forewords fattened with publication of "only the most representative" letter excerpts until a publishers'-nerves-shattering total of eighty-two pages of foreword appeared in one of the later volumes!

The problem-mail category related every variety of difficulty which can harass humanity. Multitudes which had no spiritual guide were counseled by letter and, where possible, by visits from an alerted pastor. A twenty-one-year-old from Minnesota asks if it would be wrong for her to marry a thirty-five-year-old Filipino whom she deeply loves. A woman in Quebec wonders whether it was a sin for her to institutionalize a twelve-year-old son who is mentally retarded. A freshman at the University of Oklahoma is troubled by the problem of creation versus evolution. An anguished Ohio listener seeks solace because "they are going to electrocute my brother." (His wife had jilted him, so he shot and killed her as well as a son who tried to wrest the gun away from him.) Asks the sister, "Please advise me what to do, and do you think his soul will be saved, doing what he did and dying like this?"

Doctrinal questions are posed. An Alabama listener never joined a church because he could not claim any visions of angels or burning fire or other conversion experiences demanded by the local sect. Could he still be saved? Queries like "How can I understand the Trinity?". . . . "Was Jesus really God?". . . . "What is the true church?" regularly appear. On a higher level, professors, scientists, and even theologians discuss problems of the faith.

Particularly painful were the wounds of war which would not heal:

I lost my only child in this war. He was such a good son. Nevertheless, he was killed. Why? Others whom I know to be worthless came home with not a scratch. It makes me wonder why people are foolish enough to have children. I know you won't agree with me. I have gone as far as considering taking my life, and am still thinking about it.

A few anguished cases demanded immediate attention. "I get a sort of aching in my heart which forces me to think of killing myself or someone else," confided a Minnesota man. A woman in the same state who had tuberculosis and heart trouble reported, "I was on the verge of jumping from a high bridge. Now, however, after your sermons and especially after you sent Pastor————to see me, I trust God to help me."

One Sunday morning, a lonely Ohio woman in broken health resolved on suicide and prepared her brother's revolver. As a last gesture she would banish that intruding radio minister who was preaching on hope. Just as she reached over to switch him off, the Maier voice resounded incisively, *"That's no way out!"* This shocked her into hearing the rest of the sermon, after which she buried any plans for self-destruction. Later she wrote that her spiritual rehabilitation had remedied even her health, and she was now active in a local church. Similar situations occurred, for, considered statistically, the suicide rate on each ten million listeners would normally be over one thousand annually.

Many problems, of course, were far simpler and easily metamorphosed into blessings. A childless couple in New Hampshire inquired if Dr. Maier could suggest an appropriate adoption agency. He did. A year later came a snapshot in a letter glowing with delight over a ". . . darling little blue-eyed, blond girl, Brenda Ruth. . . . We love her very much and call her 'our Lutheran Hour baby.' She knows your voice on the radio and says, 'That's Dr. Maier.' "

In other cases, the problem was converse. One mother was on relief, planned an abortion, and wrote the Hour speaker in defense of her proposed action. His immediate reply in the vigorous negative also offered to secure a free layette for her, an item provided by a church society in Rochester, New York. She agreed. The family soon turned the economic corner, her husband now held two jobs, and their layette found repeated use henceforth. Each Christmas a card arrived at House Eleven showing the "Lutheran Hour baby" a year older. Other children were also saved via such "radio layettes."

So it was that Walter A. Maier, a group of pastoral counselors at headquarters and branch offices across the world, as well as corps of alerted local clergy were able to supply help, encouragement, and a new direction to many thousands of lives in various nations each year.

Perhaps more poignant than those afflicted with a terrible, but often temporary, problem were the chronically ill, the invalids, crippled, and handicapped. "If the Lutheran Hour did nothing more than bring the Gospel of Christ's comfort to the sick, shut-ins, and hospitalized," the speaker stated, "it would well be worth several times the price we pay for it."[6] To be bedridden can involve years of personal dueling with pain; or, if pain is mercifully minimized, to be placed under house arrest by bodily incapacity can mean deadening monotony. Father had a special sensitivity for sufferers and usually offered a petition for them in his pre-sermon prayers.

Mail from this group glowed with appreciation. Occasionally such letters were startlingly prefaced, as, from North Carolina, "I am a paralytic and have been for seventy-seven years." A New Yorker typed a letter to Father by means of a stick tied to his right hand. The only thing a paralyzed Ohioan could do unassisted was to flick on her radio by means of a special switch and listen, on Sundays, to the broadcast. A patient in Pennsylvania with terminal cancer wrote that despite operations, radium, and deep X-ray therapy, the disease was spreading; yet the Hour was making a benediction of the close of her life.

A final vignette from many thousands of case histories was the predicament of one modern Job who lived in Iowa. If ever a man had faith to move mountains of pain it was he. Beginning his letter in jubilant tone—"Your program and sermons are wonderful, uplifting"—he then notes parenthetically that part of his right leg was severed in a railroad accident, his left arm and leg were totally paralyzed by a stroke, serious stomach ulcers caused him sleepless nights and restless days, vitamin and mineral deficiencies could not be overcome by his perennial liquid diet, and as he sat in his wheel chair he fought down a maelstrom of aches and pains. Nevertheless he concludes, "But I can read my Bible almost continually; so you see, God has wonderfully blessed me!"[7]

## Fourteenth Season (1946/47)

Almost a hundred more stations advanced the total to 905, and the focus on postwar international penetration now came to fruition both in the East and West. Regular "Christ to the Nations" broadcasts were transmitted in Europe for the first time over Radios Luxembourg, Normandie, and Monte Carlo. At 400,000 watts, the Luxembourg station was, and is, Europe's most popular alternative to the government-owned or -controlled networks and has an immense audience throughout the continent.

North and South Africa were further served through programming in three more languages: French, Arabic, and Afrikaans. China was again penetrated by means of stations in Shanghai, Chungking, and Kunming. And all foreign operations were supplemented through the use of several international short-wave stations in America. KJE8 at San Francisco beamed its powerful signal westward by means of huge directional antennae at 4 A.M. so that the Hour could be received one-seventh of a second later in Tokyo at 9 P.M., in Hong Kong at 8 P.M., Bangkok at 7 P.M., and Bombay at 5:30 P.M. Similarly, WBC, New York, beamed the program eastward, and it was heard in London at 8 P.M., Berlin and Rome at 9 P.M., Athens and Cairo at 10 P.M. WRC aimed at Africa in analogous fashion, and soon Boston's WIUL-WRUW-WRUX were added to the short-wave facilities.

About 400,000 letters mailed from ninety-nine lands arrived in the course of the season, while branch offices reported mounting response to foreign broadcasts.

## Australia

The forty-six station chain "down under" was beaming the Maier messages to people who reacted with proportionately large quantities of mail, and this correspondence, though English, used a new vocabulary. Missionaries at a "billabong" (lagoon) told of gathering around the "pedal" or "wireless" (radio) in surprise and pleasure. From Queensland came a sentiment repeated in thousands of such letters: "I was very much impressed by the fine Radio Session" (program) which "is receiving much popularity as it rightly deserves." Shortages of "tyres" and "petrol" prevented some ranchers in the plains from attending church, and they doubly appreciated the session unless an occasional burnt "valve" (radio tube) interfered with pedal reception. Postmarks were a geographical delight, from Sunshine and Rainbow, to Warrnambool and Gympie.

The spread and variety of listeners were the same in each new continent. A chemist (druggist) in New South Wales told customers of the "dynamic Doctor Maier," as did men and women in hundreds of other vocations in as many situations. A university student in Canberra noted that the sermons gave him peace of mind as he approached his examinations. A postman in the same province fastened the gold-cross emblem to his coat as a conversation piece and invited whole blocks to listen to the Lutheran Hour. The United Aborigines Mission at Lake Eyre, deep in the interior of the continent, tuned in regularly, and, at the edge, a religious group in Sydney requested Hour transcriptions so that they could be played over public address systems along the beaches. Then there was the ultraloyal fan in New South Wales who wrote: "We can get three stations every Sunday, and are sorry when the last is finished. We would be very happy if there were seven Sundays in a week."

*Latin America*

East across the Pacific, the broadcast reached nearly institutional status in Central and South America. The Minister of War in Bogota, Colombia, writes his appreciation of *Cristo Para Todas Las Naciones,* as does the Minister of Education at Temuco, Chile. A Sunday listeners' club gathers at a villa in Buenos Aires, while a leper in São Paulo writes that he will not miss a broadcast "until the day when God shall call me."

The proprietor of a shop in Managua, Nicaragua, invites his customers to hold their pesos until the end of the program and to sit down and listen meanwhile. Five hundred Mosquito Indians in the same country hear via interpreter and sing along with the closing "Beautiful Savior" in their native Mosquitoan language. It begins:

*Jisus Pranakira,*
*Tasba Aiska Dawan,*
*God Lupia, upla talia brin. . . .*

And in neighboring Costa Rica one modern Demetrius writes, "I was a fanatical opponent of Protestantism as a manufacturer and trafficker of images, but now I have turned to the Lord, realizing that I am saved by His grace alone."

One of the welcome aspects of response in Latin America, as in the United States, was the growing number of those who resolved to dedicate their services to the church or even to enter the Christian ministry as a direct result of the broadcast. Every country in the Americas had these volunteers, especially such cities as Nassau, Havana, Kingston, Quito, Rio de Janeiro, and Buenos Aires. (One such, a student from Huancabamba, Peru, commented, "In these days when Modernist preachers with great swelling words deny the very foundation doctrines of the faith, it is encouraging to hear a 'voice crying in the wilderness' like the voice of your speaker.")

*Africa*

Farther east across the Atlantic, correspondence from the "dark and sobbing continent" poured into the Johannesburg branch office from twenty countries. With new stations added in the next season, the Hour was aired over key multiwave outlets in Angola, the Belgian Congo, Mozambique, Madagascar, Ethiopia, Spanish Morocco, and Tangier. Transcriptions were used also in the Gold Coast, Nigeria, and Eritrea. Much of Africa, then, was penetrated by some appropriate frequency and language. The translation in Afrikaans, for example, resulted in more letter response than for any other radio program in that language.

Churchmen, of course, were heartened to find the Hour supplementing their own activities. The Sudan Interior Mission at Kano, Nigeria, invited Dr. Maier to address a series of missionary conferences there; but for a crammed schedule he would have done so. When CR7AA in Lourenço Marques first started airing the program, many registered astonishment and hundreds of letters began almost identically: "While tuning my dial, I discovered to my joy. . . ." A lonely missionary in Madagascar wrote of the broadcast, "Few can realize what it means for one placed outside the rim of civilization, who, year in and year out, never hears the Word of God spoken except at our yearly conferences." He asked for sermon copies which he would translate into Malagasy for use in his mission at Fort-Dauphin. Similarly, missionaries in the Transvaal rendered the Maier sermons into Zulu, while in North Africa, Egypt, and Palestine they were translated into Arabic.

Messages arrived from the veld, the bush, the tablelands, the villages, and cities. A plantation owner in Southern Rhodesia invited his 112 employees to the meeting hall for a wireless service. A reluctant churchgoer in George, Cape of Good Hope, listened, and said, "I have found something new in religion, something that is not a duty but a pleasure. Christ and Christianity are no longer a vague something which cannot be understood. Now Christ is Life."

There were fewer radios in Africa than in any other inhabited continent. Yet there was compensation: the wireless often became a lodestone attracting a cluster of people, whether a family, or a group, or even a tribe gathered at a mission station. Standerton in the Transvaal was one of many towns which demonstrated a "radio chain reaction." One Wednesday evening a layman heard the last of Dr. Maier's address on his set. Next week the whole family was waiting for it. The third Wednesday he invited his minister and their friends to a "wireless party." The following Sunday the pastor announced the Lutheran Hour from his Reformed pulpit, and soon ". . . the news seems to have spread around the town." Letters from Pretoria and elsewhere also reported "hundreds of people" listening.

In the vast countryside the Hour was especially valued as a living link with God. German colonists in Natal noted that their nearest church was 110 miles away and since ". . . we can't always go, we tune in your broadcasts." A similarly isolated family in the Orange Free State wrote that only a radioed fellowship with believers was possible.

North Africa heard the broadcast in Arabic, Spanish, French, and English over Radio Tangier, although local Moslems put great pressure on the station to drop the Arabic broadcasts. Response extended from Morocco to Egypt, demonstrating again that faith transcended politics. "These programs seem to have been produced in North America, but they are awakening a living interest toward the true religion," observed a listener in Melilla, Spanish Morocco. And from Samalut, Egypt, came an oratorical critique: "Dr. Maier's speech was in an Eastern manner of oratory and energy, and this kind of speech is considered highly in Egypt for its effect on the hearers."[8]

Nothing could satisfy the speaker more than such assurances that the Christian message was communicating without unnecessary identification with a white, Western, Protestant culture. The words of St. Peter applied: "Truly I perceive that God shows no partiality" (Acts 10:34).

## Fifteenth Season (1947/48)

On September 28, 1947, Walter Maier stepped before his microphone to announce with gratitude a new significance for the familiar hymns, "Oh, That I Had a Thousand Voices" and "Oh, for a Thousand Tongues to Sing." The Lutheran Hour had attained a long-coveted goal: one thousand radio stations now comprised its network, or by season's end a total of 1,022 transmissions from 43 countries, heard in 102 nations, again and from now on a new record for the broadcasting industry. Four languages were added to the program schedule: Slovak—in which the Rev. Jaroslav Pelikan, Sr. ably handled sermons and correspondence—Italian, Polish, and Chinese. Some 410,000 letters arrived during this series.

Throughout his years on the air, the Hour speaker knew that he was necessarily more a preacher than a pastor to the millions in his congregation, yet in answering problem mail he had tried to serve also as "shepherd of souls" for those who had no pastoral care. Since he wanted to minister also to untroubled listeners, he proposed a positive pastoral program to guide them into church membership or deepen the spirituality of those who were already members.

## Correspondence Courses

To structure this program, a tuition-free Lutheran Hour Bible Correspondence Course was introduced, entitled, "The Fundamentals of the Christian Faith." The materials of this study series were thirty lessons (with test sheets) written by Professor Maier specifically for his radio audience, covering the essentials of Christian theology in language people could understand. Upon completing the course, the enrollee was sent a certificate of diploma, and, if unchurched, was referred to a local minister. The series was designed also as a refresher course for regular churchgoers.

At headquarters there had been some skepticism as to whether the broadcast, which had its hands full enough, should venture into something like this. Soon, however, 70,000 had enrolled in the course, and it was proving effective, pastors reporting that graduates of the series were far better prepared for church membership. Published also in Spanish and Braille, the correspondence course especially helped those who could not attend church regularly, the shut-ins again, or the Great Lakes sailor who requested all thirty lessons at once because his ship put in to port so infrequently.

The circumstances under which the lessons were studied could be unusual enough. A hundred inmates of San Quentin Prison enrolled in the course and were tutored by San Francisco City Missionary F. H. Menzel. The warden noted an improvement in the attitudes of the group, which eventually resulted in a few paroles. Others also studied the lessons while serving time, in this case the payroll clock. A Minneapolis power station engineer did his homework during periodic breaks from dial-watching and valve-manipulating.

A year later, the Hour offered "Sunday School by Mail" for young unchurched listeners, with weekly color lesson folders in four different gradations, depending on the age level, sent to those who enrolled. This series aimed at directing children to a local Sunday school as quickly as possible. The following year another course was added to what was becoming a Lutheran Hour Correspondence Institute, "The Life of Christ." Soon "The Life of St. Paul and His New Testament Epistles" appeared in the curriculum.

Meanwhile, also, *The Lutheran Hour News* was climbing to wide circulation—over 430,000—and to acquaint the younger set with the "Christ to the Nations" cause, *The Junior Broadcaster* has been published since 1950.

*Word and Sacraments*

Walter Maier could function as pastor to an unseen congregation also in other ways. In sermons he underscored some of the same things a local minister would emphasize in counseling parishioners: prayer, and the use of the "means of grace" (theologically, the spiritual channels through which God especially announces and confers forgiveness of sins, life, and salvation), the Word of the Gospel, and the Sacraments of Holy Baptism and the Lord's Supper.

To guide hearers into closer contact with the Word, he urged regular, systematic study of Holy Scripture in family devotions and church Bible classes. And because they instilled the Word along with secular knowledge, he advocated not just Sunday schools, but also parochial schools, Christian high schools, colleges, and universities. His appeals were reflected in mail response, with a multitude of such messages as, "Family worship is now a daily joy in our home. . . ." or "We enrolled our girls in the parish school. . . ."

Obviously the speaker could not baptize his converts personally, nor administer Holy Communion to a congregation of the air. His stressing the sacraments, however, brought masses of reports like these: "In my household eight . . . have been baptized and brought to Christ through your messages."—*North Dakota.* "Holy Communion is now a necessity in our lives. . . ."—*California.*

Such lines made Walter Maier glow, because, he felt, they indicated that the conversions and reconsecrations which God had permitted to accompany his preaching would not be of the flash-in-the-pan variety. Instead, Word and sacraments could be constant nourishments of grace for converts and maintain them in the faith.

*The Far East*

The scene would be impossible now, but shortly after World War II a strange conversation took place in underground offices at Chungking, capital of Nationalist China. A group of Chinese radio officials were engrossed in a conference with Synod's missions secretary, Dr. O. H. Schmidt. His mission was to discuss with network authorities the conditions under which they would broadcast the Lutheran Hour in China. Since they were not very familiar with English and Dr. Schmidt knew even less Chinese, the officials had some difficulty in understanding his request. Presently, the director of the commission interrupted him: "I not know about program you mention, but one American program we want in China very much."

"What is that?" asked the crestfallen missions secretary.

"Is called, 'Bringing Christ to Nations'. . . ."

"But that's precisely. . . ."

"And we want bring Christ to *China!*"

Soon the broadcast (in both names) was carried over seven strong stations in Peiping, Nanking, Shanghai, Hankow, Chungking, and Kunming. It was aired in Mandarin and later also Cantonese, the native dialects of China, as well as English—an exciting start to penetration of 500 million Chinese and other Orientals.

The Chinese hold the record for immediate response to the broadcast. One Sunday afternoon in Shanghai, the Rev. R. J. Mueller, the same prewar missionary who had heard his former professor 1,000 miles up the Yangtze, answered a knock at his door shortly after the end of the Chinese Lutheran Hour program. He invited in a ranking engineer of the government highway department, Hsin Huan Ch'en, who declared that he had just heard the broadcast and now asked how he could receive further information on the Christian religion. Mueller had barely given him a delighted reply when three Chinese girls also appeared at the door. They were students at a university in Shanghai and made a similar request. After a course of instruction, the four became converts and were baptized. The girls then began working at the newly established Lutheran Hour branch office in Shanghai. It was *Foo Yin* ("happiness sound," i.e., good news) for the broadcast's entry into China.

Soon the office was receiving a brisk correspondence from a variety of Chinese, especially those in cultured classes. One Shanghai host "shanghaied" his Sunday guests into hearing the program by keeping them after dinner until air time. But *Chu Ling Wan Bang*\* penetrated to the north, west, and south as well. Super-

---

\* Or ". . . *Pang*," literally: "(the) Lord Being Brought (to) 10,000 Nations," which is the only way in which Chinese regularly expresses any large quantity.

power XGOY of Chungking easily covered most of China and brought mail from as far away as Burma and Pakistan.

Again missionaries found the Hour a great morale-booster and ally. A group of evacuee clergy in Szechwan wrote of their astonishment at hearing Dr. Maier. To a sick missionary in Wuhu he was like news from home. Another churchman, traveling by Yangtze River steamer to his mission station in Kueichou, was passing out Chinese Hour tracts to fellow passengers when one of them told him he did not need a flyer—he was already a regular listener.

While there were proportionately few radios in China, the broadcast was penetrating nevertheless—to a student in Peiping, who told classmates about *Chu Ling Wan Bang;* to an old listener in Yünnan, who had to share his earphone receiver with a group of friends and wrote Far East headquarters to send a larger radio to his village so that all could listen; and to many other Chinese.

Yet communism would change all this. The armies of Mao Tse-Tung had been advancing relentlessly through China, and on December 7, 1949, Chiang Kai-shek's forces fled to Formosa, abandoning the mainland to the Reds. The postwar ministry of the Chinese Lutheran Hour was mortally wounded, but it did not die immediately. Rather, in one of the nearly incredible episodes in the history of the program, mainland broadcasting of *Chu Ling* continued for *two years* under the Red regime! Far East headquarters, of course, cut references to communism in the Chinese versions, but what to do about the Maier transcriptions in the English program? Missionary Mueller solved that problem. Having monitored the disks, he periodically sat next to the turntable in the Shanghai studios of XORA, and with nimble fingers encouraged the tone arm into some strategic groove-hopping past any dangerous comments on communism. This worked, and what finally shut the broadcast down was the forced exodus of Lutheran missionaries from China in 1951. However, Radio Manila continued beaming *Chu Ling* via short wave, and the following season a chain of stations on Formosa carried the broadcast in Taiwanese and Chinese throughout the Nationalist-held island and into the south China mainland.

About 350 million souls were to be found in India, but repeated overtures to the government of that land failed to secure any Indian stations for the Hour. Nevertheless, short-wave transmissions were being heard, and a steady stream of letters had been arriving from many parts of that country. On July 4, 1948, the government did allow a "one-shot" program in the Tamil language over Radio Trichinopoly, but when this was not followed by additional broadcasting privileges, Directors Bertermann and Bernald turned to Portuguese Goa on India's southwestern coast. Radio Goa had powerful transmitters operating simultaneously on four frequencies, and by 1950 "Bringing Christ to the Nations" was reaching Indians and Pakistanis in Tamil, Hindustani, Urdu, Marathi, Telugu, and Bengali, as well as English.

## The Islands

The Philippines and surrounding seas were covered by seven stations in the now-independent country. Listeners who could not hear the Hour during the war wrote enthusiastic mail in welcoming back an old friend. A dentist in Manila, whose radio was bayoneted by the Japanese, had continued reading letters and sermons Dr. Maier had sent him before the war. In the same city, a girl enrolled in a deaconess course faced stern opposition from her parents until they were converted through the broadcast. A student at the University of Manila made a précis of each sermon and discussed it afterward among colleagues. From a leper colony on Luzon, the director reported, "We have a number of lepers here . . . who listen with tears in their eyes as you tell them of Jesus and His love for them." An astonishing number of Filipinos enrolled in the Spanish Lutheran Hour correspondence course, and missionaries wrote that radio converts became some of their finest church workers. One minute symptom of the program's popularity occurred when five ladies from Manila, aboard a KLM flight to Borneo, recognized peregrinating O. H. Schmidt as a clergyman and inquired as to his denomination. Upon his reply they said, "Oh, the church that has the Lutheran Hour?" Though Roman Catholic, all were regular listeners.

New Guinea was served from Manila, and few islanders were more astonished at receiving the broadcast. Wrote one fan from

Salamaua: "I picked up a voice on the 31-meter band. . . . It seemed to have an unusual energy behind it, entirely different. . . ." For some, radio was the last link with civilization: "We are the farthest inland of any white people in Papua, and are quite isolated from the outside world except for our wireless. What a thrill it was to find that we could pick up your messages rebroadcast from Manila on Sunday nights."

The government of New Zealand, despite years of negotiation, would not carry the Hour on its state-controlled radio, but it arrived nevertheless over various short-wave frequencies. And people heard. In North Auckland, a woman whose husband was an amateur wrestler wrote that he ". . . wants to wear your cross for a testimony, and he thinks the other wrestlers may ask him what it is for and that will give him an opening to speak a little word for the Lord." Up the coast, a man in Whangarei was enjoying a holiday on the beach when he tuned in accidentally on his portable wireless, became a regular listener, and found life altered for the better.

A list of the smaller Pacific islands which dispatched stacks of mail across the sea would be too lengthy for publication here. There seemed to be a direct proportion between the number of ocean miles isolating a given island and its per capita letter response. The Fiji Islands, for example, sent an incongruous amount of mail, especially from their capital, Suva, where Station VPD2 carried the program. Natives wrote in, as did British colonials. Again "wireless parties" compensated for lack of radios, and one enthusiastic host reported that although his place was filled with people, ". . . no sound could be heard or movements in the house," so intense was the listening. He concluded, "Permit me to say that my brother, sister, and I have accepted Jesus Christ through hearing your broadcasts."

Okinawa, Guam, and other American bases were each covered by military outlets playing Hour transcriptions. The Hawaiian Islands now had five stations and the Aleutians one, while Manila, San Francisco, and Quito short-waved the rest of the Pacific, which dwindled to lake size within their communications triangle.

Proportionately high mail characterized also the Atlantic islands of the Western Hemisphere. The response of the West Indies has been portrayed, but little Bermuda was a distinct bonus. The island's first commercial radio station, ZBM, Hamilton, was a-building, and headquarters wondered whether or not to move in on the ground floor. Would people in a holiday haven be apt to listen? The affirmative decision was wise, for the Lutheran Hour soon became an island favorite. In Paget East, a nine-year invalid found new courage to live, while parties along the beach traded ocean for sun-bathing when "Dr. Maier time" came around.

*Europe*

To Radios Luxembourg, Normandie, and Monte Carlo, the fifteenth season added an Austrian network including Radios Vienna, Graz, Klagenfurt, Innsbruck, and Dornbirn, as well as Radio Athens in Greece. These nine stations—particularly Luxembourg—penetrated the continent fairly well despite the fact that a predominantly government-controlled broadcasting industry in Europe did not take the Hour in some countries, repeated overtures notwithstanding. Bundles of mail had been arriving at E. George Pearce's London Lutheran Hour headquarters since the first broadcast, and later a Paris office was opened as well. Struggling out from under the debris of war and scared by the uncertainties of the new cold version, Europe was more than ready to hear a message "for such a time as this." The European press and periodicals were surprised at the magnitude of the venture and gave it considerable coverage.

Britain had been hearing the American Dr. Maier by short wave ever since 1940, but when Radio Luxembourg started beaming his broadcasts toward the island, letter response shot upward, for that station was listed in British newspaper radio pages much as any domestic outlet. The entertainment journal *What's On in London* editorialized:

Time was when Radio Luxembourg was regarded by almost every other household in the British Isles as a means of escape from the sobriety of the programmes emanating from B.B.C. stations on Sundays. It is a strange irony that listeners over here are now tuning in to the same station not for jazz and vaudeville but, of all things, for religion—and on weekdays, too.

The programme which draws the public, so we understand, is one called *Bringing Christ to the Nations*—also known as the International Lutheran Hour—which actually goes out over more than 1,000 stations throughout the world to a combined audience of some twenty million people.

And on to an article concerning Speaker Maier.[9] His cultured American accent but impassioned delivery intrigued staid Britons, and one of the landed gentry from Stoke-on-Trent remarked, "I must say as an Englishman I have not heard anything like it on English broadcasting."

A breakdown of the listening audience in England parallels the experience in the United States. Support by the clergy: an Anglican curate in Aylesbury, near Oxford, announces the "programme" from his pulpit. Supporting the clergy: a preacher in Suffolk feels his ministry a failure, considers resigning, ". . . but as I listen to the longed-for Saturday evening service from Radio Luxembourg, I receive fresh encouragement and determination to go forward." Problems solved: a veteran of His Majesty's forces in the Far East, now living in Lancaster, hears the American Dr. Maier preaching on the home and finds incentive to win back his estranged wife and their three children. The ill visited: a Yorkshire hospital carries the program throughout its wards, and patients become fans. Happiness shared: in the same county, Mr. and Mrs. G. M. Edgar, who hold weekly wireless parties, celebrate their wedding anniversary with a banquet at which the highlight is a "Christ to the Nations" broadcast. And so on, through many thousands of letters from London, Cambridge, Nottingham, Stratford, Oxford, and dozens of other -fords, -hams, -bridges, -shires, -villes, -ports, -gates, -pools, -burys, and -fields.

In Wales, a minister repeats the adjectives used most often by the British radio audience in describing Maier preaching: "clear and definite." A little boy in Aberdovey was playing with the family wireless when he came on Luxembourg and announced excitedly, "Here is the news!" Wrote his mother, "How right he was, though not in the way he thought!" (The identical thing happened on the island of Guernsey in the English channel.) Record length for any place name on any communication ever sent Walter Maier ap-

peared in the letter from a Welshman in Llanfairpwllgwyngyll-
gogerychwyrndrobwllllandyssiliogogogoch.

Ireland, orange and green, responded with Irish enthusiasm. A
housefather in Cork reported, "I pray for you every morning at
Holy Mass since I heard you." A listener in County Sligo admitted, "For years I was a confirmed atheist, but lately I have been
thinking there might be some value in Christianity, if I could
understand its message."

Unless atmospheric conditions interfered, Scotland heard clearly.
A man in Dunbarney, a woman in Ayrshire, and hundreds of
others blessed the accident in dialing which introduced them to the
program and wrote to tell about it. Listeners in Edinburgh and
Glasgow sent contributions which made Scottish frugality seem
a myth. A multitude of the letters from all parts of Scotland were
often as colorful in phraseology as the plaids of the people who
penned them.

The Continent responded with substantial mail and appreciation. In Holland, a coal shortage closed down a school in Does-
burg, and one despondent teacher was further depressed by the
enforced leisure; but he dialed Luxembourg and "received back
my joy." A woman in Hengelo requested sermon copies for others
on her block. Naturally, many of the letters were postmarked
"Amsterdam" or "Rotterdam."

Although predominantly Roman Catholic, Belgium provided a
sizeable correspondence, especially Brussels, where a large billboard in the heart of the city square advertised *"Le Christ aux
Nations."* Apparently Belgians do not procrastinate, for letters often
stated some variety of the theme, "I just tuned in to your program
and now must write. . . ."

A convert in Luxembourg used language familiar enough when
translated: "I have been brought to Christ through your radio
messages." Another commented on "so clear a proclamation," and
again these stand for many, many more.

The reaction in France ran parallel. Paris reported, as did
provinces as far away as sunny Menton, where one citizen showed
how the Lutheran Hour could be a success in a non-Protestant

country: "I am a faithful Roman Catholic but shall join my prayers . . . for understanding between all Christian churches." From Lyon a compound problem is reported and solved: "I am in the hospital and very ill. The loss of three of my children made me lose my faith in God, but I have regained that faith after listening to you." A couple in Cagnes-sur-Mer read the Bible once again, another in neighboring Nice gratefully report their marriage saved. A man in Marne tunes in by chance, writes of his conversion five weeks later, and there are many like him.

From a villa overlooking Monte Carlo in Monaco, a former Briton notes: "I find your 'Bringing Christ to the Nations' programme a comforting remembrance of my happy childhood and strict bringing-up in the Protestant Church of England." A thirty-eight-year-old Monégasque confesses himself a moral wreck and seeks help.

Spain was reached through stations in Tangier and Luxembourg, and since *Cristo Para Todas Las Naciones* had been the earliest foreign language transmission, Spanish programs had veteran experience. Letters arrived from the Pyrenees to Gibraltar, although in far lesser quantity than elsewhere. A Protestant missionary in Cadiz expressed gratitude, but so did a Roman Catholic layman from Granada.

*Cristo Per Tutte Le Nazioni* could be heard over much of Italy. One multilinguist in Genoa was edified in three languages: "I am a regular listener of 'Christ For All Nations' in Italian, French, and English. . . . it does me good." An Italian Methodist pastor in Chieti, destitute from the war, stopped en route to the reconstruction of his missionary camp and wrote Dr. Maier for sermon copies; these, he felt, would give him the necessary encouragement to continue. A laborer in San Remo did not own a radio, but made a weekly trip down the Riviera to his sister's home in Bordighera in order to hear the program. From Rome came some Catholic correspondence, as well as enthusiastic mail from members of the oldest Protestant church, that of the Waldensians, who remain a strong evangelical group in Italy.

We continue this European excursion to a land rich in classical and Christian tradition—Greece. When *Na Gnorísoun ta Ethne ton Christon* ("That the Nations May Know Christ") started broadcasting over Radio Athens in English and Greek, Walter Maier was exhilarated. For here was thoroughly Biblical territory which had figured so prominently in the career of Christendom's greatest theologian and missionary, St. Paul. Almost exactly nineteen centuries earlier, the Apostle had addressed the Athenians from the Areopagus (Acts 17), one of the pinnacles in the Greek capital, and now the sermons of a man who often quoted St. Paul also radiated from the highest point in the modern city, the transmitting tower of Radio Athens. Eastern Orthodox Christians were favorably surprised. A churchman in Athens thought the addresses "an inspiration to the performers and organizers of our own Greek religious broadcasts." Several of the large sidewalk cafes in Athens regularly piped the program via loudspeakers to customers inside and out. Elsewhere, mail from Korinthos and Thessaloniki had a genuine Biblical ring, and letters arrived even from the island of Crete.

Across the Aegean Sea in Turkey, a considerable number of Greek-speaking people in the West responded, although Turkish transmissions did not begin until later. These lines from Izmir (formerly the Smyrna of Rev. 2:8) are illustrative: "Just when Christianity seems to be taken for granted, your program by radio is like a piece of bread after years of hunger."

Back in Europe, the Balkan states would soon hear the broadcast in their own languages. Earlier response, however, came from Yugoslavia, where Slovak and German programs could already be understood by some inhabitants of that independently Communist country.

Austria, blanketed by five stations, easily heard *Christus für Alle Welt*. Here and in Germany, the addresses were personally delivered by Dr. Maier, who enjoyed preaching the German renditions of his own sermons, although to insure idiomatic precision an expert did the translating for him. Here also were parallel problems, parallel joys. A woman at Innsbruck would not miss a broadcast; she lost her husband in the war and had no other relatives. A man in Dornbirn reported, "Many families are gathered before their radios every week."

Switzerland listened and answered in its three national languages. From all sections of the picturesque country came trilingual postmarks: Bellinzona, where a man tuned in the Italian program by accident and forgot about the station he had intended; Vaud, where someone reported in fastidious French, "It was this program that first awakened me to the . . . joys of Christian life;" and the German-speaking capital, Bern, where a listener sent forty francs in gratitude for his mother's recovery.

Such letters bore out something which was surmised from the beginning of foreign broadcasting: "people are the same the world over," at least so far as their need of, and response to, the Christian message is concerned. With minor variations, most of these excerpts could have been sent from Philadelphia, or Phoenix, or Wounded Knee, South Dakota.

For a Lutheran minister in America to preach back to Germany, land of the Reformation, might seem a religious version of carrying coals to Newcastle. But it was hardly that. The war had blasted church buildings here as elsewhere in Europe, there was a serious clergy shortage, German churches had not capitalized on radio as an agency for communicating the faith, and the defeated country proved especially receptive to *Die Lutherische Stunde.* A pastor in Tettau wrote one of the earliest letters, which also sounded the keynote for penetration into Germany:

By a happy chance, my wife and I heard for the first time your Lutheran sermon this morning over the air. . . . Such sermons should be made available inasmuch as the need for a truly spiritual reformation in this country, after the last decade of idolatry [the Nazi Era] and the present consequences therefrom, seems at least in our opinion the most urgent one for the salvation of Germany, and with it, of the whole of Europe.

Similar thinking characterizes much of the large German correspondence. The word goes out in Hamburg churches about *"Die Lutherische Stunde aus Amerika,"* while several hundred miles south in Steinheim ". . . there are many listeners in my neighborhood." A counselor in Neustadt uses a series of Dr. Maier's sermons as a study unit for his Christian youth group. A patient critically ill in a hospital at Duisburg-Hamborn finds fresh courage to live because ". . . you have shown me new goals." Two students at the Roman Catholic Seminary in Bamberg express ". . . our interest in your future broadcasts." Unchurched families in Swabia wait "impatiently" for the weekly program, while a fraternity in Westphalia listens each Saturday as a group. From Baden-Württemberg comes also a glad personal touch: Father's own cousins, the Bihlers of Stuttgart and Reutlingen, hear the *Stunde* and write to inquire if this *"Doktor* Walter A. Maier" might be Emil Maier's famous son. From then on the relatives stayed in touch!

Generally, Scandinavia could hear the broadcast clearly, although not until later was programming translated into Danish, Swedish, and Norwegian. Since the Norse regularly learn two or three foreign tongues, including English, language proved no great barrier, as letters soon demonstrated. With Lutheranism comprising 97 per cent of the populations of Denmark, Norway, and Sweden, it might be anticipated that the Hour would get a good reception. It did.

Denmark was compact enough for a radio chain reaction to work effectively. A couple in Jutland, for example, wrote their daughter in Roskilde to listen to the broadcast. She tuned in, then told and wrote others, as did other new listeners from Aarhus to Bornholm. In Hans Christian Andersen's home town of Odense a housefather reported the program up and down his block. A weekly "Lutheran Hour Coffee" was held at a home in Copenhagen during broadcast time, and variations of this idea occurred elsewhere in Scandinavia, where people like their coffee.

Mail from Norway illustrated typical Scandinavian disposition: an apparently impassive mien about many things, but a flare of spirit for whatever touches a vital concern. This extract from Lillehammer in the magnificent fiord country was a case in point: "We say from our hearts: Thanks for the glorious preaching every Saturday from Luxembourg! It is the best hour in the week for me. Please keep on with it, and broadcast oftener if it is possible!" Again, the urgency in the Maier voice snared this hearer in Vestfold: "I am not normally a deeply religious person myself, but there is, I must admit, something that is convincing about your radio program."

In similar fashion, Sweden reported from Malmö and Göteborg

in the West to Stockholm and Gävle in the East. Mail arrived even from Finland, though in lesser quantity, for transmissions in Finnish would not begin for several years.[10]

Back in America, probably a majority of the population had by this time heard, or heard of, Dr. Maier, The Lutheran Hour, "Bringing Christ to the Nations," but far fewer knew the extent of the world-wide operations involved. The broadcast was like an iceberg: it was a massive affair, part of which was visible on the American scene—it had Sunday household-word status in the States—but most of whose more extensive global influence was not visible. Visiting radio, church, or secular authorities usually came away from headquarters astonished at the enterprise; and it was still growing: the next two seasons would raise the station total to 1,236. By this time the weekly listening audience had increased from an estimated 12,000,000 (*Time*, 1943), to 15,000,000 (*Collier's*, 1944), to 20,000,000 people (*Saturday Evening Post*, 1948).[11]

Did twenty million really hear Walter A. Maier each week? The skeptic's question is pertinent, for the large number of stations testifies only to the wide availability of the program, not its reception. Every radio station in the world could carry a broadcast to which no one would listen if it were bad enough. Obviously, other standards must be used to measure the radio audience.

The familiar audience measurement agency ratings are difficult to apply in the case of the Lutheran Hour for several reasons. Some of the Hooperatings for this era are no longer available, the Nielsen Radio Index did not expand to national coverage until 1946, and Trendex, Inc., did not begin operations until 1950. Moreover, they covered only multiple-network localities, whereas the Hour was heard on again as many non-network stations by transcription. But, most important, the rating services are limited to the United States alone, which is only one of the 120 lands where the broadcast was, and is, heard.

The ratings do, however, provide some interesting data. They show that the Hour's listening audience was greatest in the fall, winter, and early spring, which was borne out in the mail tally as well. They also frequently report the Lutheran Hour as holding a substantial segment of the available radio audience. For example, its Hooperating for Washington, D.C., in the winter of 1942/43 was 7.3, indicating that 7.3 per cent of all homes were listening to Dr. Maier, which was also 35 per cent of the Washington radio audience for that hour. A year later, his Hooperating for Richmond, Virginia, was 8.6, or equal to 51 per cent of the listening audience. Previously WRVA of that city had been faced with the dilemma of carrying either the New York Philharmonic concerts or the Lutheran Hour. When the station appealed to its listeners to vote, Dr. Maier gained the plurality at the polls, and the time slot, so *Variety* reported.[12]

Periodically the ratings also provided an assist. Pittsburgh's WCAE, for example, was debating whether or not to drop the Hour, for there was much pressure to replace it with another broadcast. The program director consulted the ratings and found that the Lutheran Hour at 5.4 had a much larger audience than other popular network religious programs at 1.8 and 1.3. Accordingly, the director concluded that the Hour was "in a class by itself," and it stayed on in Pittsburgh. But there is no way to arrive at definite figures for its audience size on the basis of ratings alone.[13] Other criteria must also be applied.

Mail quantity, of course, is a direct gauge of listener interest and response, as well as an indirect measure of audience size. Before the appearance of the rating agencies it was the only gauge. Many times more people will be listening to a radio program than the few who make the effort to write in, but trying to determine a proportion between writers and listeners is difficult. At any rate, with nearly a half-million letters received per year and most of these sent only on an annual basis, a projection of merely some forty listeners for one listener-writer, or one letter per eleven families, would tend to corroborate the twenty million figure. And the broadcasting industry uses a much higher multiplier for such projections. After involving evidence from ratings, mail response, coverage, and especially the world-wide outreach of "Bringing Christ to the Nations," a rough estimate of a total listening audience of twenty million hardly seems exaggerated.

Additional testimony to the size of the radio audience was local, circumstantial, unscientific—but entertaining. Taken individually, such spontaneous observations on Hour penetration as the following mean very little; taken together, something more. From Pontiac, Michigan, came a much-repeated comment: "As you walk down the street at 12:30 on Sundays, you can hear the Lutheran Hour from almost every home," although why the loyal fan was not home listening himself is not stated! The same hyperbole was used of Staten Island, Council Bluffs, Tacoma, and elsewhere. More accurate were favorable reports from station managers, who scrutinized ratings or conducted their own surveys in local listening areas. Such gauging was done also in the foreign field. For example, radio officials in Georgetown, British Guiana, wrote, "The margin of listeners on ZFY to your broadcast was a fairly wide one," and similar information arrived from other continents.

Very unofficial "polls" had been taken incidentally by Professor Maier's former students, fresh from his classes. One wrote:

When I left the Seminary I became "Missionary at Large," and spent five months canvassing from house to house in various cities and towns of New York and Pennsylvania. . . . It was indeed gratifying to see how many people listened to you regularly and to experience the warm receptions we got when the people learned we were connected with the Lutheran Hour.

Another seminary alumnus reported from Texas, "When I came here several years ago as a missionary, people looked at me rather askance when I told them that I was a Lutheran, but now I get many a greeting like this: 'Oh yes, come in! I have been hearing your Lutheran Hour.'"

Finally, the question was often raised, "How does Lutheran Hour mail response compare with that of other broadcasts?" That Walter A. Maier and "Bringing Christ to the Nations" received substantially more letters each year after 1936/37 than any other religious radio program in the world—Protestant, Roman Catholic, or Jewish—is demonstrable.[14] They also drew far more "fan mail" than secular radio shows. The speaker, however, did not know all these facts, nor was he that interested. If anything, he was glad that other religious broadcasters were using radio to glorify God and help their fellow men. And no matter who was succeeding in which enterprise: *Soli Deo Gloria.*

# 18

# Olcott

Students at Concordia Seminary watched the professor-on-leave as he walked briskly down the street to his office each morning, occasionally tossing a key ring into the air and catching it. Eventually one of them asked, "Dr. Maier, why do you toss the keys that way?" Came the roguish reply, "Everyone has to have some kind of recreation!"

The incident became a legend, and like any good legend there was exaggeration here, but more than a grain of truth. The KFUO studio saw less and less of Father in the later forties, since broadcasts often originated at rallies throughout America. These years witnessed repeated mass meetings in New York City, Washington, D.C., Cleveland, Detroit, Chicago, Milwaukee, and Minneapolis–St. Paul, as in other years, but now also highly successful incursions into such less-penetrated areas as New England, the Southeast, the deep South, the Pacific Northwest, and the Far West. Even though their Lutheran populations were comparatively small, Father spoke to huge rallies in Boston, Miami, New Orleans, Houston, Denver, Seattle, Portland, San Francisco, and Los Angeles. At Boston Garden, for example, 17,000 attended in a city which listed only 2,000 members of the speaker's own church. This conformed with experiences in radio: one brief urban mail tally, in this case from Pittsburgh, showed only 55 Lutheran letters among some 1,300 received.

The late forties, then, crowded Father's fall and spring calendars with a different out-of-town rally almost every weekend. This seemed too much, and once again Mother, together with friends of the family, urged him to lighten his schedule. A noted Chicago doctor voluntarily made a special trip to St. Louis just to warn him of the hazards of overexertion. Our family physician, Dr. Ted Hanser, cautioned, "Remember, you're now a fifty-four-year-old man!" For a moment Father was thrown for a loss, but then he rebounded, "Well in that case I'd *really* better get busy!"

With his sturdy frame, he felt he could take the pace in stride, and the Lord would take care of the rest. His medical record was short; besides items cited earlier, a tonsilectomy in 1939, and a mild diabetic inclination after 1945, but that was all. Vigor remained, and despite a slightly receding hairline and more deeply furrowed brow, he did not look his age. Never had he missed a broadcast because of illness, although twice laryngitis had softened his tone to normal oratorical standards.

Father knew how to recharge physically. In scattered hours when he did relax at home he found things to do besides tossing keys, and whatever recreation or hobby might be involved, he always plunged in with a vengeance. But, alas, the model railroad was no more. With brother Walt now studying at the seminary, and I, soon to graduate from high school and be off to Harvard, that era was passing.

However, there were new projects at House Eleven. Mother had the inconvenient habit of making close friendships in cities which were anything but close, and letter writing soon developed into a monstrous chore. Her solution was called "The St. Louis Robin," carbon copies of her letters which circulated far and wide, until even these did not suffice and her newsletter had to be mimeographed to reach nearly a thousand personal friends. Some of the Robins grew fairly long, for when Mother had something to tell, no detail escaped her.

Father's delight and main avocation was his growing rare book library. Its nucleus was his old, well-traveled Luther Bible, which found companion volumes joining it whenever he spied a good buy from time to time. To honor his silver anniversary in the ministry, members of the Lutheran Laymen's League and friends presented him with 210 rare medieval and Reformation era books and manuscripts, which had come from the Gaebelein collection in Mt. Vernon, New York. Father was in bibliophilic heaven. Thereafter, no party at House Eleven was complete until a proud host conducted guests into his study and exhibited some of the choicer items from his collection. And there was much to show. The earliest manuscript was more than eight hundred years old, a palimpsest dating back to 1120 A.D. There were incunabula, the earliest books printed, as well as first editions of Luther's writings and those of other reformers. Luther himself had signed one of the volumes, Melanchthon had made marginal notations in another, while Thomas Carlyle had interpolated a third.

Next to a number of beautifully-illuminated medieval psalters stood the pride of the collection: a complete, 1493-edition *Nürnberg Chronicle,* the bulky geography-history-picture book of the Middle Ages. It began with Adam, but neglected to mention that America had been discovered. There were other delightful idio-syncrasies: the very same woodcut had been used at different places to depict Damascus, Naples, and Verona, to say nothing of towns in Spain and Lithuania! And Adam bore more than passing re-semblance to personages many generations later. But the 1,809 woodcuts were so valuable that the St. Louis Art Museum prided itself in having just one page of the *Chronicle* under glass. When officials learned that the entire volume was in their city, they re-quested that it be put on exhibition, along with most of Father's other rare books. From there the collection was displayed at the St. Louis Public Library and in the color rotogravure section of the *Post-Dispatch,* but eventually Father got his books back.

About once a week he sallied out of the study with a new dis-covery in his collection. Grinningly he pointed to the famous mis-print in his copy of "The Wicked Bible" (London, 1653): "The unrighteous shall inherit the kingdom of God" (I Cor. 6:9); or the verse which named his "Breeches Bible" (London, 1583): Adam and Eve ". . . sewed fig leaves together, and made themselves breeches" (Gen. 3:7; "aprons" in KJV). Eagerly he translated the text of an actual papal indulgence from Pope Innocent VIII in the late 1400s. He would beam in locating professional appraisals on some of his volumes in collector's catalogues, such as "Extremely rare," "Excessively rare," "Extraordinarily rare." One was listed as "Fabulous," two others as "Only copy in the United States," and one, "Only known surviving copy."

Because international recognition had descended on the man in House Eleven, a lengthening stream of visitors called at the seminary office or at home. Those who somehow "crashed the gate" set up by Harriet or Mother included leaders in the political, cultural, or business worlds, who wanted to enlist his counsel or simply pay their respects. But among them were also obscure individuals who found his address and were in need of help. Clearly this development was a bad mistake: Father should have had better screening from callers—important or insignificant—and the problem cases referred to a counseling staff. Yet he would not turn anyone away.

Probably no one becomes a public figure without sacrificing some of his family life. While it was fun to have a famous father— on trips people would recognize him at restaurants, walking along a city street, on trains and elsewhere—we were also periodically "orphaned" when a heavy speaking schedule took Father, or both parents, out of town. On these occasions Mabel tried to keep us out of mischief.

House Eleven was always hectic just before one of Father's trips. While Mother and Mabel packed his clothes, he gave last-minute dictation to Harriet, assembled his papers, and discussed details with Rudy, who would accompany him. Walt or I had the car running in preparation for the dash to the station or airport. So close was the schedule that often we were unable to see them off, for by the time we had parked the car they were gone.

Occasionally the pace was reflected in Father's disposition. His temper somewhat resembled a benign volcano. Most of the time it was under fair control, but small jets of steam were emitted now and then which quickly dissipated. He was irritable only when under great pressure. Then the right combination of factors could trigger a Vesuvian eruption—a befriended individual letting him down, a bungling repair job on his car, or a book manuscript lost. Typical of the extroverted personality, a cloudless calm settled over the summit soon after the upheaval.

Father largely avoided interruption during that blessed institution called the summer vacation. From June through September he was not on the air, yet rarely did he go one or two weeks without preaching somewhere, usually for rallies. Then too, summer was the time to work on the Nahum project, dictate *Day by Day*, and prepare his books for publication.

Behind several of his "vacations" lurked ulterior motives which involved something besides relaxation. When the doctor had ordered our parents on a tour through Banff and Lake Louise in the Canadian Rockies to help Father recuperate from a tonsilectomy, he scouted out radio opportunities in the Northwest. The family vacation to California in 1941 was a summit of happiness, but the tour had been sparked by Father's role as voice of the Lutheran Hour in a religious motion picture being filmed in Hollywood. Winter trips to Florida and Texas saw grand afternoons at the beach, but also hours of dictation, public appearances, people.

Still, there were times when he could relax totally, even if only for a few days. Such golden hours saw what friends called "the different Doctor"—a man who could absorb a dark tan at Fort Lauderdale, go deep-sea fishing in the Gulf of Mexico near the mouth of the Rio Grande and come off with the day's top piscatorial honors, or luxuriate off Point Dume near Santa Monica in a lobster and abalone fishing party. Once the relaxation came close to being terminal: he tried to swim a bay at California's Lake Arrowhead and almost drowned but for Mother's desperate calls to "swim just one more stroke . . . one more stroke . . . one more stroke" until finally he reached a raft.

It was at Lutherland that Father met the man eventually responsible for our second summer paradise, Hugo Williams of Lockport, New York. Impressed with the Poconos, but not dazzled, Williams allowed that Pennsylvania was "nice," but "you ought to drive home through western New York and see some real country: the Finger Lakes, miles of fruit orchards, Niagara Falls, Lake Ontario, Erie, Canada just around the corner." One September the Maiers took this northern detour on their way home and promptly fell in love with western New York.

This was all Mr. Williams wanted, for now he hatched a plan which answered the solicitude of many who were concerned about the health of the Lutheran Hour speaker. What the man really needed during summer months was not the atmosphere of a busy resort, but the comparative seclusion of a seaside cottage where he could work and relax undisturbed. In the spring of 1943 Williams sent a letter which excited Father as much as the rest of us. Its message, in part:

I hope you have not yet made plans for the summer, because we heartily invite you, Mrs. Maier, and the boys to Western New York. . . . We have rented a spacious cottage for you on Lake Ontario near Olcott Beach, which is twelve miles north of Lockport. The view is beautiful, the atmosphere one in which you will not be disturbed. . . . So far as the rent is concerned, you will never receive a bill, and the discussion on that point has ended now.

Co-owner of a major department store, Mr. Williams felt that this would be an act of gratitude to God for his business success.

That summer and each season thereafter, cool, blue Lake Ontario provided the setting for some of the vividly delightful memories in our family life. Entirely isolated and undisturbed it was not—a corps of new friends in the Niagara County-Buffalo area soon saw to that—but since Father and Mother had always thrived on company, guests received the glad welcome. In fact, total isolation would probably have necessitated a severe personal adjustment.

Three years later, after a spring mass meeting in Buffalo, the Williamses drove Father, Mother, and Rudy Bertermann to Lockport in order to discuss plans for the coming summer. There had been some difficulty in renting the cottage again, and they might have to select another spot, said Williams. Upon arrival at his department store, they were greeted by a large group of friends, after which the host announced, with a strange smile, "Why don't we all take a ride down to Olcott? Mrs. Maier always enjoys seeing the lake." Although the Missourians could not quite fathom the idea, an entourage drove beachward in a car caravan. At Olcott the procession turned up a bluff road until it reached the shores of Lake Ontario a mile west of town. Here the cars halted, as everyone filed out to the edge of the bank and saw Ontario roaring against the beach, a sight the Maiers relished. Only then did they notice that they were standing on the broad lawn of a handsome, white, two-story Dutch-colonial summer house with blue roof and large picture windows.

His slight smile expanding, Mr. Williams suggested, "How

would you like to see the inside of *this* cottage?" The delegation seemed to be holding its breath.

"Well, this is a little too large to call a cottage," opined Father, "but all that glass intrigues me. Do you suppose anyone is home?" He flashed a look to Mother and Rudy which they read perfectly: "Surely Mr. Williams isn't going to rent something like *this* for us—two floors?"

Already they were escorted to the door, which was unlocked and opened. Inside was a long living room extending across the entire house, with a fireplace surrounded by built-in shelves at the far end. The decorative motif along the north wall was simply Lake Ontario: through two great picture windows and three normally large ones it could not be missed. The whole place was furnished in maple colonial—something out of a furniture fashion magazine. Williams showed them the rest of the house, while the delegation filed through after them. The kitchen was completely equipped, the two bathrooms and showers were lined with mirrors set in multicolored glass tile, and there were three bedrooms, a study, plus a spacious upstairs hall.

At the end of the inspection tour they all reassembled in the living room, where Williams asked, "Well, how do you like it?"

"I'm in love with it," admitted Mrs. Maier candidly, while her husband quickly added, "But this would be far too expensive for you to rent. . . ."

"You're right," agreed Williams, "it would." He paused, then resumed with a twinkle, "So we've made another arrangement. In behalf of your many friends in western New York who want you to spend your summers here in order to rest up for the heavy radio season each fall, I hereby convey to you a little gift from all of us." Slowly he took a key out of his pocket and handed it to them. "You are now full owners of this house, everything in it, and the two lots of 180-foot lake frontage on which it stands!"

The room burst into applause. Father blanched, tried to say something, but then choked up. Mother didn't even try. They retreated into the study where they composed themselves and offered up a prayer of earnest gratitude for such loyal friends as these. Some minutes later they emerged, and the man who had delivered a few thousand addresses in life made what was possibly the hardest speech of his career. For how does one express adequate thanks for a furnished seaside home and property? In a flood of appreciation the new owners re-explored every inch of the place.

Then the story was pieced together for them in full. Since it had become harder to rent lakeshore cottages for just the summer months—proprietors were winterizing them for year-round use—Hugo Williams and his pastor, the Rev. Herman F. Meier, discussed the matter with a group of interested friends. They appointed a committee to select and purchase a suitable summer home for Dr. Maier as his permanent retreat. "That way we can also assure his return to Niagara County each summer," suggested patriarchal Pastor Meier with a glint in his blue eyes. The Niagara Lutheran Pastoral Conference seconded this thinking and approved a fund-raising project among its congregations.

Without Father's knowledge, Rudy attended a planning conference with the same delegation which had accompanied them now. Did he think Dr. Maier would be pleased, or feel tied down for the summers by such a gift? That was one of the easiest questions Rudy ever answered.

Quick enthusiasm for the project developed in western New York church circles. For the last decade, Father had managed to address an annual Niagara County rally despite a surcharged schedule, and the people loved him for it. They now contributed a sum which almost reached the goal, and committee treasurer Williams made up the difference as his own gift.

Early that June, a throng gathered on the lawn around the house for a dedicatory service, after which Father again expressed the profound joy and gratitude of the Maier family. Later he dedicated his book, *Go Quickly and Tell*, to: "Our Friends in the Clergy and Laity of Western New York State."

During the next two months, the visitors never quite left, and on some days there were callers in the morning, afternoon, and evening, until Wednesday was finally scheduled as "Visiting Day." But who can blame them? Father often greeted people who lined up to meet him after area mass meetings with a hearty, "You must come out to the lake and see our new place!" And they did.

In succeeding summers, however, the situation corrected itself, and the welcome blanket of privacy descended on our home. Probably nothing did more to prolong the life of Walter Maier than the months spent each year at Lake Ontario. This is when we first learned that the man had a practical side after all, that he knew how to tinker at something in rare moments just like any other father. Once the family stood by and applauded when, after we dared him, he succeeded in hanging a screen door correctly.

There were projects a bit more involved than this. One summer it was to assist in building a peaked Dutch-colonial garage to match our house. Another year Father, Walt, and I decided to clear away an orchard of superannuated peach trees on the western part of our property so that we could extend the lawn and plant a rose garden for Mother. But the gnarled tree trunks were perverse about the entire plan: they had squatter's rights to the place long before we intruders appeared. After burning out the clutch on our car in trying to drag them off, we finally hired a bulldozer and the job was done. Next we erected a white, ranch-style fence around the enlarged yard and prided ourselves on having had the foresight to engage a surveyor before taking up drill and saw. But it seems the surveyor had been given the wrong abstract, and we ended up a little matter of ten feet off! The lawyers were kind.

However, the grand challenge came the following summer, a story of three men versus Lake Ontario. Because Great Lakes water levels were abnormally high in the late forties, many United States beaches, like ours, had been reduced to a scant eight or ten feet when the waters were placid. But in a storm, waves would crash against the bluffs, eroding them badly, and each year one or two feet of our lawn were sacrificed to Ontario's waters. Something had to be done to secure our part of America's northern frontier!

The logical solution would have been for United States and Canadian authorities to lower Ontario's water level by some means other than turning off Niagara Falls. Increasing the draining flow into the St. Lawrence River would have done it, but south-shore property owners would have had to battle their way up through red-taped politics in *two* national governments, not to mention fighting a hard duel with steamship interests, which liked high water levels. The only alternative was to erect a concrete seawall along the frontage of our property.

Estimates from two construction companies for such a wall were beyond the family budget. We surmised the solution even before Father braced up enough nerve to suggest it in the course of a fireside soiree: the Maier Contractors, Uninc., a nonprofit organization. Father would be supervisor, Walt foreman, and two hired hands and I, the laborers. After checking plans with contractor William Beccue, Walt drew up a preliminary estimate on total cost of materials and labor, and presented it to the supervisor. "Aaahh, now that's more like it," said he. "This we can afford. Let's go!"

At lunch time three days later a huge truck arrived from Ryerson Steel Corporation of Buffalo to deliver fat steel dowels and long reinforcing rods. Maier Contractors bounded out to face the grand challenge. During the unloading, Walt commented: "Pop, this is undoubtedly the greatest bargain in the entire operation. Thousands of pounds of steel for only $16.32!" Father agreed it was a good buy. The driver then presented Walt with the bill: $16.32 for hauling, $575.00 for the steel. Father blanched and nearly told the truckers to get all that steel off his grass. Apparently, Walt and the order secretary at Ryerson had not fully communicated during their telephone conversation.

With such a start, the project could not fail to improve as it moved along. Mercifully, Lake Ontario was calm most of that August, and after digging a footing trench down to bed rock, we slid the dowels into holes which had been drilled into the substratum by pneumatic hammer. Then the footing was poured, just twenty-four hours before a brief midsummer storm which would have ruined the entire operation had it lashed in a half-day earlier. A week later we added superstructure by wiring long wooden forms to the dowels, while a small cement mixer started chugging away atop the bluff. Every three minutes it gushed a batch of "soup" down a 40-foot trough which led to the seawall forms below. Father was captivated by each stage of the construction and interrupted his dictation every twenty minutes for a run to the water front in order to "supervise." Guests also found him down at the beach in swim trunks, heaving shore rocks into the soup between the wall forms, for this not only saved cement but gave the structure far greater strength. Standard hospitality for visitors that month was an invitation down to the beach, where Father showed them what kind of stones to heave inside the wall-to-be! By the end of August the forms were removed and the job completed. Beccue examined the structure and pronounced it seawallworthy: "Judgment Day will come before that thing moves!"

The ever-changing surface of Lake Ontario never ceased to fascinate Father. One glance to the north could provide him a dozen different sermon illustrations. And no two vistas were ever the same. There was the soft white haze of morning blending into an emerald base; the proud blue of midday, with sea imitating sky even to such detail as whitecaps for clouds; the sullen gray fury of an afternoon storm lacerating the face of the sea until, squid-like, it released its turbid bottom waters in flight before the wind; the flaming sunset, incandescent with all the hues at the red end of the spectrum and reflected by nature's own marine kaleidoscope. But the star-crusted night sky over Ontario made caricature of any description; nature herself was so impressed that she regularly turned on Aurora arc lights to advertise the spectacle.

Beauty and love were never far separated in the mind of Walter Maier—the one was connected by a direct neural linkage to the other. The stimulus gained from nature he relayed in a perennially deepening love for his wife, who mirrored the process. Every clear evening they made a private ritual of standing together at the brink of the bluff, watching the sun slip over the horizon. When in a lyric mood, they sang the German folksong, "See How the Sun Sinks Yonder," or resumed, arm in arm, the long walks of Chicago days, now more than twenty-five years in history. By starlight they often luxuriated through another chapter from the eventful past, or made plans for an even more eventful future.

On other nights they entertained guests around a blazing hearth, old associates passing through, or new friends from western New York. Mother's sisters from Indianapolis visited each July, and

Father's dinnertime joking with Paula, Lydia, and Millie bathed the place in mirth. One daily delight was his game of Russian Bank with Aunt Millie. Whenever she scored incisively, which was rare enough, Father fretted at the cards with such boyish disappointment that Millie almost preferred losing.

Mother's brother, Ted Eickhoff, and his wife drove up from Cleveland on occasion. There was a walking paradox: genial, soft-spoken, mild-mannered Ted was the man who had engineered the Thompson submachine gun! When he saw what gangland did with the "Tommy gun" he had developed for the military, Ted was just as glad the weapon was named after his boss, a former department head at Army ordnance. The Boston side of the family also dropped in with visits from the Karl Maiers, as well as Barbara and her husband, Prof. Francis O. Schmitt, the noted scientist who is head of the department of biology at M.I.T. All Hub relatives, however, were saddened by the death of brother George in 1946.

Beauty at Olcott fired a love also for work, and Father could produce at maximum efficiency along Lake Ontario. Here each summer he prepared at least one book for publication, in addition to writing all *Day by Day* meditations for the year. A firsthand account of his production rate comes from Harriet Schwenk, who spent a vacation at Olcott even though she knew the Boss would inject a little dictation into the schedule. One morning she knew it would be more than a little. At breakfast he said he wanted to try dictating a hundred *Day by Day* meditations in one day, and would she be party to such a marathon? She would, and later reported:

He began about 10:15 A.M. We worked outside on an embankment overlooking the water. Knowing the objective of the day's work, I timed the first few and suggested that he would have to produce 12½ an hour. Because a few callers dropped by to see him, the schedule lagged. He continued after dinner, and by 1:30 the next morning he had completed 150 meditations. The length of each varied from 200 to 220 words—a total of more than 30,000 words in one day! He was delighted with the output. . . .[1]

Tanned and in open-necked sport shirt, he would pace back and forth along the bluff while dictating, though sometimes he almost relished an interruption or two. If the neighbors' boxer nuzzled up to him he often "took five" and tussled violently with him, or preached at the dog through a cylinder of drain tile left over from the seawall. The voice sounded like something from another world and would send the boxer into paroxysms.

His most faithful animal fan, however, was a tame crow. One morning while dictating outdoors, Father removed his silver wristwatch and laid it on the garden table. Circling above, the crow made a power dive for the table, alighted, took the watchband in its beak, and flew off in a high arc over Lake Ontario, the watch still dangling from its bill. I had witnessed the whole episode and could not resist commenting, "My, how time flies!"

"Well don't just stand there, *do* something!" exclaimed Father in the most unoriginal line of his life.

"Well what in the world can . . . why don't you try whistling or something?"

He put his two little fingers V-shape into his mouth and generated a shrill blast. The crow turned abruptly in flight and headed back toward the table where it alighted again and deposited the watch. At first the bird stood guard over its silvery trophy, but Father whistled a different pitch and it flew off again without the watch. Even St. Francis would have been delighted.

At times Father's "influence" on nature seemed too direct, and we accused him of an unholy alliance with the nether powers. Just before crossing the Mohave desert on the trip to California, we had been warned by wilted eastbound motorists that only hell could be hotter, and even that was questionable. As we set out, Father glowered at the sky and uttered a few words in Hebrew. Soon the first rainstorm in months dropped the temperature so rapidly that we shut the car windows against the chill. Father grinned and naturally took full credit.

But he was more than a rainmaker. One dismal, wet Sunday at Camp Pioneer on Lake Erie, he sought to raise the congregational mood by switching his sermon theme to "The Blessings of Rain." Toward the close of his address, he was making eloquent the platitude about how God always sends sunshine after showers when, at that very moment, the sun's golden rays suddenly illuminated the chapel. Thereafter at Pioneer he was always serenaded with, "You Are My Sunshine."

Father could not spend June and July of 1947 at Olcott, for he was some 4,000 miles distant at the time. He had been invited by the United States War Department to fly to Europe as a member of a commission of cultural leaders to advise the Allied Military Government for Germany on educational and religious matters. He was accorded V.I.P. status and encouraged to establish broad contacts with German church and university leaders in order to make recommendations on cultural policy. He had been much concerned about conditions in postwar Europe as it was and so regarded the opportunity as a godsend.

After a briefing by the War Department in Washington, Father proceeded to Westover Field, Massachusetts, the Army base for transatlantic flights. There to see him off were Mother—a little worried because two planes had crashed that week—as well as a large delegation of relatives and friends. The flight group had seen special training films on how to stay alive in the event a ditching in the Atlantic became necessary, and even now Father prepared to board the plane decked out in standard Army flight gear, complete with parachute harness and Mae West. Somehow, Mother was not entirely comforted and could just imagine what would happen should Father, with his fear of heights, ever have to use a parachute! They commended each other to divine protection and arranged at least a spiritual communication during his three-month absence: starting with Psalm 1, they would read each day the same consecutive psalm for devotion, he at 11 P.M. in Germany, she at the same moment, 5 P.M., in America.

The military C-54, its four engines screaming, took off on the morning of May 3, and after a smooth flight over the Atlantic landed in Paris, then Berlin. During a briefing at United States Military Government headquarters, Father learned further details of his mission. Among other things, he was to survey postwar church problems and prepare a report with recommendations on religious broadcasting in Germany, which had been cut off by the Nazis. There was duck soup on that menu!

Now began exciting weeks for the visiting consultant. Aircraft were put at his disposal so that he could crisscross West Germany to confer with Allied military officials and German leaders. Especially profitable were discussions with Cardinal Graf von Preysing of the Roman Catholic church, Bishop Otto Dibelius and Dr. Martin Niemoeller of the Evangelical (Lutheran) church, and future Bundestag President, Dr. Eugen Gerstenmaier.

The results of his research were embodied in a long document which he submitted to the military government and War Department entitled, "Report and Recommendations on Religious Broadcasting in Germany."[2] The monograph surveyed the status of German radio and called for more religious programs in view of the destroyed churches and clergy shortage. It also suggested how better church broadcasts could be achieved, and here the author spelled out a philosophy and technique of religious radio.

The survey seems remarkably objective. It was written by a man who for two years had been trying to introduce the Lutheran Hour over German networks, yet his own program is not cited in the report. While employed by the government as a public servant, he would not take partisan advantage of his position. His suggestions for apportionment of religious air time also bear this out:

Each group is entitled to representation in radio programming, with the emphasis laid on . . . [the Roman Catholic and Evangelical Lutheran churches] which constitute almost 97 per cent of Germany's population. However, time allotment should not be made merely on the basis of numerical preponderance. The Jews in Germany now total only an estimated 30,000; yet their treatment during the Nazi regime, the razing of synagogues, dispersement, imprisonment, destruction, and disappearance of members and rabbis make their radio broadcast of particular importance. . . .

Religious broadcasts should be constructive presentations of the respective churches' teachings and are not to indulge in personal attacks or polemics directed against other churches.[3]

When a request by the Archbishop of Bamberg to establish a station sponsored by the Roman Catholic church was denied by the military government, Consultant Maier objected to the adverse action and advised that the Archbishop appeal the verdict. In the appendix of his report he even drew up suggested program formats for Roman Catholic, Lutheran, and Jewish broadcasts in Germany, which were commended by representatives of those faiths.

The trip to Europe also gave the professor-on-leave opportunity for the theological and scholarly exchange he always relished, but for which he had less time later in life. He engaged in a series of stimulating conferences with faculty members at the Universities of Berlin, Erlangen, Marburg, and Heidelberg. In Tübingen he met Prof. Gerhard Kittel, the noted biblical lexicographer, and the two struck up what became a warm transatlantic friendship. And before returning to the States, he attended the constituting assembly of the Lutheran World Federation at the University of Lund in Sweden. An active proponent of Lutheran unity as a first step to wider ecumenicity, he welcomed the chance to meet church leaders from all parts of the world who had gathered to discuss and demonstrate their oneness in Christ. When foreign churchmen learned that this was the Walter A. Maier whom they had known only by voice, the enthusiasm of some was unrestrained. Missionaries and other clergy from scattered areas of the globe eagerly told him of conversions through his radio crusade.

The most significant result of the mission to Europe, however, lay in another area. Amid exciting reports in Father's first letter home and a recurrent theme for Mother ("I miss you terribly"), we had sensed an undercurrent of something deeply serious tugging at his soul, which surfaced in the next correspondence:

The first week in Berlin was one of the saddest in my entire life. Conditions are beyond description. Much of the city is in ruins, most of the people are impoverished and many are undernourished. . . . Doctors told me that their resistance has weakened and masses of them are ready for tuberculosis. . . . For the first days I could hardly eat with a German. The food stuck in my throat. How the poor people carry on, I simply do not know. We must help them this fall and winter more than ever before.

Father did personal bits of relief work immediately and resolved to do far more in a short time. One typical day found him at Neuhausen in the Württemberg where his father had been born. Invited to witness the town's Corpus Christi rites, he was greeted officially by the Mayor and accompanied to a high ecclesiastical seat in the local Roman Catholic church. After services, Father stood at the door and watched the congregation file out: gaunt-faced mothers, children with bloated stomachs and spindly limbs, the people hungry and suffering from food and vitamin deficiencies.

That afternoon, he drove with his liaison officer to a nearby park where he struck up a conversation with several German families, and soon a large group had gathered about this American who handled their language so carefully. After giving a brief sermonette on hope and faith in hardship, he opened the trunk of his car and started passing out a horde of food accumulated from the PX: candy, chocolates, cheese, fruits, and the like. He never forgot the gleam which illuminated those faces—some of the children had never tasted a candy bar. But before they ate any of the food, the people lined up and sang a few *Lieder* in honor of their benefactor. Afterward, a woman who was spokesman for one family group took him aside and inquired earnestly, "Please tell me: aren't you the Angel Gabriel? Does not Scripture say that Gabriel will come to earth in human form and do much good? It must be you!" The pious woman was rational, but the situation had overwhelmed her. "No, my dear woman!" He smiled, then made a pun which is lost in translation: "I'm hardly an *Engel* (angel). It's more like a *Bengel* (rascal)!"

Whatever his role, he knew that this scene would have to be repeated hundreds of thousands of times if there was to be relief for war-torn Europe. American welfare agencies were already in operation, so there was no need to start from scratch. But he could act to throw immediate massive support behind existing relief efforts. He transcribed a series of messages which were aired at the conclusions of Lutheran Hour programs, and in one of them he told his stateside audience:

When I surveyed the almost endless rows of rubble, remembering Goering's boastful promise that if ever enemy planes bombed German cities, he would change his name; when I saw the blackened remnants of the Kroll Opera House where Hitler shouted that Germany could never be defeated, I asked God to keep the masses in America from ever putting their trust in men such as this. . . .

The need for food is unbelievably great in Europe today. No matter how many packages you have mailed in the past, keep on sending them. You cannot send too much. Without sustained help from the outside world, I cannot see how masses in Germany will survive. Following Him who told us, "Love your enemies," you can help bring real peace and blessing to suffering mankind.

Almost immediately after his return flight to New York, Father set in motion further European relief efforts. To the United States government he addressed a petition in behalf of certain refugee groups, especially for 100,000 Bessarabians who, under the leadership of their pastors, had fled Russian-controlled Northern Rumania and taken asylum in the American zone of Germany. To his radio audience he appealed for help in providing food and clothing for the starving and destitute both in Europe and the Far East, while a further plea was included also in the closing announcements of the Hour. Listeners were invited to supply ten-dollar packages through CARE in New York, six-dollar parcels via the Lutheran Emergency Planning Council, or through services provided by their own church relief organizations. The same appeal was featured at Hour-sponsored European Relief Rallies.

The response was munificent. Large sums were donated by the radio audience to various relief organizations, which wrote their appreciation. The far broader tide of gratitude, however, flowed in with messages from thousands of families in Europe for whom several CARE packages had dramatically alleviated hunger and suffering. Some listeners simply sent money, with the instructions: "Dr. Maier, please use this to send food and clothing where you think they are most needed." Accordingly, a "Walter A. Maier World Relief Fund" had to be set up with trustees who purchased CARE packages for names on a lengthy list which he had compiled in the course of his European tour and from subsequent correspondence with churchmen abroad. The fund also aided Korean relief.

The late Ernst Reuter, mayor of West Berlin at the time of the airlift crisis, made the statement: "Under the leadership of Dr.

Maier huge quantities of merchandise, food and clothing were supplied to the German people right after the war, and the Lutheran Church has continued this helpful work of rehabilitation. . . . Among the great solaces afforded to the German people in these times are the broadcasts of 'Bringing Christ to the Nations.' "[4]

Father also tended other charitable projects. He nourished a special interest in spastics and mentally-retarded children. One of his grand moments came with the news that Fred C. Rutz, a substantial Hour contributor from Ohio, had created the Walter A. Maier Foundation to benefit such unfortunates. And when the owners of the hospital in Vicksburg, Mississippi, contemplated sponsorship of the institution by a church body, Father encouraged the L.L.L. to add the "Lutheran Hospital of Vicksburg" to its list of enterprises, and he gave the dedicatory address.

A majority of his broadcast prayers had included a special petition for those in pain, physical or spiritual, as in this first published radio intercession: ". . . May Thy Word bring comfort to those who are afflicted by sickness and sorrow . . . raise the falling, cheer the cheerless, enlighten the doubting."[5] Years later, in the final prayer he broadcast, appeared these clauses: ". . . Thou didst enrich all of us, the poorest, the plainest, the most pain-ridden, with Heaven's highest treasure. . . . Give Thyself now to every searching, sorrow-filled heart, every darkened soul."[6]

Sensitivity to distress, then, remained a major motif in his career. Assisting prisoners and displaced persons in Boston as a youth, relief shipments to Europe after World War I, welfare work in St. Louis, concern for the fighting forces in World War II, and postwar European relief were different expressions of the same motif. With years of counseling the troubled in person or by mail, he could not fail to keep his hand close to the pulse of human suffering.

# 19

# Culmination

America probably recognizes achievement sooner than most countries because of her mass communications media, although these sometimes create success artificially where none should have occurred in the first place. A few starlets, popular singers, and radio-television personalities, for example, who have fame but certainly not talent, are cases in point. Conversely, the media often overlook a major development in their preoccupation with a current but transient fad.

"Bringing Christ to the Nations" is a success story in the traditional American mode—from a lone transmitter in one country to radio's largest program in many—the type of account which is usually prime grist for the mills of journalism. Yet the only mass media to discover the story before 1943 were the newspapers, and, of course, the religious magazines. Had broadcast headquarters hired a press agent the situation might have been different, but that would have been too commercializing to suit the speaker and staff, who had no passion for publicity.

In 1943, however, *Time* had broken the news with its article, which was followed by stories in *Collier's* the next year (". . . Religion Goes Global"), *Pageant* in 1945 ("The World's Largest Congregation"), the *Saturday Evening Post* in 1948 ("The Man of the Lutheran Hour"), and, posthumously, *Coronet* in 1956 ("The Word in 56 Languages"). Other high-circulation magazines also featured accounts: *Christian Herald* ("Twenty Million Hear Him Preach"), *Radio and Television Life* ("The Lutheran Hour"), as well as religious journals. *Newsweek* and *Look* also published items on Walter Maier.[1]

He was pleased that the "Christ to the Nations" story gained press recognition, because each article about the broadcast would be an entree to people in the general, not simply radio, public and alert them to the cause. And the articles showed that secular magazines could indeed serve a religious purpose. Quantities of mail now arrived from readers who had never before heard the Hour because of preconceptions against radio sermons. Many became regular listeners, some were converted.

A number of writers who interviewed him said later that their brush with Dr. Maier was one of the unusual experiences in their careers. Journalist William F. McDermott, who did the articles in *Collier's* and *Herald,* was astonished to find in the same person both a gentle and affable family man, and the whirlwind "Jeremiah of the Twentieth Century" before the microphone. At a Chicago banquet this author drew a vignette of "the Lutheran prophet with a universal message: the great common denominator of Christianity."

Another writer who followed Father from home to office, and from headquarters to KFUO, was Hartzell Spence, famed author of *One Foot in Heaven.* Assigned by the *Saturday Evening Post* to do a feature on the Lutheran Hour speaker, Spence finished his long interviews an impressed man. One of the notable moments occurred when he watched his subject prepare for a broadcast through a window in the announcer's studio. Father's casual attire surprised sartorial Spence, who dressed strictly from *Esquire,* and he turned for a moment to question announcer Elmer Knoernschild about it. When he looked back the speaker had vanished, with just seconds until air time. "Where *is* he?" worried Spence. "On the floor," replied Elmer. Edging closer to the window, he peered down at a figure on his knees with clasped hands, imploring divine blessing on the sermon. Spence said he had seen many speakers preparing for addresses and broadcasts, but never one who prayed so frankly for guidance as Dr. Maier.

For pictures to accompany the article, the *Post* had sent ace photographer-author Larry Keighley to St. Louis, and here also the contact with Father generated a friendship, and a story. In eighteen years of married life, despite his duties across the world, Keighley and his wife Dorothy had always managed to celebrate their wedding anniversary together. But anniversary number nineteen appeared to be the dismal one: on that day he had to photograph Dr. Maier before his studio microphone in St. Louis. Nevertheless, love triumphed, for Keighley called his wife: "Darling, you *must* catch a plane and 'Meet me in St. Louis'!" She did just that. When Father learned the news he became a little euphoric; here was the kind of love about which he had written in *For Better, Not for Worse*. After a quick conference with Mother and the Bertermanns, he was ready with the unexpected: Larry and Dorothy Keighley were lionized at a banquet complete with large, nineteen-candle cake and serenades from the Lutheran Hour Chorus. Rudy took Larry's camera in hand for a picture of the couple cutting the cake. When photographer Keighley fidgeted like one of his own subjects and asked, "Where do you want me to look?" it brought down the house.

The story in the June 19, 1948 *Saturday Evening Post* exemplifies some effects of such magazine articles. Highlighted in posters on newsstands from Portland, Maine, to Portland, Oregon, the feature on "The Man of the Lutheran Hour" was king-sized even for the *Post*, and it was a good summary of the Maier ministry. There were a few errors, not more than would be par for any writer or any magazine. One stated that the subject ". . . had translated the New Testament into Chinese."[2] Now Professor Maier knew a variety of languages, but Chinese was certainly not one of them. He had written a theological paper on the proper Chinese word to be used in expressing the term "God," and perhaps this was the source of the misunderstanding. Probably also it was a proof error which listed his mail count as 1,200 letters per week instead of 12,000.[3] Most of the story, however, was accurate, even to such details as the sons' contribution to family mealtime conversation. Wrote Spence: "Just now the principal question concerns how to raise funds enough to buy an outboard motor for the summer vacations. They've been working on that one for some time without too much promise."[4] We did not have to work much longer. Although the cited sentences appeared near the end of the article, a large-hearted American reading public spontaneously sent us donations labeled, "For the Outboard Motor," totaling about $450.00. And one H. B. Walker from Ohio generously sent a crated, 7½-horse-power Mercury outboard motor! The pen is mighty indeed, and people more munificent than we sometimes think.

The months of 1948 and 1949 fairly exploded with opportunities in the life of Walter Maier, fresh avenues of outreach to new and different publics in behalf of the spiritual crusade which was claiming all his energies. He had a man-killing list of rallies and engagements, but he would not slow down. He was only fifty-four, which he translated as thirty-four for his purposes. Moreover, he could not slow down: to him the cause was far greater than one life.

The cover of the *Post* issue with his story showed an artist's preview of delegates marching in demonstration at the Republican National Convention in Philadelphia a few days later. This was predictive also for Father. Carroll Reece, chairman of the Republican National Committee, had invited him to serve as a chaplain for the convention and offer one of the invocations. He accepted. Politics fascinated him, though in his public ministry he was careful to remain impartial as to parties, and he had friends in both camps. But soon after arriving in Philadelphia, he was caught up in a series of interviews by reporters and radio-television commentators, who posed some questions which could hardly be answered without betraying political sympathy. While parrying these, he did admit having his ear to the convention floor; it looked to him like a Dewey renomination.

On Thursday, June 24, Chairman Joseph W. Martin, Speaker of the House of Representatives, banged his gavel and called the convention to order. Then he introduced Dr. Walter A. Maier. A stocky figure in navy blue walked over to the bunting-covered rostrum while the tumult died abruptly and heads bowed. His words now reverberated:

Almighty and All-Merciful God, the Father of our Lord Jesus Christ:
    Within a few moments the epochal balloting begins; therefore, first of all we start this session by praising Thee for this privilege of free government. One-fourth of the earth's habitable surface is controlled by atheistic tyranny, which has torn the free ballot from the masses and regimented them for ruin. Yet by Thine undeserved mercy, Thou dost still permit our people to choose their own leader, the man of destiny for the testing time ahead, and for this we thank Thee, Father.
    Help us show our gratitude today by choosing a man . . .
                a real man, an American man
                a statesman, not a politician

a leader of character and honor . . .

an executive of truth and righteousness . . .

Above all . . . as we are met here in Philadelphia, where at the first Continental Congress, George Washington fell on his knees to beseech Thy help; as in this Convention Hall the features of Abraham Lincoln look down to remind us of his personal and protracted pleading with Thee, let us nominate as candidate for the highest office in the land

a man of prayer

a man of faith

a man of Christ, who came to serve, not to be served.

May the Holy Spirit indelibly impress on our souls that above all else the United States needs Thee, our God, the Founder of our country, the Author of our liberties, the Guardian of our blessings! Give us all a deep sense of genuine repentance for our many individual and national sins. Forgive them all by the merits and mercy of Thy Son, our Savior. . . . We ask it in that name which is above all other names, the name through which our prayers are heard—Jesus Christ, our Lord. Amen.[5]


The months continued, as exciting as they were busy. Throngs regularly overflowed every auditorium in which "Dr. Walter A. Maier" was slated to speak. His schedule looked as if it had been borrowed from an opera soloist, a prize fighter, and the Harlem Globe Trotters, with appearances in such places as Carnegie Hall, the Chicago Stadium, Hollywood Bowl, as well as auditoriums, coliseums, and sports arenas throughout the nation.

The Hollywood Bowl Rally of October 3, 1948, inaugurated the sixteenth radio season, and because it set the stage for other mass meetings that year, it should be sketched briefly. After precise preparation by the committee in charge, nearly 20,000 people left acres of cars and chartered buses in the parking lot to converge on the Bowl that bright autumn afternoon. Probably no rally had a more beautiful setting than this. Scraped into one of the Hollywood hills just north of the motion-picture capital, a soaring amphitheater fanned around the familiar shell, across which hung a great banner emblazoned, "BRINGING CHRIST TO THE NATIONS."

Organ music preluded the service, with a carillon cascading echoes down the hillsides. The Los Angeles Police Band did its finest, three mass choruses sang, and then came a new twist to rally festivities: a Hollywood motion-picture actress mounted the rostrum. The committee felt that such an appearance would be appropriate since films were the town's chief industry and the broadcast had penetrated the screen world as well. But selecting the appropriate star had been a problem. Various film celebrities had written Dr. Maier and contributed to the broadcast, including young Vera-Ellen and old "Grandma" Adeline Reynolds (*Going My Way*). Cast for this role, however, was character actress Agnes Moorehead (*Johnny Belinda*), New York Film Critics' "Best Actress of the Year" in 1942.

Miss Moorehead delivered a serious and moving monologue which emphasized the world-wide extent of divine love for all humanity, and concluded: "One world of one blood . . . one world of many nations . . . one world, God's world!" This served as introduction to "The Parade of Nations," which now physically demonstrated international response to a global broadcast of God's universal love. Down the long aisles of the bowl and up to the stage marched a procession of 400 men, women, and children dressed in the native costumes of each of 100 countries in which "Bringing Christ to the Nations" was heard. Every group carried a sign identifying one of the lands, as well as the country's flag. The effect was a symphony of color and pageantry illustrating the Hour's world-wide scope.

The Maier address seemed startlingly out of context with the pleasant environment, but it was squarely synchronized with the international situation. The year had seen Rumania and Czechoslovakia fall to Communist coups, as well as the Berlin blockade. China would soon be lost. Therefore he had chosen two brief passages of Scripture as a joint theme: "The Time Is Short! Go Quickly and Tell!" (I Cor. 7:29, Matt. 28:7) In part one, "The Warning," he stressed that the time could well be short for world peace, religious freedom, prosperity, and the reformation of American church life. Part two, "The Appeal," called for national repentance, rededication to the search for Christian unity, strengthening the home, and renewed emphasis on Christian education. As loyal citizens, laymen were not only to support the government,

but to seek political office as well. Finally, he urged the laity to publicize the story of salvation by every available means, even to the
Communist world.

At this point he reached a climax in announcing the beginning
of Russian language Lutheran Hour broadcasts beamed to the
U.S.S.R. The audience was electrified at the news and broke out
in a roar of applause. In closing, he appealed for continuing prayer
in the world crisis ahead, especially for the Russian people, including their Communist leaders, that even the latter might be brought
to faith.

It was a remarkable afternoon, one which still lives in the memories of those who attended. For some it became even more unforgettable. As the speaker greeted a long queue of well-wishers
after the rally, occasionally one of the shaking hands belonged to a
friend who had helped make the Maier California honeymoon such
an empyrean excursion twenty-four years before. Santa Monica's
Pastor and Mrs. Walter Troeger were there, as well as the Rev.
George Theisses who had so loyally defended "Spy" Maier on the
Mexican border nearly a quarter-century earlier. And at the end of
the line stood the very Dora Knief who had provided the newlyweds' cottage. She received a bear hug instead of a handclasp.

Mass meetings often proved to be crossroads for such friendships
which had not enjoyed personal contact for many years. In Boston,
boyhood friends surprised the speaker in the receiving line; in New
York, a host of Lutherland acquaintances; in Milwaukee and Chicago, the Walther League crew. Even a hometown rally in St. Louis
turned up a significant friend of yore: Emma Gihring, mother of
Herman of the crystal sets. With a broad smile, Father asked her,
"Have you forgiven me for visiting your home so often years ago
and tinkering with that crystal set?" She answered with a Bible
verse: " 'This gospel of the kingdom shall be preached in all the
world for a witness unto all nations. . . .' You are helping to fulfill
that prophecy." Father shifted the subject to Herman and how he
was doing in New Jersey.

A few weeks after the sunny day in Hollywood came a gusty
evening in New York's Times Square. Father and Rudy were hav-

ing an animated conversation as they turned and walked down a side street. Presently they stepped inside a Georgian-style building, identified by lettering in granite as "The Town Hall," and were greeted by George V. Denny, Jr., founder and moderator of *America's Town Meeting of the Air*. The nation-wide broadcast-telecast of his show that evening, December 7, 1948, would become one of the most important and memorable in the annals of *Town Meeting*.

This was suspected in advance because of the topic, "Is a United Protestant Church Possible Now?" To discuss the question Denny had assembled a formidable panel: author and missionary-evangelist Dr. E. Stanley Jones; Minnesota Governor Luther Youngdahl, a layman active also in church affairs; Dr. Truman B. Douglass, an executive of the Congregational Christian Church; and "Dr. Walter A. Maier, originator of the International Lutheran Hour."

Dr. Maier had looked forward to this appearance not only because he loved to debate, but especially in view of his concern for church unity. At a dinner for the panel preceding the show, he was in one of his exuberant moods, sizing up the opposition and thoroughly enjoying himself. Even his favorite dessert was served: strawberry parfait. Leaning over to E. Stanley Jones, he said, "You remember you were having a little trouble condensing your opening remarks to four minutes?"

"Yes . . ." replied Dr. Jones, a little nervous about the coming simulcast.

"Well, I've heard that strawberry parfait tends to coat the throat and retard the rate of speaking, so you'd probably have more trouble than ever."

Already good Dr. Jones had pushed away his dessert untouched. Meantime Father finished his, then casually eased Jones' parfait onto his own plate with a reassuring: "Actually, it would be a shame to let this go to waste. Besides, experts insist I should slow my rate of speaking anyway!"

Fortified by double dessert, Father proceeded to relish every minute of the hour-long program from the moment the red buttons glowed on the television cameras at 8:30 P.M. All four panelists had agreed on the desirability of a united Protestant church, but the point at issue was how to bring it about. Because of the continuing high significance of the ecumenical movement and since the Maier thinking on it was clearly expressed in this debate, it is briefly summarized.

In the introductory presentations, Dr. Jones submitted his plan for Federal Union: one Church of Christ in America, comprising Baptist, Lutheran, Episcopal, and other branches which would dedicate sovereignty to the Union while preserving local self-government for themselves. Thus one branch could be governed by bishops, another practice baptism by immersion, and so on; but St. Peter's confession would link all branches in the one Church: "Thou art the Christ, the Son of the living God" (Matt. 16:16).

Dr. Douglass proposed merger or amalgamation, the elimination of denominational vestiges in favor of a total organic union, which, he felt, would be better than ". . . getting a large number of denominational beads on an organizational string," his impression of the Jones plan. Youngdahl fully seconded Dr. Jones' proposal, pointing out that organic mergers could continue under this plan.

The audience accorded each of the speakers a round of applause. Now to the original record, as Mr. Denny introduces the anchor man:

Few radio listeners have not at one time or another heard our next speaker on the International Lutheran Hour. In fact, Dr. Maier, we hope that all your regular audience is with us tonight to hear you discuss this important question with your other distinguished colleagues. Dr. Maier represents a different branch of the Lutheran Church from the one represented by Governor Youngdahl, and a different point of view. Dr. Maier. . . .

*Dr. Maier:*

Now, let's get one thing straight right at the outset. The millions who think as I do and for whom I'm speaking tonight, not officially, but nevertheless in the spirit, want a united Protestant church. We pray for it; we work for it; but we do insist that it be a true God-made, not man-made, united church.

You've heard Dr. Douglass' idea of an all-out, organic Protestant union, although he's offered no specific plan whatever for action.

You've listened to the outline for Federal Union as proposed by Dr. Jones and my very good friend, Governor Luther Youngdahl, who certainly ought to be on my side tonight. (*Laughter.*)

Now my thought calls for spiritual unity as directed by the Bible. This asks for a series of conferences on Christian doctrine, one embracing all the divisions of each denomination, and at the same time representing all Protestant churches.

The discussions would start, not with the mistaken idea that Protestantism is now strongly united, but with a detailed study of the day and night differences that separate the Protestant churches when the term Protestant includes capitalists and communists, Modernists and Fundamentalists, Unitarians and Trinitarians. Churches in which some preachers lift up the cross of Jesus Christ and others speak on "Bonga, Bonga, Bonga!" "Amos 'n' Andy," "The Lewis and Clark Expedition to the Pacific Northwest"—actual subjects mentioned in our broadcast mail—are certainly not united.

These Christian unity conferences should then systematically study what God's word says in the matter of the disputed doctrines and adopt a Scriptural verdict. These other unity programs you have heard set doctrinal problems aside as secondary. Dr. Jones admits clearly, "Federal Union does by-pass these problems," and I tell you Protestantism cannot survive by such agreement to disagree. . . .

Finally, these conferences on Christian unity should formulate a detailed statement of doctrine, covering all essential teachings of Scripture. This confession of faith should be acknowledged by the individual churches and all denominations as their creed.

This will be a long, gradual process, for you cannot remove overnight and by a few resolutions a difficulty which has been centuries in the making. Nor can organization and super-organization, all purely human arrangements, alone bring the harmony we desire.

The Old Testament prophet's protest, "Not by might, nor by power, but by My Spirit, saith the Lord," still holds. Not committees and subcommittees, directors and executive officers, give the churches the guidance they need, but the Holy Spirit Himself.

. . . Give us a united Protestant church; I ask you to pray for it. But let it be fully and honestly unified in its acceptance of the faith once given, rooted in the Bible, and climaxed in Christ, the Son of God, and the Savior of the world. (*Applause.*)

*Moderator Denny:*

Thank you, Dr. Maier. Well, we see why he's on the radio. (*Laughter.*) And I'm sure that our television listeners—viewers—will agree that he did a pretty good job on television, too. (*Laughter.*)[6]

Then followed a period of give and take within the panel. Jones rebutted Douglass, who replied. Youngdahl challenged Maier's plan because doctrinal unity was a problem even within Lutheranism, not to speak of the rest of Protestantism. Maier rejoined that people in 1500 A.D. also thought a Reformation impossible, but it succeeded, and that Lutherans were now far closer doctrinally than a quarter-century earlier. Unity would come through theological effort and in God's time.

After further discussion, Moderator Denny invited questions from the floor. The transcript indicates that audience participation was unusually animated. There was also additional debate within the panel, generally the doctrinal unionist, delighting in the contest, versus the three organizational unionists. In closing, Denny directed himself to his radio-television audience: "Now, friends, what do you think about this subject tonight? Your thoughtful responses to this discussion should make a very interesting magazine article, so send your replies to us here at Town Hall, and we'll let the speakers know what you think."[7]

The public took George Denny at his word. Since many churches had announced the simulcast, an extraordinary audience had heard the debate and now reacted. Town Hall Program Manager Elizabeth Colclough reported several weeks later that the mail count for that program was the highest of the season, ". . . with about 83 per cent of those who expressed an opinion agreeing with Dr. Maier."[8] The public had spoken.

Some of the most enthusiastic letters Father ever received also arrived at St. Louis in great stacks. He had to chuckle at a few of the phrases which reappeared in the correspondence even though written by people of many faiths: "Like Luther at Worms," "Courage of the prophets," "Paul at Mars Hill," and the like, which are highly inept, but do show the involvement of people who felt that strongly on the issue. The letters Father saved came instead from the Rev. M. Hartenberger in Texas: "We were all mighty proud of 'our Wam' and consequently have now forgiven him for over half of those Hebrew finals he shot at us in the late '30s," or Pastor A. Ahlman in Nebraska, who wiped the entire slate clean: "I hereby recant all of the gripes I made about your Hebrew courses at the Sem."

## Sixteenth Season (1948/49)

Again all Lutheran Hour graphs—stations, nations, mail count, contributions—pointed upward. New accessions raised the station total to 1,100. Of these, 590 were in the United States; the remaining 510 were foreign outlets in 50 lands (see Appendix I). Letter response increased from 410,000 to 450,000, which necessitated an office staff of nearly 100 at St. Louis headquarters alone. Exactly $1,439,565.61 was received in contributions during the series, leaving an operating deficit of only $56,000, and immediate steps were taken to eliminate this. Even when income exceeded expenditure, no thought was given to building a large reserve—a naked faith in Providence.

## Soviet Eastern Europe

Foreign programming advanced from seven to twenty-five languages. Included among the new tongues were Japanese, Korean, Taiwanese, Indonesian, Siamese, Burmese, Hindustani, and Telugu for the Far East; as well as a phalanx of translations which would pierce the iron curtain along different sectors of its overhang in the West: Estonian, Latvian, Hungarian, Bulgarian, and Russian itself. Polish and Slovak transmissions were already in operation. Lithuanian, Rumanian, and Albanian would follow in a year, while Yiddish and German also served many listeners in the Soviet satellites.

This was nothing less than a twelve-pronged ideological counterattack against communism in the realm of religion and intellect, which corresponded, albeit on a smaller scale, to the activities of the Voice of America and Radio Free Europe in the political and cultural spheres. It was an ambitious venture, but more than that: the action could conceivably have East-West political consequences. On the other hand, the transmissions might pass unnoticed not only by Communist authorities, but by everyone, including the intended audience. These programs it would not be possible to advertise locally! Once again, speaker and staff could only entrust iron-curtain penetration to the Christ of the Nations who knew no such curtain.

Poland was first to respond, since Polish programming had begun with the previous season. Surprisingly, but logically, the earliest mail came from Polish refugees and displaced persons scattered throughout Western Europe, who expressed gratitude for the radioed inspiration which was helping them adjust to changed circumstances. Poignant personal tragedies were recounted, as in this note from an Austrian D.P. camp: "I am separated from my parents, who were deported into Russia. I do not know where they are. I now live in Austria. . . . My brother is in France as a displaced person." Another Pole in London expressed hope that perhaps his family, scattered across the world as a consequence of war, was at least spiritually reunited by the program. Some of the refugees were of the highest caliber: political leaders, professionals, and such churchmen as the Polish Catholic professors in Paris who regularly corresponded with the broadcast.

Many letters uttered the hope that countrymen back in the fatherland would be able to listen. In one of the dramatic chapters of Lutheran Hour history, this hope was realized. *Chrystus dla Narodów* ("Christ for Nations") was being heard in Soviet-dominated Poland. Mail to the West was officially discouraged, yet the freedom-loving Poles penned letters as enthusiastic as the Hour ever received. Like all satellite correspondence, mail arrived by devious routes and means—some was sent direct, the rest smuggled out or addressed to friends and relatives in the West for remailing.

With their occupation, Russian forces had removed many radios from the villages of Poland, leaving instead one central receiver which fed a series of loudspeakers scattered in homes and public places throughout the town. This served two purposes: plunder—the radios were sent to Russia; and control—one Communist agent could select and monitor precisely what the community would hear. Such a measure seemed necessary in rural districts, because the farmland formed one of the last lines of resistance in Poland. But Moscow-selected programming from the central radio could now pipe propaganda into homes which might otherwise have turned a deaf ear.

This very device now boomeranged in a few of the villages. While dialing the central receiver for something appropriate on Friday noons, the local functionary arrived at Radio Luxembourg and became interested in *Chrystus dla Narodów*. Now Polish Communists have always been a special breed, and soon a number of such monitors (some of them Christians in secret) became so engrossed in the program that they—and necessarily their entire villages—became regular listeners. One of them cautiously wrote:

. . . In our village, we have one radio and thirty-four loudspeakers, and every Friday I am tuning in to your broadcast *Chrystus dla Naródow*. In this way the whole village listens too. . . . We would be very satisfied if you possibly could broadcast on short wave as well, because sometimes the long waves are interrupted by neighboring stations.

Shortly afterward, the program was beamed in also via short wave. A similar letter from Maków reported one radio controlling twenty-four loudspeakers.

Communications from other villages and towns, together with scattered information passed on through refugees and relatives in Western Europe pieced together a rather remarkable story. No other religious broadcast in Polish was being heard, and news spread rapidly about this one. The result was that Friday, when *Chrystus* was scheduled, became a kind of Sunday for some in the Polish countryside. In several villages it was reported that certain shopkeepers temporarily closed their stores at 11 A.M. and some of the farmers came in from the fields to gather around the radios or speakers for worship centered on the broadcast. One host in Tarnobrzeg noted, "There are ten persons listening now, but next Friday more shall come."

As glimpses through the iron curtain, a few additional excerpts are indicated. Warsaw and the larger cities responded also, and one hearty soul in Kraków ventured these lines:

. . . I have decided to take a chance and write to you. I said "take a chance" because I don't know if my letter will be censored by the Red government or not, and maybe the consequences will be very unpleasant to me. In case it happens, the life in Poland is of no value to us. We are living with the hope of a better future because we know that God is always just and as we see in your broadcast He is not forgetting us.

Because of the clergy shortage, the situation was often like the early Christian "church in your house" (Phil. 2), only the location was Zlotów instead of Colosse: "All those who have no radios are coming to our house to hear your broadcasts just as they would to church." Many letters cautiously referred to the dreary political materialism which was affecting the public, and some of the mail signed off poignantly: "We will be listening as long as it will be possible. We can hear the truth only from America."

Czechoslovakia received the Slovak Lutheran Hour under circumstances similar to the Polish programming and responded with the same double wave, first mail arriving from Czech refugees and displaced persons in Western Europe, who enthusiastically wrote friends back in the homeland to tune in. Then came the second swell of correspondence from listeners in Czechoslovakia itself, conveying gratitude for *Rozhlas Slovenskej Luteránskej Hodiny*, "The Slovak Lutheran Hour Broadcast." The capital city of Prague as well as less familiar Chrudim, Tisovec, and dozens of other localities appeared on postmarks. The need for prayer books and devotional materials was acute, especially after Czechoslovakia was forced into Soviet satellite status in 1948. Shipments of such materials behind the iron curtain sometimes arrived intact, sometimes not. But confiscations were a small price to pay for a channel of spiritual welfare which could flow under political barriers.

Among the unusual devices used to inform Czechs of the broadcast were gas-filled balloons tagged with stacks of flyers detailing the *Hodiny*. When the wind was right, hundreds of these balloons were released from Bavaria and floated across the border deep into Bohemia, where they advertised the program.

Direct testimony that the broadcast was heard came from two members of the Czechoslovakian Air Force, whose daring flight to freedom made headlines around the world in 1953. Gustav Molnar and Vladimir Krman had been grounded by Communist authorities for pro-Western sympathies and, among other things, for listening to the Lutheran Hour. But one cold night in March, they stole into the hangar of their air base at Piest'any, near the Austrian border, drained the oil from the engine of an old ex-German Hunter 96 airplane, heated it over a stove, and then poured it back into the crankcase so that very little warm-up would be necessary. Though sluggish, the engine started and pulled their plane out of the hangar, onto the runway, and into the air. Flying almost at tree-top level, they skirted Russian MIGs waiting for them over Vienna and landed at Graz in the British zone of Austria. Later in London they reported that, despite Communist directives, many of their countrymen were listening to the Hour in secret.

Hungary, the Baltic States, and even, to a lesser extent, Rumania and Bulgaria reported in a manner analogous to the other Soviet satellites, and their nationals wrote either from their native lands or west of them. Refugee families often enclosed photographs of themselves grouped around a radio, while those who listened under less candid circumstances back in the fatherlands learned that communism could not rule religion out of the air waves or out of hearts. Some sent word by devious means, and by equally devious routes sermons, crosses, and devotional materials pierced the iron curtain.

Finally, the Soviet Union could hear the Russian Lutheran Hour, *Njesjom Krista Narodam* ("Bringing Christ to the Nations") over much of European and some of Asiatic Russia. Most of those who fled the U.S.S.R. for political reasons had taken refuge in Western Europe, and response from this group was nearly immediate, running fully parallel to that of other displaced nationals in the West. Many reported on the unhappy status of Christianity in the Soviet Union and the circumstances under which they escaped. Such refugees were particularly grateful for Bibles and religious literature in the Russian language, for much of this had long since disappeared from the Soviet book trade.

However, except for an occasional smuggled letter, no mail came from the U.S.S.R. itself. Had the broadcast failed to penetrate? No. Russians in the West stated that Radio Luxembourg could be heard clearly in the Soviet Union. Moreover, short-wave stations at different parts of the world were beaming the program in on various frequencies, and there was no record of jamming. The explanation lay rather in the fact that mail communications between Russia and the West were "severely discouraged" at this time, an expression better described as follows: during the iron-clad restrictions of the late Stalin regime, Soviet nationals who tried to correspond with relatives and friends in the West received anything from dire warning to five or ten years in the concentration camp for their pains. Writing to a Christian broadcast, then, would be subversive in the extreme!

After Stalin's death, however, there was some relaxation in Soviet policy, and a limited mail exchange with the West became possible. Now from Leningrad, Moscow, Minsk, Kiev, Odessa, and elsewhere arrived a small stream of letters, cautiously worded—some of them transmailed through friends in the satellites—but as positive as politically possible. Certainly there was no surge of correspondence, but the messages proved that the Hour was being heard in Russia, and that far more would write if they were able. Once, in a *Krista Narodam* program, hope was expressed that hearers, wherever they were, would add their "Amen" in response to the sermon. During the next few weeks, several hundred letters and cards arrived from Russian-speaking listeners, most of them unsigned, but bearing one word which told all: "Amen!" Many of these were traced to the Russian military in East Germany.[9]

The broadcast word continued to become the printed word throughout the forties. The earlier Maier books were followed by: *Victory through Christ* (1943), *America, Turn to Christ!* (1944), *Christ, Set the World Aright!* (1945), *Jesus Christ, Our Hope* (1946), *Rebuilding with Christ* (1946), *Let Us Return unto the Lord* (1947), *He Will Abundantly Pardon* (1948), *The Airwaves Proclaim Christ* (1948), *Global Broadcasts of His Grace* (1949), *One Thousand Radio Voices for Christ* (1950), and *Go Quickly and Tell* (1950). These averaged 400 pages each and again were brought out by Concordia Publishing House. From the eleventh series on, two volumes per season had become necessary because of the author's extended broadcasting schedule, and the new titles raised to twenty-one the number of major books by Walter A. Maier.

In addition to the above he wrote also the following Lenten devotional books in paperback: *Beautiful Savior* (1945), *My Suffering Redeemer* (1946), *Christ Crucified* (1947), *"Christ Died for Us"* (1948), and *"Behold the Lamb of God!"* (1949). Prayer booklets and tracts for radio mementos also came from his pen, as well as the annual *Day by Day with Jesus* meditations. Small wonder that Spence noted: "He is always writing a book. . . . and at the moment there are in his office the page proofs of one new book, the galley proofs of another, the manuscript of a third, and the uncompleted pages of a fourth."[10]

Quantity, of course, by no means connotes quality. Yet the latter seemed assured because the scholar in him persisted, and his motto for sermon preparation remained, "I must exhaust my subject." The critics appeared to agree. Most of them reviewed the books in positive terms, similar to Editor John Bradbury's report on *Go Quickly and Tell* in *The Watchman-Examiner*:

These sermons embody inspiration, comfort, and enlightenment, sincere persuasion, and earnest warning. Simply unfolded, yet eloquent in expression, illuminated with graphic phrases and classic illustrations, these messages in book form will continue to carry on Dr. Maier's great ministry.[11]

A negative critique was exceptional, but should be cited; in this case for *Rebuilding with Christ*:

Dr. Maier deals with sin, but has nothing to say about the evil conditions under which men live, which drive them through the dark moods of despair and frustration into sin. Whatever wisdom there may be in our modern culture and whatever virtue there may be in a concern for social justice are . . . unappreciated by this preacher.—*Theology Today*[12]

*The Christian Century's* review of *Let Us Return unto the Lord* took an affirmative view:

It may be that Dr. Maier has, on the Lutheran Hour, a larger weekly audience than any other preacher has now or has ever had since preaching began. Preaching must have positive qualities to attract so many listeners and to continue to hold them for so many years as this series has been going. These sermons present Christianity in vigorous, uncompromising, conservative terms, with a clear and positive answer to every question. . . . There are no loose ends or unsolved problems and no half lights of intellectual doubt or moral uncertainty. There is emotional warmth, but no ranting.[13]

The books never reached a best-seller category; a best-selling sermon volume is a rarity even among the largest nondenominational publishers. But consulted, read, or studied by clergy and church workers in America and abroad, the books carry on their own active ministry, and virtually all have been sold out. Meanwhile, *For Better, Not for Worse* would not stop selling, and Concordia's General Manager, O. A. Dorn, asked the author to prepare yet another edition.

About this time several trade publishers, particularly Doubleday & Co., the John C. Winston Co., and Fleming H. Revell Co. wrote Dr. Maier their interest in publishing his next book. G. Paul Butler numbered his among the *Best Sermons*, brought out by Harper & Brothers,[14] as did Andrew W. Blackwood in his "Anthology of Master Sermons from the Reformation to Our Own Day," *The Protestant Pulpit*, from Abingdon-Cokesbury.[15] For Walter Maier to find himself in the same volume with Luther, Wesley, Edwards, Spurgeon, Brooks, Barth, and others was a rewarding experience. The dean of American homileticians, Blackwood also set Maier sermonizing as an effective model in his textbook on preaching, *The Preparation of Sermons*,[16] and subsequently called him "the leading radio preacher of our time."

Now it was 1949, a special year for our family: on June 14 Father and Mother would celebrate their silver wedding anniversary. Yet spring began normally enough. Mass meetings took them up the East Coast to New England, then westward to a series of Canadian rallies starting at Niagara Falls, where a great gathering was held and the program carried throughout the Dominion by the Canadian Broadcasting Corporation. For once, however, it was providential to have the parents out of town. Rudy, Harriet, Walt, Mabel, and friends in various cities were preparing a surprise celebration for them on the fourteenth.

Walt sent word to Cambridge that I would positively have to take my last final examination early and fly to St. Louis in time for the festivities. Harvard was both very understanding and very traditional about it. I was permitted to take the final early, but university rules required a special "escort" in such exceptions, a proctor who was kind enough to accompany me all the way to the airport lest I be tempted to tell friends just how the exam went!

Meanwhile, Father and Mother knew that something was afoot, but they were totally unprepared for the celebrations which now took place. They were hailed by a gathering not only of the Maier-Eickhoff clan and the broadcast brotherhood, but friends from different parts of the country made festivities resemble television's *This Is Your Life,* though without the tears. On the evening of the fourteenth, they were feted at a grand banquet, for which Master of Ceremonies Bertermann had prepared a full program. This was touched off when sister Paula and brother Karl were prevailed upon to reminisce at will about that sultry night in Indiana when an executive secretary married his Junior secretary. A few of the congratulatory letters and telegrams were read, which had arrived from all parts of America and abroad. Friends or admirers in church and state from colleagues to congressmen saluted the milestone in the lives of Dr. and Mrs. Maier. Vice-President Alben Barkley sent a special message from Washington wishing them much ". . . happiness and success not only in your personal lives but in your work of service to others."

The evening crested when the fabled "On the Q" Committee was introduced: Chicago's Otto Amling and W. C. Hutchings, and Ed Kuhlman of Detroit. After appropriate banter, they ceremoniously trundled in a crate full of fresh lettuce, which would have looked fine in the local supermarket but somehow seemed a trifle out of place at a banquet. The guests of honor were invited to examine the lettuce more closely. More than puzzled, they complied until Amling pulled out a purse from the center of the crate and presented it to them ". . . in behalf of your friends everywhere who have been blessed by knowing you both!" They were directed to unzip the silver-ornamented purse. Inside were checks plus green-and-gray United States Treasury "lettuce" totaling $10,000! It was another moment when Father and Mother blanched from shock.

Insisting on the utmost secrecy, "On the Q" Committee had previously informed a wide circle of friends that a joint anniversary present was being planned, and that the letters or cards they were invited to send—with or without gift—would be included in a large memory book to be presented to the Maiers at the celebration. The generous response surprised even the "On the Q" optimists, and two large volumes became necessary.

Father and Mother were profoundly moved. With words a little halting, they expressed astonished gratitude for so extraordinary a gift, and such extraordinary friends. Father said he would give serious thought to using the $10,000 for charitable purposes. Then they admitted an even deeper cause for thanksgiving that evening —for a quarter century of one another, in which God had permitted them to be of some small service in His kingdom. The many personal commendations were genuinely appreciated, but finally misdirected, because "to God alone all glory."

The celebration shifted to our home, where more guests had gathered, and continued late into the night. The place was decked with flowers sent by well-wishers, including fifty dozen roses. Another reception for additional hundreds of friends took place the next evening with an outdoor garden party at House Eleven. Once again the gently oscillating strands of Japanese lanterns gave the waterfall, the rock garden, and the guests a soft but animated incandescence, while a string quartet on the terrace provided background music. Once again the celebration crested with Father and Mother reliving a few episodes from their twenty-five years of romance and excitement.

After everyone had gone, they took another stroll through the garden, arm in arm, reviewing the last two days. They sat down on a stone bench in front of the upper pond. Water was gurgling under the bridge, and a large moth circled a violet-white-green lantern above them. A chorus of crickets sent strident vibratos into the tepid spring night.

A silver-anniversary groom said to his bride: "Honey, we've experienced many wonderful things in our years together, but weren't the last two days a . . . a culmination of joy?"

"Oh yes!" she agreed in a glad whisper. "Those friends of ours: what loyalty and appreciation!—Just think, we'll be eighty when we

. . .," she paused abruptly, then resumed, "celebrate our . . . golden wedding."

"God willing."

Both grew very silent and stared for some moments at the ivy which was trying to choke the crystalline rocks on the hillside. Soon she saw no ivy, no rocks. Tears were filling her eyes.

"Honey, what in the world. . . ?" He was startled.

"That word culmination . . . 'culmination of joy,' you said . . . what if it *is* just that: a summit now and a terrible drop later?"

"Now how could *that* ever happen? You know I'll always love you more deeply until the. . . ."

"*Yes* . . . until the day you die! That's the point," she cried. "This joy of ours . . . I feel . . . what if we've had our measure? That terrific pace of yours—I've begged you to slow down, doctors have pleaded. You're in that age bracket now where you *must* take care of yourself."

"But I feel perfectly fine!"

"And now this terrible plan of yours to use ABC in addition to Mutual: *two* different sermons per week—*double* work. . . ."

Finally he calmed her in the only way he knew, by promising to watch himself and emphasizing that everything was in the hand of God.


To be given a furnished summer home plus $10,000 within several years would make it appear that Father's large ship had now arrived. Not quite. His entire career had been dedicated to church work, which is another way of saying that all his life he had received only a modest salary.

When Father revealed his misgivings about accepting the $10,000, Q Committee assured him that the donors had intended it solely for his personal use, not charities, which they supported on other occasions. Walt and I also commented that Father should have become a monk since he seemed content enough without property. Two weeks later Otto Amling's telegram reiterated: LET ME EMPHASIZE AGAIN WELL WISHERS INTENDED LETTUCE FOR FAMILY CONSUMPTION WITHOUT STRINGS ATTACHED.

Nevertheless, letters of thanks were sent to all contributors with these lines included: "As evidence of our gratitude to God for His many blessings on our life during this quarter century, we plan to use this gift as the beginning of a fund for missions, education, and charities. So much physical and spiritual need is presented to us personally that it will be a joy to be able to help through your generosity."

### Seventeenth Season (1949/50)

Plans for the new Lutheran Hour series called for marked advances. Speaker and staff were excited by the news that the American Broadcasting Company had decided to accept sponsored religious programs, and soon 199 stations of ABC joined the Mutual and transcription chain in the United States. Some of the accessions replaced less advantageous outlets, and the enterprise now embraced 1,236 stations.[17] Moreover, ABC scheduled the Hour at an optimum Sunday *afternoon* time, when it could gain yet another audience—"make new friends and keep the old."

ABC also offered its television facilities for the program, as, in a welcome policy breakthrough, did the CBS television network. The first Hour telecast took place on a local, experimental basis over St. Louis' KSD-TV on New Year's Day, 1949, and it was followed periodically by other such programs. With only seventeen stations in America, the television industry was still in swaddling clothes. Area churches arranged special "TV services" to view these programs, but besides the wealthy homes the only real concentration of television sets in those pioneer days was at taverns.

Before one Hour telecast, a bartender on Olive Street announced to his customers, "All right, men, let's order our spare drinks now, 'cause I don't want to be disturbed during the next program." As the telecast began he called out, "Bar's closed!" There were hoots and commotion until the sermon, when the tavern stilled to an incongruously worshipful silence. Every barfly in the place had become intrigued by "that man."

"Dr. Maier is a natural for television," observed the station manager after the initial telecast. In the radio studio Father had always gestured with facial expressions and arms even though no audience could see him. Now, dressed formally in a gown, he did the same for the telecast. If the Hour did launch into TV, such persuasive visual contact would no longer be lost on the living rooms of America.

There were other advantages. The announcer and chorus went over well on video, with the versatile camera lenses sweeping along rows of singers or zooming in and out on the principals. One idea for a fresh sermonic technique occurred to the speaker and he used it to good advantage in the first telecasts. Occasionally his illustrations were literally projected, as the camera switched to a picture card of the very thing to which he was making reference in the sermon. Film footage was utilized in similar fashion.

Back in that other medium, "Bringing Christ to the Nations" was girdling the globe from 55 broadcasting countries and being heard in 120 different lands. Programming was translated into eleven new languages—among them Turkish, Persian, and Finnish—now thirty-six tongues in all. On New Year's Day, plans called for announcing fourteen new languages, raising the total to fifty. The Hour was on its way to fulfilling the ideal of Pentecost that "each . . . in his own native language . . . hear . . . the mighty works of God" (Acts 2:8 & 11). And the mail—Rudy Bertermann called every other week to report a new record, which finally climaxed at 17,000 letters in one day, almost 30,000 in one week. Extrapolated for the rest of the season, the totals would well exceed a half-million pieces of correspondence.

Prospects for foreign broadcasting continued to multiply. In the spring of 1949, three network officials of the Broadcasting Corporation of Japan emerged from the study at House Eleven, and a beaming Father announced that their 111-station network planned to carry a Japanese Lutheran Hour. This would add 45,360,000 to the world-wide potential listening audience of 450,000,000 people. Eventually the Hour became one of the top ten programs on Japanese radio.

Later in the year an Army inquiry arrived asking if Dr. Maier would consider an invitation from General Douglas MacArthur to address a mass Easter sunrise service before the Imperial Palace in Tokyo, which would be carried on Japanese and American networks. Such a trip would hold great promise, for Father could use the opportunity to speak via interpreter to crowds in other Japanese cities as well. If the door to China was closing, another portal in the Far East had now opened.

We were distressed to learn that Father intended to prepare a completely separate series of sermon manuscripts for the ABC broadcasts, in addition to the addresses for Mutual, the transcription stations, and the German programs. That would make an average of three sermon deliveries a week, plus frequent trips to World Broadcasting Studios in Chicago to cut transcriptions. We argued that a different address for ABC was entirely unnecessary, but Father replied: "The networks might not like it if the same sermons are used. And more important, much of America will now be able to get the broadcast both Sunday mornings and afternoons. I wouldn't want anyone to have to hear the same sermon twice."

And so the fall of 1949 saw two separate Lutheran Hour programs, with similar format but different announcements, choral numbers, and addresses. For the speaker it meant the task of authoring almost fifty pages of copy a week, for he still would not sacrifice quality or his habit of dictating twice as much as he could broadcast. Besides all this, the out-of-town engagements continued. Fall mass meetings in Midwestern metropolises drew overflowing crowds, although the revised policy for the seventeenth season had called for a gradual phase-down of the rallies in view of the demands on the speaker with doubled programming.

This was too much and Father should have realized it. He was in error at failing to recognize that his body could not keep pace with his mind, which was the heart of the problem. Mentally he was able to produce in this fashion—he would not have had a nervous breakdown at three times the load—but physically he could not absorb the by-products of stress, lack of sleep, and less-than-optimum diet which were inevitable with such a schedule. Nevertheless, so long as he was able, he felt a theological necessity to continue, for it was the cost of discipleship: "If any man would come after me, let him deny himself and take up his cross and follow me. For . . . whoever loses his life for my sake and the gospel's will save it" (Mk. 8:34 f.)

But the cross would have been lighter were it not for the chronic carping directed against him by several individuals in high places and low, whatever their motivation: envy, smallness, or "concern for the truth." Wherever possible, he tried to resolve differences with such detractors in a personal, straightforward manner and hardly ever bore anyone a grudge lasting more than twenty minutes. One individual, however, constituted a genuine "thorn in the flesh," an ultraconservative layman on the seminary board of control. Periodically he launched petty but very abusive attacks on Professor Maier which were entirely without foundation and therefore rejected by the board. Though Father consistently offered his friendship, the assailant worsened his tactics until finally another member of the board formally requested the man's resignation. After various pressures, the detractor addressed a note to Father, dated December 23, 1949, in which he stated: "I am pleased to inform you that I am prepared to drop the entire matter," though without any apologies. The letter arrived on Christmas Eve, but Father did not open it. For years the sender had sought to wound him via mail, and he thought this could only be more of the same. Nothing would now spoil his Christmas joy. As it happened, he never had a chance to read that letter.

Christmas, 1949, was not marred in any way. Harriet reports that the bounce in the Boss's step picked up the closer the holiday season approached. At last he could remain at home—no more rallies for some weeks. One morning he threw open the office door with a broad grin and announced, "Just think, Harriet, in a week both of the boys will be home with us! Paul back from Harvard, and Walter can make it too. He called last night to say he'll fly in after his Christmas Eve services at Elma." Walt was now pastor of Faith Lutheran Church in suburban Buffalo, where Father had ordained and installed him that September. Soon the Rev. Walter A. Maier, Jr. would announce his engagement to a young belle of the congregation.

Once again House Eleven flared with the excitement of preparation. The basement became a mailing room in which seminary students wrapped *Day by Day* calendars and Maier books for a lengthy gift list. Parcels flowed also in the other direction, and personal Christmas cards arrived in the multiple thousands. Once again they passed in review around the dinner table, and there were the usual arguments over whether a certain Bethlehem scene should rate three or four stars, what to do with that gaunt, modern view of the Christ Child, and why some artists should study geography before painting snow into a scene from the Holy Land.

The celebration that Christmas Eve was the study in joy it had been each year: once again the bells, Father exuberantly attacking the piano, the Nativity devotion, and maximum mirth afterward. One of his gifts to me was an enormous pair of webbed, arctic snowshoes, more than six feet long. Despite the fact that St. Louis drifts rarely reach 6 inches, I tried to act pleased. In a way, I was. Someone, obviously, had sold Father the Siberian items for a song. He never outgrew his love of bargains.

Christmas Day fell on a Sunday in 1949. I accompanied Father to KFUO for the broadcasts of his sermon, "Heaven's Love Lies in the Manger." He was pleased with it and, for the first time, had decided to repeat it for the afternoon ABC program. For old times' sake, I again served as studio time-signalman, and when I flashed the two-minute warning, Father was concluding with these words:

If your Christmas joy is not complete; if you have no true peace in your heart but only fear and worry; if you have not yet learned to know what unselfish love is, don't let the day close without having God bless you with the gift of this grace! When Handel wrote *The Messiah,* which every Christmas season brings joy into millions of hearts, he locked himself in his room in London for twenty-four days, with no other printed material than the passages of Holy Scripture dealing with Christ to form the text of his masterpiece. He let everything else fade away. At meal time a servant brought him food, but the tray often remained untouched. It is recorded that the servant stood by in silence as Handel's tears dropped on page after page to mingle with his sacred score. A visitor found the composer convulsed in sorrow as he wrote the music for *"He is despised."* When he finished the "Hallelujah Chorus" and wrote at the end, above his signature, "S.D.G.," a common abbreviation for the Latin "To God alone all glory," he later confessed, "I did see all heaven before me and the great God Himself."

You can have similar joy this Christmas. Even though you cannot take twenty-four days, before this Sunday has ended you can take twenty-four minutes apart from the rush, the feasting, the merry-making, and dedicate these to the Christ Child. As you read aloud, either alone or preferably with your friends and family, the record of the Savior's birth in Saint Luke's simple story; as you pray for the Christ Child's presence and blessing in your heart and in your life, His love will warm your soul with its divine glow and . . . you will learn the high and holy lessons of self-sacrificing love. With that love Christ would enrich each of you this day. God grant that you will now receive it and ever after glorify God for it! Amen![18]

That "Amen" crowned roughly 2,500,000 words he had spoken in sixteen and one-half years on the Lutheran Hour, and it marked the conclusion to his five hundred and ninth, and final, address.

On Christmas Day, a special world-wide broadcast had been featured for the last seven years, an *International Christmas Program* arranged months in advance by Gene Bernald. Carried over a network of 1,200 stations located even in Soviet satellite nations and such non-Christian countries as the Mohammedan lands of the Arab world, Hindu India, and the Buddhist Far East, the 1949 broadcast would be heard in fifty languages. The program featured Dr. Maier giving a "Christian commentary" (sermon not permitted!) on the significance of Christmas, which was translated by a battery of foreign speakers. Coordinated from New York, the broadcast switched to the South African veld for a native choir singing carols, then to choruses in Scandinavia, India, and China, and finally to North America and Concordia Seminary for Father's concluding comment and prayer. The globe-circling tour via long and short wave had become one of the unique experiences of the holiday season and brought response from corners of the earth never before touched.

That evening, the second round of gift distribution resumed at home, and on December 27 came the anniversary of a birth which Father revered next after Christ's own—Mother's. Her birthday party was the annual Christmastide excuse for sharing happiness, and once again the house filled with a merry mélange of associates and friends. The host had finished dictating his New Year's address shortly before guests arrived, and his mind, stimulated by the sermonizing, blazed out a wit which would not turn off. After refreshments and due prodding, he rehearsed the best episodes of the past year and finally told one of his favorite stories, which is literally true:

A clergyman who is also an official at KFUO jokingly used to refer to Rudy and me as his "enemies," because KFUO is a charitable operation relying on listener contributions like the Lutheran Hour, and somehow—he thought—this made us rivals or "enemies." One evening he was officiating at his daughter's wedding in a beautiful church nearby. As bride and groom stood before him he solemnly opened his formulary to the first sentence of the ceremony, which reads: "Dearly Beloved: We are assembled here in the presence of God and these witnesses . . ." and so on. But just before starting he spied Rudy, who was in the wedding party, and me sitting with Mrs. Maier and Ruth Bertermann in the front row. Then he began eloquently: *"Dearly Beloved: We are assembled here in the presence of God and these enemies to. . . ."* He halted, blushed, coughed, cleared his throat, and started again, this time reading it the way it was written!

Before the evening was over, another good story was born—this time at Father's expense. At the close of the party he offered a birthday prayer for Mother, which ended: "Bless us all, comma, O Lord, comma, and make us a blessing to many. Amen." Now the smiles were on a red-faced man who not only prayed his prayers but dictated the punctuation as well! Actually, Father was not losing his touch: that morning he had dictated a season's worth of prayers for the 1951 *Day by Day*, complete with enough commas to carry over into his own petitions. When I joshed him about the slip, he quickly reminded me of the time I ended one of my prayers: "Yours truly, Paul L. Maier."

Two nights later Father and Mother drove with their good friends, Oscar and Emma Brauer, to a holiday party just across the Mississippi in Red Bud, Illinois. Brauer, who was chairman of the Lutheran Hour Operating Committee, reported that Father was again the life-of-the-party whether he wished it or not. Walt and I had retired, but when sounds of conversation from our returning parents filtered upstairs, we joined them for a late snack in the breakfast nook. That day we had pried some honeymoon secrets out of Mother, and now we wanted to hear Father's side of it. The banter was as ridiculous as the hour of the night.

Very early the next morning, Walt woke me with the news, "Pop's had an attack of indigestion during the night and he's feeling a little queasy." Downstairs, Mother filled in the details. She had awakened shortly after 2:30 A.M. and discovered that Father was not in bed. She found him in the breakfast nook, sipping hot water. "Darling, what's the matter?" she asked anxiously. "How long have you been here?"

"I have a sharp pain in my chest and stomach."

"I'll call the doctor at once!"

"No! Please. It's just a spell of indigestion. I shouldn't have eaten that extra ham at the party. Now I'm probably in for it."

"But why didn't you wake me?"

"I didn't want to disturb you."

Mother uttered a brief prayer, then tried to curb the pain. But neither hot water, nor lying down, nor sitting up brought much relief. Without waiting any longer for permission, she telephoned Dr. Ted Hanser about 4 A.M. He heard the symptoms, made a preliminary diagnosis which he did not reveal, then recommended that Mother summon an ambulance for Father and he would meet them at Lutheran Hospital. When the patient overheard this development he countermanded such plans. "Too much fuss! Walter or Paul can drive me down just as well," he pleaded. "An ambulance would cause too much commotion." Reluctantly, Dr. Ted agreed.

He stood the trip well and soon was resting comfortably at the hospital. Later, doctors gave him an electrocardiogram which showed the beginning of a very characteristic and dangerous pattern. They could now confirm the preliminary diagnosis: *acute anterior myocardial infarction.* Translation: *coronary thrombosis* and *occlusion.* A blood clot was lodged in one of the arteries supplying the heart, cutting off circulation to part of the cardiac muscle. In popular terminology, Father had suffered a "heart attack."

Dr. Ted took us aside and explained the situation, this time without his familiar smile and glint: "Dr. Maier is a very sick man, but he has stood the original attack well. Some people die as soon as the clot is formed, so we've won the first round. But pray hard— the critical period is within the next two weeks!"

Walt and I were stunned. We had expected only indigestion. Mother turned aside with her first tears since that night in June when she sat at the pond with the man she loved.

# 20

## "Life Everlasting"

We drove home so that Mother could bring Father's personal effects down to the hospital, and she also packed her own clothes for an indefinite stay. From that morning on she was either at his bedside or within a few minutes of it.

Harriet, Rudy, and Mabel paid a brief, reassuring visit to the Boss, who apologized for "this monstrous inconvenience" and said: "Don't let any of this leak out to the press. I don't want people to worry needlessly."

"But what happens when you don't appear before the microphone the day after tomorrow?" asked Rudy.

"Oh, I'll be all right by then," answered a weak voice. Dr. Hanser smiled, shook his head, and said, "Better not plan on it!"

We all emerged from room 142 in the hospital's south wing still shaken by the "inconvenience." It was decided that Rudy would deliver the sermon Father had prepared for the New Year's Day program, after Elmer Knoernschild announced the substitution and asked the prayers of all listeners for Dr. Maier's early recovery "from illness."

January 1, 1950 marked the first broadcast Father ever missed because of health. In the introductory prayer, Rudy inserted petitions for the recovery of the regular speaker, and it was heartening to know that an unseen congregation was now adding millions of prayers to those of the family and friends.

Later in the afternoon, telegrams and long-distance calls started arriving from a concerned public, and this continued throughout the week. On Tuesday and Wednesday the mail hit headquarters, home, and hospital with a deluge of "get well" cards and letters—the press had learned the nature of the illness—and so many flowers arrived at the hospital that they were shared with the other patients. Special prayers were offered in thousands of Protestant churches, and even in such places as the Franciscan monastery in Pulaski,

Wisconsin, where one of the brothers sent the "Prayer of Saint Francis" to Father's bedside.

One man from Minneapolis seemed to send a telegram every two or three days, signing them "Billy Graham." After several arrived, I wondered just who this Graham might be—at that time he had not yet reached national prominence. Father, however, knew, because he smiled when I held one of the telegrams up to his oxygen tent.

A year or two later we learned that when Father had spoken at a fellowship meeting in west Chicago, a lanky, likable man named the Rev. William F. Graham was so impressed by his message that he asked if he could possibly address a special celebration at his church in nearby Western Springs. Affirmative. "The fact that the great Dr. Maier took time from his crowded schedule to address the little flock of a struggling young pastor made an indelible impression on me," Billy Graham later told a mass crusade meeting in St. Louis, to which he had invited Mother and me as guests of honor on the platform. Then he related another occasion when he was ill and Dr. Maier not only sent him one of his sermon books, but made a personal bedside call when again in the area. And now the situation was reversed: hence the telegrams.

On Monday, January 2, Father was so comfortable that he started chafing at being kept in the hospital for what he thought was now only a rest. He signaled Mother to open the side of his oxygen tent, then said: "Honey, I feel all right, and I really don't think I need oxygen any longer. Tell the doctors, and then *please* get me out of here soon. Why not take me home? I can rest just as well there as here." Mother looked at his pleading eyes and nodded, much encouraged by his improvement.

The next day Dr. Hanser reported: "Pulse good, blood pressure fine, respiration normal! He's more than holding his own." Doctors recommended a gradual reduction of oxygen. Heart specialists were in charge of the case, and Dr. Ted was our liaison with them. He explained Father's condition in further detail. A clot had formed or lodged in the left anterior descending branch of the coronary artery, and all tissues of heart muscle within an area radiating in a cone shape away from the clot were deprived of blood and had therefore died. Protecting leucocytes (white blood corpuscles) had then moved in on this section to remove the gangrenous tissue, and, ten or twelve days after the attack, scar tissue would start forming in the area affected. Meanwhile, capillaries were enlarging to provide the blood-starved section with collateral circulation.

What were his chances? "Good, although he's not out of the woods yet," replied Dr. Ted. "The first two weeks are critical because we aren't certain exactly how far up the coronary artery the clot has lodged. If too far up, or if parallel circulation doesn't develop adequately, we're in trouble. It all depends upon whether the cardiac muscle eventually gets enough nourishment for the demands made on it."

Mother was now permitted to read to her patient during short intervals because he constantly requested it. The following day he called for his files in order to prepare the next radio address, something on a "Moral State of the Union" theme. But we only smiled at him in return.

January 5 was a grand Thursday. The oxygen equipment was removed entirely, and the family could visit for longer periods. Once again a bit of the old jesting resumed. Father wanted to know exactly what was wrong with him, so, with doctors' approval, we gave a candid diagnosis. He only smiled and said, "That's what I thought all along, but I didn't want to scare you." Yet he seemed optimistic about his recovery and had no real thought of impending death. It is true that on scattered evenings before Christmas he had played Bach's "Come, Sweet Death," but that was only because of the sublime music, not the lyrics. The fact that he was serious about preparing his sermon shows that he expected the best, and the many prayers in his behalf encouraged him. And he was, in fact, moving "out of the woods."

On Friday the improvement continued and well over half the critical period was now past. Then, just after supper at 7 P.M., he suddenly gasped and found breathing frighteningly difficult. For the first time his face showed ashen concern. He sat up, struggling to catch his breath, and desperately begged Mother to get him an oxygen tent. She spent the most agonizing minutes in her life convincing the appropriate nurses to cut the appropriate tape in returning a tent to his room. The physical suffering which Walter Maier had escaped most of his life now crowded in on him. For a while every breath was a fierce contest, and his chest was racked with severe pain. However, sedation and oxygen finally cut the anguish.

Doctors were distressed about the new attack. It was worse than the one which had brought him to the hospital. His blood pressure, pulse, and respiration were markedly affected. Walt and I raced to the hospital when Mother called us about the setback. Privately we asked Dr. Ted, "What's the outlook?"

"Don't tell your mother yet: *very* serious, but probably nothing immediate."

We were thunderstruck. After a vigil and an agonizing prayer at his bedside, Walt and I drove home at 3 A.M. I was a volatile mixture of grief and rebellion. Suddenly I shot out at him, "If Pop dies—*my faith in God dies!*" He was a little horrified, but I continued, "Here we have one of the most prayed-for men in history —tomorrow another broadcast prayer, another twenty million joining in. That's *forty million* separate prayers so far! What does it take to convince God?"

Walt slammed on the brakes, grabbed me by the shoulders and shook me. "Do you think God is moved by statistics?" he shouted. "Do you think His will is changed by main strength . . . of mortal men?"

I made no reply. Only later did an impetuous teen-ager learn that *one* prayer can be as effective as forty million in the divine economy, and that God was answering them—in His own way.

And yet we could not believe that Father's assignment might now be completed. He was only fifty-six. He had been running in the center prime of life, not limping on the sidelines by reason of illness or age. Somehow, in the plans of Providence, he had always managed to elude death before this. At the end of March in 1931, he had been scheduled to fly to the West Coast for Good Friday and Easter addresses, but the pressure of local responsibilities forced him to ask a cancellation of the engagements. The very flight which he had booked exploded in mid-air and crashed in flames near

Bazaar, Kansas, killing all passengers, including Notre Dame's great Knute Rockne. On another occasion the crack "Hiawatha" was hurtling along the rails from Chicago to Milwaukee when one end of a structural brace on the pullman car in which Father was riding tore loose and sank obliquely toward the ties racing past underneath. A sharp-eyed switchman almost miraculously chanced to see it in the twilight and called ahead to have the train halted. Repair crews estimated that another five minutes could have witnessed a terrible accident, with the coach in question ripped apart. Again, because he had to travel so much throughout life, he was involved in two or three serious automobile accidents, but each time climbed out of the wreckage unscathed. There were other incidents, like the near-drowning at Lake Arrowhead. In the metaphor of spiritual athletics, it seemed that divine protection was constantly running interference for Father on the broken field of life, and we could not imagine that he was already at the end zone. Perhaps even yet God would intervene once again.

However, on Sunday, January 8, between 4 and 6 A.M. came a third attack, the next day at the same time, a fourth. Since each successive relapse diminished enormously any chances for recovery, it was now only a matter of time. And still he rallied bravely after each attack, fighting for life the only way he knew—spiritually. He requested the ministrations of his former student, the Rev. Herman Etzold, who was now pastor of his beloved St. Stephen's Church. From him he received Holy Communion and strengthening Scripture readings. Walt and I shared the night vigils. Periodically, Walt also supplied spiritual assurance in this, his first occasion to minister to a dying man.

Father's greatest inspiration, however, came from the person who had provided it ever since he met her in Indianapolis on a wonderful day in May, years ago. Although her heart was slowly shattering, Mother mustered up a courageous front, trying to do the impossible in making the last days a beautiful final visit for them. Between attacks there were hours when she could communicate with him in the unexpressed reverie of a magnificent love, or in the Scripture verses they had used for the special circumstances of their lives, each now rich in connotative memory. When things were looking bleak:

If God be for us, who can be against us? . . . In all these things we are more than conquerors through Him who loved us. (Rom. 8:31,37)

The daily motto while they were separated during his mission to Europe:

Fear thou not, for I am with thee: be not dismayed; for I am thy God. . . . (Is. 41:10)

Or the climactic conclusion of St. Paul which applied now as never before:

. . . I am persuaded that neither death, nor life, nor angels, nor principalities, nor powers, nor things present, nor things to come, nor height, nor depth, nor any other creature, shall be able to separate us from the love of God, which is in Christ Jesus our Lord. (Rom. 8:38-39)

To help him rally from the fourth attack, Mother assured him that he was surrounded by a wall of prayer from people in many parts of the world and that he could never sink too low for The Almighty. "Remember," she said, "the eternal God is thy refuge, and underneath are the everlasting wings." (Deut. 33:27)

"No, Darling, 'everlasting arms,'" he corrected her in a weak voice. His intellect was clear till the very last.

Later in the day he awoke and saw me in the room. As the nurse opened his tent he smiled and whispered, "Hello, Palsy-walsy!"— the greeting he had used when, as a child, I would fly into his arms after he returned from a speaking engagement. These were his last words to me.

Now, finally, he accepted the fact that God was calling an end to his ministry, and he made a confession of faith as simple-yet-profound as Scripture itself. Wrote Mother:

". . . I heard him whisper, 'Divine justice! Divine justice!' Shortly after that, he confessed clearly and distinctly, 'All have sinned, and come short of the glory of God; being justified freely by His grace through the redemption that is in Christ Jesus.' (Rom. 3, 23, 24) A little later he continued, again in a loud, clear voice, 'If any man sin, we have an Advocate with the Father, Jesus Christ the Righteous: And He is the Propitiation for our sins: and not for ours only, but also for the sins of the whole world.' (I Jn. 2, 1, 2)

I realized that this was his last message to his radio audience. After the first verse, he exclaimed, 'Thank God, we have an Advocate!' At this point he was interrupted by a nurse's ministrations. After pausing for a moment, he asked, 'Now may I proceed?' and then he continued with the second verse. Lingeringly, with a radiant smile, he repeated, '. . . and not for ours only, but also for the sins *of the whole world!*'

"Taking his hand, I exclaimed, 'How wonderful, Darling! . . . and that same Savior . . . is here with you now, so you can go to sleep again and rest.' He repeated, 'Yes, now I can go to sleep!' With a smile on his lips, he went to sleep. Those were the last words I heard my beloved husband utter."[1] And so it was: sin and grace to the very end.

The last attack followed the next day at 1:30 P.M. His body fought on to rally from it, but his mind was already at peace. He never fully regained consciousness. Doctors told us it was only a question of hours, and the family, Rudy, Harriet, and Mabel never left his bedside. For twelve final hours his blood-starved heart limped on, amazing specialists who attended. Edema began to occlude his breathing, as cardiac insufficiency added this symptom to what was now a characteristic congestive heart failure. At midnight his respiration became halting, the pause between breaths longer and longer. Saturated in grief, we repeated, loud enough for him to hear if there were any spark of consciousness, the old German hymn-prayer Grossie had taught him as a child: *"Breit' aus die Flügel beide* (Lord Jesus, Who Dost Love Me)" and the Scripture which concluded every evening prayer of his life: "The blood of Jesus Christ, His Son, cleanseth us from all sin. Amen." During that verse his eyes half-opened and it seemed as if he were trying to join the "Amen." Then he stopped breathing.

Walter Arthur Maier died at 12:25 A.M. on January 11, 1950. This is the medical, legal, and historical statistic. It is accurate, though it does not supply all the information. Faith provides more. The man's theology is summarized from a glance at the titles to his books: Christocentricity. His life, and now his death, had centered in the Christ who said: "I am the resurrection and the life; he who believes in me, though he die, yet shall he live, and whoever lives and believes in me shall never die." For which reason the church has always confessed: "I believe . . . in the life everlasting." As this clause crowns the Creed, so it also crowned this career. The spiritual statistic reads: at 12:25 A.M. on January 11, 1950, Walter Arthur Maier returned to his Creator for entry into life everlasting.

Our grief was no longer a private thing. It became apparent that there was little need of informing relatives and friends, for the nation's press, wire services, and networks flashed the news. In newspapers from London to Sydney, from metropolitan dailies to neighborhood journals, the world learned that the familiar voice of "Bringing Christ to the Nations" was now stilled. In many American cities and towns, front-page headlines announced this death, and unusual editorial tributes followed a day or two later. The public reacted in shock, because the terminal nature of Father's successive attacks had been concealed to avoid alarming people if he did pull through.

Arne Pettersen, of the transatlantic romance, arrived at his New York office on January 11 without having read the morning newspaper or heard the radio. During lunch at India House with two friends, he could sense that they were shielding him from something. At the second cup of coffee, one of them said, "Arne, this morning a great servant of God was called home." "No! It can't be!" he protested. "Yes, Dr. Maier passed away at 12:25 this morning." Arne was crushed, called his wife Ingrid, then stopped at a telegraph office and composed a message for Mother to the meter of a Scandinavian hymn.

Cousin Ruth Virginia Maier, Karl's daughter, was a coed at Madison College in Virginia. When she walked into art class, a friend came up to her and said, "R.V., you have our very deepest sympathy." "Why?" She was startled. "Well, your uncle died early this morning; we heard it on the radio news." She left the classroom in tears. And hundreds of personal friends, millions of broadcast friends learned in a variety of ways.

The dispatch came repeatedly on network newscasts. In his Sun Oil *Three-Star Extra*, NBC's Ray Henle sympathetically an-

nounced the sadness, datelined St. Louis, and then a special story
followed at 7:15 P.M., (Eastern Standard Time), when homes
throughout America heard a veteran newscaster:

This is Morgan Beatty, speaking for Alka-Seltzer, bringing you *News
of the World.* . . . Tonight, transcribed and direct. . . . *St. Louis*—The
voice heard round the world, by millions, is stilled. . . . The story, by
Harold Grams, Station KSD . . . in St. Louis. . . .[2]

Grams did a fine feature on Father, and included recorded excerpts of his final address on the air.

Telegrams and cablegrams from America and overseas arrived
by the multiple hundreds, letters of condolence by the many, many
thousands. They came from unknowns and well-knowns, people
of every calling, religion, race, and, once the news had fully penetrated, from most of the nations on earth. Because these communications often reflected the heartfelt sentiments of people whose
lives were changed through the Maier ministry, many spoke of
"The Twentieth Century Luther," or "St. Paul," "The Modern
Jeremiah," or "Elijah," "The Voice of Lutheranism," and similar
epithets, which prove only the depth in which many held this
man, this career. It was not "adoring followers" but responsible
individuals who expressed high tributes, leaders like Senator
Alexander Wiley, who wired condolences on the "loss of a great
American," or Governor Henry Schricker who telegraphed, "The
world has lost one of its greatest preachers. . . ." Among churchmen, Archbishop (now Cardinal) Joseph E. Ritter ". . . prayed
for the repose of his devoted soul and also that the unity of faith
and charity that he worked for so energetically may be ultimately
achieved;" while Billy Graham wired, "Shocked beyond words. . . .
Christendom has lost one of its greatest leaders."

Phrases from some of the cablegrams are a study in international
sympathy:

*Paris*—FRENCH LH AUDIENCE MOURNS. . . .

*Guatemala City*— . . . LUTHERANISM LOSES ITS MAN OF HALF
    CENTURY. . . .

*Adelaide*—ALL HERE SAD AND SHAKEN . . . STAGGERING NEWS. . . .

*London*—STUNNED BY THE SAD NEWS QUOTES CHRIST WAS MAGNIFIED IN HIS BODY WHETHER BY LIFE OR BY DEATH QUOTES. . . .

*Johannesburg*—PROFOUNDLY SHOCKED. . . .

*Buenos Aires*—GRIEVED. . . .

*Heidelberg*—THE LORD BLESS AND SUSTAIN YOU. . . .

Later the shock wave registered in a flood of foreign mail, typified in this first letter opened at the Australian Hour branch office: "We know it was God's will that Dr. Maier has been called to higher service, but many hearts are aching. . . . It was through Dr. Maier that I was reinstated in Christ."

Many who held executive office felt a spontaneous urge to communicate the joint sympathy of all staff, employees, members, or students in their charge. A multitude of such messages arrived from presidents of church bodies and organizations, the broadcasting industry, universities, colleges, seminaries, corporations, societies, and clubs.

Unusually generous was the reaction of some of Father's competing colleagues in religious radio who paid him great tribute on their respective programs, especially veteran radio evangelist Dr. Charles E. Fuller on the *Old Fashioned Revival Hour,* Dr. S. F. Lowe on the *Baptist Hour,* Dr. H. M. S. Richards on the *Voice of Prophecy,* and Dr. P. H. Eldersveld on the *Back to God Hour.* Pastors of many denominations wrote excerpts of the special testimonials they included in their sermons and over local broadcasts.

Probably the most moving aspect of the condolences was their reflection of the whole spectrum of American religious life. Protestants clustered at both conservative and liberal poles voiced tribute. From the orthodox wing, Dr. Harold J. Ockenga, president of the National Association of Evangelicals, wired, in part:

GREAT LOSS IN HOME-GOING OF DR. MAIER FELT AND EXPRESSED BY 5500 CHRISTIANS MEETING IN REVIVAL AT BOSTON UNDER BILLY GRAHAM. . . . ANNOUNCEMENT MOVED MANY TO REPENTANCE.

(When Dr. Graham first learned the news in his hotel room, he and his team joined in earnest prayer that God would "send another to pick up the torch where Dr. Maier had left off." Later he stated that the Maier ministry was very instrumental in prompting him toward his own international evangelistic mission.) And from the liberal theological wing, Protestant Radio Commission Director Everett Parker of the Federal Council of Churches telegraphed deepest sympathy, adding, ". . . His voice will be sorely missed on the air." In another sector of Christendom, the many testimonials which arrived from Roman Catholics, high and low, are themselves a rebuke to anti-Catholic bigotry. Even Jews, in whom Professor Maier always had a special interest because of Semitics studies, wrote messages with almost Christian phraseology.

For headquarters staff, the L.L.L., the seminary, but especially for our family, this universal sympathy to some extent cushioned the terrible blow. It was heartening to see how much a man could be esteemed by so many people, so few of whom had ever met him. The necessity of funeral preparations and the arrival of friends and relatives from different parts of the county also helped absorb our shock.

But nothing—except the present resurrection of Walter Maier —could finally insulate against grief. A cushion may soften the impact, but the impact arrives inexorably. The man who continued to exist in dream world and in memory was no longer physically alive. Awaking each morning after January 11 brought another painful reminder of that fact. Even with the thirteen-day warning, his death still stunned us. Had we not been related to the man, yet known of him, we would have been saddened along with the church. But beyond that, this was *our* husband, *our* father. Whatever other roles he played in life, he filled these two admirably, a man with brimming concern and pride in his family.

Mother was crushed, but now started to rebound on her own strong faith. Walt and I tried to follow suit. And further sorrow was temporarily absorbed by the details and decisions now confronting us.

Father lay in state at the Beiderwieden Funeral Home on Thursday, January 12, and was transferred the next day to the chapel at Concordia Seminary, the environment where he had spent all but two of his productive years. Students provided a continual day-and-night honor guard on a shift basis, and two of them stood sentinel at the ends of his casket, just below the chancel, until the funeral service.

Both sites were filled with hosts of floral pieces, and soon there was no more room. Many of the cards accompanying the flowers or memorial wreaths constituted small pieces of the mosaic which was Father's life. But the bouquets which told the most were those like the lavender chrysanthemums with an ungarnished Christian message from "The First Presbyterian Church, Levelland, Texas." Father had never met anyone in that congregation, yet by the "miracle of radio" he was an old friend to them.

From the moment he lay in state, a nearly unbroken line of people filed past to pay their final respects. Even the small hours of the early morning found workers on night shifts stopping by to glance at the man who had become an institution in their Sunday lives. Frequently the queue was interrupted by a familiar face from a distant part of the country and a distant chapter in the life of Walter Maier. A majority of the people in those lines, however, we did not know, and they were a biopsy of the radio audience: parents holding their children up for a final glance at the man in repose; young people on their way to a basketball game, stopping in silence; clergy and laity of different faiths grieving; long rows of tearful nuns—one sister from a busload of them assuring Mother, "We don't have to pray for *him*" (in Roman Catholic theology, the same would usually be said only of saints); waiters and waitresses from the Town Hall, scene of the silver anniversary banquet exactly seven months earlier; filling station attendants still dressed in uniform, removing their caps and covering the Texaco or Standard emblems over their hearts; university professors discussing Father's place in religious history with members of the seminary faculty; occasionally a blind or crippled person assisted into the chapel "to be near him for the last time;" and countless faces we never saw before or since.

George Burbach, general manager of KSD-TV, had asked Mother for permission to televise the funeral "as a service to the city and possibly to the nation." Our first reaction was a decided negative: we would never want to make a show of this funeral, or have television equipment obstruct the worship. Mr. Burbach replied that he was thinking of Dr. Maier's many followers in the city who could not possibly crowd into the seminary chapel, as well as his far larger radio audience. If arrangements were completed, the special telecast would be transmitted via the new coaxial cable over the NBC network and become the first funeral nationally televised. As for equipment, cameras would be in the balcony out of everyone's way. Harriet, plunged in deep grief for the Boss, reminded us, "Dr. Maier would think first of others: some could be won for the faith in viewing the service." We gratefully agreed.

This decision was providential, because long before the service began on Saturday, January 14, at 2 p.m., special groups alone had filled all 900 of the reserved chapel seats: faculty colleagues, the St. Louis clergy, broadcast headquarters staff, guests from out of town, and the three participating Lutheran Hour and Seminary Choruses. But television receivers had been set up in classrooms throughout Concordia and in the large gymnasium, permitting thousands to join in the worship through distributed orders of service. KSD newscaster Frank Eschen teamed with Elmer Knoern-schild to give a dignified narration of the proceedings. Although fed to Chicago, transfer difficulty beyond that point prevented the telecast from going over the network. However, greater St. Louis participated in that service, and it was reported that radio-TV sections of city department stores were thronged with people.

The service was stately in simplicity, except for its length—two and one-half hours. Some of Father's favorite hymns were sung, including "I Know That My Redeemer Lives," "Now Rest Beneath Night's Shadow," and, of course, his signature theme, "Beautiful Savior." The choice of minister surprised some: not a famous church leader, but the pastor of Father's own St. Stephen's Church. Yet the Rev. Herman A. Etzold rose to the occasion with an admirable memorial address, which, more than mere eulogy, provided a positive thrust needed at a time of general distress. The title itself was a turnabout: "Death is the Christian's Triumphant Hour." Declaring that the family, the Lutheran church, and Christians throughout the world were sharing a great loss, he stated, in excerpt:

Humanly speaking, Dr. Maier's sudden death was untimely. He was at the peak of his great mission of Bringing Christ to the Nations over the International Lutheran Hour. The hands which clasped in warm friendship all who came within his reach—the poor and the rich, the scholar and the illiterate, the people of all races without distinction —lie folded in death; the great heart which radiated Christian love wherever he went has ceased to beat the rhythm of life; the voice which called multitudes to repentance and was the best known and most widely heard voice in the world today has been silenced. . . .

God endowed our esteemed brother with exceptional mental brilliance, power of speech, and physical endurance. He could have used these to his own advantage for the acquisition of power, fame, and wealth. He chose, instead, to use them in the Savior's service. . . .

He "fought a good fight." His voice was raised, with the clarity of a Jeremiah, against wickedness in high and low places, against godless attitudes, against religious apathy and indifference, against false teachings and philosophies which robbed men of Christ and forgiveness through His blood. He never dissipated his time and energy in vain disputings, but always came to the point with the Christian message. . . .

His work is eternal, for human souls which are at rest in God die not. Only in eternity will we know how many souls were called out of the darkness of unbelief into the light of Christ and encouraged on the way of righteousness by the faithful witness of this man of God. . . .

"Because I live, ye shall live also." If anything in the Bible is true, this assurance is. Beyond the shadow of doubt or the possibility of debate, Dr. Maier, who believed these words, is still among the living. . . . Last Wednesday morning was his hour of triumph, greater than all the applause which men might have given him. . . . he has heard the voice of Jesus say: "Well done, thou good and faithful servant. Enter thou into the joy of thy Lord.". . .[3]

Then followed an address on behalf of the Lutheran Church–Missouri Synod by its President, Dr. John W. Behnken, who expressed gratitude to God that the Church had been served in a variety of areas by a man of such extraordinary talents. The next day he would pay him further generous tribute in a memorial address over the Lutheran Hour, "Christ, Your Matchless Advocate," based on Father's dying confession.[4]

Representing the seminary and Station KFUO was the lifelong

friend from across the street, Dr. William Arndt, who stated, in part:

It was on account of his truly astounding gifts as a writer, together with his wide acquaintance with his chosen field, that his friends often discussed the question whether he should not be induced to give his time and efforts to the production of scholarly, learned commentaries on books of the Bible and other strictly theological works rather than to the radio ministry. . . . He stated that, while works of this nature are needed, there are millions of souls who are famished for want of the Gospel and that the question is not what is needed, but what is needed most urgently.[5]

The final address came from one of those most affected by his death, Dr. Eugene R. Bertermann. Just before the service, Rudy had stood at the bier for the final time, making the sign of the cross over his dearest friend—a study of sorrow, eloquent in silence. His tribute was now expressed on behalf of the Lutheran Hour and the L.L.L. Summarizing the Maierian theology and ministry as unqualified Christocentricity, he said:

The Lutheran Hour and the Lutheran Laymen's League have suffered an irreparable loss. Bringing Christ to the Nations in its present scope and size constitutes a mighty monument to the work of Dr. Walter A. Maier. . . . *"They that be wise shall shine as the brightness of the firmament, and they that turn many to righteousness as the stars forever and ever."* (Dan. 12:3).

Then he sounded a call to perpetuate the broadcast:

The mighty radio mission . . . which under God Dr. Maier has founded and brought to its present eminence, must continue. . . . The Lutheran Hour faces staggering problems; yet with God's blessing and the assurance of your prayers, they will be met and successfully surmounted. We shall sadly miss Dr. Maier's counsel, but it would be his wish that the radio ministry . . . should carry on its testimony. . . .[6]

A final prayer, benediction, and singing of "Beautiful Savior" closed the service. Numbly we filed out of the chapel and into the cortege. Hundreds of cars accompanied us to the cemetery. After a brief committal service conducted by Pastor Arthur Nitz, the body was laid to rest in Concordia Cemetery.

House Eleven was filled with flowers and food when we returned. Friends wanted to ease our first entry into a home where the head was now unavoidably absent. It was a chill evening. I recall tormenting myself with an illogical thought: it would be terribly cold for Father—outside.

A remarkable phenomenon took place on Sunday, January 15. "Memorial Services for Dr. Walter A. Maier" were held in London, Paris, and other foreign capitals; in Boston, Manhattan, Buffalo, Detroit, New Orleans, Denver, and many major cities throughout America; in Aurora, Illinois; Schuyler, Nebraska, and hundreds of smaller towns across the land. They were conducted in Lutheran churches and those of other denominations. Some were regular worship services with memorial addresses by the pastor; others were special city-wide observances, which were also scheduled in the course of the next three months.

The broadcasting industry also scheduled special commemorations. Radio officials acknowledged that an extraordinary enterprise had been flourishing in their medium, unnoticed by some of them, and telegram tributes arrived from the network presidents as well as local station managers. Typical of the latter was the gesture by the director at WNOE, New Orleans, who interrupted his program schedule on January 11 to give a few minutes' personal testimonial to "the man who literally gave his life to bring Christ to the nations."

A surprising reaction developed in foreign radio. Certain station managers in Latin America, Europe, and Australia expressed a private sorrow in the richness of their native languages, for they had been influenced by the very messages they were broadcasting. As a memorial, some of them donated air time for one or more "Christ to the Nations" programs. Radio Tangier and several other overseas stations broadcast the entire funeral service when the transcription disks arrived by air mail.

That first Sunday evening we sat in the breakfast nook for supper, as always. This was when the *Jack Benny Show* had regularly accompanied our traditional Sunday evening cold cuts, hard-boiled eggs, toast, and fruit. No one would have chuckled more heartily at the Bennyesque humor than Father. It was a bad moment for us, and morale plunged as we saw the empty place at the northeast corner of the table. Only now did the deeper sense of loss arrive with full impact. He was cut down . . . dead . . . buried . . . gone . . . categorically separated . . . never to return in this world. A mood akin to despair was moving in on the breakfast nook when Mother pulled out the *Day by Day* leaflet in order to begin family devotion. She had that one spark of comfort: Father had completed the 1950 and 1951 series, so he would continue to speak to his family for two more years in the evening meditations. She started reading, but then her pulse quickened because of the message shown in the accompanying illustration.

Somehow it was a personal communication to us, and Father had joined the devotional circle after all. Within a week, dozens of letters with that leaflet arrived from people who hoped that Mother would not miss the message in the turmoil.

Later we noticed an almost prophetic cast to some of the final words Father wrote. In his last complete sermon, which Rudy had delivered on January 1, appeared the phrases: "What can the new year bring you? . . . Almost a million and a half will die in the United States during 1950. . . . Will you be one of them?"[7] Similarly, a newly discovered partial manuscript intended for the New Year's broadcast over ABC—the *very* last thing he ever wrote—has only Part Two completed, which begins: "Good health is one of the greatest of God's gifts. For many it is beyond the possibility of purchase, since the New Year finds them afflicted with a humanly incurable disease." And on succeeding pages he gives advice on maintaining physical and spiritual health!

However predictive such passages may seem, they probably have nothing to do with any foreboding in his own life. They are coincidental, if poignantly so. But they do show that a man who "kept his pulse on human affairs" in order to have a message as applicable to as many people as possible was also keeping pulse on himself better than he ever knew.

The *why* of this death—not the medical, but the religious why—was a question which persistently posed itself in my mind during

JANUARY
15—350
**1950**
*Sunday*

**15**

MORNING
1 Chronicles 15

EVENING
1 Samuel 1, 20-28

THE SECOND SUNDAY AFTER EPIPHANY
First American passenger railroad,
the Charleston and Hamburg, 1831

---

*"The sufferings of this present time are not worthy to be compared with the glory which shall be revealed in us."*
—Romans 8, 18

The Holy Spirit help us believe the comfort contained in the Scripture text for this Lord's day, *"The sufferings of this present time are not worthy to be compared with the glory which shall be revealed in us!"* We should not let sorrow over our departed dear ones blot out the vision of the cross, the resurrection grave, the open heavens! Rather should we hear the Son of God promise, *"What I do thou knowest not now; but thou shalt know hereafter,"* and then kneel before Him with the victorious resignation, "Whatever God ordains is good!" When we believe the Gospel of Christ's atoning death for our life; when we begin to realize that one moment in heaven is worth more than centuries on earth, we will understand that God let our Christ-dedicated dear ones meet death so that they could the longer enjoy the hallowed bliss and beauty with their Redeemer. Then, washed in the blood of the Lamb, resurrected in celestial radiance, we will know in higher knowledge that our hours of agony are *"not worthy to be compared with the glory which shall be revealed in us,"* when, face to face with Jesus, the unspeakable glories of Heaven are ours.

the following weeks and months. The man was precisely in the prime of life. How much further the international radio enterprise would have expanded had he lived cannot, of course, be estimated. The expression "saturation point" was not in his vocabulary unless the goal of "every available and suitable station on earth" were reached. His future career would probably have written a new chapter in the history of religious television, where he would have

been even more effective. After this he could have retired to the life
of scholarship and theology which had been his first, if jilted, love.
He had been advancing God's kingdom: why did God take him?

The sympathy mail showed that many had asked and tried to
answer the same question. Among the explanations volunteered:
Dr. Maier had worked so hard that God was now giving him an
eternal vacation; the good die young because God loves them so;
or even, "heaven needed the extra brightness which he supplied!"
The suggestions were pious and kind, but did not go very far in
answering the question. Much correspondence, of course, brought
a high degree of accurate spiritual comfort, though finally the action
of Providence could not fully be understood this side of eternity.

Shortly after my return to Harvard following the funeral, I wrote
this letter:

> Dunster C-42
> Cambridge 38, Mass.
> January 24, 1950

Dear Mother and Walt:

The very salutation to just two of you is very difficult. My feelings of
resentment have somewhat given place to a Christian resignation, yet
I cannot seem to digest the awful reality that my dear father is really
gone. When I think of sickly friends whom we had somewhat sorrow-
fully dismissed as candidates for heaven, and then of vigorous, healthy
Pop, who was good for another 25 years, I ask *"Why?"* Considering
that—

—many people get over a coronary without too many ill effects;
—a cure could have done nothing but strengthen the faith of millions who prayed for him: out of this prodigious number of people
   I cannot help but think that there must be some weak believers
   who were shocked out of their faith by Pop's passing;
—Pop would have led such an abundantly useful life as a theologian,
   and his success here could possibly have exceeded even that of
   his radio ministry;
the thought comes: was not the blood clot, after all, just a biological
malfunction in an unsupernatural world where the course of the disease was in no way affected by human prayer or divine intervention?

The above thought, which seems so logical to a detached outlook, fades before the deeper realization that, if Christianity were false, then—

> —my dear, sane father was a tragic devotee of a hollow superstition, and used the talents which could have gained him wealth, high station, and a longer life for a useless cause.
>
> —Pop's interment would have been the last time I would ever see him.

But conscience and faith condemn these conclusions. Therefore *one cannot help but be a Christian*, now, for more reasons than ever before!

Everyone writes me that you are doing wonderfully, Mother. Keep it up! I'll make it home for Easter, since we have spring vacation then. Tell me what immediate decisions you are facing, and *don't* sign anything without letting me know.—Now I must grind for final exams!

Love,
*Paul*

The letter was written by a sophomore, and parts of it are sophomoric, but some of the implications remain true: only Christianity has a final solution to the problem and tragedy of death. No other religion or philosophy has advanced any adequate alternative or answer.

For this reason the Rev. W.A.M., Jr., in his letter of the same date, could write above his grief: "Mother, may our Heavenly Father enable you to recognize the glory of the deliverance which death brings to all who trust in Him, and now direct you to your life's future work. 'Trust in the Lord with all thine heart. . . . and He shall direct thy paths.'"

The question *why?* had other partial answers. In accomplishing the tasks which Providence had assigned him, Walter Maier had packed three or four careers into one life, as friends commented. In that sense he had lived a very long life indeed. And by now it was time to retire the question, for in his own *Day by Day* message:

We should not let sorrow . . . blot out the vision of the cross, the resurrection grave, the open heavens! Rather should we hear the Son of God promise, *"What I do thou knowest not now; but thou shalt know hereafter,"* and then kneel before Him with the victorious resignation, "Whatever God ordains is good!"

# Epilogue: "He Still Speaks"

The life of Walter A. Maier ended more than a decade ago, but his ministry did not. The paradox is hardly puzzling. "He died, but through his faith he is still speaking" (Heb.11:4) is the Scripture verse which many applied in this instance, for since January, 1950, it was discovered that this man did continue to speak, as he would in years to come.

He was resting in peace, but people would not let his memory rest. They determined that this man should not be forgotten.

We were astonished that the phrase *Dr. Walter A. Maier Memorial* could be attached spontaneously to such a variety of things, intangible or concrete. There were memorial poems. Wrote Dr. W. G. Polack, "Never in my twenty-five years of work on *The Lutheran Witness* has any one event moved so many to express their feelings in poetry."[1] There were memorial hymns and wedding music, a large number of Maier Memorial concerts in various cities across America by choral groups, orchestras, string quartets, and the like. Articles in theological and secular journals were dedicated to his memory, as were paintings, such as an anonymous presentation to the seminary (by Gene Bernald) of the celebrated Doré original, "Soldiers of the Cross." There were Maier Memorial displays, exhibits, bronze plaques, stained glass windows, sets of his books presented to key libraries which were missing copies, and resolutions from a variety of organizations. There were even memorial children, whose first two names were "Walter Maier ———," as also during his lifetime.

More extensive memorials were erected. Some time after the funeral, a group of Father's confidants gathered in St. Louis and proposed setting up a trust fund to provide for his widow as a first tangible tribute to their deceased friend. One of the men, Edmund Kuhlman, had better information: "That won't be necessary, gentlemen. Many years ago, Dr. Maier asked me to begin an invest-

376

ment program for him in Detroit. Although he could send me only a pittance each month—I've never seen anything like it—the investments I made for him always did *far* better than my own! With reinvestment the sum grew, and, together with life insurance and Synod's pension fund, Mrs. Maier will be provided for." In these few words, "the man who drove the Maiers on their honeymoon" summarized a lifetime of service to our family.

Much relieved, the men next inquired as to what was being planned in the way of a monument at Father's grave. Mother showed them sketches of an idea she had had in mind, but dismissed as too expensive for her. They were so impressed with the plans that they formed on the spot the Dr. Walter A. Maier Memorial Association, Inc., a nonprofit organization to gather funds for this project and in other ways also "to perpetuate the ministry and memory of the man who brought Christ to the nations." Most of the officers' names are familiar: Ed Kuhlman, president; Chicago's Walter Pitann, vice-president; Fred Rutz, treasurer; and the man who was the motive force in so many church projects, W. F. Meyer of Chicago, executive secretary. "W.F." blended consecration with organizing genius, and his participation was insurance enough for the venture.

Mother intended the monument to be as typical of her husband in death as in life, and the least common denominator of that life was speaking for Christ. Instead of a cold mausoleum, therefore, the memorial would be a figure of the beckoning Christus in front of a tall, dorsal screen in modified Gothic lines, flanked by smaller wing screens which symbolized Father's specialized ministry, and then arced by two semicircular walls with built-in benches—the entire structure in ageless granite. The passer-by would be invited to sit down and meditate, for on the walls would be chiseled several of the Scripture passages which had figured so prominently in the life of Walter Maier.

With these directions, seminarian Martin E. Marty, the future author and editor, made a preliminary sketch of the monument which Mother sent to Jones Brothers Guardian Memorials of Barre, Vermont. Their chief designer and officials became enthused with the project, prepared a serene and graceful plan, and pared prices to the bone in tribute to the Maier ministry.

Funds arose almost spontaneously. As it was, many people had inquired if a memorial of some kind were being planned, and perhaps the spirit of the Sunday school at Zion Church in Painesville, Ohio, is representative. Teachers wondered out loud whether the children would like to have a part in "Dr. Maier's monument." Not only was there an emphatic "Yes!" but the offering was triple the usual collection.

Since there would not be enough room for the structure in Concordia Cemetery, the church which Professor Maier served part-time as assistant pastor in the twenties donated several acres of its Our Redeemer Cemetery for the Maier Memorial Gardens at the highest point in St. Louis County. Accordingly, the burial vault was exhumed, moved, and reinterred at the new site after construction was completed.

On Sunday, October 7, 1951, a multitude gathered at the Gardens for the dedication of the monument. The structure in light gray granite was even more handsome than the design, especially against a background overlooking St. Louis in the distance. Commemorative services continue to be held here annually, and hardly a week passes without visitors stopping to pay silent tribute.

There are also structural memorials. Concordia Bronxville dedicated its spacious, new Walter A. Maier Library; St. Stephen's, its Maier Education Building. The Walther League announced plans for a Maier Memorial Chapel at its Chicago headquarters. The L.L.L. erected its Maier Memorial Christ of the Nations Chapel at St. Louis headquarters, and Concordia Seminary, its Maier Rare Book Library. Institutions which had no immediate connection with his career also commemorated him, as the Walter A. Maier Lutheran High School in Los Angeles. Overseas, the Maier Broadcasting Station at Tangier beams "Christ to the Nations" programs via short wave Monday through Friday in seventeen languages.

However, there is a living memorial more appropriate than any monument, chapel, or school: the international radio enterprise did continue. After the death of its founding voice, the Lutheran Hour naturally faced grave difficulties. A series of guest speakers was scheduled until Dr. Lawrence Acker, L.L.L. pastoral advisor, became interim speaker. His successor and for two years the next regular speaker was Prof. Armin C. Oldsen of Valparaiso University. A Walter A. Maier Lutheran Hour Fund had also been established to help perpetuate the broadcast and coordinate the large sums contributed *in memoriam* after January, 1950. Further continuity was assured by Dr. Rudy Bertermann remaining at headquarters for the next nine years.

One of the brightest seminarians in Professor Maier's classes in Old Testament had been strapping, six-foot Oswald ("Ossie") Hoffmann, and for that distinction he was made student assistant. Later, after teaching at Concordia Bronxville, he became director of public relations for the Lutheran church and subsequently also advised in the production of the films *Martin Luther* and *Question 7*. It was Dr. Oswald Hoffmann who delivered a remarkable memorial address in Manhattan on the Sunday following his teacher's death. Several excerpts:

. . . It is safe to say that no man in the first half of this century—anywhere in the world—so touched the hearts of the suffering masses in this country and abroad as Walter Maier did. . . . No one pointed earlier or with greater clarity to the massive peril presented to the world by the growing power and influence of atheistic Communism. . . . In the cultivated accents of Harvard, he spoke of Christ to the common man. Whatever he touched leaped into life. . . . His breath was on the neck of the entire church, urging it forward in its mission for Christ, since, he asserted, the time is short. . . .[2]

In September, 1955, Dr. Hoffmann became the third regular, and present, Lutheran Hour speaker. An "unusual combination of good-natured, relaxed extrovert, scholar and passionate man of the Lord," as *Coronet* characterized him,[3] Oswald Hoffmann preaches in a style somewhat different from that of Walter Maier, but his resonant bass voice communicates the same message very successfully.

At this writing, "Bringing Christ to the Nations" is still the largest nongovernment broadcasting enterprise in the world, and is heard globally over more than 1,200 stations in 40 languages, continuing as the "modern mission miracle" its founder had envisioned. Some foreign programming is now indigenous—produced by Christians in the respective areas. In the Far East, a branch office was opened in Tokyo to handle the 90,000 letters which arrive there annually. The Japanese Lutheran Hour employs a dramatic format, like television's *This Is the Life*, and many listeners enroll in the Japanese Bible correspondence course. Iron- and bamboo-curtain penetration has continued as well, as fascinating letters on file at headquarters can testify.

"He still speaks" also in other ways, sometimes literally. Periodically a few of his hundreds of different transcription disks are played for commemorative or special events and even broadcast. In London, for example, a Reformation program featured "the late Dr. Walter A. Maier" speaking on "God Give Us Another Reformation!"[4] And from Shanghai he continued preaching to Communist China for two years after his death, probably the first time in history that a deceased person was heard on a regular radio program, and under such circumstances! He also remained on the air for some time in Australia, Europe, and elsewhere.

But it is through his writings that he continues to speak regularly. Three of his books were published posthumously, and these with the score of his other volumes continue to be read and used. Today, ministers of many denominations refer to them for homiletical helps and illustrations in their weekly sermon preparation. While the Maier bookshelf is a familiar sight in American church offices and libraries, it has also emigrated to different parts of the world. The sermons have even been repreached by lay workers at foreign mission stations.

Strangely, his last published book showed the author in the very first of his varied interests: Semitics scholarship. In 1959, Concordia brought out his long-researched, long-neglected, but long-awaited *The Book of Nahum*. It was a commentary on the short, thirty-fourth book of the Old Testament, written by one of the most overlooked minor prophets in the Bible. Whereas most people have hobbies which contrast with their vocations, doing this book had been Father's pet leisure-time project. Before his death, the manuscript was complete but for checking references and finishing the bibliography.

He was not to see it through the press. For some years the voluminous typescript gathered dust, but Dr. Bertermann kept interest in the project alive and readied the manuscript. Concordia's General Manager, Dr. O. A. Dorn, resolved to publish *Nahum*, and Father's friend and Old Testament colleague, Prof. George V. Schick, edited the book.

More than 700 years before Christ, the bloody, all-conquering Assyrian Empire invaded Israel and vanquished the ten northern tribes so brutally that they virtually disappeared from history. One of the Hebrew cousins of the lost Israelites lived in Judea c. 650 B.C., the prophet Nahum, who boldly predicted in detail the fall of Nineveh, capital of Assyria, some forty years before the event at a time when she was still flourishing. And when Nineveh fell in 612 B.C.—one of the key events in ancient history—she was destroyed in a manner almost precisely as Nahum had prophesied.

But this did not impress the German higher-critical school of Old Testament studies, which, with much liberal scholarship, simply regards the book, or such prophetic sections, as having been written *after* the events they "predicted." Nahum himself was often dismissed as a false prophet of narrow nationalism or even an uncouth rustic. To Professor Maier here was a fascinating challenge to apply his competencies in the field of the ancient Near East and learn whether Nahum had prophesied or not. It was a case history in the nature of Old Testament prophecy.

His research resulted in what for some scholars meant a correction in view on Nahum as prophet, and his book as prophecies. He shows that the man was a deeply religious figure who coupled intellect with patriotism and a "rare, almost unequaled gift of vivid presentation."[5] In page after page he duels with the objections of critic after critic, marshaling new evidence to demonstrate that Nahum *did* write his prophecies years before the event. As a climax the author discusses twenty-two separate details in Nahum's prophecies which were literally fulfilled in the fall of Nineveh. To Walter Maier, this vindicated the book as Scripture: "The pages of Nahum are of extraordinary value in underscoring the validity of

OT prophecy and the divine nature of these Scriptures. No human document of such restricted size has ever attempted to foretell in detail the march of future events; and none ever could. . . ."[6]

Another reason Nahum intrigued Father was the contemporary application of what he termed "the world's greatest indictment of militarism."[7] The modern relevance of an Old Testament prophet is set forth in this excerpt, which also illustrates the author's style:

. . . The warning against the pride of Assyrian haughtiness that insolently resists God (1:1) should be invoked to rebuke parallel tendencies in our times. . . . The destiny of Nineveh, the vampire queen of the nations, who had ruled with unchecked oppression, should deter those twentieth-century dictatorial empire builders who would stride ruthlessly over prostrate nations in adding conquest to conquest. The fortresses that fall like ripe figs, the hastily erected defenses, the fleeing armies, the heaped corpses—these symbols of a doomed, bloated militarism, bristling in its own might and then dying in its own blood, are replete with meaningful warnings for our world, which has seen the most widespread wars of aggression.[8]

Book reviewers were surprised at the versatility of a man who could be practical preacher and specializing scholar at the same time. Many also pointed up the appropriateness that America's prophetic voice should have concentrated on the prophetic message of Nahum. *The Watchman-Examiner* found the book ". . . scintillating with thought and spiritual vitality,"[9] and the *Moody Monthly* concluded that the volume ". . . brings renewed thanks to God for the life and ministry of Walter Maier."[10] One of the most extensive reviews, however, appeared in *The Christian Century*, which, theologically, is poles apart from the above journals. In his long report, "Rehabilitating Nahum," J. Philip Hyatt wrote, in part:

. . . Maier lists 22 details of the actual fall of Ninevah which were predicted by Nahum and can be verified from literary or archaeological sources. Incidentally, the author gives much interesting and valuable information about Ninevah's history and the modern excavations at the site, near modern Mosul in Iraq. . . .

This volume offers an excellent translation of the prophecy of Nahum, with detailed technical comments on every verse. Maier knew well the relevant scholarly literature in several languages. He may not have succeeded fully in rehabilitating the reputation of a neglected and sometimes abused prophet. But his book proves that a man who has native ability along with a good education and the proper tools can be both a great preacher and a good technical scholar.[11]

He can also be a great technical scholar—if he has the time. Father wanted to do more commentaries on Biblical books, and Nahum was to be "only the beginning." His dream for the time when he would "retire" was this: Walt and I were to handle the Greek, he the Hebrew, and we three would write a series of commentaries on books in the Old and New Testaments. I remember joshing him, using one of his pet phrases, "Oh, I get it . . . 'To use every available and suitable . . .' book in the Bible!" At least he aimed high.

It turned out that Father had left a final message for us anyway, which he never formally had a chance to express in the last hours. Only he had written it two years earlier in a C-54 aircraft which was grinding its way across the Atlantic at 7,000 feet. In reporting on his trip, he also included a meaningful sentence or two in separate letters to each of us "just in case," which is the only time he used that phrase. To Mother he wrote: "What happy days we've had together! How clearly I realize the Lord's blessing in giving you to me!" To Walt: "You know what a marvelous mother you have. If anything happens to me, I know you will carry her over any rough places." And to me: "Nothing you can do for Mother, who has taken such good care of us three men, will be too much."

There were rough places for Mrs. Maier. Adjustment is hard for any widow—and how shocked she was the first time she called herself that—but it was somewhat harder for her. Friends throughout the country, by their questions and correspondence, innocently served to deepen the sense of loss.

Yet she was busy enough, especially in the first difficult year. Messages of sympathy had arrived in such quantity that seven seminarians helped in just opening the stacks of letters, while faculty wives assisted her with replies. She personally answered thousands of condolences and turned large sums over to the Lutheran Hour in memorial contributions from her own mail. Planning the monument and appearing at dedications consumed the rest of her time.

Six months after the funeral, she moved from House Eleven to neighboring San Bonita Avenue. Since this was just a block from the Concordia campus, Mother could retain her old associations and remain included in seminary functions. Living with her at the new address are loyal "daughter" Mabel Breckenkamp, now of the Concordia library staff, and another good friend, Norma Bellmann, also from the library.

In the next years came frequent suggestions that Hulda A. Maier write her memoirs about life with Father. She wrote several chapters of manuscript, then succumbed to interruptions, visitors, correspondence, and speaking engagements. During parts of each year she was on the road nearly as much as her husband had been. Church groups and women's rallies invited her to speak on Dr. Maier, the broadcast, or inspirational topics. She did take time for a few literary projects, including a tract booklet, *Bringing Christ to the Sorrowing*, which charts an odyssey from grief back to joy via the comfort of Scripture.[12]

This brings the story of Walter A. Maier up to date. A final appraisal must await more studies on other aspects of his thought, a different perspective than a son's. A few brief guidelines for evaluation can, however, be suggested.

The man had his shortcomings, of which he was conscious, and some have already been cited. Others appear if the subject is approached analytically. As a professor, for example, he might have used his Harvard-honed abilities to more extensive advantage in Semitics and Old Testament scholarship. Although he came to a broad encounter with higher criticism in his chosen field, the objection is possible that he did not give it an adequate hearing. Some have criticized his interpretation of the Old Testament as too conservative. Others, of course, have just as readily championed it.

As a theologian he might better have clarified his position vis-à-vis Fundamentalism: where he was in sympathy with the movement and where he decidedly differed. Again, he was a combination of orthodox doctrine and progressive practice, but why did he not formally express this synthesis in a systematic theology?

Such "whys" and "might haves" are answerable to some extent: because of his involvement in radio, although he had the ability to develop along other lines, he did not have the time. Such activity he had intended for the golden years of life, but those years never came.

What about his broadcasting ministry? Any criticism here cannot be neutralized by resort to lack of time, since this is where he devoted most of it. Some intellectuals faulted Maier sermons for containing the age-old, rephrased-but-regularly-expressed message of sin and grace. This problem bothered Father himself. "How does one express basic gospel in a fresh fashion each time?" he often asked. Yet, by varying the thought progression, analogy, illustration, and technique, he succeeded, thought most. And abandon the heart of the Christian message he could not. Certainly he would have liked to preach from the top of his intellect, but that would lose the many to gain the few, whereas his approach by no means lost all of the few in gaining the many. In this respect he was in good company, for it was Luther who said, "When I preach here at Wittenberg. . . . I do not look at the doctors and magistrates, of whom about forty are present, but at the hundred or thousand . . . people. To these I preach; to these I address myself. They need instruction. If the others do not want to listen—the door is open."[13]

Perhaps in his role as a "modern Jeremiah" Father was sometimes overprophetic (critical) in his denunciation of evils in church, state, and society. Few will quarrel with his strictures on social sins and maladies; more controversial would be his protest against wrongs in politics and government, though again much was warranted. But some of his later censure of contemporary church life was probably too severe. While it was accurate in the thirties, the critical refrains might have been reduced when America's spiritual tone started improving in the next decade.

St. Paul wrote, "Christ's . . . gifts were that some should be apostles, some prophets, some evangelists, some pastors and teachers . . . for building up the body of Christ" (Eph. 4:7-12). In this sense, Walter Maier had received spiritual largess, for he was permitted to function in four out of the five categories. Let others assess these roles.

As "pastor" to youth, one of his Walther League successors, Dr. O. H. Theiss, styled him "a leader of . . . boundless courage and energy. . . . Through its [*Messenger's*] pages, the vision of Dr. Maier became the vision of the church he served."[14] At other times in life he could serve as pastor to prisoners, downtowners, and, by mail, to the troubled everywhere.

As "teacher," colleague Prof. Paul M. Bretscher named him a "champion of Christian education" because of his contributions at various levels of learning.[15] And in view of his versatile academic career, the Lutheran World Federation paid him unusual tribute at its 1957 world convention in Minneapolis by including him with Melanchthon, Kant, Kierkegaard, Nygren, and others in its display entitled, "Great School Men of Four Centuries."[16]

He was "prophet and evangelist"—sin-denouncer and grace-announcer—whatever his medium, voice or pen. In church history, Walter Maier will probably be remembered only for these latter roles, as they were expressed in his world-wide ministry, "Bringing Christ to the Nations." It was long after January, 1950, when we finally had a chance to read some of the editorial tributes paid him by newspapers and magazines here and abroad. Since editorials are usually the most careful writing in the press, they should be useful in evaluating this phase of his ministry. Several brief, but representative excerpts, starting at home:

> Probably no St. Louisan of our time was more widely known or was more influential in his field than Dr. Walter A. Maier, whose death early yesterday ended a notable career dedicated to serving his fellow man. It is not an exaggeration to say that Dr. Maier was one of the great spiritual leaders of modern Protestantism. His trenchant sermons were literally heard round the world. . . .
>
> —*St. Louis Globe-Democrat*[17]

His voice was one of the best known of any civilian non-ruler in the world. He never had a pastoral charge, yet he preached to a "congregation" of millions. . . .                                   —*Cleveland Press*[18]

. . . one of the most influential Christian leaders of this or any other land. . . . This great preacher . . . was able also, out of his overflowing energy and inspiration, to write almost a score of books. . . . Christian forces of the nation have lost a great leader. . . .

—*Houston Chronicle*[19]

The countryside sorrow . . . is especially acute on the Niagara frontier. . . . Dr. Maier was an institution in two fields of American activity—religion and radio. . . . one of the greatest teachers of contemporary American life, a leader who has left an imprint upon our thinking that will survive. . . .

—*Niagara Falls Gazette*[20]

Dr. Maier was one of the world's best-known Lutheran preachers. . . . His death stilled a most vigorous voice and energetic personality which since 1930 had built a two-station radio program into a coast-to-coast and finally a world-wide spiritual crusade. . . . Every two months his cumulative audience was the equivalent of the population of the United States. . . .

—*New York Times* (obituary)[21]

When Dr. Walter A. Maier went off the air to accept Higher Service, radio lost its greatest Protestant voice. Without ever being offensive, always scholarly, never less than evangelical. . . . Walter A. Maier was the pre-eminent voice of Protestant faith and practice. . . .

—Daniel A. Poling in *Christian Herald*[22]

Whether or not the editorials speak accurately, the reader will judge for himself. Beyond question, the man's contributions to his own church body, as well as Lutheranism in general, were substantial. "He put the Lutheran church on the American map" is a repeated refrain, though this is overstatement to convey a point. His church was on the map before this, but often misunderstood as German, insular, and Midwestern. After the Maier ministry it was none of these, nor thought to be so.

However, as editorials indicated, his influence far exceeded his own denomination. Theologically, he assisted orthodoxy at a critical time in American Protestantism. If Modernism had confronted a conservatism which was all piety but no perception, all inspiration but no intelligence, it might have carried the day, and Protestantism could have been either a Christianity minus the classical faith, or a dichotomy of two extreme camps, the excesses of which most reasonable believers would find distasteful. Professor Maier and other orthodox scholars, however, helped provide traditional Christianity with an intellectual undergirding, and his preaching added to its superstructure. With a significant percentage of American churchmen listening to his messages each Sunday, clergy and laity were encouraged to speak out for the historic faith in local, regional, and national church councils. Many of their letters also reported an increase in Christic preaching in their congregations, which they attributed in part to the Maier radio ministry.

So far as broader spiritual influence is concerned, the consensus is that Walter A. Maier made a substantially greater grass-roots impact on the people of his time than is generally known. To the extent that there has been a return to religion since World War II —symptomatized in record church membership, attendance, and support, as well as religious content in the mass media—there can be little doubt that Maier was one of the major heralds and instruments of this spiritual revitalization. The religious climate attending his death at mid-century was far different from that marking his start in the ministry, when Christianity was not only on the defensive against humanistic and materialistic philosophies, but itself laced with secularization and indifference.

"Only in eternity will we know how many souls were called . . . by this man of God," said the funeral speaker, which is true enough, for we cannot arrive at definite statistics. One sampling of a minute fraction of those who wrote to the broadcast during a single season reported conversions even here in the several thousands.[23] Therefore the total number of conversions would project to a vast figure, the reconsecrations more than that, those spiritually edified in the many millions. Had headquarters endeavored to keep an accurate record on the total number of converts, according to the rules of radio listener response the great majority would not have reported such a change to the broadcast. Nor was this necessary. The fact that a person was actually brought to faith or strengthened in it was important, not the statistic recording this fact.

Walter Arthur Maier was the first person in history heard around the world on a regular basis, the first to preach to a cumulative total of some two-thirds billion people annually, the first to have his words translated and aired each week in thirty-six languages, the first to receive daily masses of correspondence from 120 nations and territories, and probably the first American churchman whose published works exceeded 15,000 pages. Authorities have stated that "the most heard preacher in history" ought to occupy a place eventually on the pages of church history in the post-Pauline succession of the great preachers and missionaries of Christendom: Chrysostom, Boniface, Luther, Wesley, Edwards, Whitefield, Carey, Livingston, Spurgeon, Maclaren, and others. Perhaps this is overstatement. At any rate, in just one sermon Maier addressed more people than the cumulative total congregations of all these greats over a lifetime of preaching.

But interesting firsts, facts, and totals are not the best summary of the life of Walter Maier. They would not especially delight him, for nothing is so cold and impersonal as a statistic, nothing can more easily be misinterpreted as a prideful rather than grateful epitome of a God-given privilege. Accordingly, he would have jettisoned much of this epilogue.

What did gladden the man, what excited him with a joy he could hardly contain was the correspondence, proving that his microphone was a spiritual gateway into human lives: the penny post card with just two sentences which told all—"I am a sinner. Your message has led me to Christ;"—the letters which mirrored the happiness of a man or woman who had found the dimension of faith . . . which reported the invigorated morale of men in the Armed Forces . . . which uncovered the difficulties of the problem-burdened so that they could find solution and relief . . . which related decisions to study for the ministry . . . which reported homes saved . . . which testified that the Word could pierce the iron curtain . . . which proved that the faith is universal—that "In Christ There Is No East Nor West," no black or white, rich or poor, that the Lord of the church is something more than a Lutheran, or Roman Catholic, or Methodist . . . which demonstrated that one message for millions in any nation could only be the good news about God in Christ, saving what He had created.

Father's other major source of gladness was the woman he loved. After his death, she adjusted to the new role thrust upon her, but a touch of poignancy was periodic, especially during the summer days at Lake Ontario. Their happiness had been at its best here, the place where Father shed years and rediscovered nature and beauty with a boyish fascination.

One such occasion came late in August of 1961 after an evening party in the Olcott summer home. In previous years, this had been the hour when the host and hostess took a stroll down the lakeside path before retiring. Hulda Maier slipped out alone into a quiet night, bright with a Lake Ontario moon and warm with a fragrant offshore breeze from peach orchards to the south. The lake was so calm that an inner tube could have been paddled across to Toronto, and there was just a muffled lapping sound at the shore to give the crickets some competition.

Along that lake they had refreshed the record of a romance which began and never really ended. Once again she reminisced, as they both had many times, but the vignette of memory was remarkably vivid that night. Walter Maier was beside her in mental image, and together they lived through a girl reporting at a convention, when a man walked in and sat down in her life . . . League days, love days . . . a honeymoon cottage in Santa Monica . . . attacking the hillside at House Eleven . . . the blaze of *Truth Triumphant* . . . the Poconos . . . the man on the rostrum . . . at his side in every state of the Union . . . Christmas . . . the breakfast nook . . . the silver-anniversary groom . . . "What happy days we've had together!" . . . Ontario.

By this time it was late, a little more chilly. A long cloud bank had rolled onto the northern horizon, and the sky now came alive with an early aurora. Pillars of pale green light started wandering nervously among the stars. But her eyes were much too blurred to notice.

Just before walking into the house, she suddenly seemed to hear, with the mind's ear, his voice speaking the *Day by Day* meditation: "We should not let sorrow . . . blot out the vision of the cross, the resurrection, the open heavens. . . ." Then it stopped. Turning, she now caught sight of the open-heavened radiance presented by the northern lights in the sky over Ontario. Momentarily it seemed as if two great beams of the aurora intersected to form a natural cross in heroic dimension. She thought it another symbol for those realities which gave meaning to her present existence—the resurrection and the life everlasting.

This is the story of a man who read Christ's final words on earth and was given the grace to help fulfill them, since God had provided the opportunity to *"Go into all the world and preach the gospel to the whole creation."*

# Appendix I

PENETRATION OF "BRINGING CHRIST TO THE NATIONS"
As of 1950, quantity mail response arrived from the 120 following countries and territories. The 55 italicized lands indicate those with stations broadcasting The Lutheran Hour.

Admiralty Islands
*Alaska*
Algeria
*Angola*
*Argentina*
*Australia*
*Austria*
Bahama Islands
Basutoland
Bechuanaland
*Belgian Congo*
Belgium
*Bermuda*
*Bolivia*
*Brazil*
British East Africa
*British Guiana*
British Honduras
*British West Indies*
*Canada*
Canal Zone
*Canary Islands*
Ceylon
*Chile*
*China*
*Colombia*
Costa Rica
Crete
*Cuba*
Curaçao
Cyprus
Czechoslovakia
Denmark
*Dominican Republic*
*Dutch Guiana*
*Ecuador*
Egypt
*El Salvador*
England
Estonia

*Ethiopia*
Falkland Islands
*Fiji Islands* & Melanesia
Finland
*Formosa*
*France*
French Morocco
Germany
Gibraltar
*Goa*
Gold Coast (Ghana)
*Greece*
Greenland
*Guam*
*Guatemala*
*Haiti*
*Hawaii*
*Honduras*
Hong Kong
Hungary
*Iceland*
India
Indonesia
Iran
Ireland
Italy
Jamaica
Japan
Jordan
Korea
Latvia
Liberia
Lithuania
*Luxembourg*
*Macao*
*Madagascar*
Malaya
Malta
Marshall Islands
*Martinique*

Mauritius
*Mexico*
*Monaco*
*Mozambique*
Netherlands
New Guinea
New Zealand
*Nicaragua*
Nigeria
Northern Rhodesia
Norway
*Okinawa*
*Panama*
*Paraguay*
Peru
*Philippine Islands*
Poland
Portugal
*Puerto Rico*
Samoa
Scotland
*Siam*
Solomon Islands
Southern Rhodesia
South West Africa
Spain
*Spanish Morocco*
Sweden
Switzerland
Tanganyika
*Tangier*
*Tasmania*
Turkey
Union of South Africa
*United States*
*Uruguay*
*Venezuela*
Virgin Islands
Wales
Yugoslavia

# Appendix II

## LUTHERAN HOUR LANGUAGES

As of 1950, Th Lutheran Hour was broadcast in the 36 following languages:

| | | | |
|---|---|---|---|
| Afrikaans | Finnish | Korean | Siamese |
| Albanian | French | Latvian | Slovak |
| Arabic | German | Lithuanian | Spanish |
| Bengali | Greek | Marathi | Taiwanese |
| Bulgarian | Hindustani | Persian | Tamil |
| Burmese | Hungarian | Polish | Telugu |
| Chinese | Indonesian | Portuguese | Turkish |
| English | Italian | Rumanian | Urdu |
| Estonian | Japanese | Russian | Yiddish |

## BRANCH OFFICES by 1950

| Lutheran Hour Branch Offices | Location | Branch Directors |
|---|---|---|
| For Eastern Canada | Waterloo, Ontario | The Rev. C. T. Wetzstein |
| For Western Canada | Edmonton, Alberta | The Rev. W. A. Raedeke |
| For Portuguese Latin America | Rio de Janeiro, Brazil | The Rev. Rudolph Hasse |
| For Spanish Latin America | Buenos Aires, Argentina | The Rev. A. L. Muniz |
| For Central America | Guatemala City, Guatemala | The Rev. Robert F. Gussick |
| For Australia | Adelaide, South Australia | The Rev. Clarence Zweck and Dr. J. Darsow |
| For Africa | Johannesburg, South Africa | G. J. McHarry |
| For Europe | London, England | The Rev. E. George Pearce |
| For France | Paris, France | The Rev. Fred C. Kreiss |
| For the Far East | Hankow, China | The Rev. Paul Kreyling |

# Notes

Prologue

1. *Christian Herald*, March, 1950, p. 16. Cp. also p. 12.
2. From telegram of Dr. Billy Graham to Mrs. Walter A. Maier, January 11, 1950.
3. *Fort Wayne Journal-Gazette*, January 13, 1950.
4. *New York Times*, January 12, 1950.

Chapter 1. AT THE HUB

1. Orrin E. Dunlap, Jr., *Marconi, the Man and his Wireless* (New York: The Macmillan Company, 1937), pp. 13 ff.

Chapter 2. STUDENT WAM

1. *The Echo*, issued by Concordia (Bronxville) Class of 1912, Lewis Hildebrand, ed. (New York: Paul Overhage Publ., 1912), p. 33.
2. *Ibid.*, p. 21.
3. *Daily Argus* (Westchester County), June 29, 1912.

Chapter 3. BACK TO BOSTON

1. *Clinton Daily Item*, August 6, 1917.
2. *Ibid.*, October 26, 1917.
3. *Old Colony Memorial* (Plymouth), December 6, 1918.
4. Elmer A. Kettner, *Grossie* (Grand Rapids: Wm. B. Eerdmans Publishing Company, 1949), p. 83.
5. From letter of Karl H. Maier to author, September 29, 1959.
6. Technically, W.A.M.'s position was that of "Camp Pastor" rather than chaplain in the later sense of the term. He was sponsored by the Lutheran church, but officially approved and uniformed by the United States Army. This arrangement preceded the present chaplaincy system.
7. From letter of Carl C. Hirbecker, Legation of Switzerland, Washington, D.C., to W.A.M., as published in the *Boston American*, June 8, 1919, as well as other Boston newspapers, June 8 or 9, 1919.
8. *Boston Globe*, June 9, 1919.

Chapter 4. LEAGUE AND LOVE

1. Kettner, *op. cit.*, p. 87. Cp. also W.A.M., "The Story of a Successful Effort," *The Walther League Messenger* (hereafter cited as *Messenger*), XXX (1922), 498 ff.
2. See *Messenger*, XXXI (1923), 270–71; 482–83; XXXIII (1925), 294 ff.

Chapter 5. "FOR BETTER, NOT FOR WORSE"

1. *The Evangelical Lutheran Sanitarium Review* (Wheat Ridge, Colo.), XIX (1923), 11–12.
2. *Omaha Daily News*, July 19, 1922.
3. "An Ideal Union," *St. Louis Walther League Flashes*, IV (July, 1924), 1.

Chapter 6.   BRIDEGROOM–PROFESSOR

1. Helen M. Fessenden, *Fessenden–Builder of Tomorrows* (New York: Coward-McCann, Inc., 1940), pp. 153–54.
2. W.A.M., "This Is Station KFUO," *Messenger*, XXXIII (1925), 272–73; also 336–37.
3. *New York Times*, July 17, 1929, datelined Fort Wayne, Ind., July 16 (AP).
4. *Omaha Daily News*, July 18, 1922.
5. *Ibid.*
6. The Associated Press, datelined Chicago, July 15 (1933).
7. *New York Evening Post*, June 25, 1929, datelined River Forest, Ill. (AP).
8. Excerpts from text of entire sermon as published in *The Lutheran*, VII (August 27, 1925), 8–9, 21. Used by permission.

Chapter 7.   "WITH FLYING COLORS"

1. The figure 70,000 is a compromise of various estimates ranging from "more than 60,000" (*Chicago Tribune*, June 24, 1929) to "over 100,000" (*The Christian Century*, July 10, 1929).
2. *New York Times, Chicago Tribune, et al.*, June 24, 1929.
3. *St. Louis Globe-Democrat*, November 4, 1929. Cp. also *St. Louis Post-Dispatch, Star*, and *Times* of that date.

Chapter 8.   "THE IMPOSSIBLE CHURCH"

1. W.A.M.'s concern for student mission activity even preceded his arrival as professor; see *Alma Mater* (Concordia Seminary, St. Louis), XII (January, 1922), 125–28.
2. *St. Louis Times*, March 29, 1930.
3. From letter of Dr. Richard Kretzschmar to W.A.M., January 6, 1930. However Dr. Kretzschmar soon changed his mind about the mission and preached an enthusiastic sermon at its dedication.
4. *St. Louis Globe-Democrat*, March 26 and April 1, 1930; *St. Louis Times*, March 29, 1930. Cp. also *St. Louis Star-Times*, May 14, 1934.
5. Statistics from letter of the Rev. Edwin W. Licht, present pastor of St. Stephen's, to the author, August 13, 1962.

Chapter 9.   THE LUTHERAN HOUR

1. See the following editorials by W.A.M. in the *Messenger*: XXXI (1922/23), 314, 378, 434 ff.; XXXII (1923/24), 104, 356 ff, Cp. also XXXIII (1924/25), 109, 272, 336, 400, 464, 526, 592, 668 ff.; XXXIV (1925/26), 26, 408, 550.
2. "Minutes of the KFUO Radio Committee," November 15, 1929.
3. *Ibid.*, April 24, 1930.
4. Cp. "The Greater Possibilities of Radio," *Lutheran Laymen's League Bulletin*, I (November 15, 1929), 28 f.; and "A Lutheran Hour on the National Network–When?" *ibid.*, I (April 15, 1930), 85.
5. Board members in 1929–1930 included Edwin H. Faster, president; A. G. Brauer, Henry Dahlen, A. A. Grossmann, Dr. Lawrence Meyer, E. W. Schultz, L. F. Volkman, and Louis H. Waltke.
6. For full resolution, see *ibid.*, I (June 16, 1930), 117.

7. Early Lutheran Hour advertisements and publications suggest both the L.L.L. and the Walther League as sponsors of the first series, although officially the L.L.L. remained sole sponsor.

8. "Minutes of the Executive Committee Meeting" of the L.L.L., August 13, 1930.

9. W.A.M.'s statement, adapted into the present tense from the booklet, *Bringing Christ to the Nations* (St. Louis: Concordia Publishing House, 1935), p. 2.

10. From W.A.M.'s original broadcast manuscript, "There *Is* A God," October 2, 1930, pp. 1-2, supplied through the courtesy of Dr. Arthur Carl Piepkorn. Cp. Walter A. Maier, *The Lutheran Hour* (St. Louis: Concordia Publishing House, 1931), pp. 45–46.

11. *Ibid.*, pp. 6–7 of manuscript; cp. pp. 52–53 of book.

12. Sources for this and following samplings of listener response during the first Lutheran Hour season are found in: *Messenger*, XXXIX (1930/31), 71, 82, 139, 150, 207, 226, 275, 360, 420, 490, 556, 626, 692 ff.; *L.L.L. Bulletin*, II (September 15, 1930 through June 22, 1931); Maier, *op. cit.*, pp. 309–24; and extant letters from files of the first series.

13. At this time Station KFAB was located in Lincoln, Nebraska; today it is in Omaha.

14. Detail from letter of Henry A. Dahlen to the author, February 24, 1961.

15. The meeting in Chicago, on February 27, 1931, was chaired by Dr. Theodore Graebner. Director of the underwriting plan was the Rev. Theophil Strieter, assisted by Dr. O. H. Pannkoke. See *Messenger*, XXXIX (May, 1931), 556 ff.

16. "Why the Lutheran Hour was Suspended," *L.L.L. Bulletin*, II (June 22, 1931), 157–58.

17. *Federal Council Bulletin*, XIII (March, 1930), 22, lists "over 50,000" letters, and *ibid.*, XIV (February, 1931), 13, cites "38,000" as annual statistics for mail received by all religious programs sponsored by the Federal Council. Cp. also *Messenger*, XXXIX (May, 1931), 557.

## Chapter 10.   OTHER IRONS

1. Walter A. Maier, *The Jeffersonian Ideals of Religious Liberty* (St. Louis: Concordia Publishing House, 1930), p. 7.

2. *Ibid.*, p. 8.

3. *Ibid.*, pp. 10, 13.

4. *Ibid.*, pp. 19–22.

5. *Ibid.*, pp. 17 f.

6. *Ibid.*, p. 21.

7. *New York Times*, August 6, 1930.

8. The original letter is written in pen, but all words and punctuation are faithfully reproduced. The letterhead contains additional detail on the Society and its officers.

9. *St. Louis Post-Dispatch*, January 23, 1933.

10. The Associated Press, Chicago, August 26, 1930. One of the announcements concerning the possibility of a forthcoming Darrow-Maier debate had been made in New York City, but—in fairness to the Atheist Society of Chicago—the news seems to have reached the press somewhat prematurely.

11. From letter of James E. Even to W.A.M., September 4, 1930.
12. From letter of W.A.M. to James E. Even, September 5, 1930.
13. From letter of James E. Even to W.A.M., September 10, 1930.
14. From letter of E. W. Eggleston of the Atheist Society of Chicago to W.A.M., September 25, 1930.
15. "Three Fanatics," *Fifth Annual Report of 4 A—1930*, p. 13.
16. *St. Louis Post-Dispatch*, October 27, 1930.
17. *St. Louis Globe-Democrat, Post-Dispatch*, and *Star*, October 27, 1930. Cp. also *St. Louis Post-Dispatch* rotogravure, November 2, 1930.
18. *St. Louis Times*, October 27, 1930.
19. *Time*, July 27, 1931, p. 28. Courtesy *Time;* copyright Time Inc. 1931. While the tawdry antics cited may seem unfamiliar today, some churches in that era did, in fact, resort to such measures. For full text of the address, see *The Lutheran*, XIII (August 13, 1931), 7–9.
20. *Chicago Tribune*, July 15, 1933, and Associated Press releases.
21. *Detroit News*, November 5, 1932; *Detroit Free Press*, November 7, 1932. Press references to 20,000 in attendance at the bicentennial substantially exceed the present capacity of the State Fair Coliseum.
22. *Detroit Free Press*, October 9, 1933. Cp. *ibid.*, October 15, 1933, and *Detroit News*, October 9, 1933.
23. *Time*, September 4, 1933, p. 24. Courtesy *Time;* copyright Time Inc. 1933. *Time* reported the "Back to Luther" address delivered several months earlier at Ocean Grove, which W.A.M. repeated at Detroit—a rare instance. The *Time* citation is used here since it is the only extant source for the address.
24. See editorial, "Back to Christ," *Our Sunday Visitor*, XXII (September 24, 1933), 2.
25. *Ibid.*, XXXIV (May 20, 1945), 2. Cp. also XXXIII (October 1, 1944), 2.
26. See editorial, "Our Lutheran Friend," *The Western Catholic*, September 1, 1933.
27. The Associated Press, datelined Pocono Pines, Pa., August 19 (1933). In following months, this statement was widely reported in other Roman Catholic journals.
28. *St. Louis Globe-Democrat Sunday Magazine*, September 4, 1932, pp. 6 ff.

*Chapter 11.  "THE HAPPIEST HOME"*

1. Walter A. Maier, *The Happiest Home* (St. Louis: Lutheran Laymen's League, 1941), p. 3.
2. The Dizzy Dean quotation appeared on Grape-Nuts packages from May through December, 1936; information courtesy of W. J. Betts of the Post Division, General Foods Corporation, Battle Creek, Michigan. Since no catalogue of prizes from this promotion is extant or available, the cost options for prizes cited are the author's estimates from memory.
3. *Daily Express* (Manchester, England), December 8, 1932.
4. The Associated Press, datelined Pocono Pines, Pa., July 23 (1932).
5. *New York Times*, June 21, 1931.
6. *New York American*, July 25, 1931. Used by permission of King Features Syndicate, Inc.
7. The Associated Press, datelined Mount Pocono, Pa., September 3 (1932).
8. *Commercial Appeal* (Memphis), November 13, 1932.

9. *The American Weekly*, October 16, 1932, p. 5.
10. *Messenger*, XLI (December, 1932), 205.
11. Walter A. Maier, *For Better, Not for Worse* (3rd ed.; St. Louis: Concordia Publishing House, 1939), p. 19.
12. *Time*, December 9, 1935, pp. 41–42. Mention in the article that W.A.M. ". . . speaks with a slight German accent . . ." is incorrect.
13. *The Lutheran Witness*, LV (February 25, 1936), 61.
14. *The Lutheran*, March 13, 1940, p. 20.
15. *The Presbyterian*, 1936.
16. *Christianity Today*, Winter, 1940–41, p. 72.
17. *The Augustana Quarterly*, October, 1941, pp. 367–68.

## Chapter 12.  TO THE NATIONS

1. From "Foreward" in Maier, *The Lutheran Hour*, pp. vi–vii.
2. W.A.M. spoke here on January 17 and November 6, 1932, as well as October 8, 1933, in connection with mass meetings in Detroit. Trinity Church —the Rev. Gilbert Otte, pastor—had been constructed as the personal gift of Mr. Charles Gauss, who also supported the Detroit *Lutheran Hour*.
3. Sources for samplings of listener response during the second season are found in: *Messenger*, XLIII (1934/35), 462, 526, 598 ff.; Walter A. Maier, *Christ for Every Crisis* (St. Louis: Concordia Publishing House, 1935), pp. 150–74; and letters from files of the second series.
4. Walter A. Maier, *Christ for the Nation* (St. Louis: Concordia Publishing House, 1936), pp. 11–13. Used by permission.
5. Sources for the third season are: *Messenger*, XLIV (1935/36), 84, 105, 164, 206, 272, 336, 398, 462, 526 ff.; *The Lutheran Layman* (hereafter cited as *Layman*), VI (October 7, 1935) through VII (August 1, 1936); and extant letters.
6. Sources for the fourth season are: *Messenger*, XLV (1936/37), 162, 210, 292, 340, 352, 422, 486, 554 ff.; *Layman*, VII (October 10, 1936) through VIII (August 16, 1937); and extant letters.
7. Walter A. Maier, *Fourth Lutheran Hour* (St. Louis: Concordia Publishing House, 1937), p. iii.
8. Sources for the fifth season are: *Messenger*, XLVI (1937/38), 160, 232, 296, 366, 434, 502, 566 ff.; *Layman*, VIII (October 8, 1937) through IX (June 1, 1938); and extant letters.
9. Sources for the sixth season are: *Messenger*, XLVII (1938/39), 234, 312, 376, 440, 508, 576, 658 ff.; *Layman*, IX (October 10, 1938) through X (August 1, 1939); and extant letters.
10. Sources for the seventh season are: *Messenger*, XLVIII (1939/40), 77, 206, 276, 336, 394, 454, 510 ff.; *Layman*, X (October 1, 1939) through XI (August 12, 1940); and extant letters.
11. Sources for the eighth season are: *Messenger*, XLIX (1940/41), 142, 206, 274, 328, 394, 450, 512, 566 ff.; *Layman*, XI (October 15, 1940) through XII (August 1, 1941); and extant letters.
12. *Messenger*, XLIX (January, 1941), 267.
13. Walter A. Maier, *For Christ and Country* (St. Louis: Concordia Publishing House, 1942), p. xi.
14. See end of chapter 17 for a discussion of audience measurement. Sources for

the ninth season are: *Messenger,* L (1941/42), 18, 80, 142, 212, 270, 322, 384, 450, 496, 560 ff.; *Layman,* XII (October 13, 1941) through XIII (August 14, 1942); Maier, *op. cit.,* pp. iii–xviii; and extant letters.

15. Walter A. Maier, *The Radio for Christ* (St. Louis: Concordia Publishing House, 1939), p. vii.
16. *Time,* April 11, 1938, p. 47. Cp. also W.A.M., "Free Radio Time—But Not for Us," *Messenger,* XLV (February, 1937), 340 f.
17. *Messenger,* XLIII (June, 1935), 586 ff.
18. *Time,* April 11, 1938, p. 48. Courtesy *Time;* copyright Time Inc. 1938.
19. *Tide,* November 1, 1939, p. 34.
20. See Maier, *For Christ and Country,* pp. xvi–xvii.

Chapter 13.    WHY SUCCESS?

1. *Newsweek,* January 22, 1945, p. 74.
2. Henry LaCossitt, "TV's Most Surprising Hit," *The Saturday Evening Post,* November 14, 1953, pp. 38 ff.
3. Harriet E. Schwenk, "Jubilate . . ." *Christmas Echoes* (Minneapolis: Messenger Press, 1950), p. 52. Used by permission.
4. Walter A. Maier, *Courage in Christ* (St. Louis: Concordia Publishing House, 1941), p. xi.
5. The Concordia Seminary Chorus of Springfield, Illinois, under the direction of Prof. Fred L. Precht, and the Valparaiso University Chorus, conducted by Prof. Theodore Hoelty-Nickel, also sang for the broadcast on occasion, as did other choral groups too numerous to list here.
6. Kenneth Hartley Sulston, "A Rhetorical Criticism of the Radio Preaching of Walter Arthur Maier" (Evanston, Ill.: doctoral dissertation, Northwestern University, 1958). Cp. also Lester Erwin Zeitler, "An Investigation of the Factors of Persuasion in the Sermons of Dr. Walter A. Maier" (St. Louis: M.S.T. dissertation, Concordia Seminary, 1956), as well as other monographs cited below.
7. Dates for these and similar sermon titles are significant; for example: "Faith Faces the Future" (1931), "God's Program for National Recovery" (1935), "Light for the Lengthening Shadows" (1937), "A Permanent Armistice on Hatred" (1939), "America, Embattled, Turn to Christ!" (1941), "For Christ and Country" (1942), "Full Freedom from Fear" (1943), "What Is God's Purpose in War?" (1944), "The Victory is the Lord's" (1945), "Must We Fight World War III?" (1946), "Communism—Its Curse and Cure" (1949). Cp. also Sulston, *op. cit.,* pp. 194 ff.
8. Similarly, Mrs. Bernard Keiser and Bertha Wernsing generously contributed their time, as, occasionally, did others.
9. Zeitler, *op. cit.,* p. 79. The sermon so charted is "God Says 'Hurry!'" April 4, 1948.
10. *Collier's,* May 6, 1944, p. 50.
11. *Pageant,* February, 1945, p. 120.
12. *Time,* October 18, 1943, p. 49.
13. *Christian Herald,* March, 1947, p. 43.
14. *The Saturday Evening Post,* June 19, 1948, p. 88.
15. Zeitler, *op. cit.,* pp. 81 f.

16. *Boston Globe*, January 23, 1932, reviewing *The Lutheran Hour*.
17. *Dallas Times-Herald*, January 24, 1932, reviewing *ibid*.
18. *The Christian Century*, XLIX (February 24, 1932), 258, reviewing *ibid*.
19. *The Presbyterian*, October 21, 1937, reviewing *Fourth Lutheran Hour*.
20. Cp. Paul L. Maier, "Fundamentalism and Conservative Lutheranism," *Seminarian* (Concordia Seminary, St. Louis), XLVI (March, 1955), 16–20.
21. Maier, *Courage in Christ*, p. v. However, W.A.M. was not careful enough with his use of the term "Fundamentalism," and therefore journalists sometimes inaccurately identified him as a Fundamentalist without further qualification.
22. Sulston, *op. cit.*, p. 513.

Chapter 14. *"FOR CHRIST AND COUNTRY"*

1. From sermon of December 7, 1941, published in Maier, *For Christ and Country*, pp. 87 ff.
2. The published version of this prayer appears in *ibid.*, p. 102.
3. Correspondents of *Time, Life*, and *Fortune, December 7–The First Thirty Hours* (New York: Alfred A. Knopf, 1942), p. 91.
4. *Messenger*, XLVI (November, 1937), 146 ff.
5. *Ibid.*, XLIII (December, 1934), 230.
6. *Ibid.*, XLIII (June, 1935), 584; XLVII (May, 1939), 564 ff.; XLVIII (October, 1939), 60 ff.; XLIX (January, 1941), 266 ff.
7. *Ibid.*, XLI (April, 1933), 491; XLII (March, 1934), 429; XLIV (May, 1936), 522. For a fuller discussion, see Herman Otten, "The Political and Economic Thought of Dr. Walter A. Maier" (St. Louis: B.D. dissertation, Concordia Seminary, 1957).
8. *Messenger*, XLI (July, 1933), 662 ff.; XLII (January, 1934), 270 ff.; XLIII (March, 1935), 398 ff. W.A.M. was not the only observer who failed to recognize early Fascism as a menace. The list of those who made a political miscalculation at this point would be long and impressive, ranging from church leaders to politicians, here and abroad.
9. *Ibid.*, XLII (February, 1934), 328; XLIII (May, 1935), 522 ff.
10. *Ibid.*, XLIV (June, 1936), 588 f.; XLI (April, 1933), 491.
11. *Ibid.*, XLV (January, 1937), 274 f.
12. *Ibid.*, XLVII (February, 1939), 358 ff.
13. *Ibid.*, XLIX (January, 1941), 267.
14. *Ibid.*, XLII (March, 1934), 429; XLIII (January, 1935), 263.
15. *Ibid.*, XLVIII (August-September, 1939), 12.
16. *Ibid.*, L (January, 1942), 260; 262 ff.
17. *Ibid.*, L (February, 1942), 357.
18. With later slight revision from its first published form in Maier, *op. cit.*, p. 86.
19. Winston S. Churchill, *The Second World War—The Hinge of Fate* (Boston: Houghton Mifflin Company, 1950), p. 92.
20. The story came through a wounded American sergeant who had learned it from former British prisoners of the Japanese while recuperating at a hospital in New Guinea.
21. Sources for samplings of military and civilian response during World War II

are found in references for the eighth through twelfth Lutheran Hour seasons noted above and below.

22. *New York Times*, August 6, 1939.
23. *Time*, October 18, 1943, p. 48; and Walter A. Maier, *America, Turn to Christ!* (St. Louis: Concordia Publishing House, 1944), pp. 134–35.
24. *Chicago Tribune*, October 4, 1943.
25. *Time*, October 18, 1943, pp. 46–49.
26. After W.A.M. dedicated his third sermon volume "To the Memory of my Father," and the fourth "To the Members of the Lutheran Laymen's League," the successive dedications indicate those who were of prime assistance in his life: Mr. and Mrs. Louis H. Waltke, Edmund Seuel, Mr. and Mrs. Charles J. Staerker, Herman A. Hanser, M.D. and Theodore H. Hanser, M.D., Mr. and Mrs. Harry J. W. Niehaus, Mr. and Mrs. Charles G. Lang, Ernest J. Gallmeyer, Hugo F. Williams, Otto H. Amling, Edmund Kuhlman, Mr. and Mrs. Fred C. Rutz, Mr. and Mrs. Paul Weiss, Albert P. Williams, Mr. and Mrs. Otto C. Kuntze, Paul Brandt, and "Our Friends in the Clergy and Laity of Western New York State."
27. *Congressional Record*, 87 (November 5, 1941), 8740. "Lowing clouds" in *CR* should read "lowering clouds."
28. From letter of Rep. Brooks Hays to W.A.M., January 10, 1945.
29. From letter of Abraham Vereide to W.A.M., January 10, 1945.
30. *Ibid.*, February 3, 1945.

### Chapter 15.   MEANWHILE, BACK AT HOUSE ELEVEN . . .

1. Report on Stamps For Missions courtesy of Raymond E. Hodges, president, in letter to the author, April 5, 1961.
2. Report on the Lutheran Hour Pencil Club courtesy of Otto C. Kuntze, manager, in letter to the author, April 14, 1961.
3. *The Saturday Evening Post*, June 19, 1948, p. 92.

### Chapter 16.   CRANKS, CRITICISM, AND COMMUNISM

1. Letter to W.A.M., September 10, 1946, name of sender not disclosed out of courtesy. The other living quarters are cited in chapter 18, a summer cottage in Western New York.
2. *Proceedings of the Fortieth Regular Convention* of the Evangelical Lutheran Synod of Missouri, Ohio, and other States (St. Louis: Concordia Publishing House, 1947), pp. 48 f.; 56.
3. *Concordia Historical Institute Quarterly* (St. Louis), XXIII (July, 1950), 49–58; and (October, 1950), 132–35.
4. Address of October 23, 1949, over the ABC network.
5. Walter A. Maier, *The Airwaves Proclaim Christ* (St. Louis: Concordia Publishing House, 1948), p. 86.
6. *Messenger*, XLII (December, 1933), 239.
7. *Ibid.*, XXXII (August–September, 1923), 10; XXIV (October, 1925), 104, and *passim*.
8. *Ibid.*, XLII (December, 1933), 202 ff.
9. *Ibid.*, XLII (March, 1934), 428.
10. *Ibid.*, XXXIII (April, 1925), 488.

11. Maier, *The Lutheran Hour*, p. 49.
12. *Messenger*, L (December, 1941), 200.
13. *Ibid.*, LI (March, 1943), 366 ff.; (June, 1943), 544 ff.; LII (March, 1944), 288 ff. are particularly significant.
14. *Ibid.*, LIII (January, 1945), 190 ff.
15. From press releases, dated July 9, 1945.
16. *The Billboard*, July 21, 1945, p. 5, datelined New York, July 16.
17. For further detail on Leon M. Birkhead and the Friends of Democracy, Inc., see Ralph Lord Roy, *Apostles of Discord* (Boston: The Beacon Press, 1953), pp. 32, 43, *et al.* For a negative view, cp. also "Extension of Remarks of Hon. Clare E. Hoffman in the House of Representatives," December 2, 1943, *Appendix to the Congressional Record*, p. A5309.
18. From letter of Robert L. Sweazy to Leon M. Birkhead and the Friends of Democracy, Inc., July 23, 1945, as reported in the press, July 24 and 25, 1945.
19. As quoted in J. Edgar Hoover, *Masters of Deceit* (New York: Henry Holt and Company, 1958), p. 326.
20. Eleanor Roosevelt, *My Day*, datelined Atlanta, Ga., September 8 (1949), and published in the syndicated press the following day.
21. From letter of W.A.M. to Mrs. Franklin D. Roosevelt, September 10, 1949, and press of that date.
22. Eleanor Roosevelt, *My Day*, December 10, 1949, and press accounts the following day.
23. From press and wire services, December 11, 1949.
24. *Messenger*, LIII (September, 1944), 12 ff.

### Chapter 17.   WORLD'S LARGEST BROADCAST

1. Sources for samplings of listener response during the tenth season are found in: *Messenger*, LI (1942/43), 56, 62, 80, 144, 210, 274, 328, 380, 430, 490, 550, 602 ff.; *Layman*, XIII (October 8, 1942) through XIV (September 3, 1943); Walter A. Maier, *Victory through Christ* (St. Louis: Concordia Publishing House, 1943), pp. vii–xxiv; and letters from files of the tenth series.
2. Sources for the eleventh season are: *Messenger*, LII (1943/44), 18, 60, 108, 160, 208, 252, 296, 340, 386, 426, 472 ff.; *Layman*, XIV (November 5, 1943) through XV (August 22, 1944); *The Lutheran Hour News* (hereafter cited as *LH News*), April, 1944; Maier, *America, Turn to Christ!*, pp. viii–xxix; Walter A. Maier, *Christ, Set the World Aright!* (St. Louis: Concordia Publishing House, 1945), pp. vii–xxxii; and extant letters.
3. Walter A. Maier, *Jesus Christ, Our Hope* (St. Louis: Concordia Publishing House, 1946), pp. vii–viii.
4. Sources for the twelfth season are: *Messenger*, LIII (1944/45), 16, 60, 104, 150, 200, 244, 288, 330, 384, 428, 474 ff.; *Layman*, XV (October 30, 1944) through XVI (July 10, 1945); *LH News*, Christmas, 1944; Easter, 1945; Maier, *op. cit.*, pp. viii–xxxii; Walter A. Maier, *Rebuilding with Christ* (St. Louis: Concordia Publishing House, 1946), pp. ix–xl; and extant letters.
5. Walter A. Maier, *He Will Abundantly Pardon* (St. Louis: Concordia Publishing House, 1948), p. vii.

6. *Ibid.*, p. xxvi.
7. Sources for the thirteenth season are: *Messenger,* LIV (1945/46), 16, 22, 39 ff.; (November, 1945), 23; (February, 1946), 25; (March, 1946), 21; (April, 1946), 29; *Layman,* XVI (October 2, 1945) through XVII (September 16, 1946); *LH News,* October, Christmas, 1945; Lent-Easter, 1946; Maier, *op. cit.,* pp. viii-lvii; Walter A. Maier, *Let Us Return unto the Lord* (St. Louis: Concordia Publishing House, 1947), pp. ix–lxii; and extant letters.
8. Sources for the fourteenth season are: *LH News,* October, Christmas, 1946; Lent-Easter, 1947; *Layman,* XVII (November 22, 1946) through XVIII (June 30, 1947); Maier, *The Airwaves Proclaim Christ,* pp. viii–lxix; Walter A. Maier, *Global Broadcasts of His Grace* (St. Louis: Concordia Publishing House, 1949), pp. x–lxxix; and extant letters.
9. *What's On in London,* November 5th, 1948, p. 12. Used by permission.
10. Sources for the fifteenth season are: *LH News,* October, Christmas, 1947; Lent-Easter, 1948; *Layman,* XVIII (September 1, 1947) through XIX (May 15, 1948); Walter A. Maier, *One Thousand Radio Voices for Christ* (St. Louis: Concordia Publishing House, 1950), pp. 375–454; Walter A. Maier, *Go Quickly and Tell* (St. Louis: Concordia Publishing House, 1950), pp. 380–444; and extant letters.
11. See notes 10, 12, 14 to chapter 13.
12. *Variety,* February 3, 1938.
13. For evaluation of ratings, the author's gratitude is due Robert D. Atkinson of C. E. Hooper, Inc., New York, and Wynn Bussmann of the A. C. Nielsen Co., Chicago.
14. The Lutheran Hour seems to have been the only network religious broadcast which maintained accurate records of mail response during this era. Correspondence with the National Council of the Churches of Christ in the U.S.A., successor to the Federal Council (sponsor of the *National Radio Pulpit,* the *National Vespers, et al.*) as well as with the National Council of Catholic Men (sponsor of the *Catholic Hour*) and the Gospel Broadcasting Association (sponsor of the *Old Fashioned Revival Hour*) was unable to secure mail response figures other than listed below. This was also the experience of Sulston, *op. cit.,* p. 64.

| Year | Program | Source | Total Mail Count | Lutheran Hour Mail Count |
|---|---|---|---|---|
| 1931 | *All* programs sponsored by the Federal Council of Churches | *Federal Council Bulletin,* XIV (Feb., 1931), 13. | 38,000 | 57,000 |
| 1931 | The *Catholic Hour* | N.C.C.M. pamphlet, "Eight Years of the Catholic Hour," p. 3. | 21,899 | 57,000 |
| 1938/39 | The *Catholic Hour* | *Monthly Bulletin* of the N.C.C.M., VI (March, 1939), 4. | 50,968 | 140,000 |

| 1939/40 | The *Catholic Hour* | *The Catholic World*, 150 (March, 1940), 748. | 147,000 (11 mos.) | 176,508 |
| 1943 | The *National Radio Pulpit* | *Pageant*, I (Feb., 1945), p. 123. | 139,000 | 330,000 |
| 1944 | *All* Federal Council programs on NBC | *Ibid.* | 200,000 | 340,000 |

Evidence that the Lutheran Hour received more "fan mail" than secular programs was gained from a comparison tally with the public relations departments of the major networks. The assumptions that the Hour also received more mail than any non-Christian or foreign religious program seem safe enough in view of the preponderance of Christianity and American broadcasting.

### Chapter 18.  OLCOTT

1. Schwenk, "Jubilate . . ." *Christmas Echoes*, pp. 53 f. Used by permission.
2. Walter Arthur Maier, "Report and Recommendations on Religious Broadcasting in Germany (United States Zone)," unpublished manuscript "submitted to the Chief, Education and Religious Affairs, Office of Military Government for Germany (United States); and to the Chief, Civil Affairs Division, War Department," June 30, 1947.
3. *Ibid.*, pp. 26–28.
4. From message of Dr. Ernst Reuter, Mayor of West Berlin, to the Lutheran Laymen's League Convention in New York City, July, 1952.
5. Maier, *Christ for the Nation*, p. 11.
6. Prayer for December 25, 1949, over the Mutual and ABC networks.

### Chapter 19.  CULMINATION

1. For references to these and other magazine articles concerning W.A.M., see bibliography.
2. *The Saturday Evening Post*, June 19, 1948, p. 17.
3. *Ibid.*, p. 89.
4. *Ibid.*, p. 94.
5. *Philadelphia Inquirer*, June 25, 1948, p. 2, and press of that date.
6. "Is a United Protestant Church Possible Now?" *Town Meeting* (New York: The Town Hall, Inc.), XIV (December 7, 1948), pp. 9–11. Used by permission.
7. *Ibid.*, p. 23.
8. From letter of Elizabeth S. Colclough to Eugene R. Bertermann, December 23, 1948.
9. Sources for the sixteenth season are: *LH News*, October, Christmas, 1948; Lent-Easter, 1949; *Layman*, XIX (September 1, 1948) through XX (May, 1949); *International Lutheran Hour Bulletin* (E. Bernald, ed.), I (November, 1951) ff.; and extant letters.
10. *The Saturday Evening Post*, June 19, 1948, p. 92.
11. *The Watchman-Examiner*, 133 (September 20, 1951), 903.
12. *Theology Today*, IV (July 1, 1947), 295 f., reviewed by Harold E. Nicely.

13. *The Christian Century*, LXIV (August 27, 1947), 1022, reviewed by Winfred Ernest Garrison. Used by permission.
14. G. Paul Butler, ed., *Best Sermons, 1949–50 Edition* (New York: Harper & Brothers, 1949), pp. 105–111.
15. Andrew Watterson Blackwood, *The Protestant Pulpit* (New York: Abingdon-Cokesbury, 1947), pp. 231–37, 314.
16. Andrew Watterson Blackwood, *The Preparation of Sermons* (New York: Abingdon-Cokesbury, 1948), pp. 113, 224.
17. Technically there were 1,236 "station-transmissions." Since some foreign outlets, such as Radio Luxembourg, transmitted a dozen or more Hour programs each week in different languages on various wave lengths, headquarters rated such multiple stations more than one in the 1,236 total.
18. *The Dr. Walter A. Maier Memorial Booklet* (St. Louis: Lutheran Laymen's League, 1950), pp. 18–19.

Chapter 20.   *"LIFE EVERLASTING"*

1. *Ibid.*, p. 5.
2. From live broadcast, confirmed with the Central Files of the National Broadcasting Company, New York, continuity of January 11, 1950: *News of the World* program, 7:15 P.M. (E.S.T.). Used by permission of Morgan Beatty and William R. McAndrew, executive vice-president, NBC News.
3. *Maier Memorial Booklet*, pp. 35–40.
4. *Ibid.*, pp. 41–42, 52–59.
5. *Ibid.*, pp. 43–45.
6. *Ibid.*, pp. 46–51.
7. *Ibid.*, p. 23.

Epilogue:   *"HE STILL SPEAKS"*

1. *The Lutheran Witness*, LXIX (February 7, 1950), 45.
2. *The American Lutheran*, XXXIII (February, 1950), 4.
3. *Coronet*, February, 1956, p. 143.
4. *The English Churchman*, October 27, 1950, p. 517, with much of the sermon published on p. 520. This program was arranged by the Rev. E. George Pearce.
5. Walter A. Maier, *The Book of Nahum* (St. Louis: Concordia Publishing House, 1959), p. 20.
6. *Ibid.*, p. 86.
7. Cp. Virginia Tracy, "Dr. W. A. Maier Cites 'Greatest Indictment of Militarism,'" *St. Louis Globe-Democrat*, February 28, 1942.
8. Maier, *op. cit.*, p. 85.
9. *The Watchman-Examiner*, January 15, 1959, p. 71.
10. *Moody Monthly*, February, 1959, p. 71.
11. *The Christian Century*, LXXVI (July 22, 1959), 852. Used by permission.
12. Mrs. Walter A. Maier, *Bringing Christ to the Sorrowing* (Chicago: Moody Press, 1955).
13. D. *Martin Luthers Werke*. (Weimar, 1883 ff.) *Tischreden*, III, No. 3573, as quoted in Ewald M. Plass, *What Luther Says* (St. Louis: Concordia Publishing House, 1959), III, 1119.

14. *Messenger*, LVIII (March, 1950), 10 ff.
15. *Lutheran Education*, LXXXV (March, 1950), 325–28.
16. The caption under his portrait read: "Walter Arthur Maier, Ph.D., 1893–1950, America's great preacher, writer, educator, and world-wide radio pastor—professor, Concordia Theological Seminary, St. Louis, Mo."
17. *St. Louis Globe-Democrat*, January 12, 1950.
18. *Cleveland Press*, January 12, 1950.
19. *Houston Chronicle*, January 20, 1950.
20. *Niagara Falls Gazette*, January 14, 1950.
21. *New York Times*, January 12, 1950, obituary.
22. *Christian Herald*, March, 1950, p. 16. Cp. also "Amen!" *ibid.*, p. 12.
23. In *He Will Abundantly Pardon*, p. ix, W.A.M. wrote: "In a recent volume we reported on a survey made during the twelfth Lutheran Hour. This, based on 9,678 replies (only a fraction of one per cent of those who have sent us letters), showed that 2,650 souls had received Christ as their Redeemer through this broadcast. During the thirteenth broadcasting season, a smaller sample survey was held, but the percentage of converts was larger; 2,340 replies stated that to their knowledge a total of 1,025 had been brought to Jesus. If these proportions hold for the entire Lutheran Hour mail, which is now going on toward the four million mark, what overabundant reason we have to praise the Almighty!"

# Bibliography

## I. PRIMARY SOURCES: WORKS BY WALTER A. MAIER

The Maier books are listed on pages 159, 211, 341–42 and 380. The *Day by Day with Jesus* series is cited on page 247. References for booklets and shorter works are provided in the Notes.

The periodical articles authored by Walter A. Maier—well over 800—are too numerous for separate listing here. Many are conveniently available in the twenty-five volumes of *The Walther League Messenger*, XXIX (December, 1920), through LIII (July, 1945), as well as *The American Lutheran*, V (April, 1922) and following volumes, and *Concordia Theological Monthly*, III (March, 1932) and following volumes. A complete list of articles and addresses by W.A.M. in these and other periodicals is available from the Maier Archives at Concordia Seminary, St. Louis, Mo.

## II. SECONDARY SOURCES

The following is only that literature which deals specifically and substantially with the career of Walter A. Maier. This listing does not include newspaper articles or minor sources cited in the Notes.

Albus, Harry J., "The Lutheran Hour Girdles the Globe," *The Way*, 5 (October, 1945), 11–16; 49.

Arbaugh, William G., "Ha Muerto El Dr. Maier," *El Testigo* (San Juan), XXXIII (Marzo de 1950), 1 ff.

Arndt, Wm., "Walter Arthur Maier," *Concordia Theological Monthly*, XXI (March, 1950), 163 f.

"BCTN . . . das grösste religiöse Programm der Welt," *Die Radio-Woche* (Austria), V (20–27 März, 1949), 22.

Bertermann, Eugene R., and W.A.M., *Bringing Christ to the Nations*. St. Louis: Lutheran Laymen's League, 1942.

——, and Harriet E. Schwenk (eds.), *The Dr. Walter A. Maier Memorial Booklet*. St. Louis: Lutheran Laymen's League, 1950.

——, (ed.), *The Lutheran Hour News*, 1944 through 1953.

——, "Preaching Peace by Jesus Christ," *The Sunday School Times*, February 2, 1946, pp. 87–89.

——, series of articles in *The Walther League Messenger*, L (December, 1941) through LIV (April, 1946).

Bretscher, Paul M., "Dr. Walter A. Maier a Champion of Christian Education," *Lutheran Education*, 85 (March, 1950), 325–28.

Darsow, J., "Dr. Walter Arthur Maier," *The Australian Lutheran*, January 25, 1950, pp. 20 ff.

Dell, J. A., "Walter Maier's Ministry," *The Lutheran Outlook*, XV (March, 1950), 67 f.

Eggers, T. G., series of articles in *The Walther League Messenger*, XLIV (December, 1935) through L (November, 1941).

Fierla, Wladyslaw, "Godzina Luterska Pracuje," *Posel Ewangelicki* (London), V (Grudzien, 1949), 3 f.

Gross, Ben, "The World's Largest Congregation," *Pageant*, I (February, 1945), 119–23.

Hoffmann, Oswald C. J., "Walter Arthur Maier," *The American Lutheran*, XXXIII (February, 1950), 4.

Hoke, Donald E., "He Throws Inkwells On The Air," *Sunday*, 7 (April, 1945), 13 ff.; (May, 1945), 20 ff.

Kettner, Elmer A., "Gratitude to God for Dr. Maier," *Advance*, 7 (January, 1960), 27 f.

——, *Grossie*–"The Woman Everyone Loved." Grand Rapids: Wm. B. Eerdmans Publishing Company, 1949.

——, "Grossie Trusted in God," *Moody Monthly*, 60 (August, 1960), 14–16, 22 f.

Kreiss, F., "La plus vaste Paroisse du Monde en deuil–Dr. Walter A. Maier," *Le Luthérien Français* (Paris), Janvier–Février 1950, p. 1.

*The Lutheran Layman*, I through XXII.

"Die Lutherische Stunde im Rundfunk," *Der Lutheraner* (*Frankfurt*), Januar 1950, p. 6.

McDermott, William F., "Old-Time Religion Goes Global," *Collier's*, 113 (May 6, 1944), 50.

——, "Twenty Million hear him preach," *Christian Herald*, 70 (March, 1947), 43 ff. Trans. by P. Garrido as "El Doctor Walter A. Maier," *La Estrella de la Mañana* (Maracaibo), XLIII (15 de Junio de 1950), 136 ff.

Maguire, Judy, "The Lutheran Hour," *Radio and Television Life*, 18 (October 31, 1948), 34, 39.

"Maier, Rev. Dr. Walter Arthur," *World Biography*, II. New York: Institute For Research In Biography, 1948, pp. 2975 f.

"Maier, Walter A(rthur), Rev.," *Current Biography*, 8 (May, 1947), 37–39; yearbook, 420–22; obit., 11 (February, 1950), 376.

Mark, Graham, "The Word in 56 Languages," *Coronet*, 39 (February, 1956), 141–44.

Moore, Cedric, "The Man of The Hour," *The Christian Herald* (London), April 23, 1949.

*Newsweek:* "The Lutheran Hour," XVI (November 4, 1940), 66. Cp. also XV (March 25, 1940), 51, and "Transition," XXXV (January 23, 1950), 59.

Pearce, The Rev. E. Geo., "A Mustard Seed Which Became A Great Tree," *A Memorial* . . . London: International Lutheran Hour, 1950.

"Pelo Mundo Religioso," *Mensageiro Luterano* (Rio de Janeiro), March, 1950, p. 26.

Piepkorn, Arthur Carl, series of articles in *The Walther League Messenger*, XXXIX (November, 1930) through (July, 1931).

Polack, W. G., "Walter Arthur Maier," *The Lutheran Witness*, LXIX (January 24, 1950), 24, 27–28; (February 7, 1950), 45.

Rudnick, Milton L., "Walter A. Maier–Ambassador to Fundamentalism," chap. IX in "Fundamentalism and the Missouri Synod." St. Louis: doctoral dissertation, Concordia Seminary, 1963.

Schwenk, Harriet E., "Dr. Walter A. Maier's Undeviating Stand Against Atheistic Communism," *Concordia Historical Institute Quarterly*, XXIII (July, 1950), 49–58; and (October, 1950), 132–35.

——, "Jubilate . . . Walter A. Maier Served the Lord with Gladness," *Christmas Echoes*. Minneapolis: Messenger Press, 1950. Pp. 10–13 ff.

Smith, E. F. R., "Bringing Christ to the Nations," *The English Churchman and St. James's Chronicle* (London), February 11, 1949, p. 67.

Spence, Hartzell, "The Man of the Lutheran Hour," *The Saturday Evening Post*, 220 (June 19, 1948), 17, 88–94.

Stellhorn, A. C., "Dr. Walter A. Maier and Education," *Parish Education*, 28 (February, 1950), 19–20.

Strömberg, Finn, "Miraklet i moderne misjonshistorie," *Kristen Ungdom* (Oslo), 13. Februar, 1954, p. 5.

Sulston, Kenneth Hartley, "A Rhetorical Criticism of the Radio Preaching of Walter Arthur Maier." Evanston: doctoral dissertation, Northwestern University, 1958.

Theiss, O. H., "The Strength of His Years," *The Walther League Messenger*, 58 (March, 1950), 10–11, 25–26.

*Tide:* "Radio Gospel," XIII (November 1, 1939), pp. 34 f.

*Time:* "Seven Follies," XVIII (July 27, 1931), 28; "Back to Luther," XXII (September 4, 1933), 24; "Marriage," XXVI (December 9, 1935), 41–42; "Maier v. Council," XXXI (April 11, 1938), 47–48; "Lutherans," XLII (October 18, 1943), 46–49. See also LII (October 11, 1948), 87; "Milestones," LV (January 23, 1950), 63.

"¡Veinte millones escuchan sus sermones!" *Estampas Radiales* (Ciudad Trujillo), I (Junio, 1940), 26, 28.

"Walter A. Maier," *Puerto Rico Evangélico*, XXXVII (25 de mayo de 1949), 1, 15.

"Walter Arthur Maier," *Who's Who in America*. Vols. XVII through XXVI. Chicago: A. N. Marquis Co., 1932–1951. See also *Who Was Who in America*, II (1943–1950), 342.

Wilkie, Katharine E., "The Lutherans," *Classmate*, LVII (November 5, 1950), 3, 6.

Zacharis, Lambros, "Dia Na Gnorisoun ta Ethne ton Christon," *Oikogeniake Zoe* (Athens), Iounios, 1948, pp. 3475–76.

Zeitler, Lester Erwin, "An Investigation of the Factors of Persuasion in the Sermons of Dr. Walter A. Maier." St. Louis: M.S.T. dissertation, Concordia Seminary, 1956.

Zweck, C. E., A. Cheney, et al., series of articles in *The Australian Lutheran*, August 8, 1945, through February 8, 1950.